THE PHILOSOPHICAL THEOLOGY
OF ST. THOMAS AQUINAS

STUDIEN UND TEXTE ZUR GEISTESGESCHICHTE DES MITTELALTERS

HERAUSGEGEBEN VON

Dr. ALBERT ZIMMERMANN

PROFESSOR AN DER UNIVERSITÄT KÖLN

BAND XXVI

THE PHILOSOPHICAL THEOLOGY
OF ST. THOMAS AQUINAS

TUTA SUB AEGIDE PALLAS
·1683·

THE PHILOSOPHICAL THEOLOGY
OF ST. THOMAS AQUINAS

BY

LEO J. ELDERS S.V.D.

E.J. BRILL
LEIDEN • NEW YORK • KØBENHAVN • KÖLN
1990

Library of Congress Cataloging-in-Publication Data

Elders, Leo.
  The philosophical theology of St. Thomas Aquinas / by L. J. Elders.
    p.   cm.—(Studien und Texte zur Geistesgeschichte des
Mittelalters, ISSN 0169-8125; Bd. 28)
  Includes bibliographical references and indexes.
  ISBN 90-04-09156-4
  1. Philosophical theology—History of doctrines—Middle Ages.
800-1500. 2. Thomas, Aquinas, Saint, 1225?-1274—Contributions in
philosophical theology. I. Title. II. Title: Philosophical
theology of Saint Thomas Aquinas. III. Series.
BT40.E54   1990   90-42384
                                                                    CIP

ISSN 0169-8125
ISBN 90 04 09156 4

PRINTED IN THE NETHERLANDS

TABLE OF CONTENTS

PREFACE

This study of St. Thomas Aquinas' "philosophical theology" is the second part of *The Metaphysics of St. Thomas Aquinas in a Historical Perspective*. The partition of metaphysics into two distinct parts should not be understood as a division of disciplines. It is a practical device called for by the immensity of the subject matter of first philosophy. It has its basis in Aquinas' conviction that we must proceed from the study of common being to that of its cause[1]. This division, however, has some drawbacks. It might give the impression that the study of God were subordinated to that of common being. Moreover, the unity of metaphysics and the compenetration of themes is so great, that a clean cut separation between the study of common being and that of its cause is not possible. As a matter of fact, at several points in the first volume reference has already been made to the First Cause[2].

To bring out better the origin of the various problems and to show the originality of the positions of Aquinas or, in some cases, his indebtedness to others the historical context is stressed throughout our study. A succinct but, as we hope, objective and balanced survey of later positions is added in order to shed more light on the character of Aquinas' metaphysics and to illustrate its significance for our time. Those who dislike such sketchy examinations of philosophical positions may find some comfort in the fact that for methodological reasons Aristotle and St. Thomas also resorted to similar surveys of opinions.

Nietzsche proclaimed the death of the God of christianity and of classical metaphysics at large. Heidegger was convinced that Nietzsche's prophecy has now been fulfilled and that this is an irreversible event: man has entered a godless period of his history. In this view a work on St. Thomas Aquinas' philosophical theology is anachronistic. If it is not a mere historical study, it can be no more than a plea for a perhaps noble but lost cause. Our entire book is intended as an answer to this position. Anticipating our long and often difficult analyses we say that the existence of God can be demonstrated with certitude by natural reason. Moreover, if one looks beyond the sphere of infuence of our secularised culture, it becomes clear that the position of atheist or agnostic Western philosophers is far from being shared by people living elsewhere on the globe. More important still, man remains free with regard to dominant trends of thought in his environment. Even if it is true that

---

[1] See the Proem to the *Expositio in libros Metaphysicorum*.
[2] Reference was made to God in the chapters on truth, on actuality and potency, on the real distinction, on being, on participation, on order, etc.

in our society God is dead in the sense that a considerable number of people think and act without reference to God, one cannot deny that the sacred is re-entering our culture in a variety of ways. The problem of God is as much alive as ever before. A growing number of the younger generation, indeed, refuse the shallowness of secularised culture and desire to reach a more metaphysical view of life.

What the reader may expect from a work like this is that it presents a readable account of the main points of Aquinas' philosophical theology and takes into consideration the interpretations given by the classical commentators as well as by recent scholars. This study follows the order of subjects as found in the First Part of the *Summa theologiae*, while it omits those questions which were already treated in the first volume (such as the nature of goodness, truth and unity) as well as the articles and questions which belong to sacred theology only. This creates a problem: to what extent may the First Part of the *Summa theologiae* be used as a source-book of Aquinas' *philosophical* theology?

There can be no doubt that St. Thomas inserted and incorporated philosophical elements into sacred theology and that this discipline, despite these elements, possesses its own unity[3]. Our concern is not so much with the unity of sacred doctrine as with the possibility of using these "philosophical elements" independently of their theological context. With regard to this question one could say that the *overall* order of the *Summa theologiae* is dependent on revelation: in his wisdom and goodness God, existing in a Trinity of Persons, creates the world, all movements and activities of which are directed to him. This return to God takes place in a novel and sublime way through and in Christ. Despite this overall theological order the *inner* arrangement of the treatises on God, on creation, on man, etc. appears to obey the requirements of ordering reason and is not immediately derived from revelation. This is obvious in the arrangement of the Five Ways to demonstrate

---

[3] Cf. E. Gilson, *Le thomisme*[6], Paris 1972, 16ff.; W. Kluxen, *Philosophische Ethik bei Thomas von Aquin*[2], Hamburg 1980, 6ff. Gilson raises the question of how philosophical arguments can be used without endangering the unity of theology, The answer to Gilson's difficulty is that theology is based on revelation with regard to its subject (God who reveals himself), its essence (theology is the science of God himself). It is specified, as to its participated form by the condition of divine faith in the human recipient. Now faith is non-evident knowledge which uses concepts of the natural order to signify supernatural realities. This is possible, for there is an analogy between both orders, because God is the author of both. Reason must assist faith in the analysis, ordering and further elaboration of what is revealed. This is precisely what Aquinas does: philosophical insights and natural truths are used *within* sacred theology, becoming integral parts of it (without them theology is not possible) and they partake in the nature of theology as long as they are used by it. But they can also be detached from it. One may compare their function to that of the chemical elements and reactions in the living organism. Outside the organism they occur in their own right, but in the organism they are subservient to the principle of life and taken up into a higher unity.

God's existence, in the order of divine attributes, in the treatise on creation, etc. For this reason one may safely assume that it is also the order Aquinas would have used if he had written a merely philosophical theology.

But there is more. In many articles of the *S.Th.* the *corpus articuli* introduces an argument from natural reason intended to prove a point proposed by divine revelation (as stated by the argument *Sed contra*). In other articles, however, the main argument develops a definition or a philosophical thesis the conclusion of which will be used in the further study of divine truth. Finally, in many articles, we have to do with an analysis of or a reflection on something which is only known to us by revelation. We are not now concerned with this latter case. The first group of articles does present a more complex situation. The arguments of the *corpus articuli* appear to be purely philosophical, yet the *Sed contra* suggests that here philosophical reason is invited to carry out a reflection in order to bring itself into agreement with that which revelation teaches us. What is, in these cases, the precise role of revelation? It is guiding and helping reason to think along certain lines. But is it also a *conditio sine qua non*? To give an example, is the revelation of God's name to Moses a necessary condition for reaching the insight that God is selfsubsistent being itself? If so, such an insight is not demonstrated by reason alone and is out of place in a philosophical treatise. The existence of angels is most likely a subject which only revelation can give certitude about, but in other cases a particular theme can be demonstrated by reason alone. If so, it can be taken out of its theological context and presented as a philosophical argument. What we are saying applies to the existence of God, divine attributes, God's knowledge and will, the analogy between created things and God, creation. In this way the *Summa theologiae* provides the chapters of a philosophical theology, although it is itself a work belonging to sacred doctrine.

While in our study we follow the order of the questions about God in the *St.Th.*, these questions are preceded by an Introduction on the nature and history as well as the importance of philosophical theology and a chapter on the idea of God and its negation.

While preparing this study I have attempted to consult at least a considerable part of the immense literature which exists in various languages on St. Thomas' doctrine of God. The undoubtedly numerous oversights are unintentional. The Latin quotations of the *S.Th.* are taken from the Leonina, those of the other works mostly of the Marietti edition. For the English text of the *S.Th.* the translation of the English Dominicans has been used. Sometimes slight corrections were made.

I wish to thank all those who over the years helped me to collect the material and to write this book, in particular Dr. S. Theron for reading the English version of the text.

Leo J. ELDERS S.V.D.

INTRODUCTION

Philosophical theology is the systematic inquiry about God's existence and being. We find it in Aristotle's *Metaphysics*, in Cicero's *De natura deorum*, as well as in the debate of the early Christian authors and the Church Fathers with pagan philosophers. In the Middle Ages we encounter it in the works of Arab and Jewish authors, but also in those of the great Christian theologians, even if it is a matter for debate to what extent we can speak of a philosophical theology of St. Thomas Aquinas and, much more so, of St. Bonaventure.

Although natural theology was relegated to the background in the late Middle Ages as well as in the period of the Renaissance and Reformation, it had made its comeback by the middle of the 17th century and from then on it held a prominent position for some two hundred years. However, at the present time its very nature and place among the philosophical disciplines have become questionable. Some think that philosophical theology has no scientific value whatsoever and is a relic of bygone ages. One author, Schubert Ogden, even says that Aquinas' philosophical theology is an example of a pernicious doctrine of God which has held sway since Philo, but which now has become the major obstacle in dealing with the problem of God[1]. Others would like to reduce it to the science of comparative religion which studies the different forms of religious belief but does not set forth a specific doctrine about God. There are authors who feel that natural theology is not really philosophical but depends on religious views. Francis Cornford argued that Greek philosophy is an attempt to express religious convictions in scientific terminology[2]. Christopher Dawson wrote that "every school of Natural Theology is preceded by a revealed theology"[3] and A. Pegis even suggests that St. Thomas was exclusively led by revelation and did not have a philosophical theology[4]. For certain Protestant authors the very attempt to set up such a theology deforms man's knowledge of God or, rather, is idolatrous.

For some of our contemporaties the question of God seems to have lost its interest. In a recent book which treats themes for philosophy classes at French

---

[1] *Reality of God*, New York (Harper) 1966, 19.

[2] F. Cornford, *From Religion to Philosophy. A Study of the Origins of Western Speculation*, New York (edit. Harper), VI. What Cornford writes applies not only to the pre-Socratics, but also to Plato. See C.J. Webb, *Studies in the History of Natural Theology*, Oxford 1915, 134: "We see ... that Natural Theology, even in the hands of so great a thinker as Plato, is not independent of what, whether we call it revealed religion or no, we may at any rate ... call institutional religion".

[3] Cf. Ch. Dawson, *Religion and Culture*, (Meridian Edition) 43.

[4] A.C. Pegis, "*Sub ratione Dei*: A Reply to Professor Anderson", *The New Scholasticism* 39 (1965) 141-157.

Lycées[5] a discussion of the question of God is relegated to a few pages on mysticism which find their place after the chapter on art and a curious text on *Faith and Revolution*. Some people apparently believe and want to make others believe that the question has lost its relevance and meaning in philosophy, but this is belied by the amazing number of books and articles year after year devoted to precisely this topic as well as by a real upsurge of all sorts of religious movements.

The importance of the question of God for ethics has often been emphasised by philosophers, educators and statesmen. Kant was convinced that without God ethics loses its meaning ("ohne Gott schwindet der Sinn der Moral")[6].

Others have argued that without God man's behaviour tends to become a struggle without compassion, except perhaps for his immediate kin. On the other hand, it is also often pointed out that in the past God was used as a sort of dubious sanction where arguments in favour of a particular action were lacking; but now, modern man has become an adult in ethics and can himself decide. All these statements require qualification. Let us only remark that God means much more to ethics than the above remarks imply, viz. he is the object of man's most basic love[7].

One could also speak of the importance of the question of God for man himself and, remarkably enough, for philosophy. In a lecture to the members of the *Académie des sciences morales et politiques* in Paris on the theme, "Ever since God is dead, philosophy is dying", Ferdinand Alquié argued that without God as an encompassing Being who is the origin of the human mind and of the material universe there is no way for man to regain his bearings and his certitude[8].

The Nature of Philosophical Theology According to Aquinas

In this introduction we have to deal with philosophical theology, and more in particular with that of St. Thomas Aquinas. A first question is whether St. Thomas did develop such a theology. Some have denied it[9], but I do think

---

[5] Christian Delacampagne et Robert Maggiori, *Philosopher. Les interrogations contemporaines. Matériaux pour un enseignement*, Paris 1980.

[6] *Kritik der reinen Vernunft*, A 223. Dostoievski wrote: "if God does not exist, anything is allowed".

[7] D. Mieth, "Brauchen wir Gott für die Moral?", *FZPhTh* 29 (1982) 210-233.

[8] See *Le Monde* of January 23, 1980, under the heading "De la mort de Dieu à la mort de la philosophie".

[9] This is the position of Gilson: St. Thomas' metaphysics is a Christian metaphysics because it is dependent on the revelation of God's name. A.C. Pegis rallies to this line of thought when he writes: "if St. Thomas did not create an autonomous philosophy, no one else can do it for him" (*o.c.*, n.4, 145).

that St. Thomas definitely upholds the possibility of natural theology and worked out himself a considerable part of it. This is not to deny the guiding influence of revelation, but autonomous philosophy obtains where arguments by reason alone demonstrate the conclusions. St. Thomas affirms the possibility of philosophical theology in his *Expositio in Boetii De Trinitate*, q.5, a.4, where he writes that the philosophers consider the *res divinae* only in so far as they are the principles of all things, and as such they are studied in metaphysics[10]. St. Thomas affirms the same in his *Summa contra Gentiles* I, c.3 and in the proem to the *Commentary on the Metaphysics*, where he says that God falls under the study of metaphysics in so far as he is the cause of being, although he himself exceeds by far what man can understand by natural reason.

To the second question of whether St. Thomas himself has written such a philosophical theology the answer is also affirmative with some restrictions: The first book and a number of chapters of the second and third books of the *Summa contra Gentiles* come quite close to such a philosophy of God. In his commentary on the *Metaphysics* St. Thomas was bound by the order of the 12 books he commented upon and the chapters of Aristotle's text. Nevertheless the commentary offers a wealth of insights of St. Thomas himself some of which amount to the elements of a philosophical theology. We can even collect a fairly complete treatise from the first part of the *Summa theologiae*. Above all the order of the themes treated provides a good indication of how reason would set up an arrangement of the different parts of a philosophical theology.

Another observation is called for. In order to enter theology a special preparation is required: one should first become acquainted with the philosophy of nature and the metaphysics of common being. Without such preparation it is extremely difficult to grasp the principles to be used[11]. Quite a number of philosophers and non-Catholic authors who write on God now consult St. Thomas and consider him an important philosopher. This is certainly a most satisfying development to all those Thomists who over the years have been stressing the paramount value of St. Thomas' philosophy. But there is a serious drawback to this. Several of those who do read St. Thomas are beguiled by the apparent simplicity of his text and do not hesitate to accept or to reject his arguments according to their first impressions. To give an example: the well-known Five Ways by which St. Thomas demonstrates the existence of God are the very basis and centre of his natural theology. But

---

[10] See also *ibid.*, q.2 a.2 where St. Thomas writes that science implies that we *conclude* from premises. See R. McInerny, "On Behalf of Natural Theology", in *Philosophical Knowledge. Proc. of the Amer. Cath. Philos. Assoc.*, LIV, Washington D.C. 1980, 63-73.

[11] Cf. G.P. Klubertanz, "St. Thomas on Learning Metaphysics", *Gregorianum* 35 (1954) 3-17. See *In VI Ethic.*, 1.7, n.1209 and *In VII Phys.*, 1.6, nn.919-927.

there is such a coherence and inner unity in St. Thomas' thought, that one cannot just accept or reject part of it according to one's own rapid impression. Thus R. Swinburne's remark to the effect that the first four of these Five Ways are among the least successful pieces of Aquinas' philosophy is rather rash and does not make much sense, if one is to attach any value at all to St. Thomas' thought [12].

In addition to this we should mention another more pervasive difficulty: modern man still feels the need of the absolute, of an encompassing truth and love, but he has become so subjective and so much aware of his own freedom that he hesitates to commit himself. Many of our contemporaries, moreover, have become so totally directed toward this material world, that they do not know what to make of the spiritual. Their universe is to a large extent that of the sciences, their thinking is limited to technical knowledge and their horizon is that of the *homo positivus*. To understand philosophical theology one has first to admit the value of a type of knowledge which does not seek *to do* something with its insights, but which is contemplative. Precisely because the aims of theology lie at a level which is non-utilitarian, they are not related to the passing vicissitudes of human life but to the deepest ontological structure of man's being.

The philosophical theology of St. Thomas presupposes at the same time the metaphysics of realism and the trustworthiness of reason. While reductive empiricism is discarded, rationalism is also excluded: the philosopher finds himself standing before the mystery of God which he cannot penetrate; the negative aspect of all our knowledge about God is constantly stressed.

An outline of the History of Philosophical Theology

Turning now to the history of the term theology, we notice that *theologos* occurs for the first time in Plato [13]. It denotes the poets and wise men who spoke about the gods. In Aristotle's works the word *theologia* signifies discourse about the gods by poets such as Homer, Hesiod or Pherecydes. The term may well imply inspiration or revelation given by the gods [14]. Thus *theologia* is not just knowledge about the gods but divine science. To denote scientific theology *theologiké (episteme)* is used [15].

---

[12] *The Existence of God*, Oxford 1979, 119.

[13] *Rep.* 379a. Cf. *Metaph.* 983 a 1-6.

[14] See F. Kattenbusch, "Die Entstehung einer christlichen Theologie. Zur Geschichte der Ausdrücke θεολογία, θεολογεῖν, θεολογός", *ZThK, NF* 11 (1930) 161-205.

[15] *Metaphysics* VI, 1. Cf. *Meteor.* 353 a 35, where Aristotle sees a connection between mythology and scientific theology. In *De mundo* 391 b 4 θεολογεῖν means the scientific study of God. For the history of the term see also A. Festugière, *La révélation d'Hermès Trismégiste, II: Le dieu cosmique*, Paris 1949, 598-605.

This term occurs in Aristotle's tripartition of the theoretical sciences. It is not clear to which extent this science of God is identical with the science of being *qua* being, of which Aristotle speaks at the beginning of Book IV of the *Metaphysics*. A certain ambiguity persisted among the Greek commentators: Alexander of Aphrodisias says that the highest knowledge is the science of being *qua* being, so that theology is apparently incorporated into metaphysics[16]. However, in his commentary on Book E, the authenticity of which is not undisputed, he writes that it is the highest, most valuable being which is the subject of metaphysics[17]. In this connection he uses the word theology in the sense of the philosophical study of the highest principle[18]. According to Asclepius the study of being *qua* being is that of the highest being; therefore metaphysics is theology[19].

Philoponus and Simplicius follow this (Neoplatonic) line of interpretation[20]. Theology is the highest form of all scientific pursuits: the other branches of philosophy are a gradual preparation. This variety of interpretations was to lead to the contrasting views of Avicenna and Averroes, but before dealing with the great Arab philosophers we should mention a division of philosophy as used by the Stoa and widespread in the Roman Empire and the early Middle Ages, viz. that into rational, physical and moral philosophy. Theology is part of physics. The Latin author Varro divides theology into three branches: rational theology, mythology and civil religion (the knowledge of the state ceremonies of civil life); only the first gives true knowledge about God[21].

The Christian authors, in particular Origenes and Eusebius, mention theology as (revealed) doctrine about God and Christ[22], but such Latin authors[23] as St. Cyprianus, St. Ambrose, St. Gregory the Great and Boethius do not use the term to denote sacred theology[24]. Avicenna made being qua being the subject of metaphysics[25], whereas Averroes declared God to be this

---

[16] *In Metaph.* 11, 6; 239, 16-23.

[17] *In Metaph.* 447, 24-36.

[18] *In Metaph.* 661, 29ff. Cf. Simplicius, *In Phys.* 359, 6.

[19] *In Metaph.* 1, 24; 3, 21.

[20] *In Categ.* 5, 1-5; *In Phys.* 1, 17-21. Cf. K. Kremer, *Der Metaphysikbegriff in den Aristoteleskommentaren der Ammoniusschule. BGPTMA*, 39, 1, Münster 1960.

[21] *Apud Augustinum, De civ. Dei* VI 5: theologia est ratio de diis.

[22] *Contra Celsum* VI 18. Dionysius also uses the term in this sense. See R. Roques, *Structures théologiques. De la gnose à Richard de Saint-Victor*, Paris 1962, 136.

[23] An exception is St. Augustine who in his discussion with pagan authors speaks of *vera theologia*. Abelard also uses the term in the modern sense of the systematic study of revealed doctrine.

[24] On St. Thomas' use of the term see his *Expositio in Boetii De Trinitate*, q.5, a.4.

[25] *Metaphysica* 70 vc (*Liber de philosophia prima* (Van Riet), 13, 47ff.). According to Avicenna God is studied in metaphysics insofar as he is the cause of being.

subject[26]. Their divergent views gave rise to a protracted discussion in the Middle Ages[27].

In a concise introduction it is impossible to cover the vast field of the history of natural theology in the Middle Ages. We can only recall some more outstanding positions and authors. The first to be mentioned is St. Anselm. Although in his works no clear distinction is drawn between natural and revealed theology, he nevertheless tries to argue for God's existence and attributes from reason alone. In the *Proslogion* he develops his famous argument for the existence of God (the so-called ontological proof), while in the *Monologion* Anselm tries to answer the question of what God is. He presents a thoroughly reasoned and fairly complete treatise of God's attributes.

A second important philosopher is Abelard. In his *Dialogue between a Christian, a Jew and a Philosopher*, he expounds many themes of what later came to be called natural theology. Abelard, however, went far beyond the limits of natural reason inasmuch as he sought evidence in the writings of pagan authors in favour of specifically Christian dogmas such as that about the Person and mission of the Holy Spirit.

St. Albert expresses his view of philosophical theology in his important *Commentary on the Metaphysics*. Despite some texts where he seems to make God part of the subject of metaphysics his considered opinion is that this subject is being (*esse*), which he understood in the Neoplatonic sense as the *prima effluxio Dei et creatum primum*[28].

St. Thomas himself is unwavering in his assertion that being *qua* being, i.e. common being or, simply, being is the subject of metaphysics. It is his merit to have made clear the epistemological status of metaphysics: this discipline really is a study of being[29]. Not God, but common being is the subject matter of metaphysics[30]. On account of the fact that only created being is immediately accessible to man, God is known insofar as he is the extrinsic

---

[26] Averroes, *In Physicam* I, comm. 83.

[27] A. Zimmermann, *Ontologie oder Metaphysik? Die Diskussion über den Gegenstand der Metaphysik im 13. und 14. Jahrhundert*, Leiden-Köln 1965.

[28] L. Elders, "La naturaleza de la metafísica según San Alberto Magno y Santo Tomás de Aquino", *Scripta theologica* (Pamplona) 12 (1980) 547-561.

[29] See our *Die Metaphysik des Thomas von Aquin in historischer Perspektive*, I, Salzburg-München 1985, 21ff.

[30] *In libros Metaphysicorum*, Proemium: "... ut subiectum solum ipsum ens commune". Arguing against L. Dewan, "Being *per se*, Being *per accidens* and St. Thomas' Metaphysics", in *Science et Esprit* 30 (1978) 169-184 (170, n.4) J. Owens suggests that, if we take *subject* to mean the topics discussed in a science, God is certainly included in the subject of metaphysics. But if we take subject to mean that which specifies a science, God is not the subject of metaphysics. See his "Existence and the Subject of Metaphysics", in *Science et Esprit* 32 (1980) 255-260. We must notice, however that St. Thomas uses the term subject to denote the reality immediately given to us which we deal with in a science. Now God does not belong to this reality.

cause of being[31]. One cannot sufficiently insist on this point: God is the subject matter neither of metaphysics nor of philosophical theology because he is not directly knowable and is not comprised under common being. There is no philosophical theology distinct from metaphysics. Nevertheless the knowledge of God is the end of metaphysical knowledge[32]. This doctrine of St. Thomas, then, qualifies our knowledge of God which is very much limited and is above all a negative knowledge. Thus it safeguards God's transcendence and prevents us from making God subject to man's intellect. The importance of this will become clear as we pursue our survey of the history of natural theology.

Finally, Aquinas' conception keeps philosophical and theological knowledge (in the sense of sacred theology) clearly apart and so it answers the objections which certain Protestant authors have raised against natural theology, some of whom even go so far as to speak of human concepts being made the Absolute.

In this connection one may raise the following question: if the study of God belongs to metaphysics, where does God come in? The obvious answer is that the analysis of common being, that is the resolution to its causes, leads to the conclusion that God exists. Now the more widespread view among Thomists seems to be that one should first very carefully study common being before proceeding to establish God's existence[33]. One can adduce in its favour that the *Commentary on the Metaphysics* does not begin the inquiry about God until it reaches Book XII: the consideration of being and its properties, first principles, essence, substance, act and potency precedes. However, Joseph Owens dissents and argues that we must go from a first exploration of the subject of metaphysics to the quest of its principles and establish God's existence in order to return to the study of common being: "By far the greater part of the work in metaphysics remains to be done after the existence and nature of God have been established"[34].—Father Owens is partially right inasmuch as the study of being (e.g. of ontological truth, logical possibility, participation

---

[31] *Expos. in Boetii De Trin.*, q.5, a.4: "There is one theology in which we treat of divine things, not as the subject of the science, but as the principles of the subject and this is the sort of theology pursued by the philosophers and wich is also called metaphysics" (transl. by A. Maurer, *St. Thomas Aquinas, The Division and Methods of the Sciences*, Toronto 1953, 41. In the Proem to the *Commentary on the Metaphysics* St. Thomas writes likewise: "Praedictae substantiae separatae sunt universales et primae causae essendi". As such they are known in metaphysics.
[32] *Expos. in Libros Metaphysicorum*, Proemium: "Nam cognitio causarum alicuius generis est finis ad quem consideratio scientiae pertingit".—Avicenna also held this position. Reacting against the dominant view of Islamic authors he declares that God is not the subject of metaphysics. He learned this insight from Alfarabi. See D. Gutas, *Avicenna and the Aristotelian Tradition*, Leiden 1988, 238ff.
[33] This is also the author's position. Cf. Thomas C. O'Brien, *Metaphysics and the Existence of God*, Washington D.C. 1960.
[34] See his review of O'Brien's book in *The New Scholasticism* 36 (1962) 250-253.

etc.) requires the previous demonstration of God's existence, at least for a
more profound understanding of the issues involved,—but he is wrong in so
far as he assumes that *existential being* is the exclusive subject of metaphysics
from which we would pass immediately to God. In his view even the real
distinction between essence and existence is made dependent on the previous
knowledge of God's being.

Pursuing our survey of the more important positions on the nature of
philosophical theology we come to Duns Scotus who holds that common
being is the subject of metaphysics. Common being is undifferentiated and
common to God and to creatures. The first division of being is that into finite
and infinite being. In this way Scotus makes God dependent on our concept
of being, although, on the other hand, he correctly defends God's
transcendence by stating that in philosophy we cannot grasp God
adequately [35].

The height of philosophical speculation reached by the great thinkers of the
13th century and in particular by St. Thomas Aquinas was not destined to
mark a definitive acquisition of the Western mind. Toward the middle of the
following century distrust became widespread with regard to the capacity of
the intellect to reach certitude as to God's existence. William of Ockham held
that human reason cannot definitely establish the existence of God nor reach
certain knowledge about God's nature. In this way Ockham cut the connection between metaphysics and sacred doctrine and tried to destroy
philosophical theology. Ockham's influence remained very strong for the next
hundred years. We must turn now to the scholasticism of the Renaissance.

The important Spanish philosopher Suarez follows Scotus to a certain
extent, asserting that the division into created and infinite being is the first
division of being: God is comprehended under our knowledge of being and
the first principles [36]. Suarez treats God before he deals with finite being and
considers God to be the "primum et praecipuum obiectum huius scientiae" [37].
Suarez, therefore, maintains the unity of philosophical theology and
metaphysics. With Suarez the question of man's knowledge and its certitude
came to the fore; it precedes so to say that of God's existence. The road was
now open for Descartes, "a disciple of the disciples of Suarez" [38].

---

[35] *Ordinatio* I, d.3, I, q.3 (*Opera omnia* III, 68). Cf. *Quaest. in Metaph.* I, 1, m.33; J. Owens,
"Up to what point is God included in the Metaphysics of Duns Scotus?", in *Mediaeval Studies*
X (1948) 163-177; E. Gilson, *Jean Duns Scot. Introduction à ses positions fondamentales*, Paris
1952, 91-94.
[36] *Disp. metaph.* I, 1, 19 & 28, 1, 5. For Suarez being as a noun is the object of metaphysics.
This discipline, therefore, becomes a study of concepts.
[37] *Disp. metaph.* 29, 1, 1.
[38] E. Gilson, *L'être et l'essence*, Paris 1948, 155. Cf. G. Siewerth, *Das Schicksal der
Metaphysik von Thomas zu Heidegger*, Einsiedeln 1959, 120ff.

But before we consider the place theology occupied in Descartes' philosophy attention must be drawn to a development shaping up in the 14th and 15th centuries. The rise of formalism among scholastics, the struggle between the schools and their subtle differences made philosophical theology more and more independent of religion. The debate about the *potentia Dei absoluta* versus the *potentia Dei ordinata* also led to an attitude which no longer saw God's goodness and wisdom reflected in the world. Man now sought a more immediate contact with God in his own heart[39]. In a recent book A. Louth argues that in the closing centuries of the Middle Ages a dissociation of thought from physical reality as perceived by the senses, its beauty and order occurred, so that theology began to whither[40]. The rise of philosophical and religious scepticism also contributed to the decline of natural theology. However, about the middle of the seventeenth century a reaction set in[41].

The most important development in that century was undoubtedly Descartes' attempt to connect philosophical thought about God with man's quest for certitude: when we doubt about al things, the reality of our own thought and of the self still stands out as evident. For Descartes God comes in to guarantee that man's daily perceptions of the world do not normally deceive him. God's existence is given with the idea of a most perfect being which man finds in his mind. God's properties are deduced in a sometimes casual way. Since for Descartes there no longer is any being or event in the physical universe from which God's existence can be inferred, God becomes relative to human thought. From there it is only one step to argue that God is dependent on man's mind or is its product[42].

Descartes' influence on philosophy did not remain restricted to the above. By promoting the study of the quantitative aspects of nature he deprived the physical world of its reference to God. Physical bodies are just three-dimensional entities without the secondary sensible qualities. God has apparently withdrawn himself from the world after having devised the mechanism of the universe. In view of these consequences it is not surprising that Henry More, one of the leading Cambridge Platonists, sharply criticised Descartes' philosophy because he felt it led to atheism[43]. Pascal was sharp-

---

[39] See P. Vignaux, *Nominalisme au XIVe siècle*, Montréal-Paris 1948, 12ff.; H. Obermann, "Some Notes on the Theology of Nominalism", *Harvard Theological Review* 53 (1960) 47-76.
[40] *Discerning the Mystery. An Essay on the Nature of Theology*, Oxford 1983.
[41] Cf. R.H. Popkin, *The History of Scepticsism from Erasmus to Spinoza*, Berkeley 1979, ch. VI: "The Counter-attack Begins". See also T. Penelhulm, *God and Scepticism. A study in Scepticism and Fideism*, Dordrecht 1983.—In Germany such authors as Ch. Scheibler, J. Musaeus, J.G. Canz and H.S. Reimarus published influential works on natural theology, perhaps partly inspired by the metaphysics of Suarez.
[42] See E. Jüngel, *Gott als Geheimnis der Welt*, Tübingen 1978, on the epochal significance of Descartes' position.
[43] *Enchiridium metaphysicum*, I 6, 4-6.

sighted enough to protest against the Cartesian representation of God and thought that this brand of deism was almost as far removed from Christian religion as atheism[44].

During the major part of the 17th century the idea of God was still a dominant concern. From Descartes' principles issued the ontologism of Malebranche which is entirely centered on God. The enormous influence of Descartes' rationalism and his method are also evident in the writings of Spinoza. It has been said that "Spinoza was drunken with God". Nevertheless in Spinoza's monism God is no longer above nature, but becomes its very essence and its universal reality. God is immanent and not transcendent, still less the Creator. He takes on the characteristics Descartes assigned to the two types of finite substance, viz. thought and extension. Theology is also both cosmology and ethics.—Leibniz developed his *theodicea* to show God's justice at work in the world and to defend God's government against criticisms. The greatest disadvantage of Leibniz's rational theology is its tendency to make the order of the world the supreme value to which even God himself is subjected. God directs things as carefully as a good engineer tends his machines. There is nevertheless in Leibniz's *theodicea* some space left for the incomprehensible mystery of God's wisdom, so that the reproach that Leibniz reduced theology to mechanics and logic is not fully justified[45].

At about the same time in officially established Calvinism natural theology made a comeback: it was felt to offer an escape from the uncertainties resulting from theological debate. Attempts were made to rationalize the creed (the so-called *Vernunftsorthodoxie*)[46]. The sceptic Bayle opposed this tendency: reason has nothing to do with religion; faith and philosophy should be separated[47].

While on the continent rationalism dominated, empiricism was on the rise in England. Francis Bacon separates natural theology from metaphysics. The latter discipline is unable to carry us beyond nature. The sharply reduced role he assigns to natural theology is that of dealing with God's existence and power, but it cannot give us any certitude[48]. There is no direct experience of God and so there is hardly a place for him in philosophy.

---

[44] H. Gouhier, *Pascal. Oeuvres complètes*, Paris 1963, 449.

[45] See Ph. Némo, *Job et l'excès du mal*, Paris 1978 and P.-Ph. Druet, "La théodicée comme tribunal de la raison", in *(coll.) Pour une philosophie chrétienne*, Paris-Namur 1983, 43-62.

[46] J.L. Leuba, "Rousseau et le milieu calviniste de sa jeunesse", in (coll.) *Jean-Jacques Rousseau et la crise contemporaine de la conscience*, Paris 1980, 11-46.

[47] S. Goyard-Fabre, *La philosophie des lumières en France*, Paris 1972, 87.

[48] See J. Collins, *God and Modern Philosophy*, Chicago 1959, chapter four: "Empiricism and the Neutralizing of God".—Francis Bacon claimed to have freed natural theology from metaphysics and to have placed it on its own feet. He did acknowledge a proof of God's existence from the order of nature (*The Advancement of Learning, The Works of Francis Bacon*, edit. by Spedding and Ellis, 3, 350ff).—Hobbes, who ascribed necessary existence to the world, did not see the need of creation and rejected natural theology.

Against Descartes Locke argues that there is no innate idea of God; even without recourse to God our knowledge is reliable. Locke is quite circumstantial in his explanations of how we form the complex idea of God from such other ideas as being, autonomy, infinity, thinking etc.—David Hume went far beyond Locke in rejecting philosophical theology as a dream of a sickly mind[49]. But Hume's position was far from being typical of the dominant attitude in 18th century England.

The general tendency was to show scepticism or indifference with regard to revealed religion and to set up a philosophical theology. In this line of thought we have Toland's *Christianity not mysterious* (1696) and Tindal's *Christianity as old as the Creation* (1730): what is wholly above our understanding has no meaning and we do not even know whether it exists or not.

Thus the importance of natural theology grew and it obtained a new status in a Europe which realised that it had lost its religious unity[50]. As such it held a great attraction, for, as Christopher Dawson writes, scientists and philosophers could not yet dispense with the idea of God, the author of nature and its order. Natural theology was to flourish as long as the scientists were in contact with a living religion[51]. Newton lent support to this development in that he pointed out that we must assume the existence of God to account for the initial order and the beginning of process in the world. From Newton there issued a group of authors on natural theology. However, "what had begun as an attempt to show that much of what was essential to christianity could be established by reason, ended by claiming that only what could be rationally defended, was essential"[52]. To mention some authors of this tendency: S. Clarke wrote a *Demonstration of the Being and the Attributes of God*; William Whiston published his *Philosophical Principles of Natural Religion* and John Graig *Theologiae christianae Principia mathematica*. John Ray wrote *The Wisdom of God manifested in the Works of Creation*. Other names in this upsurge of so-called physical theology are William Derham, Boerhaave and Swammerdam in Holland and the abbé Pluche in France. The most influential book out of this vast literature was to be William Paley's *Natural Theology*, which even impressed Charles Darwin.

---

[49] *Natural History of Religion*, Section XV.—It is difficult to interpret Hume's view of God and religion. Recently J.C.A. Gaskin has argued in favour of calling Hume an "attenuated deist". See his "Hume's Attenuated Deism", in *Archiv f. Geschichte der Philosophie*, 65 (1983) 160-173.

[50] For example, there was a remarkable interest in natural theology in the Netherlands around the middle of the 18th century. See F. Sassen, "John Lullofs (1711-1768) en de reformatorische verlichting in de Nederlanden", *Mededelingen van de Koninkl. Nederl. Acad. der Wetenschappen*, D 28 (1965) 277-340.Suarez' influence made itself felt even in Calvinist Holland.

[51] *Religion and Culture* (Meridian Books, New York 1958, 6ff.

[52] James Noxon, *Hume's Philosophical Development*, Oxford 1973, 66.

During a long period the Christian faith had been an important cultural force. But when faith grew dim, a superficial clarity of reason was sought instead; a philosophy about essences and order was set up to take the place of the philosophy of being. Deism became the dominant frame of mind[53]. Deism juxtaposes God and man. It may be seen as an attempt to assign a place to God in the universe of modern physics.

Now the word deism can be used with several meanings as it denotes a philosophical position about God standing between Christian faith and atheism. Samuel Clarke distinguishes four groups of deists:
(a) those who say that they believe in the existence of an eternal God but deny his providence; (b) a group of authors who uphold God's government of the world but say that God is indifferent with regard to human conduct; (c) others, again, admit divine providence but reject the immortality of the human soul; (d) finally some refuse to admit divine revelation.

We should have to place Voltaire with the second group, or perhaps even with the first, since he excludes divine providence. God to him is the God of the physical world[54]. Diderot takes a different stand: people have banished divinity from their lives and shut God up in a protected place, but this narrows the range of human thought. It would be better either to admit God to the full extent or to be an atheist[55]. Apparently the insincere and ambiguous deism of the late 18th and early 19th centuries prepared the road for atheism. In the sciences the return to atomism and the belief in an eternally existent matter became quite widespread. Homogeneous explanations of phenomena were sought. According to Laplace we must envisage the present state of the universe as an effect of a previous state and as the cause of that which is to follow[56]. In this view God is a superfluous hypothesis. Scientific knowledge was now considered by many to be the only valid form of intellectual pursuit. This view was spread by Auguste Comte: the theological and mystical stages of history must give way to the realism of the sciences. Comte's work made a considerable impression in France and abroad. In England it confirmed Darwin in his positivist frame of mind. Natural theology had to leave the scene. The battle to impose these ideas was fought in England during Darwin's lifetime, but also in Germany.

When studying the development of philosophical thought in Germany in the 18th and 19th centuries we notice Leibniz's influence. In 1710 this great

---

[53] In his *Dictionnaire historique et critique* (1696) Bayle credits the Protestant author Virat with being the first to use the term deism (1563). It denoted a certain religious universalism, comprizing a number of tenets on God and man. Herbert of Cherbury, in his *De religione gentilium*, was one of the first advocates of deism.

[54] S. Goyard-Fabre, *op.cit.* (n.45), 121f.

[55] *Pensées philosophiques*, XXVI.

[56] *Essai philosophique sur la probabilité* (1814), in *Oeuvres complètes* VI, VI.

philosopher published his *Theodicy. Essays on the Goodness of God, the Freedom of Man and the Origin of Evil*. Leibniz is deeply concerned with the religious issues of his day but shows at the same time a rather strong rationalist tendency. We owe to Leibniz the term theodicy, which he chose as the title of his book because he is dealing with human freedom, evil and God's causality. It has been argued that there is a noticeable gap between Leibniz's logical and metaphysical tenets on the one hand and his Christian theodicy on the other.

The rationalism of the Enlightenment is even more apparent in the work of Christian Wolff (1679-1754). Important for our survey is Wolff's division of theoretical philosophy (metaphysics) into four branches: ontology, rational psychology, cosmology and natural theology. The separation of theology from ontology is radical. Wolff had been preceded by Clauberg in this. It would seem that Wolff's division was influenced by Suarez, who had juxtaposed the metaphysics of infinite being to that of finite being; both are preceded by a general metaphysics. In Wolff's lifetime the rise of rationalism provoked a reaction: pantheistic mysticism began to spread and many people turned to an anti-dogmatic pietism, which is perhaps related to medieval negative theology.

Since Baumgarten (1714-1762) metaphysics came to be divided into *metaphysica generalis* (ontology) and *metaphysica specialis* which has three parts (respectively on the soul, the world and God)[57]. This division is based upon Platonic views and admits a dualistic separation of the material from the spiritual world. Baumgarten's theory of reality and his corresponding division of philosophy prevailed for quite some time. More than a century later Nietzsche felt obliged to reject this type of metaphysics in which there was no place for becoming.

Against this backdrop the figure of Immanuel Kant appeared. In his works there is an outspoken contrast between the world of science (where God is no longer required) and that of thought related to God. Kant holds that the questions of God, freedom and immortality are the main concerns of man[58]; the knowledge of God is the crown of man's intellectual pursuits[59].

He distinguishes between different types of theology, viz. a cosmo-theology (which attempts to deduce the existence of God from the experience of the outside world); onto-theology (which does so from a concept and is a development of the ontological argument). Both are so-called transcendental theologies. Then there is natural theology which holds that one can not only deduce God's existence but also his attributes. This theology can either be

---

[57] *Metaphysica* (edit. 2), Halle-Magdeburg-Leipzig 1743, §4.
[58] *Kritik der reinen Vernunft*, Einleitung B7/A3.
[59] *O.c.*, B670/A642

physico-theology or moral theology[60]. However, Kant himself is convinced that it is not possible to demonstrate God's existence and that all attempts to set up a philosophical theology are doomed to failure[61]. As is known, Kant bases our knowledge of God on man's quest for happiness: the postulate of God's existence is necessary for a well-ordered human life. It is no disadvantage, Kant writes, that we do not know what God is in himself, as long we know what he means for our moral life[62]. Throughout his works Kant uses the Christian concept of God and makes God the ideal of the human mind.

Fichte follows Kant and is emphatic that a finite intellect cannot have any knowledge of the infinite. How could one deduce God's necessary being from the contingent existence of the world? Hence theology as the study of God's being is patently impossible[63]. Fichte tries to rescue philosophical theology by insisting on man's indestructible faith in freedom and the voice of conscience. Conscience gives man the certitude that he belongs to a supra-sensible world[64]. In his later years, however, Fichte came to adhere to a total idealism: all being is knowledge; knowledge is the appearance of freedom and of an ultimate we call God. The possibility of understanding God and of being God lies in religious man himself[65]. Thus Fichte ends up by identifying God and man.

Hegel speaks of the philosophy of religion instead of natural theology and this change is significant because it indicates that for him what we do in metaphysics is to investigate what is in the human mind and to follow ourselves its dialectical movement. The Absolute Idea realizes itself: it calls up the finite, denies it and so returns to itself. God alone is the absolute; to him all reality belongs. Instead of having a philosophical theology we end up with considerations about an assumed eternal dialectical process of the Absolute[66]. The German idealist sees a certain order of our actions as if they were directed to God and God were real, but in fact only what happens in man's mind is real[67].

Feuerbach criticised this pantheistic point of view and rejected what he calls the non-sense of the Absolute[68]. Instead of saying with Hegel that man's consciousness is the expression of God, he states that in man there is nothing

---

[60] *O.c.*, B659-660/A631-632.

[61] *O.c.*, B664/A636.

[62] *Die Religion innerhalb der Grenzen der blossen Vernunft*, edit. Weischedel, IV, 806.

[63] J.G. Fichte, *Werke. Auswahl in sechs Bänden*, hrsg. von F. Medicus, Leipzig *s.a.*, 250.

[64] *Op.cit.*, III, 165.

[65] *Ibid.*, IV, 383.

[66] W. Weischedel, *Der Gott der Philosophen. Grundlegung einer philosophischen Theologie im Zeitalter des Nihilismus*, I: *Wesen, Aufstieg und Verfall der philosophischen Theologie*, Darmstadt 1971, 328ff.

[67] See his *Geschichte der Philosophie* (Jubil. ausgabe, Stuttgart 1927, XIX), 8.

[68] *Feuerbachs Sämtliche Werke*, hrsg. von W. Bolin und F. Jodl, 10 Bde, II, 227.

besides man himself. The so-called consciousness of God is nothing else but the self-consciousness of man[69]. This implies that theology is nothing but anthropology[70]. "Knowing about God is the knowledge of man about himself, about his own being"[71]. By this theory Feuerbach reaffirms the reality of the material world and makes anthropology a comprehensive science: "Man is himself the measure of all things and of all reality"[72].

Nietzsche wholly rejects metaphysics and philosophical theology. Metaphysics is the science of human errors which gave precedence to being over becoming. But Nietzsche saw the catastrophic consequences which follow from a denial of God. The world and man himself lose their meaning and their foundation. Without God the universe will be characterised by icy emptiness and man will have to break with age old convictions.

Leaving now the German scene we see that in England physico-theology was shaken to its very foundations by Darwin's attempt to explain the apparition of living beings in their amazing variety without any recourse to God and so to strike at what had long been considered the mainstay of the proof from cosmological order. Clinging to natural theology now was considered to be out of tune with the best insights of modern science. Had not Lord Macaulay already somewhat earlier observed that "natural theology is not a progressive science"[73].

In France Bergson held a somewhat dubious position. He placed God in the centre of his philosophy: the intuition of our own duration brings us in contact with a continuous Duration. God, indeed, is living eternity and consequently he is changing even now. God is concentration of reality and energy whereas materiality is dissipation. God is known to us because he lives in us: he makes himself in us (*il se fait en nous*). God appears as a centre from which the worlds stream forth as beams and this centre is a continuous upsurge[74]. Bergson's philosophy is a sort of pantheistic creationism[75]. God cannot be conceived without the world. With regard to the first period of Bergson's philosophy one can hardly speak of physics or metaphysics. We have to do with a sort of all-embracing monism.

In the USA philosophical theology was rejected by such pragmatists as W. James and John Dewey. James even put forth arguments against its very possibility: philosophical theology is not generally agreed upon and cannot

[69] VI, 15.—Quotations after Weischedel, *o.c.*, 391-395.

[70] II, 222.

[71] VI, 278.

[72] VI, 27.

[73] "The Ecclesiastical and Political History of the Popes by L. Ranke", in the *Edinburgh Review* 72 (1841) 23.

[74] *Evolution créatrice*, 270.

[75] Cf. J. Maritain, *La philosophie bergsonienne*, Paris 1948, 196.

really be called a science[76]. A very different voice is that of Alfred North Whitehead. His process theology is a sort of theological physics. God must exist because he is the foundational process of creativity and at the same time its fulfilment; God is, indeed, dipolar. There is an impact of God on the world and of the world on God.—Process theology exercises a strong appeal to many. Its attractiveness must probably be explained by the fact that people feel that with its help they can uphold theism in a world dominated by positivist science and psychologism. But the price they pay for espousing Whitehead's system is very high. They fall into much confusion on the difference between mind and matter and abandon basic principles of being, such as: a being cannot give a perfection it does not yet have. Scientific viewpoints such as the law of action and reaction henceforth determine the relationship between God and the world. God's being is divided into a primordial and derivative nature.

Whitehead argues that the combination of the Christian notion of God with the Aristotelean theory of the Unmoved Mover was highly unfortunate because (he thinks) it gave rise to the doctrine of a transcendent Creator. Precisely this doctrine is responsible for a tragedy, for God came to be represented in the image of the Egyptian, Persian and Roman rulers[77]. This representation of God as well as the idea of God as moral energy has to be abandoned[78].

The more prominent contemporary philosophers have little or nothing to say about philosophical theology. Merleau-Ponty and Sartre do not even discuss it, and Heidegger firmly refuses to identify philosophy with theories held by Christians. He reproaches Thomism and Hegelianism for reducing philosophy to theology and wholly excludes the idea that God can be approached in terms of the philosophy of being[79]. Heidegger profoundly influenced a good number of Protestant and even Catholic authors and led them to denounce onto-theology in all its forms[80].

Paul Tillich considers natural theology, which he chooses not to call theology, a description of human self-transcendence and of questions to which there are no sufficient answers. Living religion has to come to our aid if we want to make our thinking about God meaningful[81].

---

[76] *The Varieties of Religious Experience*, Lecture 18. We must admit the fact of a wide variety of opinions, mentioned by James, but consider it a sign of the frailty of man's intellectual enterprises rather than of the impossibility of a natural theology. Cf. St. Thomas, *S.C.G.* I, c.4.

[77] *Process and Reality*, New York 1941, 519-520.

[78] B.Z. Cooper, *The Idea of God. A Whiteheadian Critique of St. Thomas Aquinas' Concept of God*, The Hague 1974, 5.

[79] See his *Einführung in die Metaphysik* and R. Kearney in *Heidegger et la question de Dieu*, edited by R. Kearney and St. O'Leary, Paris 1980, 129ff.

[80] Cf. J. Greiset, "La contrée de la sérénité et l'horizon de l'espérance", *o.c.* (n.79), 186-193, 170.

[81] *Systematic Theology*, V, II, 1a.

With the rise of neopositivism the question of the sources of philosophical knowledge has gained importance, in particular after the debacle of physicotheology and deism. Several neopositivists argue that God ought to be excluded from philosophical discourse because experience provides no basis for any knowledge about God. John Wisdom's tale of two explorers who came upon a clearing in the jungle is revealing for this way of thinking. One of them feels that there must be a gardener tending the plot, but all attempts to see him fail. His colleague points out that there thus remains no basis whatever for his assumption [82]. The tale is meant to explain how although in the past God could be made responsible for the order in the world there is now no longer any reason to resort to a divine cause of the world, since science provides us with the answers to our basic questions. According to a widespread feeling, indeed, philosophical theology is a relic of an uncritical past and does not agree with the modern scientific frame of mind. As P. F. Strawson writes, "It is with very moderate enthusiasm that a 20th century philosopher enters the field of philosophical theology even to follow Kant's exposure of its illusions"[83]. Exit philosophical theology.

Experience of God?

One of the compelling reasons why a good number of neopositivist and analytical philosophers reject natural theology is their conviction that experience is the source and criterion of all scientific knowledge and that there is no experience of God. There are, however, authors who argue the opposite point of view. Rudolf Otto describes the various forms man's experience of the holy can take. Bergson and Scheler speak of an intuition of God[84]. The American philosopher Samuel Peirce writes that apprehending God is a matter of direct experience, although this experience does not amount to seeing God and must be developed into a demonstration[85]. W. James is convinced that feeling is the deeper source of religion, but natural theology is of little if any value: "causation is too obscure a principle to bear the weight of the whole structure of theology"[86]. Applying the pragmatic principle to natural theology and its arguments, James concluded that the latter are destitute of all intelligible significance. Only that is true which we can see immediately; what is inferred by reason is notional rather than real.

---

[82] See his *Logic and Language*, I, Oxford 1961, chapter ten.

[83] *The Bounds of Sense*, London 1966, 207.

[84] For the texts see H.T.L. Penido, "Sur l'intuition naturelle de Dieu", in *RScPhTh* 21 (1932) 549-561.

[85] *Values in a Universe of Change*, in *Selected Writings*, edit. by Ph. Wiener, New York 1958, 10.

[86] *The Varieties of Religious Experience*, Lecture XVIII

Outside the domain of philosophy both the denial of the possibility of experience of God and a more positive attitude can be found. A good number of the younger generation show a certain desire for religion and may even resort to new techniques to secure an encounter with the Eternal Self, the Infinite or the personal God of Christianity. Hence we cannot avoid the question of the role of experience in philosophical theology, in particular in that of St. Thomas. Aquinas does admit a spontaneous knowledge of God which people acquire through the experience of their own limits and of their dependence upon other beings[87]. It would seem that this spontaneous conviction reposes on a sort of reasoning of which one may not even become aware, such as that what does not explain itself requires another being as its cause. Also there is in us a natural tendency toward the ground of our being as well as to the good as such. This tendency may lead to an implicit knowledge of God[88]. Aquinas does, however, exclude any direct experience of God by natural man: God is Being which totally transcends man, while human knowledge is subject to the restrictions of man's embodiment. The above mentioned experiences only play an extrinsic role in the elaboration of natural theology. Nevertheless for St. Thomas experience is basic in philosophical theology inasmuch as the Five Ways all begin with facts of daily experience, viz. the experience of the physical world. We may add that St. Thomas throughout his study of God's being is aware of the fact that all our knowledge of God hinges on our knowledge of the physical universe. Thus instead of developing a chain of arguments such as those which deduce God's properties from his being pure actuality St. Thomas whenever possible seeks to revive the contact with the world of experience.

There is a further sense in which experience may be said to have a place in philosophical theology. Arguing that God is present in things St. Thomas writes that effects represent their cause. The term *repraesentare* here means to show the presence of God in his effects and to convey that he is actively acting in them so that, when touching the effect, one also touches God's causality.

It goes without saying that St. Thomas' metaphysics is very different from 18th century deism: God is intimately present in all things as the source of their being and their sustaining force. From this it follows that philosophical theology is not a sort of abstract discipline but a matter of "to be of not to be", because it conveys to us the knowledge of God "in whom we live, move and have our being".

---

[87] Cf. *S.Th*. I, 13, 8 and II-II, 85, 1.
[88] See *S.Th*. I, 60, 5.

God the Object of Man's Knowledge?

One of the major questions in contemporary philosophical theology is whether God can be the *object* of philosophical knowledge. Some authors question this possibility and debate has become so widespread that some even speak of the process of God's objectivity. To introduce the reader to the subject we recall a remark made by Gabriel Marcel to the effect that the Five Ways are "a trap of causalistic interpretation" and have "a materialising effect"[89]. Marcel apparently feels that God must be approached as a person and that instead of thinking *about* him man should turn *to* God and pray to him. In a somewhat similar way Karl Barth has called natural theology an attempt of sinful man to get hold of God: it has no function in the Church, even if in the course of history it has time and again manifested itself. "Natural theology must be rejected... *a limine* and kept removed even from the threshold of Christianity. It can only be advantageous to the theology and church of the Anti-Christ"[90]. Barth applies the Protestant theory of the corruption of human nature by the fall even to the field of knowledge. Rudolf Bultmann has a similar view: all human discourse about God outside the faith is not talking about God, but about the devil[91]. As recently as 1982 the French author J.-L. Marion launched a vicious attack against Aquinas accusing him of making God an idol because he pretends to grasp God by means of a man-made concept[92].

Other Protestant authors hold a more moderate position. E. Brunner admits that there is a natural knowledge of God, although he adds that such knowledge is easily and rapidly corrupted[93]. This view is shared by E. Jüngel who writes in a recent publication that in the history of Western philosophy the thought of God has led to a dissolution of all thought of God[94].

Confronted with such a strong-worded rejection of philosophical theology by some authors one wonders whether there is not a deeper reason behind their position than the one they indicate (viz. the opposition of rational thought to the Word of God). Upon closer inspection this suspicion is confirmed. It would seem that Barth's position is tributary to that of Feuerbach

---

[89] "Dieu et la causalité", in *Recherches de Philosophie II et IV: de la connaissance de Dieu*, Paris 1958, 28-29.

[90] K. Barth, "Nein! Antwort an Emil Brunner", in *Theologische Existenz heute*, Heft 14, München 1934, 63.

[91] Rudolf Bultmann, "Das Problem der natürlichen Theologie", in *Glauben und Verstehen. Gesammelte Aufsätze*, Tübingen 1933, 303.

[92] J.-L. Marion, *Dieu sans l'être. Hors-texte*, Paris 1982.

[93] E. Brunner, *Offenbarung und Vernunft. Die Lehre von christlicher Glaubenserkenntnis*, Zürich 1941, 64ff. Cf. H. Bouillard, "Le refus de la théologie naturelle dans la thélogie protestante contemporaine", in aa. vv., *L'existence de Dieu*, Tournai 1961, 95-108.

[94] *Gott als Geheimnis der Welt*, Tübingen 1978.

who thinks that religion is but the self-expression of man[95] and that, therefore, all thinking about God is a projection of man's own being. This position, in its turn, is connected with German idealistic philosophy, according to
which the concept of God is a product of the human mind. We also find this
in Schleiermacher's works. This theologian, who has been called the Protestant Church-Father of the 19th century, considered dogmatic theology a
reflection on human experience. In his view religion is the pious self-
awareness of man. In this connection one could say that Barth has brought
about a Copernican revolution in Protestant theology by stating that we
should not attempt to go from man to God, but must only consider God
approaching man. Barth's position is not without exaggeration when he says
that human religion is unbelief and the affair of godless man. For in natural
religion we do find, besides gross representations of human phantasies, a
sincere desire for God and a prayerful attitude of asking to receive his gifts.
It would be improper to qualify these feelings as idolatry. St. Paul himself
shows appreciation of this natural quest of God[96] and the Church has always
considered these religious convictions a *praeparatio evangelica*.

If one asks what may have brought Barth and Bultmann to hold their rather
extreme view of natural theology, the answer lies, it would seem, primarily in
the Lutheran theological tradition and, in the second place, in the
philosophical situation in Germany. Luther himself sharply criticised the
theologians who were using Aristotelian categories: they only know a false
God whereas the true God dwells in our innermost heart. The 'objectivity of
God' as taught by Scholastic theology, is an idle speculation of pagan thinking. Feuerbach described this tendency in Luther's thought as follows: Prot-
estantism has given up knowing God in himself and is only interested in him
insofar as man can experience him. With regard to the philosophical situation
in Germany the influence of Kant on theological thought must be recalled.
According to Kant the copula of the judgment does not refer to things but to
concepts. It is the human intellect which posits the beyond of concepts: what
the mind declares to exist is its object. The mind has the tendency to consider
objective what it thinks, although it may well be in an illusion regarding
outside reality. A further illustration of this position is what Kant calls the
cosmological proof of God: in order to explain contingent being necessary
being is required. But this argument only holds for man in his reasoning and
we are not allowed to exteriorize the conclusion. Needless to say, Aquinas'
doctrine is wholly different: in our judgements we can reach reality itself and
things come to us in our thinking: we do not know concepts but things. It is
wrong to claim that God belongs to the subjective order of the mind only.

---

[95] *Das Wesen der Religion (1948), 3rd conference.*
[96] *Acts* 17, 27-28. Cf. 14, 15-17.

Rather, he belongs to objective reality which the intellect acknowledges as real and independent of its own subjectivity.

Kant's view of objectivity was sharply criticised by Hegel: we should consider the content of thought not from the point of view of whether it is subjective or objective, but only by itself. Hegel then gives a description of what is called subjective and objective and defines Kant's view of subjectivity as the thesis which asserts that what we think is only subjective. Hegel himself, on the contrary, believes that true objectivity means that our thoughts are not only just *our* thoughts, but at the same time the *An sich* of things. For Kant, on the other hand, the contents of thought are objective only in this sense that the universal as formulated by us is contrasted with sense-experience of individual things[97]. For Hegel himself all objectivity implies subjectivity and vice versa. Subjectivity is marked by liberty, objectivity by the thing as it is or as it constitutes itself in the physical world[98]. Consequently God's objectivity is God as he unfolds himself in trinitarian life and in creation as well as in incarnation (which is continued in history).

It would seem that Hegel sacrifices the objectivity of God as God is in himself for he lets it flow over into creation and into human subjectivity. Apparently something of Luther's "God-for-me" (instead of God-in-himself) went into Hegel's system.

Kierkegaard sharply protested against Hegel's attempt to melt subjectivity into objectivity and vice versa: the absolute Subject cannot become the absolute Object. It could well be that Barth was influenced by Kierkegaard in his assertion that God is nothing but a subject and that any attempt at describing God is idolatrous. Objective knowledge is in his view unable to express the personal aspect of our encounter with God.

The rent between man and the physical world, made by Kant, continued to pose a problem for later philosophers. Husserl attempted to overcome the separation between the subject and the object by connecting the object with consciousness: it is made a determination of the field of consciousness. However, Husserl finally returned to an idealistic position: in human knowledge the physical world as it is in itself cannot be known; man's approach and observation decisively influence his knowledge.

Heidegger argues that prior to Plato and Aristotle the world was not experienced as an object; it was a reality facing man, but not opposed to him. Heidegger advocates a return to this pre-Socratic attitude. But even Heidegger

---

[97] See Hegel's *Enzyklopädie*, §41, Zusatz 2.
[98] *Ibid.* §46, Anmerkung. See also *Phänomenologie*, Vorrede, 22. On the influence of Luther on subjectivism see also Hegel's *Vorlesungen über die Geschichte der Philosophie* III, 228-230 (Michelet[2]): "So ist hier das Prinzip der Subjektivität, der reinen Beziehung auf mich, die Freiheit, nicht nur anerkannt, sondern es ist schlechthin gefordert, dass es im Kultus der Religion nur darauf ankomme".

failed to reach the study of the thing as such, because for him the phenomenological point of view remains primary. Being appears, shows or does not show itself to us. On account of this unforeseeable appearance of being a truly ontological and objective approach to reality does not seem possible. Heidegger thinks that it is a mistake to consider thought a reflection or a comprehension of being[99].

As Claude Geffré observes, it is striking that so many Protestant authors reject what they call the objectification of God on the ground that this 'objectification' would be an intrusion of philosophy into the domain of the faith, while they do not seem to be aware how much their own position is dependent on a particular philosophical view. In fact, Kant and Hegel seem to provide the inspiration for their extreme rejection of philosophical theology.

Answering these criticisms of natural theology requires entering into a discussion of metaphysics and theories of knowledge. At this juncture we may perhaps remark that when in Thomistic metaphysics the objectivity of God is affirmed, an objectivity wholly different from that of the physical world is meant: God, indeed, is outside and above all categories and not contained under our concept of being. For St. Thomas God is never "an object", for God is far above our understanding[100]. Moreover, God's objectivity is not something outside us, for God is present in the very roots of our being and our thinking. The human intellect has a basic capacity to receive knowledge of whatever is real. Although in its activity the intellect is bound by its formal object, which is the quiddity of material things, it can nevertheless affirm, by means of a judgement, the existence of a transcendent Cause of which it denies the limitations proper to material beings. Philosophical theology is a predominantly negative knowledge.

The Use of Philosophical Theology

Our discussion thus far has raised the question of the meaning and use of philosophical theology, that is of a scientific study of God by natural reason, independent of revelation. When we say 'independent' we do not exclude that it may be developed and worked out with the extrinsic guidance and inspiring assistance of the faith, as was the case for the metaphysics of St. Thomas.

Speaking about the *use* of theology we must keep in mind that metaphysics as such is useless knowledge in this sense that it is not a means to some other knowledge but is an end. It nevertheless bestows considerable benefits on man. In the first place philosophical theology shows that true religion is not

---

[99] Cf. CL. Geffré, *Le problème théologique de l'objectivité de Dieu*, Paris 1969, 241-263; A. Dumas, "La critique de l'objectivité de Dieu dans la théologie protestante", in *RScPhTh* 52 (1968) 408-426.
[100] *Expos. in libr. de causis*, prop. 6 (Saffrey, 47).

a product of man's anxiety or self-protective urges. The proper idea of God is not a projection of subjective psychic data. Religion has its foundation in man's being insofar as man is ontologically ordained to God, lives, moves and exists in God. Religion does not just belong to the field of so-called mystical phenomena and much less is it dependent on the domain of feeling or on individual taste. It has an objective basis, inasmuch as all man's faculties should accompany and agree with that which reason discovers about God. In this way philosophical theology gives a sound and solid basis to man's quest for the holy as well as to a much needed evaluation of the different religions and religious movements on the scene.

Philosophical theology is furthermore of importance for seeing the sense of human life and for understanding the ultimate meaning of the physical universe. There is little doubt as to what has been called the crisis of contemporary Western man, who in many ways seems to have lost sight of what he himself is. Despite the fact that with regard to what is at the surface of his life, he is able to procure for himself more pleasure and protection than ever before, at a more metaphysical level modern man feels disorientated and hollow in an indifferent world. Some speak of a crisis of reason, inasmuch as the universal rule and the common good are forgotten and individual interests as well as subjective views are pursued. Neopositivism and existentialism each in their own way witness to this failure of reason to make itself heard. In the field of moral life heteronomy is exchanged for a rather cheap autonomy. Anxiety, solitude and guilt feelings are widespread. Philosophical theology helps one to understand man as a person who finds his true greatness in being *capax Dei*.

Likewise when the transcendent cause, God, is disregarded or denied, the world, his work, begins to lose its value. We observe indeed a remarkable event in the history of modern philosophy. To the Greeks the world was in many ways a marvellous and divine place; to Christians it is God's beautiful work, full of wisdom and goodness. But ever since Bacon and Hobbes philosophers have been arguing that truth, goodness and beauty are ideas which man ascribes to things, but which basically are not present in extramental reality. In this way the world becomes an indifferent, dark or even threatening reality which is neither good nor beautiful, so that it has little left to make modern man feel at home. The Marxists and John Dewey assert that the admission of God's existence disrupts the homogeneity of reality and promotes a devaluation of the world[101], but Thomism argues just the opposite: the denial of God destroys the meaning and goodness of the physical world.

---

[101] Cf. J. Dewey's *The Quest of Certainty* and F. Smith, "A Thomistic Appraisal of the Philosophy of John Dewey", in *The Thomist* 18 (1955) 127-185.

A most important task lying ahead of us is somehow to create a common philosophy which will help to keep our society together in an age of pluralism. Now that the Christian heritage we have been living off in our post-Christian society is almost exhausted, people begin to realize how necessary a common philosophy and common ethics are. The contemporary discussion about the relationship of religion and the state provides an example of the problem we are referring to. It would seem that here philosophical theology has a role to play: if people who do not share supernatural faith, nevertheless admit the elements of religion as the soul of their culture, the trend toward a most dangerous total secularisation can perhaps be stopped or reversed. It is here that natural theology can be helpful. It will also contribute to the growth of natural law ethics. In carrying out its task it will, however, have to meet contemporary atheism and religious indifferentism as well as various underlying ideologies such as materialism, monism, extreme empiricism, etc. Philosophical theology will help us to understand these currents of thought somewhat better by examining the roots of atheism. Just as in the first ages of the Christian Church ecclesiastical authors and the Fathers argued with non-Christians in the terms of natural theology a similar, although probably more difficult task now lies ahead of us. Thus philosophical theology should examine the implications of the coexistence of the Absolute with finite being. Some of our contemporaries feel that if God exists, man's freedom is threatened. Merleau-Ponty even writes that the doctrine of the Absolute renders all thought superfluous and suppresses all human endeavours: "Il n'y a plus rien à faire"[102].

The answer to this and similar difficulties is obvious: the relationship between God and man is wholly different from that between an Absolute, imagined along the lines of other things, and ourselves. Moreover, the metaphysics of love introduces an entirely new perspective where sharing and loving communion are the goal that is aspired to.

The above mentioned tasks of philosophical theology are part of its preparatory function with regard to the faith. A further task it has is to assist sacred theology in its patient endeavour to meditate on divine revelation. Some have said that Aquinas' philosophical theology is an impossible synthesis of pagan thinking and Christian elements. This issue must be cleared up. We hope to show that, on the contrary, it is exclusively based on realism and the metaphysics of being. Precisely because of this closeness to reality, God's work, it is also in harmony with the doctrine of the faith.

---

[102] *Sens et non-sens*, 39.

CHAPTER ONE

MAN's QUEST OF GOD

I. *The Idea of God in Western Philosophy*

The philosopher who undertakes to study what has been called the problem of God notes that the idea of God or the divine is present in the thought of religious people regardless of the culture to which they belong. God's existence appears to be affirmed almost spontaneously by man and religion developed before philosophy established a systematic reflection on the nature of the divine.

This is not to say that philosophical theology is identical with the philosophy of religion. The former proceeds by means of the study of being in which it discovers a dependence on a transcendent Cause. For that matter it is independent of religious life and thought although religious convictions and experiences can be a source of inspiration to it, something which actually happened in Greek philosophy as well as in Aquinas' metaphysics. Philosophers such as Aristotle and St. Thomas see such a connection between their conclusions about the existence of God and religious beliefs ("et hoc omnes dicunt Deum"); Descartes, Leibniz, Kant and the deists took over the main traits of the idea of God as proposed by Christianity.

Religion often reflects the spontaneous insights of man, which, however, are frequently mixed with representations which do not stand the test of reason. Xenophanes and Plato provide samples of a philosophical criticism of anthropomorphic representations in popular religion. Nevertheless it is not the first task of philosophy to promote religious life or to lead man to intimacy with God: its purpose is to reach certain knowledge of God and his work. This knowledge may become a basis for thanksgiving and adoration, but when a philosopher turns to prayer, he leaves behind the realm of philosophy.

This does not mean that the God of philosophical theology stands beside the God of religion. For Aquinas God is not an abstract idea or a remote principle of being about which man theorizes but which has no importance for his life. On the contrary, God is the source of being, truth and goodness, in whom we live, move and exist; God is more intimately present to us than we are to ourselves. Hence after having demonstrated the existence of God St. Thomas will point out, as Aristotle had done before him, that the Being discovered at the terminus of the Five Ways is the same as the God of right religion.

In the Indo-European languages different words are used to denote God, viz. θεός, deus, God. While the name Zeus is derived from the root *di* (to shine), the etymology of θεός, is not fully certain. The Greek themselves proposed three explanations: Aeschylus and Herodotus see in it the root of the verb τίθημι: God establishes the order of the world and governs all things [1]; in his *Cratylus* Plato derives the term from θεῖν (to run) so that it would signify the restless movement of the celestial bodies. Plutarchus suggests that θεός has the same root as θεᾶσθαι [2]. Some Christian authors took over this explanation. Cassiodorus [3] and Isidorus [4] connect both θεός and *deus* with *timor* (fear). It would seem, however, that θεός is derived from *dhes*, a term which probably signified a rite or an object used in religious rite [5]. The Latin *deus* '(Dio, Dios, Dieu) is related to the word *divum* (sky).—"God" is a Teutonic word, of which the original meaning was probably quite close to the Latin *numen*. There are two Indo-European roots from which it may have been derived, meaning respectively "what is invoked" and "what is worshipped" [6].

The divine has been conceived and represented by man in a variety of ways, but no cultures have been found which did not have some form of religion. How does one account for this universal presence of religious views and practices? This question was already raised by Aristotle who pointed to two sources of religious belief, viz. cosmic phenomena and impressions in the human soul such as dreams and premonitions [7]. In his contacts with the physical world man experiences a reality which surpasses him: the cycle of the seasons, the coming-into-being of plants and animals, the pageantry of the starry heaven, storms, thunder and lightning, earthquakes and rain possess an impressive grandeur. Although these phenomena do not depend on man, they are nevertheless fundamental for his life. Astonishment and admiration lead man to the conclusion that these phenomena have a cause and master [8]. This insight is obviously not a projection of subjective feelings [9]. Rather it is based on an implicit argument: cosmic events demand an encompassing cause.

To this we may add that man, when not hampered by a superficial or limited way of looking at things, sees in them a certain depth. Thus a tree is more than a piece of wood, for it reveals vigour, strength and duration. In this way it points beyond itself to a more perfect reality in which it shares and of which it is a reflection. An example is the use of the term "divine" by

---

[1] See *Persae* 283 and *Hist.* II 52.
[2] *De Iside et Osiride* 375 C.
[3] *Expos. in Psalmum* XXI 2.
[4] *Etym.* VII 1,5.
[5] E. Beneviste, *Le vocabulaire des institutions indo-européenes*, II 134.
[6] *The Oxford English Dictionary*.
[7] *The philosophia* fr. 10 R.
[8] This conclusion apparently results from a premiss which uses the principle of causality but of the use of which one may not be aware. See *S.Th.* II-II 85, 1 and I 13, 10 obi. 3.
[9] On Feuerbach's theory of projection see the second part of this chapter.

Homer to denote this particular aspect of persons and things[10]. In Aquinas' metaphysics the underlying process of thought is explained by means of participation: formal perfections or essential contents partake of a source of reality in which they exist in an unlimited form[11].

In addition to these modes of implicit reasoning[12] there are experiences which may lead to an acknowledgement of a divine Reality. An example one may refer to is the so called voice of conscience with regard to what is right and wrong.

Man has given different expressions to these experiences of a source of being, a supreme person or power. The science of comparative religion distinguishes between mana, totemism, animism, anthropomorphic representations, etc. The natural and cultural environment of a tribe or nation often has a pervading influence on the way these religious representations are elaborated.

As soon as in other sciences the evolutionary viewpoint came to be widely admitted, scholars attempted also to set up a scheme of the stages through which religious representations would develop in their march forward. At an early stage the divine or the holy would have been conceived as an impersonal power[13]. Later it would have been represented as soul (animism) and as human beings (anthropomorphism). R. Otto speaks of several stages through which religion develops: charms, veneration of the dead, representation of the soul, the numinous, personification etc.[14].

This theory found a resourceful and zealous opponent in Wilhelm Schmidt who collected an impressive array of facts to argue that it is wrong to start from the assumption that the older forms of religion are the most primitive ones. Schmidt was convinced that "primitive" man cannot have had an impersonal idea of the divine. He also rejects the view of L. Lévy-Bruhl[15] that

---

[10] Cf. W.F. Otto, *Die Götter Griechenlands*, 1929, 55ff.

[11] Cf. vol. I, ch.14 (Intr., n. 29) with the relevant texts of St. Thomas.—J. Maritain speaks in this connection of the law of transgression: each perfection we know refers to something higher and leaves a certain desire behind in the mind for greater perfection. See also R. Guardini, *Religion und Offenbarung*, Würzburg 1958, ch.1.

[12] When formalized into an argument this reasoning becomes the Fourth Way (see below chapter three).

[13] Cf. N. Söderblom, *Das Werden des Gottesglaubens. Untersuchungen über die Anfänge der Religion*, 1916.

[14] R. Otto, *Das Heilige*, 1917. From the later part of the 19th century onwards numerous theories were proposed of the origin of religion: ancestor worship, fetishism, totemism, dynamism, animism, etc. The idea of a progressive development of the conceptions of the divine partly depends on the (secularised) Christian and Augustinian view that there has been progress in revelation. This belief in progress appears in Lessing's *Von der Erziehung des Menschengeschlechtes* and Herder's *Ideen zur Philosophie der Geschichte der Menschheit*. In his *Cours de philosophie positive*, vol. 5 A. Comte, when speaking of the theological age of history, divides it into the stages of fetishism, polytheism and monotheism.

[15] *La mentalité primitive*, Paris 1921.

primitive man was "prelogical". Evidence such as the religious beliefs of the
Pigmies points to a very simple sort of monotheism as the earliest known stage
of religious life; the general direction of evolution is that of a loss of the
grandeur of this initial idea of God[16]. Schmidt even thought that the beauty
of the oldest forms of religious belief can hardly be explained unless one
admits that they spring from an original revelation given to man[17]. Schmidt
could indeed point to the fact that in almost all "primitive religions"[18] a
supreme being is acknowledged and venerated, which is also frequently
regarded as the Creator. Changes in religious beliefs and development occur,
but the so-called successive stages of religion actually seem to coexist in a
changing balance. What some have called a development may not be more
than decadence provoked by changes in a way of life, by contamination with
other cultures or by a unilateral influence of certain representations or
philosophical ideas[19].

Turning now to our Western philosophical tradition we shall attempt to
give a concise description of the main philosophical theories about God. This
account is intended to be the background against which St. Thomas' natural
theology will be expounded. Obviously our survey will be sketchy and far
from complete.

Aristotle reached an idea of God of extraordinary depth but not unlike
most great ideas fashioned by man it owes a good deal to its predecessors.
Aristotle himself draws attention to Anaximander's representation of the
apeiron (the infinite): it performs the task both of a material principle and of
the cause of change and cosmic process. Another link in the chain of Greek
philosophical thought leading to the theory of the First Unmoved Mover is
Xenophanes of Colophon, a poet, satirist and philosopher who asserted that
God is one and unmoved[20]; although he moves the world he is identified
with[21]. With Xenophanes a philosophical monism arose which stands in sharp

---

[16] Cf. his "Der Ursprung der Gottesideee. Eine weiterführende Ueberschau", in *Anthropos*
16/17 (1921/1922) 1006-1051 and his work in twelve volumes *Der Ursprung der Gottesidee*,
Münster i.Westph. 1912-1955.—In addition to the evidence from primitive cultures collected by
Schmidt and his collaborators one may also point to the ancient Chinese who considered God the
universal rule of the world, the creator of man and the guarantor of the moral order. See P.M.
D'Elia, "Il Dio degli Antichi Cinesi", in *Gregorianum* 38 (1957) 193-256.
[17] *Der Ursprung der Gottesidee* IV (1935) 494. See also S. Pajak, *Urreligion und Uroffen-
barung bei P.W. Schmidt*, Sankt-Augustin 1978, 207ff.; E. Brandewie, *Wilhelm Schmidt and the
Origin of God*, (UPA) Lanham MD 1983.
[18] S. means those religions which in all likelihood are the oldest forms of religious life known
to us.
[19] Something similar may have happened in India and China.
[20] Fragm. 26. Xenophanes means that God remains in the same place. He does not exclude
other movements from God. See W.K.C. Guthrie, *HGrPh* I, 382.
[21] Aristotle, *Metaph.* 986 b 21-25.

contrast to the prevaling polytheism[22]. His criticism of anthropomorphic beliefs and his insistence on God's incomprehensibility opened up a new road and may be considered a starting point for philosophical theology[23].

As W. K. C. Guthrie writes "the thinkers of the sixth and fifth centuries shared, in outline, a common notion of the universe... There is the cosmic sphere, bounded by the sky, with the earth at its centre, the fixed stars at the circumference... But this cosmos is not the whole of reality. There is also 'that which surrounds', a quantity of the untransformed primal substance or *arche* which for some at least of the Presocratics was infinite or indefinite in extent. This was of a purer, higher nature than the opposites within the cosmos which had in some way been 'separated out' or 'condensed' from it. It was everlasting, alive and active, itself the initiator of the changes which formed the cosmos, which it not only surrounded but directed or 'steered'. It was in fact divine"[24]. As we have seen Anaximander's thought provides a good illustration of such an underlying conviction, but we find it also in Heraclitus. The Logos-fire of which he speaks surrounds the cosmos, directs all changes and even enters itself into cosmic process. It is a divine principle which is both external and immanent to the world[25].

With the Sophists a shift began away from the study of the physical universe to concern with man and society. Several Sophists criticised the views of traditional Greek religion. Protagoras shrouds himself in agnosticism[26]. Prodicus advances a rational explanation of the belief in the gods: human persons as well as things which were particularly useful to man, were elevated to divine rank[27]. The atomist Democritus considered the idea of God the result of man's fear of frightening physical phenomena[28]. In the second half of the fifth century B.C. criticism was widespread of traditional representations of the divine and religious rites. According to Aristophanes Socrates would have compared the traditional gods to coins no longer in circulation[29]. In one of Euripides' tragedies we read that people only believe in the gods by the force of convention[30].

---

[22] Cf. C. Ramnoux, "Sur un monothéisme grec", in *RPhL* 82 (1984) 175-198. See also W. Jaeger, *The Theology of the Early Greek Philosophers*, Oxford 1947, 38ff.; O. Gigon, "Die Theologie der Vorsokratiker", in *Studien zur Antiken Philosophie*, Berlin 1972, 41-68 points out that Theophrastus' Φυσικῶν δόξαι, our main source for ancient Greek theology, only gives scanty information. Theophrastus probably felt that most of the opinions of the Presocratics should not be considered scientific theology at all.

[23] See Xenophanes, A 1 (Diels-Kranz, *FVS* I 114, 3: ... ἀκατάληπτα εἶναι τὰ πάντα.

[24] *A History of Greek Philosophy*, vol. I, Cambridge 1962, 470.

[25] Guthrie, *op.cit.*, 471. In popular Greek religion the divine and the gods were generally considered immanent in the world.

[26] *FVS* II, B4.

[27] *FVS* II, B5.

[28] *Ibidem.*

[29] *Nubes*, 246.

[30] *Hecuba*, 799.

Nevertheless the denial of the gods was felt as a threat against the state[31]. Shortly before the beginning of the Peloponnesian war a law was passed in Athens which made atheism punishable[32]. Unfortunately this law of Diopheites did not distinguish between those who rejected naive representations and straightforward atheists. Criticism of gross anthropomorphic views aiming at the purification of religious belief and practice is a far cry from atheism. In his tragedies Euripides repeatedly suggests that gods who behave in an immoral way are no gods[33]. Philosophical reflection shows that the gods cannot act immorally and do not need anything from man[34]. In a somewhat similar line of thought the Hippocratic treatise *De morbo sacro* states that the cause of a mysterious disease is not a god: diseases have natural causes.

The philosopher Anaxagoras upholds similar views: mind is the cause of cosmic order. This mind exists in itself and is unmixed with the material of which the physical universe is made, but it has a knowledge of everything. However, Anaxagoras does not make it clear how this intellect works in causal processes[35].

The criticism of traditional religion by the Sophists also produced some positive results: the idea of God was purified. God now came to be conceived as the mind which influences cosmic process and governs things. Socrates seems to have subscribed to the criticism of anthropomorphic representations, but he did not yet reach a very precise idea of God. The attacks on traditional religion by the atheists led others to devise proofs of God's existence[36].

Already in his earliest dialogues Plato expresses his conviction about the divine: God is good and knows no envy with regard to man. Plato criticises the anthropomorphic representations of the poets: the gods are righteous and do not inflict injury[37]. Because the demiurg himself is good, he desires that all things resemble him so far as possible[38]. Plato's use of the terms 'god' and 'divine' is not without difficulty, because they signify a gamut of things from the ideas to good men. More specifically 'divine' denotes excellence; the divine is reality above this visible world subject to endless change[39]. The higher the place a thing has in the hierarchy of being the more divine it is. In

---

[31] Cf. Cotta's words in Cicero's *De natura deorum* I 42, 117: "Horum enim sententiae omnium non modo superstitionem tollunt, in qua inest timor inanis deorum, sed etiam religionem quae deorum cultu pio continetur".

[32] Cf. Plutarchus, *Vita Pericl.* 32.

[33] *Heracles*, 1341ff.; *Bellerophon*, fr. 292, 7.

[34] Antiphon, B 10.

[35] See W. Jaeger, *op.cit.*, 164.

[36] Cf. Xenophon, *Memorabilia* I, 4; Plato, *Laws* 996 c; Aristotle, *De caelo* I and *Metaph.* XII, cc. 6-7.

[37] *Rep.* 379-383.

[38] *Tim.* 29 e.

[39] Cf. J. Van Camp et P. Canart, *Le sens du mot 'theios' chez Platon.* Louvain 1956.

this way the divine is also that which is more universal and comprehensive[40]. In Stoic and Neoplatonic philosophy tinged with monism 'divine' continues to be used to qualify the world.

In his later dialogues Plato increasingly pays attention to the celestial bodies: the regularity of their revolutions as well as their apparent immutability were felt to be a sign of their divine nature. As a matter of fact in the fourth century B.C. the so-called cosmic religion began to spread in the Greek world. Its rise may be explained by Egyptian and Persian influences as well as by the philosophical criticism of traditional anthropomorphic religion; the progress of astronomy and the interest in the regularity of the movements of the celestial bodies in an age in which social and political structures were subject to constant change also contributed to this new religious feeling[41]. In his last dialogue Plato writes that astronomy provides the best foundation for piety and that the study of the heavens brings peace to man[42].

Fragment 13 of Aristotle's *De philosophia* also witnesses to the ascendency of cosmic religion: whoever sees the beauty of the universe will consider the celestial bodies as gods and the work of gods. Aristotle's theology is likely to have developed along the following lines: at first he probably placed the divine in the ideas or made the first heaven a supreme god[43], while later he worked out his celebrated doctrine of God as actuality and the First Unmoved Mover of the universe; desire of his perfection sets everything in movement; his activity is self-knowledge. His description of God as Thought of thought may be considered the culmination of Greek philosophy[44]. Nevertheless Aristotle's theology was not fully worked out. He did not solve the question of the unicity or plurality of the unmoved movers and his theory led him to exclude from God both knowledge of the world and providential care.

Compared to Aristotle's doctrine Epicurus' view of the gods is a retrogression: divine transcendence and unity are abandoned; supreme self-knowledge in contemplation is replaced by a happiness which is not much better than freedom from disturbance. Divine providence is rejected: the gods have no interest in man, since such a concern would impair their peaceful life[45]. Therefore under no circumstances should man fear the gods. Epicurus did indeed intend to free people from the bondage the fear of the gods imposed upon them. Man should live as a practical atheist. The only reference to the gods

[40] See W.J. Verdenius, "Platons Gottesbegriff", in *La notion du divin depuis Homère jusqu'à Platon. Entretiens sur l'antiquité classique*, I, Vandoeuvres-Genève 1954, 241-271; F. Solmsen, *Plato's Theology*, New York 1942.
[41] Cf. A.-J. Festugière, *La révélation d'Hermès Trismégiste, II: Le Dieu Cosmique*, Paris 1949, 75ff.
[42] *Laws* 967 a.
[43] Cf. L. Elders, *Aristotle's Cosmology*, Assen 1966, 39.
[44] See *id., Aristotle's Theology*, Assen 1972.
[45] *Epist. ad Menoeceum* (apud Diog. Lart. X 123).

still acknowledged is that their happiness is an example for the quiet life man
should strive to attain[46]. Lucretius would draw the consequences of this denial
of providence[47].

Epicurus himself admitted several proofs of the existence of the gods: all
nations have an inkling (πρόληψις) of the existence of the gods[48]. Impressions
of the gods come to us in our sleep[49]. The equilibrium of the world order
requires that the numerous perishable things are balanced by an equally large
number of imperishable beings[50].

With the Ancient Stoa a novel view is presented: man has no further destiny
beyond his present life, which he should conduct in full autonomy; he has no
need of grace or redemption and divine assistance is superfluous. Nevertheless
the wise man is religiously minded insofar as he contemplates with admiration
the order of the universe in which the Logos manifests itself. The Stoa does
in fact admit God's causality in the world and holds that God's existence can
be demonstrated. A presumption in favour of this is the fact that there is no
nation which does not believe in the gods[51]. Moreover, if God does not exist,
man's having a spiritual mind does not make sense[52]. Finally, powerful
cosmic phenomena as well as the degrees in perfection we observe point to the
existence of God[53]. God must be conceived as the soul of the world; he gives
movement to all things and his government encompasses whatever happens in
the world.

In sharp contrast with the monistic theology of the Stoa Philo of Alexandria reaffirms God's transcendence. God is higher than the world and he is
above knowledge, virtue and goodness[54]. Uncomposite and eternal he is the
one who really is. Philo introduces important modifications into Plato's
metaphysics inasmuch as he considers God a personal being, in whose thought
the ideas are present as the models of the things he creates.

In the second century A.D. the transcendence of deity was taught by
Albinus, who laid the groundwork of negative theology. God's being cannot

---

[46] This does not prevent the Epicureans from actively participating in popular religious
festivals, thereby imitating the joy and leisure of the gods. Cf. A.-J. Festugière, *Epicurus and his
Gods*, Cambridge Mass. 1956, 52ff. and 62; D. Lemke, *Die Theologie Epikurs. Versuch einer
Rekonstruktion*, München 1973, 101: for Epicurus the gods are the perfect realisation of ideal
happiness. See also J. Moreau, "Epicure et la physique des dieux", *Revue des études anciennes*,
1968, 286-294.

[47] *De natura deorum* V, 165ff.

[48] *O.c.*, I 43.

[49] Sextus Empiricus, *Adv. Mathem.* IX 25.

[50] *De natura deorum* I 19, 50. See also K. Kleve, *Gnosis Theon. Die Lehre von der natürlichen
Gotteserkenntnis in der epikureischen Theologie*, Oslo 1963.

[51] Cicero, *Leg.* I 24.

[52] This is the sense of Zeno's statement. See *SVF* I 152.

[53] Cleanthes insisted on these arguments. See Pierre Boyancé, "Les preuves stoïciennes de
l'existence des Dieux", in *Hermes* (1962) 45ff.

[54] *De opif.* 2, 8.

be expressed in words. God is so perfect that no attribute adequately captures his essence. God is neither good nor bad nor neither of these. He is neither endowed with attributes nor deprived of them[55]. Along the same lines of thought Maximus of Tyre points out that it is difficult to know God in the manner in which he is, because God surpasses whatever we affirm about him. We can only form analogous concepts to express his being[56].

Numenius, who prepared the way for Neoplatonism, places development in God: the first God is in himself; his being is uncompounded and unspeakable. He is the Father of the second god, the demiurge who by his thought makes the world. The third god is the world as thought by the demiurge[57]. With Plotinus a profoundly religious and even mystical view of God comes to the fore. Plotinus does not propose any proofs of God's existence, for the absolute principle can be experienced. All things flow forth from it. But by this emanation the principle, the One, does not lose anything. All things must turn toward their origin and strive to be re-united to the One. By means of purification, concentration and contemplation the soul accomplishes this return to its origin. Ecstasy is the highest level attainable to the human mind. Nevertheless the One remains hidden transcending as it does all knowledge[58]. We cannot predicate any attribute of God because God is above all perfections: omniperfection involves multiplicity. Because God is supremely one and real, he is above being and thought. The One remains in itself[59]. Plotinus himself does not use the expression "the unknown God", but it became current in later Neoplatonism[60]. A negative theology developed which placed God above any determination, above substance and life and even above thought[61].

Greek philosophy is only one of the sources of St. Thomas' natural theology. Biblical revelation, as is obvious, also had a pervading influence on the idea of God held by Christian philosophers. For this reason we must briefly consider the Biblical conception of God.

It is perhaps true that in the oldest utterances of the Bible about Yahveh traces can be found of an animistic mountain god, but these are soon effaced by the characteristics Israel attributes to its God. Yahweh who speaks to

---

[55] *Didaskalikos*, 10.

[56] *Oratio* XVII.

[57] Cf. Proclus, *In Timaeum* 1303, 27ff. (= fragm. 21 Des Places; Fragm. 24 Leeman); A.-J. Festugière, *La révélation d'Hermès Trismégiste, IV: Le dieu inconnu et la gnose*, Paris 1954, 275f.; J. Dillon, *The Middle Platonists*, London 1977, 366ff.

[58] *Enn.* V 4; VI 8, 19; VI 9, 10-11.

[59] *Enn.* VI 8. See also L. Sweeney, "Metaphysics and God: Plotinus and Aquinas", in P. Wilpert (hrsg), *Miscellanea Mediaevalia, 2: Die Metaphysik im Mittelalter*, Berlin 1963, 232-239. J. Rist, "Theos and the One in Some Texts of Plotinus", in *Mediaeval Studies* 24 (1962) 169-180.

[60] Cf. St. Augustine, *Sermo* 117, 3, 5: "qui scitur melius nesciendo"; *De ordine* 16, 44.

[61] See E. Benz, *Marius Victorinus und die Entwicklung der abendländischen Willensethik*, II: *Die Ansätze der Metaphysik Viktorins im plotinischen Denken*, Stuttgart 1932, 189ff.

Abraham is a living person, with whom Abraham is on intimate terms although he does not know him very well. God, on the other hand, respects Abraham's free choice: he calls him, but does not force him. He expects Abraham to attain moral perfection[62]. At this stage God is not yet known as the unique and universal Creator of the world.

With Moses Israel reached a deeper understanding: God saves his people and gives it its own territory and its own law. God is the holy one, the one who is immutable and who always remains faithful to his people. The implications of his name which he revealed to Moses, viz. "I am the one I am"[63], are that he is being and the very foundation of all things. God is one; the gods of other peoples are not real. In this way animism, polytheism and anthropomorphism are discarded. God is a spirit and cares for man who, for his part, must keep God's commandments (natural law). The religion of nature is replaced by religion based upon a personal relationship. Once God is known as the Creator of the world, he is acknowledged as the universal Lord.

The Jewish people occupied Palestine and turned to agriculture. In the process it underwent the influence of the cultural and religious traditions of the local inhabitants as well as of the neighbouring tribes. When it began to lose its original belief prophets arose who attempted to bring Israel back to faith in Yahweh. Time and again they reminded the people that God is not to be identified with natural phenomena. God is above the material world and man, for he is the Creator who by a free decision effortlessly produced the entire universe. In his wisdom God knows all things and every secret of man. Because he is good and merciful, he never abandons those who seek him[64].

In the New Testament the revelation of God is carried further: God exists in a Trinity of Persons who share the same divine nature in unity. God is love and invites man to participate in his triune life.

The idea of God presented in the Bible is that of the almighty Creator who extends his loving care to the world and supervises man's doings as a Judge and even more as a forgiving Father. This relationship with creation and in particular with man seems to introduce contingent and accidental factors into God's being. Hence some scholars have argued that there is an unbridgeable gap between the Biblical and the Greek idea of God[65]. Jewish and Christian thinkers, however, were always reluctant to admit such a cleft. Philo was one of the first to attempt to combine Biblical thinking with Greek philosophy: the philosophical study of God's existence and being leads to a purification of one's mind so that it is better prepared to receive the illumination of the

---

[62] *Genesis* 17, 1.
[63] *Exodus* 3, 13-14.
[64] Cf. *Kings* 19, 11ff.; *Genesis* 1; *Is.* 43, 13; 49, 13; 55, 9; *Jer.* 31; *Dan.* 14, 37; *Joel* 2, 13.
[65] See below the chapter on God's immutability.

faith. The Christian apologists also moved toward this solution. While they used Platonic and Stoic material, they conceived philosophy as a preparation of greater or lesser value to the faith.

The doctrine the Greek and Latin Fathers profess about God is inspired by Holy Scripture but when they speak about God they nevertheless use terms and expressions borrowed from philosophy. As Plato had done before him Clement of Alexandria derives the term *theós* from the verb *theein*[66]. God is called *apathès* (unchangeable), *amerès* (without parts), *akatalèptos* (incomprehensible); he is not in physical space (*achoorètos*)[67]. Most Fathers point out that God while penetrating all things, nevertheless transcends them[68]. God is immaterial; he is not the result of a process of becoming (*agennètos*). Some Fathers, apparently under the influence of Neoplatonism, even hesitate to ascribe *ousía* to God[69].

St. Augustine follows the Neoplatonic theory of God's unknowability[70]. God's essence is being (*esse*) itself[71]. Dionysius Areopagita also emphasizes God's transcendence and speaks of a *hyperdea divinitas*[72] or of God's *supersubstantialitas*[73].

With these materials the Scholastics elaborated their philosophical theology. However, Christianity's idea of God also became normative for most modern philosophers. Until the recent past authors speaking about God meant the God of the Christian faith, the personal being, the eternal, infinite and immutable Spirit who created the world. The general trend, however, has been toward the gradual abandonment of the metaphysics of being. On account of this God is given a more limited task such as that of preserving the world within the context of mechanism, but he is no longer the Being in whom we live, move and exist. Furthermore the connection between the God of philosophy and the God of religious worship is severed[74].

---

[66] Cf. Plato, *Cratylus* 397 c.

[67] See Hippolytus, *Refut.* 5, 9, 5.

[68] St. Gregory of Nyssa, *Epist.* 2, 39.

[69] See G. L. Prestige, *God in Patristic Thought*[2], London 1950; A.-J. Festugière, *La révélation* IV (n.57), 92ff.; G. Christopher Stead, "The Concept of Divine Substance", *Vigiliae Christianae* 29 (1975) 1-14.

[70] *De ordine* 18, 47.

[71] *De mor.eccl.* 14, 24.

[72] *De div. nom.* II, 42.

[73] *O.c.*, I 5. See also W.M. Neidl, *Thearchia. Die Frage nach dem Sinn von Gott bei Pseudo-Dionysius Areopagita und Thomas von Aquin*, Regensburg 1976.

[74] See E. Gilson, *God and Philosophy*, New Haven 1941, 88.—Descartes' idea of God is that of Christian tradition: "Par le nom de Dieu j'entends une substance infinie, éternelle, immuable, indépendante, toute-connaissante, toute-puissante et par laquelle moi-même et toutes les autres choses qui sont (s'il est vrai qu'il y en ait qui existent) ont été créées" (*Médit.* III: Adam et Tannery VII, 45). Descartes' theory of the idea of an infinite perfection in which God is present as its formal cause (see the next chapter) is a remote preparation for idealism. Cf. the *Quatrième réponse*, A. et T., VII, 241. On a subtle innovation in Descartes' idea of God see E. Gilson,

While in the system of Descartes deity remained somewhat aloof from the world, other thinkers attempted to construct a relation between God and the physical universe by making infinite space a property of God[75]. The tendency behind this was to work out a theory by means of which one could embrace in one single view God and the universe. Malebranche, Spinoza and Leibniz tried, each in a different way, to set up such an encompassing system. Yet God was still given the properties of the Christian God, except, of course, in the monism of Spinoza[76]. However, deism tended to reduce or set aside at least some of God's attributes. It is, for this reason, not so surprising that over the past 150 years other reductions, of God's infinitude and immutability, for instance, have been proposed.

Due to his empiricism John Locke refused to admit God's function as the ground of the certitude of our knowledge which Descartes, Malebranche and others had ascribed to him. It is superfluous to resort to God as guarantor of knowledge. Moreover man does not have an innate idea of God but constructs it out of materials gathered from sense experience[77].

David Hume went far beyond Locke in drawing a sharp distinction between rational and irrational belief. Severely critical of the latter his position was that the order found in the world lends some probability to the opinion that God exists as its author. But Hume holds that this probable knowledge concerns some of God's ontological properties (such as his power) but not his moral attributes. Hume wonders whether in view of the evil in the world it is not better to assume that God is a finite being. In this way Hume neutralised God separating him totally from man's scientific, moral and social life[78].

In scientific deism God was still conceived as a necessary and eternal being who is the cause of the universe. Voltaire denied God's freedom in creating the world and asserted that God remains far aloof from man's happiness or bad fortune. "The God of modern times has withdrawn himself from man's

*Etudes sur le rôle de la pensée médiévale dans la formation du système catésien*⁴, Paris 1975, 224ff.

[75] Cf. A. Koyré, *From the Closed World to the Infinite Universe*, New York (Harper Torch Edition) 1957, 190-225. See also Newton's *Philosophiae naturalis principia mathematica*, §527; H.S. Thayer (edit.), *Newton's Philosophy of Nature*, New York 1953, 41-67.

[76] Spinoza's God is no longer an individual being, but a universal reality and the totality of being in which things are present as finite modes. God is an immanent, not a transcendent self-causing power; thought and extension are the modes (attributes) of God through which we ascend to his deepest reality. As a matter of fact, God is a substance consisting of an infinite number of attributes, each of which expresses eternal and infinite essence. But we only know extension and thought (*Letter* II: Van Vloten-Land III, 5). Hence Spinoza's tendency to pantheism is unmistakable.

[77] *An Essay Concerning Human Understanding*, IV, ch.10.

[78] On Hume's position see R. Hurlbutt "David Hume and Scientific Theism", in *Journal of the History of Ideas* 17 (1956) 486-497; James Noxon, *Hume's Philosophical Development*, Oxford 1973, 165-187. Noxon's study is of importance with regard to the relation between Newton and Hume. See also Hume's *Dialogues Concerning Natural Religion* XII.

world of thought"[79]. If people still resort to him, it is so as to get an explanation of otherwise unexplainable facts. They use God to stop the gaps. Rousseau, on the other hand, stressed God's freedom of choice, although he admitted eternal matter coexistent with God[80].

According to Kant the question of God is one of the main problems of philosophy. He argues that God's existence cannot be demonstrated by theoretical reason, but is a postulate man needs to conduct his life meaningfully. Kant's concept of God is still that of Christian philosophical tradition and the idea of God is far from being meaningless: it constitutes the unity of thought and had a functional use forbidding us, as it does, to apply the properties of material things to beings-in-themselves. More than anything else God is the guarantor of moral order. Moral law is autonomous, but it nevertheless proposes a supreme good for man. God is needed to secure that virtue is rewarded. Although Kant holds that we cannot know God's atributes in God himself, he speaks about him as the good ruler of the universe. The question of whether Kant modified his theory of God in his *Opus postumum* (*ca* 1796-1802) is a matter for debate. Some see traces of a development into the direction of idealistic positions although others maintain that for Kant one who thinks God above himself and the world in the last analysis reconstructs rather than constructs God and the world (as idealism does).

Contrary to what Kant had done Hegel introduced an entirely novel idea of God as the Absolute, that is as the identity of the subject and the object, of thought and of being. The Absolute carries the finite within itself. In this way there is movement and process in God who is the idea which realizes itself by positing the finite, negating it and returning to itself. Hegel also speaks of God as the Absolute Spirit which expresses itself in the human spirit and through it returns to itself. It is the nature of spirit to produce itself, to make itself an object: it becomes knowledge of the finite and in this way it is reconciled to itself. Hegel sometimes expresses this in the following way: the Absolute passes from universality to particularity, from where it returns again to itself. This dialectical process in the Absolute is eternal. The Absolute Spirit becomes the other to acknowledge it as itself.

One may characterize Hegel's philosophy of God as a monism with stages or levels: God is the totality and universality; the physical world is God in a latent way; the human mind shares in the dialectical process of God. The apex of divinity is without personality and even without self-consciousness[81].

---

[79] G. Gusdorf, *Dieu, la nature et l'homme au siècle des lumières*, Paris 1972, 253. See also S. Goyard-Fabre, *La philosophie des lumières en France*, Paris 1972, 121-122.

[80] See in Rousseau's *Emile* the Profession of Faith of the Savoyard Vicar.

[81] In many ways Hegel's concept of God is baffling. He holds that the Absolute cannot be considered by itself but only in relation to other things (without the world God is no longer God). In our explanation we have made use of such texts as are found in his *Wissenschaft der Logik*,

Hegel's God is Becoming and God is immanent to what becomes out of him and what makes him exist. The entire universe no less than man and his history are the becoming of God.

Hegel's theory which attempted to combine some shreds of Christian dogma with Neoplatonic elements and the pantheism of Spinoza, has revolutionised the idea of God: the transcendent Absolute is introduced into space and time and becomes aware of itself in and through man. God is now indissolubly tied to man and man is divinised. Man even relates to God in social and political organisation as well as in the development of culture and philosophy. Traditional religion separates God from man. It is Hegel's conviction that man should consider himself a development and expression of the divine life which is man's nature in a more universal way. The finite as such is not truly real. Man, therefore, is taken up into the dialectical process of God becoming God. Because Christianity does not fully reveal this nature of God, it must leave the scene so as to make place for Hegel's dialectical monism. As J. Collins points out[82] the Left Wing Hegelians did away with the Absolute or Infinite Spirit and made man or the human community the absolute. Hegel's impressive theory turned intellectuals away from Christianity and in this way it promoted atheism. On the other hand, it also prepared evolutionary and finitist views of God.

John Stuart Mill is one of the first modern philosophers to defend the view that God is finite[83]. He believes with Comte that mankind is now leaving behind the theological and metaphysical age: in the present period of transition it would be premature, he thinks, to exclude religion entirely[84]. God as the demiurg of the world need not be infinite or omnipotent. Mills believes that the design observed in the world points to a limited God, for there is evil and suffering. If God would be infinitely powerful, each human individual would lead a morally perfect life[85].

Mill's writings influenced William James who returned from agnosticism or atheist humanism to belief in a finite God. However, he never regarded God as the Creator of the world. The truth of the idea of God can be verified in a pragmatic way (by means of a mystical experience); it is helpful for sound

---

Philosophie der Geschichte and *Vorlesungen über die Philosophie der Religion*. One may also compare F. Grégoire, "Idée absolue et panthéisme" in *Etudes hégéliennes. Les points capitaux du système*, Louvain-Paris 1958, 140-217; James Collins, *God in Modern Philosophy*, Chicago 1959, 201-237; W. Weischedel, *Der Gott der Philosophen* I, Darmstadt 1971, 289-312; W. Jaeschke, *Die Relionsphilosophie Hegels*, Darmstadt 1983.

[82] *O.c.,* (n.81) 236f.

[83] In a sense Voltaire and other rationalists had already imposed limits on their concept of God, excluding as they did divine providence.

[84] Mill's position is stated in his *Three Essays on Religion*, London 1874, and also in some of his letters. See the edition *The Letters of John Stuart Mill* 2 vols, London 1910, by H.S.R. Elliot.

[85] *Three Essays*, I, 93.

morals and fits in with a scientific view of the world. Man can further God's design and, surprisingly, he can even enrich God's being itself. In the full sense of the term man is God's partner. In James' view God is not the Absolute of monist philosophers but a supreme individual with moral perfections. James rejects the entitative attributes traditional theology assigned to God: they are devoid of practical significance. In short James' basic idea is that there is a plurality of finite beings who must cooperate the one with the other[86].

James' view was further developed by Alfred North Whitehead. However, before presenting an outline of the latter's theory we must briefly mention Bergson's intuitionism. According to this French philosopher we must insert ourselves in an experience of the duration of things. Duration is self-constituting: through contact with an ascending series of durations we reach an intensity of duration called eternity or God who is the source of all duration. According to Bergson the only reality is Becoming and so he is not very clear on the distinction between God and the world. He seems to consider it a difference of degree rather than a basic otherness, although he himself always denied that his philosophy is pantheistic. In particular in his earlier period Bergson while stressing certain aspects of deity such as energy, duration and intensity, neglected other ones. He did not consider God as subsistent thought or provident love. As a matter of fact his approach is anti-intellectualistic. Hence those attributes of God reached by intellectual deduction are of no value: God is emotional creativity[87].

In his later work *The Two Sources of Morality and Religion* (1952) Bergson is feeling his way to the basic truths of Christian metaphysics, although this does not mean that the gist of Bergson's theories is now in agreement with traditional philosophical theology. With Maritain we should distinguish between a Bergsonianism *de facto* and another Bergsonianism according to its deeper intention, which is an attempt to free modern thought from the limits imposed on it by idealistic philosophy as well as positivism. It is an invitation to return to reality although from the point of view of Aquinas' principles the extent to which Bergson himself realised such a return remains inadequate[88].

Bergson's view of God as a centre from which the worlds shoot forth as rays of an immense bouquet[89], that is of an evolving Absolute, is an anticipation

---

[86] Collins, *o.c.*, 313.

[87] In his *Les deux sources de la morale et de la religion*, 256 Bergson writes in a Pascalian vein that the God of philosophers is so different from the God of religion that ordinary people will not recognize the one in the other.

[88] On Bergson's philosophy of God and its relation to Christian thought see J. Maritain, *La philosophie bergsonienne. Etudes critiques*[3], Paris 1948, 169ff. T. Penido, *Dieu dans le bergsonisme*, Tournai 1934; J. Nabert, "L'intuition bergsonienne et la conscience de Dieu", in *Revue de métaphysique et de morale* (1941); M. Carion, *Bergson et le fait mystique*, Paris 1976.

[89] *Evolution créatrice*, 270.

of Whitehead's process theology or theological physics. Whitehead proposes
to give an explanation of the ultimate constitution of the universe: the world
consists of a plurality of interconnected centres of experience which are somehow mind-like and in constant process. In his so-called primordial nature or
mental pole God is the foundational starting-point of cosmic process. However, there is another side to the nature of God. He is also the end of process
in that his nature is completed into a fulness of feeling: "the concrescent
creature is objectified in God"[90]. God's consequent or derivative nature is
constituted by the creative advance of the world. As we already pointed out
in the Introduction Whitehead rejects the doctrine of a transcendent Creator
and, as he critically observes, an Imperial Ruler[91]. In its place we get a totally
secularised God who seems to fit in better with modern theories about the
physical universe[92]. God is arrived at as an entity required by the facts of the
physical world. God is the cause by which the possible is actualised in a
creative advance. God's function is also limitative since being connected with
God means for a physical fact that it is of this precise type.
Whitehead's theory has met with considerable acclaim in the Anglo-Saxon
world: it is credited with placing dynamic process in God, something traditional metaphysics failed to accomplish. Moreover God now seems to have
come much closer to the physical universe[93]. However, Whitehead's approach
seems to be based on the assumed duality of mind and body in man. It is an
extrapolation of certain physical facts and evident principles of being such as
"the more cannot come from the less" are discarded[94]. As J. Collins observes
"there seem to have been two major impulses animating the finitist movement: naturalistic and humanistic"[95]. A modern theory of God, it is felt, must
be connected with natural science and the ceaseless becoming we experience[96].
Furthermore, the theory's supporters argue, the presence of evil shows that
there must be growth in God's consequential nature so that evil will decrease.

---

[90] *Process and Reality*, New York 1929, 523.

[91] Whitehead not only discards the Semitic concept of God as it is expressed in the Old Testament and in Christian theology, he also wants to oppose immanentism and monism. Cf. his
Religion in the Making, New York 1926, 68ff. However from our metaphysical point of view his
auto-creationism is but a veiled monism.

[92] God never loses what has accrued to him and may even let this acquired wealth reflect back
upon the physical universe.

[93] See B. Z. Cooper, *The Idea of God. A Whiteheadian Critique of St. Thomas Aquinas' Concept of God*, The Hague 1974.

[94] Denied, for instance, is the principle that a cause must be at least as perfect as its effect.
See L.A. Foley, *A Critique of the Philosophy of Being of A.N. Whitehead in the Light of
Thomist Philosophy*, Washington D.C. 1946.

[95] *O.c.*, 322f.

[96] Newton's account of God's causality with regard to the world intimated that God
should not be thought of in isolation from the physical universe. See his *Philosophiae Naturalis
principia mathematica*, §527.

The answer of Aquinas to this theory will be expounded in the following chapters[97].

It would seem that no other significant theories concerning the idea of God have been advanced in modern philosophy so that we must now turn to the study of the denial of God's existence.

II. *A History of the Idea of God in the Negative*

Atheism is the denial of God's existence as the dominant religion in a particular culture conceives it. In the Western world atheism is the denial of one or more constitutive elements of the notion of God as held by the Christian faith and elaborated in Christian philosophy[98]. In Attic Greek the terms ἄθεος is used in the more general sense of 'godless' and 'abandoned by the gods'.In Plato's *Apologia* 26c it means a person who denies the gods, in particular those recognized by the state[99]. In later Greek the term ἀθεότης (godlessness) is found. The New Testament has ἄθεος and ἀσεβής. St. Ignatius of Antiochia calls the pagans atheists[100], whereas Simplicius applies the same term to the Christians themselves because they deny the divinity of the cosmos[101].

Atheism can be divided into theoretical and practical atheism. The former is either an explicit or an implicit denial of God's existence[102]. One is a practical atheist when one refuses, in one's life and actions, to take God's existence into account[103]. Atheism is a phenomenon mainly restricted to the Christian world. However there were a number of atheists in fifth century Athens. Some texts of the Sophists, certain of Euripides' tragedies as well as of Aristophanes' plays reflect unbelief or agnosticism[104]. Plato considered atheism the greatest threat to the commonweal, but he is convinced that the proper education, true learning, a morally good life and above all the

---

[97] In particular below c.3.

[98] Cf. E. Gilson, *L'athéisme difficile*, Paris 1979, 12.

[99] Plato uses ἀσέβεια to denote ungodliness and impiety.

[100] Cf. also Justinus, *Apol. 6, 1-2*.

[101] *In De caelo* 370, 30-371, 4.

[102] From the point of view of Christian metaphysics the denial of such attributes as transcendence, omnipotence, infinity, immutability and providence is tantamount to a refusal to admit God's existence and therefore it is objectively a form of atheism.

[103] Cf. St. Paul's *Letter to Titus* 3, 3. One may also use the term unbelief to denote the refusal to admit Christian doctrine. This form of unbelief does not necessarily imply atheism, although historically speaking it has often been a stepping stone to it. Cf. S. Budd, *Varieties of Unbelief. Atheists and Agnostics in English Society, 1850-1860*, London 1977, 105. See also the excellent study by G.M.M. Cottier, "Athéisme religieux", in *Nova et Vetera*, 1968, 36-55.

[104] Prodicus, fragm. 5 (DK). See Guthrie, , *o.c.*, III, 241ff.; Euripides, *Cyclops* 316ff.; V. Ehrenberg, *The People of Aristophanes*, Cambridge Mass. 1951, 272. According to Democritus religion is a product of fear.

approach of old age help people to give a positive answer to the question whether the gods exist[105].

Changes in Greek social and political life in the fifth and fourth centuries B.C. led to a religious crisis. Something similar took place in France in the early decades of the seventeenth century. In the wake of the wars of religion a rather virulent atheism appeared. The changing view of the world, political upheavals, the rise of individualism and the intrusion of Epicureanism furthered agnosticism and unbelief. Perhaps not without some exaggeration Mersenne sighed that Paris alone was plagued by 50,000 atheists. Surprisingly atheism as a fairly widespread trend in intellectual life soon declined until it appeared again about the middle of the 19th century. It could be argued though that such philosophers as Spinoza, Fichte and Hegel modified the idea of God to such an extent that they must be considered atheists[106].

The recrudescence of atheism in the 19th century was caused by a number of factors: a rationalistic attitude made people exclude from the field of knowledge whatever is transcendent[107]. The rise of the sciences was accompanied by a positivist attitude toward religion; it was widely believed that theology and metaphysics must now be replaced by the sciences[108]. In fact, metaphysics had already been weakened so much that God was generally conceived as a cause wholly extrinsic to the universe. Deism had taken the place of philosophical theology. In a further development recourse to God as a cause beyond the physical world came to be considered unscientific. Laplace introduced the theory of homogeneous explanation by means of causes of the same order[109]. Moreover the universe the scientists were now in the process of discovering was so magnificent that they lost interest in the invisible God.

Others were led to reject religion by the desire to change certain political structures which were felt to be connected with Christianity[110]. Growing awareness of one's liberty made people reject God in order to assert their autonomy. In a letter of the fourth of February 1795 Schelling writes to Hegel that he has no longer any use for the concept of a personal God; he had become a Spinozian although he replaced the All of Spinoza by the Ego[111].

---

[105] *Laws* 888 aff. Cf. H. Görgemans, *Beiträge zur Interpretation von Platons Nomoi*, München 1960, 85-100. In *Laws* 908 b-e. Plato distinguishes between atheists who lead a morally correct life and others who in addition to their atheism lack self-control.

[106] See. C. Fabro, *Introduzione all'ateismo moderno*, Roma (Ediz. Studium), 127-167.

[107] Cf. J.H. Newman, *An Essay on the Development of Christian Doctrine*, 357.

[108] A. Comte, *Cours de philosophie positive*, I, 1° leçon.

[109] See his *Essai philosophique sur les probabilités* (1814) in *Oeuvres complètes* VI (1886), VI. Charles Lyell, the father of modern geology, Darwin and others shared Laplace's view of the exclusive recourse to homogeneous causes.

[110] Cf. F. Gregory, *Scientific Materialism in Nineteenth Century Germany*, Dordrecht 1977.

[111] One may compare *Fichte. Briefe von und an Hegel*, hrsg. von J. Hoffmeister, Hamburg 1952, I, 22. See also Engels' *Poem on Heroes (Marx-Engels. Historisch-kritische Gesamtausgabe I, 2, p. 257)* where he writes of Hegel:

We have already had an opportunity to mention Hegel's pantheistic idealism clothed in a terminology which evokes Christian doctrine. For some decades Hegel's thought held sway over Germany, but then it began to meet with fierce opposition. Schopenhauer affirmed the godlessness of reality. In Nietzsche's words he was "the first unflinching atheist philosopher in Germany"[112]. But the influence of the pessimistic Schopenhauer was far surpassed by that of Ludwig Feuerbach. The latter's *The Essence of Christianity* was greeted with enthusiasm by the younger generation who became partisans of his view. Religion arises when man projects his sense of dependence onto the idea of God. This God is nothing else but man's own essence placed before him; his own thoughts and desires are made an object to be adored. In his prayers and sacrifices man turns to this being his own imagination has created and personified; man even makes himself an object for this imaginary projection[113]. In short religion is totally subjective and theology is anthropology.

Feuerbach's theory of religion as a projection was taken over by Friedrich Engels and Karl Marx. What is new in the latter's presentation of the issue is their stress on the social factors contributing to such a projection. "Religion is the self-consciousness and self-experience of man who has not yet taken possession of himself or who has again lost himself... It is a reverse awareness of the world..., its moral sanction, its solemn complement, the general basis for consolation and justification. It is the imaginary realisation of man's essence, for man's essence is not real.... The misery of religion is at the same time the expression of real misery and ... a protest against it. Religion is the yearning of creatures in distress, the sensitivity of a world without heart as well as it is the spirit of a spiritless situation. It is the opium of the people. The real happiness of the people requires doing away with religion as their illusory happiness. The demand to give up illusions about one's situation is the demand to give up a situation which needs these illusions.... Religion is the illusory sun revolving about man as long as man does not revolve about himself. It is the task of history to establish the truth of this world after the disappearance of the beyond of truth. It is in the first place the task of philosophy which is at the service of history to strip the sacral forms of human self-alienation of their disguise and to unmask this alienation in its profane forms. Thus the criticism of the heaven turns into a criticism of the earth, the

---

Mein ganzes Leben weiht'ich der Wissenschaft,
Den Atheismus lehrte ich mit ganzer Kraft.
Das Selbstbewusstsein hob zum Throne ich,
Gott zu bewältigen, glaubte ich schon.

[112] *Die fröhliche Wissenschaft* V (Schlechta II 226).
[113] *Das Wesen des Christentums*, Leipzig 1909, 37.

criticism of religion into criticism of prevailing laws, the criticism of theology into that of politics''[114].

Marx's atheism is intrinsically dependent on Feuerbach's theory of projection. But to understand its nature and implications its connection with Hegelianism must also be kept in mind. Marx transposes Hegel's Absolute assigning its characteristics to man[115]. Thus the Absolute Spirit is replaced by man who, according to Marx, is a universal subject (*Gattungswesen*). Aseity, the prerogative of God, is attributed to man. In the Christian view created being does not have its ground in itself, but for Marx it is absolutely self-sufficient and has no cause[116]. Thus Marx preaches the total autonomy of man who must renounce entertaining dangerous evasions of reality and must achieve his own redemption by reshaping the world. Atheism is a stage in the dialectical development of history: it is the negation of a thesis (the existence of God) and a stage through which we must pass to reach a new idea of man, viz. man who assumes the characteristics of God[117]. Heaven is now replaced by the earth as the historical space where man unfolds his activity[118]. But this does not mean that eventually Marxism will no longer be anti-religious once all social misery has vanished. Religion alienates man from himself and from his true tasks. For this reason it must disappear: man is for himself the highest being and must vigorously extirpate those conditions which reduce him to a humiliated and despicable being[119]. He should not live by the grace of someone else[120].

Marx's view of theism as a dangerous evasion from man's real being and tasks was taken over not only by his followers but also by a number of existentialist authors. Although some Marxist philosophers do not seem to make atheism a key issue[121], in official Marxism as well as in the mind of most of its adepts the idea of God must be abandoned as a worn out and even dangerous symbol which has lost its use[122]. The question has been raised whether the Marxist analysis of the economic and social situation can be

[114] *Zur Kritik der Hegelschen Rechtsphilosophie. Einleitung.* (*Karl Marx. Frühe Schriften*, B.I, hrsg. v. H.J. Lieber und Peter Furth, Darmstadt 1971, 488f.).

[115] While Hegel's Absolute is the only being and nothing else can exist outside it, Marx reintroduced multiplicity.

[116] G.M.M. Cottier, *L'athéisme du jeune Marx: ses origines hégéliennes*, Paris 1959, 342.

[117] *Ökonomisch-philosophische Manuskripte aus dem Jahre 1844*, in *Marx-Engels. Werke*, Berlin 1957-1968, Ergänzungsband I, 583.

[118] Hegel had already written that without the world God is not God. See his *Vorlesungen über die Philosophie der Religion* I, 1 A & B (Theorie Werkausgabe 92ff.).

[119] *Zur Kritik der Hegelschen Rechtsphilosophie* (cf. n.114), 297.

[120] *Ökonomisch-philosophische Manuskripte* (n.117), 606.

[121] Roger Garaudy, Leszek Kolakowski, M. Horkheimer, Th. Adorno, J. Habermas.

[122] On E. Bloch's view see W. Kern, ''Grundmodelle des humanistischen Atheismus'', in *Stimmen der Zeit*, 1972, 291-304. For a statement of the official Marxist doctrine cf. the manual *Grundlegung des Marxismus-Leninismus*², Berlin 1963, 8, where religion is categorically rejected and man's only field of activity is said to be the earth.

accepted without admitting the Marxist ideology in general. The answer must be negative because the analysis itself is dependent on dialectical materialism and marked by the theory of the struggle between the classes in society[123].

The rise of atheism in Germany was considerably furthered by Friedrich Nietzsche. Understanding and interpreting Nietzsche is a difficult undertaking, more so than that of other contemporary philosophers. The reason for this lies in the peculiar nature of his thought and writings. Taking Nietzsche's statements at their face value risks overlooking the fact that he is a poet and prophet who formulates problems in ever new ways. Qualifications of Nietzsche as an atheist, a nihilist or a new Prometheus are one-sided. In our survey we shall attempt to indicate how Nietzsche was commonly understood and how his ideas influenced others.

Nietzsche thinks the time has come to give up belief in God. The death of God will be the beginning of a new era in history. The roots of this position are to be found in the spirit of age: the growing awareness of man's autonomy, the new materialism and the theory of evolution. Nietzsche's anti-rationalism also contributed to his rejection of Christianity. God is inconceivable. If God's eye were watching us, we could no longer live in undisturbed self-possession. Nietzsche shared Schopenhauer's conviction of the *Ungöttlichkeit* of human life, which has no meaning[124].

Nietzsche almost always speaks of God as a human invention, a lie, a mistake of man and a projection caused by fear. Man called his own weakness God[125] and never embraces anything but clouds. The idea of God is the collection of idealised desires and of our lower needs, such as the need of a master. Nietzsche rebels against this situation: projected ideals must die so that life may triumph; man must remain faithful to the earth at all costs; what he has revered as God is in reality harmful; the idea of God is the greatest obstacle to an untrammeled human existence; it is a declaration of war against life. Dionysius, that is the stream of life and the vital force, must replace the moderating influence of Christian religion, science and technology. Christianity has obstructed and repressed the body, its instincts and passions and even the exercise of the powers of the mind.

---

[123] Cf. the *Letter* by P. Aruppe S.J., published in *Ateismo e Dialogo* 16 (1981) 114-117.

[124] *Der Wille zur Macht* (Schlechta III, 748ff. *et passim*). In his *Die fröhliche Wissenschaft*, 357 Nietzsche raises the question whether Schopenhauer's atheism is a typically German product. The answer is negative: "the victory of scientific atheism is an all-European event". The Germans, and in particular Hegel, retarded the rise of atheism. Schopenhauer was the first inflexible atheist the Germans had. According to N. atheism is rather the result of an auto-destructive tendency in Christianity itself. For Christianity makes people seek greater freedom although it attempts to keep them submitted to God.

[125] *Der Wille zur Macht* (Schlechta, III, 574); *Menschliches, Allzumenschliches* (s., I, 518ff.); *Morgenröte* I, 91 (S., I, 1071f.). Critically speaking N.'s analyses are tendentious and full of gross and naive misunderstandings.

Obsessed by the idea of God Nietzsche looked for a substitute. Eternal recurrence and the superman, this higher form of human existence, must take the place of God. Nietzsche considered himself an atheist and even an anti-theist, although in his inner self he seems to have felt a constant craving for religious worship.

After God and Christianity will have been set aside an era of new possibilities wil open up before us. Man will take the place of God and create his own values. However, Nietzsche was sharp-sighted enough to foresee the enormous consequences of the denial of God's existence: the universe is deprived of warmth and light; the earth circles around aimlessly; man has no co-ordinates to get his bearings and darkness fills infinite space. Now that man has killed God the break with man's past is total[126]. The death of God is followed by the collapse of moral values hitherto admitted. There is no longer a universal moral law.

Nietzsche found a good number of followers who urged doing away with more than 2000 years of reason, law and order to surrender instead to one's spontaneous urges as well as to the forays, whatever direction they take, of technology, industrialization and experimentation; in short, to make extreme subjectivity and convenience the supreme law[127]. Others who also claimed to be inspired by Nietzsche, chose to transform his "will to power" into the inex-orable progress of history and his superman into a society without classes.

Even if some interpretations and uses of Nietzsche's writings go beyond what he had in mind himself, it would be dishonest not to see in him one of the most destructive forces in the history of Western man[128]. Despite his accomplishments as an author and a most acute observer of human psychology, despite even his prophetic gifts Nietzsche must be considered an atheist whose works had a tremendous impact on the spiritual destiny of Western man.

Nietzsche's account of nihilism made a profound impression on Heidegger, who considers the statement that God is dead a declaration of fact: the metaphysical order of values which for so many ages has guided thought and actions has now collapsed. The Platonic-Christian God has now definitely left

---

[126] *Die fröhliche Wissenschaft*, I, 125 (S., II, 127).

[127] Cf. J.J. Goux, *Les Iconoclastes*, Paris 1978; B.-H. Lévy, *Le testament de Dieu*, Paris 1979, 121: "On manque l'essentiel de *Mein Kampf* sans la volonté folle d'abolir trois mille ans de rationalité, d'affirmation de la Loi, de médiation "paternelle" et, pour tout dire, de monothéisme". Other authors, not unlike Nietzsche, extol boundless change and spontaneity. Cf. Ph. Benoist, *Tyrannie du Logos*, Paris 1975, 14-20.

[128] See A. Camus, *L'homme révolté*. One may also compare K. Jaspers, "Zur Nietzsches Bedeutung in der Geschichte der Philosophie", in *Neue Rundschau* 61 (1950) 346-358. The author suggests one finds in Nietzsche not a specific doctrine but a criticism of convention and inauthen-ticity.

us. In the modern world there is no place for him any more[129]. Heidegger does not seem to regret it for this God was only an unfortunate expedient of man for freeing himself from his inevitable temporality and limitations[130].

The question must be raised whether Heidegger still sees a possibility of affirming God's existence and assigning some meaning to the idea of God. Among the students of Heidegger the partisans of transcendental philosophy attempted to identify Heidegger's Being (*Sein*) as the Ground of reality with God[131]. For Heidegger Being is, indeed, the mysterious ground which becomes present in the *Dasein*. It is a source and origin (*Ursprung*) which gives rise to beings without losing itself in what comes forth from it. Nevertheless Heidegger repeatedly and emphatically rejected the identification[132]. Being can never be thought of as the foundation of God or as his essence. Heidegger adds that, as Luther correctly understood, faith does not need the philosophy of being. It is a fascinating question why Heidegger discards so emphatically any relation between philosophy and religion. One of the reasons might be that he has a (preconceived) idea of God wholly different from that of the Absolute Ground of being[133]. Heidegger starts somewhat 'unmetaphysically' from a position which holds that reality appears and disappears without any connection with an ultimate Cause. This view is quite close to an abdication by reason of clear and evident principles. Instead of subscribing to a methodical and critical analysis such as the philosophy of being carries out, Heidegger wants to make his own the *dichtend-denkende Grunderfahrung des Seins*, i.e. the basic experience of being in its poetic and noetic expression by the early Greek philosophers[134]. Contradictions are to be experienced and not to be judged and it is meaningless to propose refutations in the battle between philosophers[135]. Despite all contrasts they allow us an ecstatic dwelling in the vicinity of being[136]. Apparently we have to do here with the giving up of a logico-critical position in thought and the decision to stay within a subjective experience of being[137]. On account of this choice Heidegger does not go beyond a contact with certain aspects of being.

---

[129] In a sense this may be considered a corollary of Luther's radical separation of faith from reason. Cf. Th. Süss, *Luther*, Paris 1969, 42f. Luther, in fact, declared reason a-religious and even godless. God disappeared from the temporal order.

[130] *Holzwege*, 196f.

[131] See E.-R. Korn, "La question de l'être chez Martin Heidegger", II, in *Revue Thomiste* 70 (1970) 560-603, 585.

[132] One of Heidegger's most outspoken statements on this subject is a reply to a group of students of the University of Zürich. We follow the text published by R. Kearney and J.S. O'Leary (edit.), *Heidegger et la question de Dieu*, Paris 1980, 333f.

[133] See below on what is implied by Heidegger's "Fourfold".

[134] *Einführung in die Metaphysik* (edit. 1953), 11.

[135] *Brief über den Humanismus*, 185ff. (in *Wegmarken*, Frankfurt a.M. 1967).

[136] *O.c.*, 173.

[137] One may perhaps connect this position with Luther's attitude "whose religious and theological thought consciously, willingly and consistently contains contradictory elements" (J.

In all this Heidegger lets himself be guided by an unuttered assumption ("eine unausgesprochene Vermutung")[138]: he chose this position he writes, because he felt it would be a road to freedom[139]. Without even realizing it Heidegger was very much influenced by a central tenet of Luther. In a remarkable essay E. R., Korn explains how Heidegger in his early lectures on *Augustinus und der Neuplatonismus* (1912) sets forth Luther's thesis that God is not knowable through his works; Christian faith is identified with subjective experience; true knowledge is acquired by a step backward, that is by undoing the critical and notional thought of the philosophical and theological tradition,—our state of sin. Heidegger wanted his philosophy to be a soteriology: his Being concerns man. But he parts with Luther insofar as he sets forth a quasi-self-redemption by man, viz. his auto-transcending[140].

His poetic and non-committal approach led Heidegger to set forth the strange theory of the Four(fold) or Quadrate ("das Geviert"): heaven and earth, the divine and mortal man. The Four are in interplay and none of them is their centre[141]. The centre is the primeval whole or the yawning chasm. Heidegger, as we have seen, starts from the unproven assumption of the not-grounded appearance of being. Instead of a true metaphysics of being he presents a poetic lingering in appearances, but in this way Heidegger paradoxically relapses into essentialism. Obviously in this procedure God is no more than a secondary aspect. In his *Letter on Humanism* Heidegger writes that from the truth of being (its appearance) one comes to think the essence of the holy and from there the divine (*die Gottheit*). It is only in the light of the divine that we can say what the word God means. Indeed, God can only be thought within the framework of the holy[142]. But for Heidegger the holy is the intangible ether, i.e. an aspect of the physical world[143]. God is hidden in this kind of reality. Heidegger probably wants to say that by means of an experience of the whole cosmos we may arrive at the apprehension of a certain depth of things. God appears in, or as, a region of the cosmos. Whether we receive such an experience of the holy and such a perception of the divine depends on Being[144], but the divine itself lies outside the field of Being and

---

Lortz, *Die Reformation in Deutschland*, I 153. Luther's new logic is based on the rejection of the mean in syllogisms and in this way it became a logic of contradiction. See G.M.M. Cottier, "De Luther à Hegel. Aux origines de la dialectique", in *Nova et Vetera* 45 (1970) 114-131.

[138] *Was ist Metaphysik?*, Pfullingen 1949, 13.

[139] *Unterwegs zur Sprache*, Pfullingen 1959, 137.

[140] See the important essay by E.-R. Korn, "Aux origines de la pensée moderne: le drame luthérien", in *Revue thomiste* 71 (1971) 329-348. Cf. also M. Corvez, "La pensée de l'être chez Martin Heidegger", in *Revue thomiste* 65 (1965) 536-553, 550.

[141] *Einführung in die Metaphysik*, 25.

[142] *Wegmarken*, Frankfurt a.M. 1967, 145-194, 181-182.

[143] *Holzwege*, Frankfurt a.M. 1950, 272.

[144] "Die Kehre", in *Die Frage nach der Technik*, Pfullingen 1962, 45. Cf. H. Köchler, *Skepsis und Gesellschaftsethik im Denken Heideggers*, Meisenheim 1978, 47. Luther appears to have had a pervasive influence on Heidegger. See also n.137 above.

outside metaphysics. For faith and religion have nothing to do with philosophy.

From the above it follows that Heidegger's holy and the divine are a sort of cosmic dimension, but not the Subsistent Source of Being[145]. From the point of view of Christian philosophy Heidegger's position is atheistic. His restless concern with being results in an inability (or refusal) to reach Subsistent Being Itself. It also ends in the desperation of not being able to reach truth and to share the possession of truth with others[146].

In many ways the atheism of J.-P. Sartre continues Nietzsche's nihilism. According to the French existentialist man himself must establish the meaning of his life. As the slogan says: "To do and by doing to make oneself and be nothing else but what one has made oneself into"[147]. God cannot exist, Sartre writes, because then man would no longer be free. Man must make his own laws[148]. Sartre also uses the Nietzschean theme of God's stare (*regard*) as an argument in favour of atheism: God's stare destroys our subjectivity and therefore we must deny his existence[149]. The argument that God is nothing but a projection of man's desire to become being-in-itself (*être-en-soi*) also occurs[150].

Sartre was keenly aware of the consequences of his denial of God: "It is very embarrassing that God does not exist, for together with him disappears any possibility of finding values in an intelligible world; there can no longer be an *a priori* good, because there is no infinite consciousness to conceive it"[151].

Maurice Merleau-Ponty begins his discussion of the question of God's existence by insisting on the marvel of the emergence of subjectivity in the world. Subjectivity, that is the presence of human subjects, is the starting-point of thought, choice and action. Attempts at explaining subjectivity destroy it[152]. This takes us to Merleau-Ponty's arguments against the existence

---

[145] Cf. R. Fornet Betancourt, "Heidegger et le christianisme", *RScPhTh* 66 (1982) 375-396,395.

[146] E. R. Korn, "La question de l'être chez Martin Heidegger", in *Revue thomiste* 70 (1970) 227-263; 560-603; 71 (1971) 33-58, 43. B. Welte, "La métaphysique de saint Thomas d'Aquin et la pensée de l'être chez Heidegger", *RScPhTh* 50 (1966) 601-614 shows that St. Thomas escapes Heidegger's criticism, but he has not seen the limits of Heidegger's approach.

[147] "Faire et, en se faisant, se faire et rien d'autre de ce qu'on s'est fait". See his "Mise au point" in *Action*, du 27 décembre 1944.

[148] *Les mouches*, 84ff.

[149] Cf. the experience of his boyhood he describes in *Les mots*, 83.

[150] See H. Paissaic, *Le dieu de Sartre*, Paris 1950; R. Verneaux, *Leçons sur l'athéisme contemporain*, Paris s.a., 57ff.; L. Elders, *Jean-Paul Sartre, El ser y la nada*, Madrid 1977, 45-52.

[151] *L'existentialisme est un humanisme*, 35-36.

[152] *Phénoménologie de la perception*, 2; *Eloge de la philosophie*, 61. D. De Petter argues against this position as follows: if the contingency of certain things obliges us to admit a Necessary Being as their First Cause, it is ridiculous to say that this Being destroys the contingency of things. See his "Le caractère métaphysique de la preuve de l'existence de Dieu et la pensée contemporaine", in aa. vv., *L'existence de Dieu*, Tournai 1961, 167-178; 172.

of God. Man is the "project" of the world, i.e. he must be understood
through his relation and communion with the world[153]. Since the world is
man's horizon it does not make sense to place man's destiny in God[154].

Throughout his works the French philosopher keeps coming back to his
thesis that the assumption of an absolute Being destroys contingence and
freedom[155]. Related to this argument is his assertion that if an infinitely perfect God exists, there is nothing left to do[156]. If God is the cause of man, man
is no longer free. However, we must observe that Merleau-Ponty's difficulty
is caused by the fact that he conceives the Absolute and its causality in a
univocal and almost quantitative way so that an infinite being makes
everything else beside itself superfluous or totally determines it so that
freedom is lost[157]. Merleau-Ponty's thesis "if God exists, man is not"[158] is
widely held by existentialists. It rests upon a wrong way of conceiving the relationship of God to the world and even more upon the desire to make man
autonomous to the point of rejecting the possibility of reaching definite truth
about the origin of things. A final knowledge of the physical world is not
possible because it is its essence only to be known in a series of aspects or
approximative sketches[159].

Other arguments brought forward by Merleau-Ponty against the existence
of God include those of the presence of evil and of the contradictory character
of the notion of God (which tries to combine immanence and transcendence).
People, however, resort with impunity to the notion of God because what they
present as God lies beyond experience and cannot be belied by it[160].

---

[153] *Phénoménologie de la perception* (*PP*), 463.

[154] Man himself would not be more than "une vue du monde", that is a special way of looking
at the world (*PP*, 465). See F. VandenBussche, "Les approches du problème de Dieu dans la
philosophie de M. Merleau-Ponty", in *De Deo in philosophia s. Thomae et in hodierna
philosophia. Acta VI Congressus Thomistici internationalis*, t. II, Romae 1966, 339-344.

[155] *Sens et non-sens*, 166: "Quand il n'est pas inutile, le recours à un fondement absolu détruit
cela même qu'il doit fonder"; 167: "La conscience métaphysique et morale meurt au contact de
l'absolu". Cf. *ibidem* 350ff.

[156] *Sens et non-sens*, 309. Voir R. Jolivet, "Le problème de l'absolu dans la philosophie de
Merleau-Ponty", in *Tijdschrift voor Philosophie* 1957, 63ff.; W. Luijpen, *Fenomenologie en
atheisme*, Leuven 1979. 344-359.

[157] God as a cause need not impose necessity on his effects, as even G. Marcel seems to think
("Dieu et la causalité", in *aa. vv., De la connaissance de Dieu*, (Desclée) 1958, 27-33. Cf. St.
Thomas, *Q.d.de malo* 17, a.7 ad 15: "voluntas divina est supra ordinem necessarii et con-
tingentis..."; *In I Periherm.*, lectio 14: "nam voluntas divina est intelligenda ut extra ordinem
entium existens sicut causa quaedam profundens totum ens et omnes eius differentias".

[158] *PP* XV. Surprisingly this relativism stops short at the phenomenological principle which is
declared to be universally valid. In phenomenology the relation of consciousness and the world
is conceived in terms of "founding" and "constituting": consciousness constitutes the sense of
things which in this way lose their full independence. Being becomes being-for-me.

[159] *PP* 453; *Signes*, 185. Cf. also *Sens et non-sens*, 189-190: "J'ai le droit de soustraire mes
jugements au contrôle d'autrui".

[160] *Sens et non-sens*, 193.

One of the most powerful currents in twentieth century philosophy is positivism which defends the maxim that only what the senses perceive can be the content of knowledge. Within this general movement the so-called Wiener Kreis put forward the principle of verifiability: only those propositions are meaningful which can be verified (by experience). Only verification by the senses or by scientific experiments is admitted. With this thesis neopositivism limits valid knowledge to that of the material world[161]. In this view a good number of statements by philosophers and most of religious language become meaningless. Moreover the task of philosophy itself shifts to that of the criticism of language.

Several neopositivist authors such as A. I. Ayer and A. Flew hold a radical agnosticism or atheism. "We know that non-empirical propositions can never be anything more than probable. It follows that there is no possibility of demonstrating the existence of God.... And our view that all utterances about the nature of God are nonsensical ... is actually incompatible with them"[162]. We cannot here discuss the variety of positions taken by neopositivist authors with regard to the existence of God. We must mention, however, that Wittgenstein himself never excluded the possibility of faith in God. He felt that religion and religious ethics belong to a mystical dimension of man and cannot be the object of scientific research. This does not mean that they were not important to Wittgenstein. On the contrary, that about which one cannot speak and one must keep silent about is of paramount importance. In this connection Wittgenstein even calls God the sense of life.

Wittgenstein's later theory of pluralistic signification leaves room for religious language. However, an unfortunate consequence of neopositivist theories is that the impression was created that there is an irreducible gap between the world of science and facts on the one hand and that of religion on the other[163]. Scientific knowledge about God is declared to be impossible.

---

[161] St. Thomas would agree with positivists that all our knowledge comes from the senses and that there is no "pure thinking" without the assistance of the senses. But over and against this empiricism he holds that the intellect sees more in the sense data than the senses themselves discern; there is knowledge of the universal. The first principles, such as that of causality are apprehended on the basis of sense experience, but are known as universally true and applying to all being. With their help we discover a source of being behind material reality. The verification used is the reflection on the very evidence of these first principles and the insight that one cannot deny them without falling into absurdity.

[162] *Language, Truth and Logic* (Dover publications), 114. See also A. Flew, "Theology and Falsification", in A. Flew and A. MacIntyre (edit.), *New Essays in Philosophical Theology*, London 1955, 106-108. —In his essay "Ueberwindung der Metaphysik durch Analyse der Sprache", in *Erkenntnis* 2 (1932) R. Carnap analyses the uses of the term God: besides a mythical sense (visible appearances of divine beings) and a theological use the term has no definite meaning whatsoever. There is a metaphysical use of the term which is nonsensical. General terms such as First Cause or Infinite Being have no verifiable meaning.

[163] See M.J. Charlesworth, "Athéisme et philosophie analytique" in J. Girardi and J.F. Six, *L'athéisme dans la philosophie contemporaine*, Tournai 1970, 623-675, 671. See also in the same

In a sense Wittgenstein seems to come close to the ancient theory of dual truth: totally separate from and sometimes at variance with our scientific understanding of the world there is a sort of mystical experience of unutterable reality[164].

These and similar theories were adopted by the so-called Barthian atheists who assert that the Christian faith can be combined with philosophical agnosticism or atheism. P. Van Buren thinks that for us, secularised men, the term God no longer has any meaning[165]; Th. J. Altizer writes that incarnation is the negation of transcendence and that the death of God is a joyful event to be celebrated cheerfully[166].

In addition to neopositivism we must also briefly mention naturalism which holds that nature is the whole of being and the ground of all phenomena. It reduces metaphysics, theology and ethics to nature. While 18th and 19th century naturalism was not opposed to the admission of God's existence (although it rejected revelation), a more recent current of naturalism in the United States denied the existence of God and the immortality of the human soul. John Dewey argues that by accepting God's existence one disrupts the homogeneity of reality and promotes a devaluation of the world; those who seek the contemplation of God are deficient in their worldly tasks[167]. Needless to say we have here to do with a simplistic monism: transcendence is denied and reality is believed to be only material.

Atheism entered not only contemporary philosophy; it is also found in literature and art which frequently witness to the absence of God or insist on the presence of evil, absurdity and disorder in the world. What are the causes of this widespread denial of the existence of God?

In the first place the personal choice of man should be mentioned who wants to be free and autonomous instead of subject to God. Primitive representations of God, the revolt against the moral doctrine of Christianity or the conviction that the coexistence of an infinite God and finite creatures is impossible sometimes provoke a decision no longer to acknowledge God. Among other factors which could be of a psychological nature, the

---

volume the excellent essay by J. Ladrière, "Athéisme et néopositivisme", 555-621; cf. J.-F. Malherbe, "Athéisme scientiste et métaphysique de la représentation", in *Revue théologique de Louvain* 13 (1982) 31-48.

[164] See W. Baum, "Ludwig Wittgenstein und die Religion", in *Philos. Jahrb.* 86 (1979) 272-299. On "God-language" see below the chapter on the names of God.

[165] *The Secular Meaning of the Gospel*, New York 1963, 103. For a pertinent criticism of this position see E.L. Mascall, *The Secularization of Christianity*, London 1963. Cf. J. Ch. Cooper, *The Roots of Radical Theology*, Philadelphia 1967 and P.J. Etges, *Kritik der analytischen Theologie*, Hamburg 1973.

[166] *The Gospel of Christian Atheism*, Philadelphia 1966.

[167] See Dewey's *The Quest for Certainty* and *Reconstruction in Philosophy*. For a critical analysis of Dewey's position one may consult J. Collins, *o.c.*, 272-276 and F. Smith, "A Thomistic Appraisal of the Philosophy of John Dewey", in *The Thomist* 18 (1955) 127-185.

metaphysical option in favour of atheism taken by several philosophers deserves to be emphasized. When he was 24 years old, Karl Marx decided to become an atheist[168] and to place the divine in the material world. Analogous events are mentioned by J.-P. Sartre[169] and S. de Beauvoir[170]. As our description suggested, even in Heidegger's view there are signs of a choice in favour of a clear rupture between metaphysics and religion. Freud also rejected, mainly for personal reasons, any dependence on God[171]. Hume's sceptical position with regard to the existence of God may well have been dictated by his desire not to be dependent on anyone else. In this connection we may also recall Schopenhauer's words that "Atheism is an assumption to start from (eine Voraussetzung) and the affective *a priori* of the refusal of God (das affektive Apriori der Ablehnung Gottes)".

As is commonly agreed upon there are no real arguments for the non-existence of God. According to Christian philosophy the universe as well as man himself bear witness to God's existence. Moreover, God being the Infinite Good in which all other goods participate, in whatever man seeks to attain he is actually seeking God[172]. However, when man considers certain effects of God, such as the moral order, brought home to him through the basic inclinations of his personal human nature, he may experience these and thus God himself as hampering the fulfillment of some of his wishes. A rejection of God may also be provoked by wrong representations of deity or a mistaken idea of evil. However, in the last analysis the decisive factor is man's free choice by which he refuses to admit the transcendent First Being and reduces reality to matter or prefers to proclaim the irrelevancy of God and to banish him from all human considerations[173]. Atheism is an expression of man's will to break all supposed chains and to be his own master. However, man cannot escape from being inserted in an ontological order which is dependent on and directed to God.

A second group of factors which sometimes contribute to the option of atheism are neurotic problems. People who were educated in such a way that God was represented to them as a severe judge, condemning and punishing

---

[168] In a letter to his father he describes his abandonment of the Christian faith in veiled terms: "Ein Vorhang ist gefallen, mein Allerheiligstes zerrissen, und es müssten neue Götter hineingesetzt werden" (*Frühe Schriften*, I, hrsg von H.-J. Lieber und P. Furth, Darmstadt 1962, 13).

[169] *Les mots*, 169.

[170] *Mémoires d'une jeune fille rangée*, 137f.: "Je compris que rien ne me ferait renoncer aux joies terrestres... Je ne crois plus en Dieu, me dis-je, sans grand étonnement. J'avais toujours pensé qu'au prix de l'éternel, ce monde comptait pour rien; il "comptait" puisque je l'aimais, et c'était Dieu soudain qui ne faisait pas le poids; il fallait que son nom ne recouvrît plus qu'un mirage".

[171] *Gesammelte Werke*, Frankfurt a.M. 1952-1958, XIV, 346.

[172] *C.G.* III, cc.18-20.—Cf. also G. Cottier, "Définition et typologie de l'athéisme", in *Nova et Vetera* 55 (1980) 241-259, 248. Cf. also Cajetanus, *In Summam theologiae* II-II, 34, 1 and 2.

[173] See Th. Molnar, *Theists and Atheists. A Typology of Non-Belief*, The Hague 1980.

even the slightest weakness, may try to escape from reprimands and punishment by denying God's existence. Likewise people who had to suffer from ministers of religion or who saw their desires thwarted by religious prohibitions may resort to a declaration in favour of atheism in order to escape from what has become a sort of an obsession to them[174]. It is not unlikely that Nietzsche's atheism is at least in part dependent on psychic factors. Certain psychological data also influence one's position with regard to God. Childhood, adolescence, maturity, old age may all either promote or hamper religious life. A crisis during one's childhood or adolescence may lead to atheism, whereas in the words of Plato old age often brings people back to the admission of God's existence[175].

Agnosticism or atheism have also been promoted by a number of developments in modern science and society. According to Freud the idea of God is the product of man himself, of his fears or desires that is. Primitive man, he believes, personified the uncanny forces of nature. To placate them he began to use the same means he would resort to to regain the favour of his superiors. In a further development these personified natural forces lost their human traits. The divine is somewhat separated from nature which is yet supplemented by it where nature is wanting[176]. In this way religion is a self-imposed illusion or rather a neurosis by means of which people seek to free themselves from fear and guilt feelings. It is the result of the inevitable frustrations of our desires which we have to cope with in our lives. In his *Totem und Tabu*[177] Freud delves deeper into what he believes to be the roots of the Father-image man gives to the divine. In this connection he advances his fantastic and gratuitous theory of the murder of a vicious and tyrannical ancestor. This murder was followed by remorse and atonement and so it led to religious veneration.

Besides these specific theories about the origin of religion the psychology of Freud and his followers tended to reduce man's entire life to the level of animal urges and so it became a factor which undermines the Christian view of man and God. Religious representations have no objective value whatever but are the product of certain desires. In the wake of Freud some psychoanalysts even went so far as to reproach Christianity with oppressing the normal urges of the human heart with its religious monotheism.

Karl Jung is much more positive with regard to religion. He considers the idea of God as an archetype, i.e. as a basic model in man's psyche, which must be taken account of to ensure man's health. Neglect of this idea easily leads to psychic deviations. According to Jung Western man misleads himself when

[174] See I. Lepp, *Psychanalyse de l'athéisme contemporain*, Paris 1961.
[175] Cf. R. Guardini, *Die Lebensalter*, Würzburg 1953.
[176] This is the thesis of *Die Zukunft einer Illusion* (1927) (*Gesammelte Werke*, XIV, 337).
[177] *Ges. Werke* IX, 169ff. Cf. also his *Moses und der Monotheismus* (1939).

he thinks that he no longer needs God and religion[178]. However Jung does not pronounce judgment on the objective existence of God. To him religion is subservient to man's psychological equilibrium.

A psychoanalysis conducted according to the principles of Freud and protracted over a long period of may will bring people to depreciate their religious feelings. On the positive side, however, we must notice that when judiciously used psychoanalysis may contribute to the purification of man's attitude in his quest of God[179].

Turning now to the examination of the influence of modern science on belief in God we notice that there is a rather wide spread conviction that the rise of science and technology has contributed to the loss of the idea of God. It is, indeed, a fact that a number of scientists have argued that the development of scientific knowledge has now relegated all religious explanations of the world to the domain of myth. It has also been observed that the study of the sciences apparently causes a number of people to give up their traditional religious beliefs[180]. To the contrary, however, we have the testimony of those scientists who do not have the least difficulty in admitting God's existence and religious practice. Apparently there is no easy answer to the question of what is the precise relationship between modern science and theology. In general, Christianity has always enthusiastically favoured scientific research and received new insights or discoveries with interest. There was no question of any real conflict until the beginning of the seventeenth century. The introduction of the mathematical method into science as well as the rise of positivism brought about the change. Researchers now became sometimes prone to neglect or to deny whatever could not be expressed in mathematical formulae. The ontological dependence of the world on God was lost sight of. Homogeneous explanations of phenomena by causes of the same type were considered to be sufficient to understand all of reality. The world as it is now is the product of natural forces already present in a previous state[181]. Recourse to an outside heterogeneous cause was rejected as unscientific. In the 18th and 19th centuries progress in the sciences had been so rapid and their

[178] See his *Modern Man in Search of a Soul*, New York 1933 and Victor White, *God and the Unconscious*, London 1952.

[179] J. Nuttin, *Psychoanalyse en spiritualistische opvatting van de mens*, Utrecht-Antwerpen 1959; J. Durandeaux, *Chrétiens au feu de la psychanalyse*, Paris 1972; M. Bellet, *Foi et psychanalyse*, Paris 1973; E. Amado Lévy-Valensi, *Les voies et les pièges de la psychanalyse*, Paris 1968.

[180] See F. Gregory, *Scientific Materialism in 19th Century Germany*, Dordrecht 1977. On the case of Charles Darwin see L. Elders, "El transfondo religioso y filosófico de la teoría de la evolución de Charles Darwin", in *aa. vv., Comemoración del centenario de Darwin*, Madrid 1983, 179-216, 209.

[181] S. Jaki, *The Road of Science and the Ways to God*, Chicago 1978. On this problematic see also L. Elders, "Die Naturwissenschaften und die Existenz Gottes", in *Salzburger Jahrbuch für Philosophie*, 30 (1985) 73-86.

influence on society, education and culture so pervasive that they came to be considered the only true form of rational knowledge[182]. In the past theology had been the centre of learning: it provided answers to man's basic questions about the origin and destiny of the world and the meaning of human life. But by now it had lost its privileged position and people began to turn to the sciences for the answers[183]. Simultaneously the type of explanations provided underwent a profound change. The answers given by the scientists no longer aim at an ultimate intelligibility but at knowledge of the quantitative and measurable aspects of things. This knowledge is turned to practical use so that our mastery of material reality increased rapidly.

The scientific approach as it came to be practised certainly provides objective knowledge, but this alone is not a comprehensive and sufficient interpretation of reality. Some scientists are aware of this and declare that there is no opposition between the assertion that God exists and the insights gained by modern science, because each type of knowledge is at a different level. Others, however, make scientific method the only valid approach to reality and are inspired by certain philosophical options in their interpretation of the results of scientific research. Such options may provide a certain depth and unity to the scientifically established facts. Sometimes they are metaphysically unobjectionable, but frequently materialism and monism prevail in the attempts at ultimate explanations[184].

In the 20th century a new development took place: the insight began to gain ground that scientific theories and formulae have only a limited objectivity. The scientist, many believe, must choose a framework of ideas with the help of which he has to interpret nature, but which is no more than a limited approach. Especially the greater minds among the scientists become aware of the limits of their discipline and refrain from statements on metaphysical problems[185]. However, this attitude is still far from general. Particularly at

---

[182] This process is part of what has been called the secularization of the European mind, a development, that is, by which certain fields of man's activity gradually lose their connection with God or with religion. The term was first used to signify the passing of Church possessions into the hands of secular powers at the end of the Thirty Years War. Some call the state of culture or way of life from which God is absent modernity.

[183] By scientism is meant the systematic reduction of all knowledge to that given by the sciences; it holds that the method of the latter is the only admissible one and that the sciences will provide the answers to all questions.

[184] This is quite obvious in the case of such authors as Bertrand Russell and Jacques Monod, but also Darwin's later agnosticism or atheism was not dictated by his scientific discoveries. He read his discoveries in the light of his own inner development (his growing positivism, his desire to keep God out of the domain of living beings where, Darwin felt, so many shocking and cruel things occur, of which one may not make God responsible). One might say that positivism became a creed to many a scientist: whatever happens in the world is caused by material factors only; whatever lies outside the field of science belongs to a mythological world.

[185] I. Prigogine and I. Stenger, *La nouvelle alliance*, Paris 1979; R. Harré, *The Philosophies of Science. An Introductory Survey*, Oxford 1972.

the level of popular publications one frequently encounters statements on the origin and meaning of the physical universe and man which exclude God as first cause. In this way the sciences may contribute to religious indifferentism, to shallow thinking and to atheism.

Modern technology has also been a factor in the growing secularisation of human life. When people constantly have to do with forces such as electricity and nuclear energy which were made available by man's efforts it is tempting for them to believe that there is no other master of the physical world than man himself. Moreover things are considered mainly from the point of view of their usefulness while their ontological status is overlooked. This "inversion of technology leads to the progressive obliteration of the world of mystery which is at the same time that of presence and hope"[186].

In a technological culture the role left for religion is insignificant and the thought of God tends to disappear from daily life. People are to a large extent conditioned by a technological way of thinking and apply its principles and viewpoints even outside the field of industrial activity. This not only leads to an eclipse of the idea of God and of religion but also to a depersonalisation of human life. The result is that man experiences a certain emptiness of things, of which, however, he is himself the cause[187].

From the time of Socrates onwards the existence of evil has been considered sufficient reason to reject the idea of God. We shall return to this after the discussion of the Five Ways. An immoral life has also brought some to a denial of God's existence in order to avoid being confronted with a superior authority which disapproves their conduct. Others again refuse religion because they are against the existing social order for which they make religious ideas responsible.

Our survey shows that atheism is a complex phenomenon which may depend on several factors. Formally speaking we define it as the refusal to admit God's existence.

The slowly spreading agnosticism and atheism as well as religious indifference place us before a most important question: is modern man losing the sense of God and does he really restrict the range of his mind and aspirations to himself and the finite things he finds around him? Were all past speculation on God and religious practice a mistake or a phenomenon typical of the childhood of mankind? Or is the present situation a cul-de-sac and a threat to the very survival of mankind?

To find the answers to these questions we must retrace the road philosophical thinking has taken down through the centuries and reconsider the evidence in favour of God's existence as well as its implications for us.

---

[186] G. Marcel, *Les hommes contre l'humain*, 70.

[187] Cf. Ellul, *Les nouveaux possédés*, Paris 1973; *id., Le système technicien*, Paris 1977; A. Brunner, "Technik und Religion", in *Stimmen der Zeit*, 1977, 677-682.

CHAPTER TWO

THE KNOWABILITY OF GOD

I. *Is God's Existence Evident?*

In the previous chapter the idea of God as present in our Western culture was discussed and a survey was also given of the denial of God in its various forms. More widespread than atheism is agnosticism or indifferentism. For a variety of reasons people decide that one just does not know with certitude whether God exists or not. Others feel that it does not make any practical difference whether God exists or not, for God is irrelevant to man's needs and pursuits.

In order to shed some light on these problems we must examine to what extent and by what means we can come to know God by our natural reason. With regard to this question different answers have been given. Besides the forthright denial of the possibility to know anything whatsoever about God there is a fairly widespread position which admits God as a spiritual reality but does not think it possible to go beyond such a vague conviction; attempts to elaborate scientific demonstrations of God's existence are doomed to failure. Some pragmatists such as William James and Samuel Peirce accepted the idea of God as a highly probable hypothesis, but they did not admit any philosophical arguments in favour of his existence nor any scientific knowledge about his being.

A similar view is upheld by R. Bultmann and K. Barth. The former admits in man an existential awareness of God's existence which takes the form of a searching question concerning the meaning of human life[1]. When this radical experience is expressed in concepts and arguments, man is removing himself from the true God, for in doing so he makes God an object of his thought. Sinful man can only approach God in faith to the extent that God himself comes to man[2]. Using almost the same reasoning K. Barth asserts that when sinful man tries to assert something definite about God he is actually creating an idol. For such natural knowledge is nothing but a projection of man's own views and desires. Therefore philosophical theology is to be rejected[3].

---

[1] *Glauben und Verstehen*, II, 231f.
[2] *Ibid.*, IV (Tübingen 1965) 135. Cf. also L. Malevez, "La théologie naturelle de Rudolf Bultmann", *Gregorianum* 47 (1966) 226-253; Klaus Kremer, "Der Gottesgedanke bei Rudolf Bultmann", in *Philos. Jahrbuch* 73 (1965-1966) 322-338.
[3] Cf. his *Credo* (1935), 14-15.

Over and against this opinion of two leading Protestant theologians one could point to some texts of the Bible which affirm the possibility of a natural knowledge of God, viz. *Romans* 1, 18ff and *Acts* 17, 16ff. In agreement with Biblical revelation the Catholic Church holds that God as the Cause and the End of things can be known with certitude by natural reason from the things he has made[4].

But this does not quite solve the question *how* man knows God. Different answers are given to it. What one might call a maximalized reply is that of ontologism: every man has an immediate knowledge of God so that no demonstration of God's existence is necessary[5]. Malebranche argues his point as follows: our ideas express and contain immutable objects. As such these objects cannot be created things but exist in the mind of God. In knowing them we perceive God directly[6]. All our ideas are God's infinite essence inasmuch as it can be participated in by created things. Obviously this position is not without serious difficulties. Malebranche tries to solve them by pointing out that not our ideas as such but only the object expressed by them is God's being. Moreover our intuition of God's essence is not a total comprehension of God in his simplicity: we only see one aspect under which God reveals himself at a given moment. But Malebranche fails to explain why when considering God's being we only see one aspect of it. Because our knowledge is knowledge of the divine essence it also reveals God's existence[7]. God is in such a way present in us that to know is to know in God and to know God. Only God can bring about in us the intellectual insight by means of which we know the truth[8].

Malebranche's theory has a profound religious inspiration and it stresses man's entire dependence on God. Combining insights of St. Augustine and Descartes it survived in the ontologism of such 19th century philosophers as G. Ubaghs, V. Gioberti and A. S. Rosmini. In the last analysis this position is the outcome of Descartes' rationalism which regards God as the immediate ground of man's certitude about the physical universe[9]. Malebranche added

---

[4] Vaticanum I, *Const. dogm. De Fide catholica*, c.2, DS 3004: "Eadem sancta mater Ecclesia tenet et docet, Deum, rerum omnium principium et finem, naturali humanae rationis lumine e rebus creatis certo cognosci posse". The text then quotes *Rom.* I, 20, The so-called anti-modernist oath added to this definition "tamquam causam per effectus, certo cognosci adeoque demonstrari etiam posse ..." (DS 3538).

[5] Malebranche, *Entretiens sur la métaphysique et la religion*, VIII, 9.

[6] "C'est en Dieu, uniquement et immédiatement, que nous contemplons l'objet de toutes nos idées intellectuelles" (*l.c.*).

[7] *Entretiens*, II, 5.

[8] Malebranche's theory leads to the assertion that God is the only efficient cause in the universe; created things receive from God the state of exercising activity which, in reality, is only a sign of causality.

[9] Collins, *o.c.*, 88.

that the objective content of our mind lies in God's essence. God is the embracing *locus* of all intellectual activity.

Malebranche himself appeals for his theory to St. Augustine. The Bishop of Hippo does indeed teach that God illuminates man inwardly so that he begins to understand what he could not grasp at first[10]. St. Augustine, however, distinguishes between our knowledge of the material world and that of immaterial things. The first comes about through the senses, the second by means of an illumination of the mind[11]. God is the spiritual sun which makes these realities known to us[12]. In this connection St. Augustine refers to Plotinus[13] for whom the concept of ἔλλαμψις has indeed a central place, for it signifies any emanation from the highest principle[14]. St. Augustine writes that God is "pater intelligibilis lucis" or "pater illuminationis nostrae", but these expressions are clearly metaphors[15]. For St. Augustine does acknowledge that man himself has cognitive faculties and an activity of his own. Divine illumination actually leads to a created human insight[16]. Even the knowledge of God's ideas (which he sometimes describes as a seeing) is not a direct apprehension of God but rather the illuminating and regulating influence of God in our mind[17]. This is the meaning of such texts as: "God is the intelligible light in which and from which and by which intelligibly shine all things which intelligibly shine"[18].

St. Augustine's theological language is not formally precise and so it gave rise to far reaching interpretations. His theory of illumination was combined with the Aristotelian doctrine of the agent intellect. Certain mediaeval doctors identified the agent intellect with God while others, such as St. Bonaventure, admitted the theory of abstraction to explain our knowledge of the material things, while resorting to divine illumination to explain how we come to know spiritual realities. According to the Franciscan doctor God immediately influences the human mind[19]. He is the ground of our intellectual understanding. He is present in the soul, which actually grasps ("actu capit") him[20]. There

---

[10] *De magistro* XII, 40.

[11] Cf. *De Trinitate* IX, 3, 3: "mens ipsa, sicut corporearum rerum notitias per sensus corporis colligit, sic incorporearum per semetipsam novit, quia est incorporea".

[12] *Solil.* I, 6, 12.

[13] *De civ. Dei* X, 2.

[14] *Enn.* V, 3, 17. Cf. also II, 9, 2.

[15] E. Gilson, *Introduction à l'Etude de saint Augustin*, 105.

[16] Cf. *De Trin.* IX, 15, 24.

[17] *De lib. arbitrio* II, 10, 29.

[18] *Solil.* I, 1.

[19] *In II Sent.*, d. 1, II, a.2, q.2 ad 1: "Deus immediate influit in mentem et ipsa mens immediate a prima Veritate formatur"; *De donis Spiritus Sancti*, coll. 8: "Secundum quod Deus est ratio intellegendi, intrat in animam".

[20] *Itinerarium mentis in Deum*, c.3, n.2. See J. Bissen, *L'exemplarisme divin selon saint Bonaventure*, Paris 1929, 178-187. Elsewhere St. Bonaventure writes that the truth of God's

is no innate idea of God, but a special presence of God's light in certitudinal knowledge and in the attraction exercised on man by the Infinite Good which is his happiness. The human mind "cannot define or judge or reason or take counsel or desire without finding the ultimate and justifying ground of its activity in God"[21]. Man cannot even fully grasp himself without discovering that God works in the very core of his being.

St. Thomas rejects this way of describing our knowledge. Although God is present in our mind, we cannot directly touch him, because our intellect is not adapted to spiritual reality which it can only come to know through the medium of sensible things. Arguments are needed to pass from the material world to its hidden cause. Moreover, Aquinas observes, the parallelism "what the sun is to the eye, God is to the intellect" is not correct because the eye is at the same level as the material light of the sun, but one cannot say so of the human intellect in respect of God[22]. To St. Augustine's assertion that all things are known in the First Truth, St. Thomas answers that one should not understand these words as saying that God is the proximate principle by which we know and judge. Rather they mean that we know and judge by means of a light given to us which is a likeness of God. Our intellectual light only acts through the First Light. As the light in the material world is not always the first thing we perceive (often we first notice an illuminated object), so even the created intellectual light we carry within us is not the first thing we know. It makes things known and on this account we know it in and through the things we perceive[23].

This explanation by Aquinas is also a reply to those intuitionist philosophers who claim that man has access to God in the innermost experiences of his heart[23a]. It is certainly true that for many people the proofs of the existence of God, if these are to meet with assent, require the presence of certain experiences, which some call intuitive knowledge. Thomists contend, however, that in those cases either there are hidden or implicit forms of argumentation at work, or desires lead to assent[23b].

---

existence is so great that no one can assert with conviction that God does not exist, unless one would not know what is meant by the name 'God' (*In I Sent.*, d.8, 1, a.1, q.2 (Q.I, 154).

[21] A.C. Pegis, "The Bonaventurean Way to God", in *Mediaeval Studies* 29 (1967) 206-242, 233.

[22] *In I Sent.*, d.3, q.1, a.2 ad 2.—This criticism also applies to S. Peirce who holds that apprehending God is a matter of direct experience (although man does not *see* divinity). See his *Values in a Universe of Change (Selected Writings* (Edit. Ph. Wiener), New York 1958) 10.

[23] *In Boetii De Trinitate*, q.1, a.3 ad 1.

[23a] S. Kowalczyk, "Connaissance intuitive et philosophie de Dieu", in *Divus Thomas* (Piac.) 87 (1984) 165-204, 194f. argues in favour of what he calls a "mitigated intuitionism", which he attributes to J.-H. Newman, H. Bergson, W. Otto and M. Scheler. It would seem, however, that "intuition" is a rather vague term. Before one can meaningfully speak of intuition as used by different philosophers, one must first present their theory of knowledge.

[23b] See M.T.L. Penido, "Sur l'intuition naturelle de Dieu", in *RScPhTh* 2 (1932) 549-561; E. Rolland, "L'intuition philosophique de Dieu", in *Sciences ecclésiastiques* 1962, 253-264; J.

An impressive number of philosophers hold that man has an innate idea of
God or at least acquires his idea of God by the natural spontaneous function-
ing of the mind. The latter view was upheld by Stoic philosophers: the ideas
which come to us by nature (ἔμφυται προλήψεις) are not inborn in the Platonic
sense, but arise spontaneously in man without toilsome reasoning[24]. This
position met with wide acclaim in the ancient world[25] and was also admitted
by a good number of Christian authors[26]. Cicero has given it its classic
expression[27].

St. Thomas rejects this view. That which we have heard about ever since
we were children and which therefore seems self-evident must not be con-
founded with the "naturally known"[28]. However, in a more general sense the
knowledge of God's existence may be said" to be implanted in us by nature
inasmuch as God is our beatitude. Man naturally desires happiness and what
is naturally desired by man is naturally known by him. This, however, is not
to know in an absolute sense that God exists; just as to know that someone
is approaching is not the same as to know that Peter is approaching, even
though it is Peter who is approaching. For there are many who imagine that
man's perfect good, which is happiness, consists in riches and others in
pleasure and others is something else"[29]. A certain knowledge of God is contained in our concept of happiness although some people identify their happiness with something else. We may therefore say that the knowledge of God's
existence is implanted in us by nature insofar as nature has given us knowledge
from which we can arrive at the knowledge of God[30]. But God's existence is
not self-evident to us. "A proposition is self-evident because the predicate is
included in the essence of the subject". St. Thomas quotes some examples,
e.g. the first principles of demonstration. But when the essence of the subject
and/or the predicate are unknown to us, a proposition may be self-evident in
itself, although it is not to us.

Bobik, "Intuition and God and Some New Metaphysicians", in *id., New Themes in Christian
Philosophy*, Notre Dame 1968, 254-274.

[24] See F.H. Sandbach, "Ἔννοια and Πρόληψις in the Stoic Theory of Knowledge", in *Classical
Quarterly* 24 (1930) 44-51. Cf. M. Pohlenz, *Die Stoa*, I, 58.

[25] See, for instance, Seneca, *Epist.* 117, 6; Dio Chrysostomus, *Oratio* XII, 27; Sextus
Empiricus, *Adv. Phys.* I 62-63.

[26] Justinus, *Apol.* II 6; Clemens Alex., *Strom.* V 14, 133; Tertullianus, *De testimonio animae*
II, 1; Gregorius Nyss., *De beat., Oratio* 5 and others such as Didymus and Cyrillus of Jerusalem.
With regard to Irenaeus' view see L. Escoula, "Saint Irénée et la connaissance naturelle de Dieu",
Revues des sciences philos. et théol. 20 (1940) 252-270; A. Orbe, "San Ireneo y el conocimiento
natural de Dios", *Gregorianum* 47 (1966) 441-471; 710-747.

[27] *De natura deorum* II, 12: "omnibus enim innatum est et in anima quasi insculptum esse
deos".

[28] *S.C.G.* I 10.

[29] *S.Th.* I 2, 1 ad 1.—St. Augustine's *Conf.* X 20, 29, is the source of this reply to the first
objection: when we desire happiness, we desire God.

[30] *Q.d. de veritate* 10, a.12 ad 1.

To reach certitude concerning God's existence we must use arguments. One could allege against this conclusion that apparently a great number of people reach the firm conviction that God exists without their being aware of using specific arguments in support of it[31]. In reality, however, their conviction, if not the fruit of tradition, rests on arguments such as "the order of the world requires a cause".

Summing up we say that God's existence is not self-evident to us because we do not know his essence. As a matter of fact the statement that we do not know God's essence recurs on countless occasions in the *Summa theologiae*. It follows from the agreement between our way of being and our knowledge, whereas God's mode of being is totally different. As will be shown later God's essence is subsistent being itself so that, if one would know God's essence, his existence would appear as necessary. Hence the proposition "God exists" is evident in itself, for the predicate is the same as the subject. To us, on the other hand, it is not thus evident and hence needs demonstration[32].

It is sometimes objected that even if we do not immediately know God's essence, we nevertheless have a knowledge of the name of God as a reality than which nothing greater can be conceived. "That which actually exists is greater than that which exists only mentally. Therefore, since as soon as the name God is understood, its exists mentally, it also follows that it exists actually"[33]. St. Thomas here mentions the proof of God's existence proposed by St. Anselm, which was later called the ontological argument. It holds the middle ground between the theory of an intuitive knowledge of God and arguments which take concrete experience as their starting point. St. Anselm presents his original argument in the *Proslogion*[34]. St. Thomas gives a succinct version of it placing it deliberately in a philosophical setting. St. Anselm himself "seems to have wanted to create a mood of heightened spiritual awareness in his reader" before presenting his argument in a context which invites to prayer[35]. "Anselm stands baffled before the divine unapproachability" and he "wants assurance from God on two points of faith, namely that God exists and that he is what we believe him to be"[36].

---

[31] H. de Lubac, *Sur les chemins de Dieu*, Paris 1956, 194ff., deduces from *S.Th.* I 2, 1 ad 1 that man "possesses" God by living in contact with nature and in community with others. To demonstrate God's existence is to become aware of what is already given. One may agree with the author provided philosophical arguments are sufficiently distinguished from confuse feelings.

[32] *S,Th.* I 2, 1.

[33] *L.c.*, obj. 2.

[34] Chapter 2.—A slightly different version is found in his *Quid ad haec respondeat editor huius libelli*, i.e. in his answer to Gaulino who reproached Anselm with making a jump from the logical order to real existence.

[35] G.R. Evans, *Anselm and Talking about God*, Oxford 1978, 41.

[36] A.C. Pegis, "St. Anselm and the Argument of the Proslogion", *Mediaeval Studies* 28 (1966) 228-267, 244f. Pegis thinks that Anselm regarded his questions in the light of the metaphysics of participation. Others, however, such as K. Barth, have defended the theological character of the

The argument runs as follows: God is something than which nothing greater can be thought. An unbeliever hears it, understands it and what he understands is in his mind. But what exists in the mind and in reality too is greater than that which exists in the mind alone. Hence that than which nothing greater can be thought cannot be that which exists only in the mind. It follows that God must exist in reality.

When we analyse the argument we notice that the concept of something than which nothing better or greater can be thought already occurs in Cicero[37]. St. Augustine applied it to God[38], as did Boethius[39]. The insight that reality is intrinsic to truth and to thinking is typical of Plotinus' philosophy[40]. To St. Anselm something is greater when it exists than when it is only an essence (conceived in thought). His way of stating this depends on a metaphysics of essences in which existence is a further perfection to be added to the already given perfection of the essence as such. This is the upshot of his answer to Gaunilo. Anselm did not think that his argument passes from a subjective concept to objective reality. His starting point is God's essence as imperfectly known by us; in its shining truth it shows itself as that which is most perfect and therefore it also possesses existence.

Some interpreters such as A. Pegis suggest that Anselm means God's essence as known in his likeness in created things; these likenesses can be reduced to their source; in this way the idea of God originates and its contents are something real. However, St. Anselm insists rather on the fact that when we mention the idea of an essence than which a greater one cannot be conceived everyone understands us and has this idea (which may also be called God). Hence the starting-point of the proof lies much more at the level of logical discourse than at that of a study of participation.

St. Thomas criticises the argument without mentioning St. Anselm by name (although elsewhere in the *Summa theologiae* he quotes St. Anselm as an authority some thirty times). Aquinas observes in the first place that it is not so certain that everyone has the idea of God as something greater than which

---

argument. See H. Bouillard, "La preuve de Dieu dans le 'Proslogion' et son interprétation par Karl Barth", *Spicilegium Beccense. Ier Congrès international du IXe centenaire de l'arrivée d'Anselme au Bec*, Paris 1959, 191-207.

[37] *De natura deorum* II 18: "... sed ne cogitari quicquam melius potest".

[38] *De doctrina christ.* I 7, 7-8; *Conf.* VII 4-6. On the 'Deus semper maior' theme see Athanasius, *De incarn. Verbi.* c.16; Gregorius Nyss., *De beatitudinibus, orat.* 6, 2; Gregorius Naz., *Oratio* 2, 76; 38, 8; Dionysius, *De div. nom.*, 13, 3; Tertullianus, *De test. animae* II, 1; *Adv. Marcionem* 1, 4-5; Hilarius, *Liber de Trinitate*, c.2. St. Bonaventure repeats that "Deus enim dicit simpliciter summum et in re et in opinione cogitantis" (*In I Sent.*, d.2, art. unic., q.1: Q.I, 52).

[39] *De consol. philosophiae* III, prose 10: *PL* 63, 763f.

[40] See J. Trouillard, *La purification plotinienne*, Paris 1955, 89-90. See also K. Kremer, *Die Neuplatonische Seinsphilosophie und ihre Wirkung auf Thomas von Aquin*[2], Leiden 1971, 135.

nothing can be thought. For many have a materialistic view of God[41]. Against this one might object that everyone must nevertheless have the idea of a highest and a best. Hence St. Thomas does not further insist and grants that everyone understands that by this name 'God' is signified something than which nothing greater can be thought[42]. But even granted this assumption it does not follow that people think that God exists; many atheists hold, in fact, that God does not exist. According to St. Thomas true knowledge has its origin in reality. From the presence of a concept we cannot conclude that what is represented by it really exists unless we first gain this concept, immediately or mediately, from reality[43]. One cannot object with Pegis[44] that St. Thomas misunderstood Anselm because he interpreted him from Aristotelian presuppositions whereas he should have understood him within the framework of Plato's metaphysics. St. Thomas' philosophy of being is neither that of Aristotle nor that of Plato, but is Aquinas' own.

St. Thomas brings in Anselm's argument in the context of the question whether the existence of God is *per se* known to man. Scotus remarks that Anselm does not say that God's existence is immediately known for his argument implies two syllogisms[45]. Formally this is correct. Nevertheless one may call this proposition immediately known in a broader sense of the term since it is by immediate implication that we are supposed to see that God exists. As F. Van Steenberghen writes, it is remarkable that St. Thomas, in an age when many admitted the immediate evidence of God's existence, nevertheless asserted that our road to God must start from (created) things and that his existence has to be demonstrated[46].

Those mediaeval doctors who did not share Aquinas' realism were tempted to accept the argument of Anselm. It occurs, for instance, in the works of St. Bonaventure[47]. Descartes presents a somewhat similar proof: we notice in ourselves a desire for perfection so that apparently we have the idea of a being

---

[41] Cf. for further details our commentary below on *S.Th.* I 3, 1. See also *S.C.G.* I 20, St. Augustine, *De civ. Dei* VIII 2, 5 and *De gen. ad litt.* X 25.

[42] A good number of people are likely to form this idea of a maximum in the various classes of perfection. The insight behind this idea is stated in the principle of formal causality "omnia quae sunt in aliquo genere derivantur a principio illius generis" (I-II 1, 1) or "propter quod unumquodque (tale) illud magis" (I 87, 2 ad 3).

[43] Cf. W. Basler, "Die Kritik des Thomas von Aquin am ontologischen Gottesbeweis", *Franziskanischen Studien* 55 (1973) 97-190.

[44] *O.c.*, n.36, 261.

[45] *Op. oxon.* I, d.2, q.2, n.8.

[46] "Saint Thomas d'Aquin contre l'évidence de l'existence de Dieu", in *Rivista di filosofia neoscolastica* 66 (1974) 671-681, 681. St. Thomas interpreted the famous saying of St. John Damascene "the knowledge of God is naturally implanted in us" as signifying only a confused knowledge, contained in certain principles, so that man has to reason in order to reach a clear understanding. St. Bonaventure, however, understood the words literally. Cf. E. Gilson, *La philosophie de saint Bonaventure*[3], Paris 1963, 108.

[47] *De mysterio Trinitatis* I 1, 20 (Q. V, 47).

more perfect than ourselves[48]. Its objective content is not produced by
ourselves, but requires a cause. Descartes is thinking here of a formal, not of
an efficient cause. This formal cause is intrinsically present in this idea as its
source and ground[49]. This cause is God. A similar type of argument is used
by Spinoza[50] and Leibniz. Leibniz completes the argument in the following
way: only after it has been shown that a perfect being is possible has God's
existence been demonstrated geometrically[51]. A being is possible so long as a
contradiction in its essence has not been proved[52].

Kant used the name "ontological proof" and thinks that the argument runs
as follows: contingent being requires a necessary being as its ground. Now
necessary being is identified with total perfection (*omnitudo realitatis*). It is
precisely this identification which is problematic. At this juncture Kant uses
the example of the 100 thalers, which he took from Bering. The thought of
this sum of money is not the same as its reality. Kant criticised the proof not
only because it entails a transition from thought to reality (as St. Thomas
does). Such an unwarranted transition may also occur in other cases (e.g.,
attributes which do not really belong to something but are applied to it in
thought). The reason why he ultimately rejects the ontological argument is,
that he came to consider "necessary" an apriori category of the mind.
Existence cannot be inferred from it. In his *Critique of Pure Reason* Kant
even reduces all other speculative proofs to the so-called ontological argument, sc. what is contingent requires a necessary being as its cause[53].

Hegel takes up Anselm's argument with enthusiasm. In his view subjectivity
and its object are the same. This unity finds its purest expression in the
ontological proof. Thus Hegel understands the argument in a different way
inasmuch as he holds that the concept objectifies itself and becomes idea
(= objectivity). It is precisely this auto-determination of the concept which he
calls the ontological argument. In it logic and the philosophy of religion are
welded together[54].

[48] *Méditation* VII, 47. This Being is autonomous, all-knowing, etc. In our commentary we
follow the *Third Meditation*.
[49] See P. Fontan, "Une certaine idée de Dieu. Lecture de Descartes", *Revue thomiste* 71 (1971)
349-366. The idea of an infinite and perfect being, inasmuch as it is a concept, is produced by
the intellect. In order to do so the latter does not need any materials from sense perception, for
the contents of this concept depend on God. However, Descartes sometimes appears to suggest
that man just has this idea as somehow innate. Throughout his proof he assumes that that which
man clearly perceives as true, is true.
[50] See P. Siwek, "La preuve ontologique dans la philosophie de Spinoza", *Gregorianum* 33
(1952) 621-627. Cf. H. Wolfson, *The Philosophy of Spinoza*, Cambridge Mass. 1934, I 177.
[51] C. Boyer, "Leibniz et l'argument ontologique", *Gregorianum* 14 (1937) 302-310.
[52] *Nouveaux Essais, IV, c.10.*
[53] D. Heinrich, *Der ontologische Gottesbeweis. Sein Problem und seine Geschichte in der
Neuzeit*, Tübingen 1960, 120ff.
[54] See *Enzyklop.*, § 193; Heinrich, *o.c.* (n.53) 189 ff; W. Jaeschke, *Die Religionsphilosophie
Hegels*, Darmstadt 1983.

In the twentieth century many philosophers still show a great deal of interest in the ontological proof. This is especially true of those who give up the Five Ways. These authors attempt to show that God is already present in man's mind before the latter explicitly starts to investigate God's existence. But in doing so they do not sufficiently distinguish between God's ontological presence in man and his presence as an object to be known[55].

Kant's assertion that existence is not a predicate is taken up by some neopositivist authors. "Anselm's ontological proof of the *Proslogion*, ch. 2, is fallacious because it rests on the false doctrine that existence is a perfection and therefore a real predicate"[56]. This view has been discussed in vol. I, ch. 11: being (*esse*) means actuality and perfection and only in the second place the copula. Hence it can be used as a predicate. Analytical philosophers assert that existence is always contingent. For instance, G. Ryle argues that "any assertion of the existence of something can be denied without logical absurdity"[57]. This was already David Hume's view: "Whatever we conceive as existent, we can also conceive as non-existent"[58]. When applied to contingent created beings we may readily admit this maxim, but Hume fails to show that it also holds true for transcendental being[59].

II. *Can God's existence be demonstrated? (S.Th. I,2,2)*

In the preceding article St. Thomas concluded that "because we do not know the essence of God, the proposition "God exists" is not evident to us and needs to be demonstrated through things that are more known to us, although they are less knowable in their nature, i.e. through God's effects". This conclusion is shared by most theologians of the 13th century. For instance, Alex-

---

[55] Cf. B. Montagnes, "Le Dieu de la philosophie et le Dieu de la foi", in (coll.) *Procès de l'objectivité de Dieu*, Paris 1969, 215-231, 222.—A. Poppi sees in Anselm's argument an application of the principle of contradiction: "La struttura elenctica dell'argomento anselmiano", in *Verifiche* 10 (Padova 1981) 195-203. However, while the principle of contradiction is a proposition which states a law of being, Anselm speaks of an idea which possesses existence (because it is perfect). Even if we express it in the form of a proposition, it is not an assertion.

[56] N. Malcolm, "Anselm's Ontological Arguments", in John Hick (edit.), *The Existence of God. Readings Selected, Edited and Furnished with an Introduction*, New York 1964, 48-70.—As to Kant's position see his *Kritik der reinen Vernunft* B627/A599: "Sein ist offenbar kein reales Prädikat, d.i. ein Begriff von irgend etwas, was zu dem Begriffe eines Dinges hinzukommen könne".

[57] *The Nature of Metaphysics* (edit. by D.F. Pears), New York 1957, 150. For further statements to the same effect by J.J.C. Smart and J.N. Findlay see A.N. Flew and A. MacIntyre (edit.), *New Essays in Philosophical Theology*, London 1955, 34 and 154.

[58] *Dialogues Concerning Natural Religion*, part IX.

[59] On the ontological argument see also H. Scholz, "Der Anselmische Gottesbeweis", in H. Hermes (hrsg.), *Mathesis universalis*, 1961, 62-74, and A. Plantinga (edit.), *The Ontological Argument from St. Anselm to Contemporary Philosophers*, New York 1965.

ander of Hales states that in this life God can be known only through an
intermediary[60]. Such is also the opinion of St. Albert the Great[61].

Aquinas now further explains this point. There are, he writes, two ways of
(philosophical) demonstration, viz. through the cause to the effect (this is
called a demonstration *propter quid*) and, when the effect is better known to
us than its cause, through the effect to its proper cause (this is called a demonstration *quia*). "Since every effect depends on its cause, if the effect exists,
the cause must preexist". A demonstration *quia* shows that a cause must exist
but it does not indicate the proper physical or metaphysical *ratio* of its
existence[62]. This type of argument consists of a syllogism and hence there is
a middle term.

This middle term, Aquinas adds, is the meaning of the name God. This is
obvious when we write out the argument in full: by 'God' we understand
supreme reality; this supreme reality exists; hence God exists. Or: God is the
being which is necessary by itself; a being necessary by itself exists; hence God
exists.

The major of these syllogisms is known through religious tradition or by a
previous quasi-spontaneous process of reasoning of which one is hardly
aware[63]. On the assumption that someone would not know this major, it
nevertheless remains possible to develop the arguments of the Five Ways. In
this case further reflection on the conclusion reached must show that this
reality (e.g. a First Unmoved Mover, a First Efficient Cause, etc.) is one and
the same thing for each of the Five Ways[64].

As will be shown later God's essence is pure being (*esse*). There is nothing
prior to it so that a demonstration *propter quid* is not possible. If, on the other
hand, we would intuitively see God we would know that God is subsistent
being through himself. But this intuition is not accessible to natural reason.
Hence the only way left to show that God exists is to conclude from the effects
that their cause exists[65].

---

[60] *Summa theologica*, tract. introd., q.2, m.3, c.1 (31a).

[61] *Summa theologica*, I, tr.3, q.15, m.1.

[62] The distinction goes back to Aristotle, *An. Post.* I 13, 78 a 22. See St. Thomas, *In I Anal.
Post.*, lectio 20.

[63] St. Thomas mentions such a quasi-spontaneous knowledge of God in I 13, 8 and 10 (by the
word 'God' people understand something excellent, the one who exercises universal providence)
and II-II 85, 1 (something superior, whatever it may be).

[64] If follows that for proving God's existence the nominal definition of God is necessary as the
middle term (cf. Suarez, *Disput. metaph.* XXIX, sectio 2, 4) but this does not mean that one must
already have such a nominal definition in order to set out along the Five Ways. If one commences
the argumentation without such a nominal definition, the conclusion reached (e.g. an Unmoved
First Mover) is simply not seen to be God. Cf. Th. O'Brien, *Metaphysics and the Existence of
God*, Washington D.C., 1960, 207.

[65] This solves the difficulty of those who hold that God's existence cannot be proved because
he is being itself and cannot not be. See E. Severino, "Ritorno a Parmenide", in *Rivista di
filosofia neoscolastica* 56 (1964) 150-153.

The third objection against the possibility of demonstrating God's existence points out that God's effects are not proportioned to Him because He is infinite and his effects are finite. This objection has been brought forward time and again. St. Albert the Great felt that the argument from the effects to their cause is not a syllogism when the effects are not convertible with their cause. The only rigorous demonstration of God's existence would be by way of a reduction to absurdity (if God would not exist)[66]. Duns Scotus felt that the proof from the effects rather leads us to erroneous conclusions[67]. Kant, for his part, insists that it is impossible to make the contingent reality of the world the foundation of the proof of the existence of a necessary being: one cannot build a house on a heap of stones[68]. A. N. Whitehead also holds that "there is an essence to the universe which forbids relationships beyond itself as a violation of its rationality"[69]. P. Tillich argues that when we deduce the existence of God from the world, God cannot be a being which transcends the world but becomes a link in a chain[70]. Austin Farrer advances a similar view: God has nothing in common with other beings; whatever we might say of him could only apply to created things, not to God; the principle of causality does not allow us to go beyond this world[71].

St. Thomas' answer to these difficulties is that "from effects not proportioned to the cause, no perfect knowledge of that cause can be obtained. Yet from every effect the existence of the cause can be clearly demonstrated, and so we can demonstrate the existence of God from his effects, though from them we cannot know God perfectly as he is in his essence"[72].

It is simply not true to assert that in the proofs contingent being becomes the basis for God's existence; it becomes the basis for our knowing about God. Likewise it is not true to say that God and created things have nothing in common, for even if God wholly transcends the world, his effects must nevertheless have some likeness to him. The principles we use in the Five Ways such as, for instance, the principle of causality, apply not only to this material universe but to being as such and hence also to divine reality. We know with certitude that God is not not-God (the principle of contradiction) or that if he were a composite being, there would have to be a cause of such composi-

---

[66] See St. Albert, *Summa theologica* I, tract. 3, q.15 (Borgnet, vol. 31).

[67] *Opus oxon.*, prol., q.1, a.2, 4.14.

[68] *Kritik der reinen Vernunft* B631/A603ff.

[69] According to Whitehead God is bound to cosmic process. The Ultimate is creativity beyond God. See his *Process and Reality*, 339.

[70] *Systematic Theology* I 243.

[71] *Finite and Infinite*, Westminster 1943, 7ff. Cf. J.H. Walgrave, "Kritik und Interpretation der Gottesbeweise bei den Oxford-Thomisten", in W.P. Eckert (hrsg), *Thomas von Aquin. Interpretation und Rezeption*, Mainz 1974, 144-157.

[72] I 2, 2 ad 3.

tion which he himself could not be[73]. The problem with the objection we mentioned and others similar to these is that they make use of a one-sided view of causality and proceed within the framework of monism or empiricism.

Before we consider in detail the Five Ways of St. Thomas and the historical origins of each of these arguments we must briefly examine the history of the proofs of God's existence in general. It is, of course, not our intention to present a complete history of such arguments. We want only to place St. Thomas' Ways in their historical setting.

Where religion is concerned with nature no need is felt to demonstrate God's existence: the divine is the almost palpable depth of things, the mysterious power behind cosmic movements and the growth of living beings. Only when forms of religious belief thus far admitted by all come under attack and the cosmos as well as human life are de-sacralized the need is felt to show with arguments that divinity really exists. As a matter of fact the first proofs of God's existence were elaborated after the Sophists had voiced doubts about the reality of the traditional gods and atheism had made its appearance during the Enlightenment of the fifth century B.C.[74]. Plato and Aristotle develop arguments which already anticipate some of the Five Ways: the ascent through the degrees of perfection (such as arguing from beautiful things to the existence of Beauty itself); the teleological argument; the demonstration of an ultimate source of movement, etc. Especially in his earlier period Aristotle was looking for ways of proving God's existence[75]. As we have seen Epicurus also admitted several proofs of the existence of the gods[76] as did the philosophers of the Stoa[77]. The latter explicitly asserted that scientific demonstrations are possible and devoted a special chapter of their treatises on the cosmos to this question (the "an sit"). Cleanthes enumerates four factors which cause in us the representation of the gods: oracles; the awareness that we owe our existence to others; fear produced by the forces of nature; the order and beauty of the cosmos[78]. Cleanthes also knew of a demonstration based upon the degrees of perfection[79].

---

[73] Behind a great deal of arguments of this sort lies the basic conviction of empiricism that we cannot go beyond this physical universe. Cf. also Kant's *Kritik der reinen Vernunft* B637f./A609f.: What is contingent cannot produce a synthetical proposition (such as the principle of causality). We shall return to this below.

[74] The first extant example of a proof is probably that reported by Xenophon, *Memor.* I 4; IV 3. See A.J. Festugière, *La révélation d'Hermès Trismégiste, II. Le Dieu cosmique*, Paris 1949, 75ff.

[75] Especially in his earlier period Aristotle was looking for ways to prove God's existence. See A.H. Chroust, "A Cosmological Proof for the Existence of God in Aristotle's Lost Dialogue *On Philosophy*", in *The New Scholasticism* 40 (1966) 447-463.

[76] See above chapter one, notes 48, 49, 50.

[77] P. Boyancé, "Les preuves stoïciennes de l'existence des Dieux", in *Hermes* 90 (1962), 45ff.

[78] *SVF* I 528.

[79] *SVF* I 529.

The Fathers of the Church did not fail to make use of the arguments they found in philosophical literature[80]. The proofs they propose often show the influence of Stoic thought. St. Augustine developed a demonstration based upon Neoplatonic ontology: since the intelligibles are in the intellect and are always true, there is eternal truth in the human mind. This must be a reflection of God's illuminating action. If truth exists, God exists[81].

Mediaeval Arab and Jewish philosophers adopt the Aristotelian demonstration of a First Unmoved Mover, adding to this sometimes the teleological argument. Al-Kindi (9th century) proposes a demonstration based upon the unity and plurality of predicables. The latter (for instance, 'man') do not possess their unity essentially. If this were the case, they would not be predicated of many. It follows that unity exists essentially outside of them[81a]. Al-Farabi uses the argument from movement but he also introduces the proof from the possible and the necessary and so prepares the way for the Third Demonstration of St. Thomas[82]. Avicenna advances this proof in his *Metaphysics* and *Book of Directions and Observations*. He even knows a proof from the consideration of being inasmuch as one abstracts from its particular mode of realization[83]. Averroes holds that the arguments showing that God exists belong to the philosophy of nature. He prefers by far the proof from motion and thinks that the teleological argument is only probable. He reformulates Avicenna's proof from the possible and the necessary[84].

In his treatise of the demonstration of God's existence the Jewish philosopher Maimonides is closer to Avicenna. His account of the proofs prepared the ground for some of the Ways of St. Thomas[85]. In the Latin West Boethius

---

[80] For an excellent concise history of the proofs see M.-D. Philippe, *De l'être à Dieu. De la philosophie première à la sagesse*, Paris 1977, 25-308.

[81] *De libero arbitrio* II, cc.3-16. Cf. Plotinus, *Enn.* V 5, 1 and Lloyd Gerson, "Augustine's Neoplatonic Argument for the Existence of God", *The Thomist* 45 (1981) 570-584. See also Ch.-V. Héris, "La preuve de l'existence de Dieu par les vérités éternelles", in *Revue thomiste* 31 (1926) 330-341. For the history of the proofs in the Middle Ages see G. Grunwald, *Geschichte der Gottesbeweise im Mittelalter bis zum Anfang der Hochscholastik. BGPhMA* VI 3, Münster 1907.

[81a] See M.E. Marmura and J.M. Rist, "Al-Kindi's Discussion of Divine Existence and Oneness", in *Medieval Studies* 25 (1963) 338-354, 338.

[82] Cf. A. Badawi, *Histoire de la philosophie en Islam*, II, Paris 1972, 534. See also A.J. Wensink, *Les preuves de l'existence de Dieu dans la théologique musulmane. Mededelingen der Koninklijke Akademie der Wetenschappen*, Afd. Letterk., 81, serie A, Amsterdam 1931, 16ff.

[83] Cf. M.-D. Philippe, *De l'être à Dieu. Topique historique*, II, Paris 1978, 252. According to St. Thomas' realism we may distinguish between being as such and modes of being, but we cannot separate being as such to use it in an argument, because we do not know yet whether being as such exists by itself.

We may add to our account that the great theologian Algazel (Ghazzali) proposes a demonstration from movement in which the world is claimed to have had a beginning. See S. de Beaurecueil et G.C. Anawati, "Une preuve de l'existence de Dieu chez Ghazzali et S. Thomas", *Mélanges de l'Institut Dominicain d'études orientales* 3 (1956) 207-258.

[84] For Averroes see L. Gauthier, *Ibn Rochd (Averroès)*, Paris 1948, 144ff.

[85] With regard to Maimonides' list of four proofs (*Dux perplexorum* II, cc.1-2) see G. Wieland, "Die Gottesbeweise des Moses Maimonides und die Ewigkeit der Welt", in *Philos. Jahrb.* 82

knows the arguments from the degrees of being and the order of the world[86].
In the Christian Middle Ages the universe, filled as it is with order and beauty,
could not even be envisaged without God. John Scot Eriugena writes that the
totality of things consists of God and the world. Created being reveals its
Maker. St. Anselm proposes a proof based on the idea of participation which
is related to the argument from the degrees of perfection[87]. His impressive
ontological argument has been discussed above. Abelard cites Cicero's demonstration of the existence of God[88]. His formulation, however, is quite loose.
As appears from his *Dialogue Between a Christian, a Jew and a Philosopher*,
where he sets forth the proof from design, in Abelard's opinion the arguments
in favour of God's existence are persuasive rather than demonstrative. Since
there are no proofs against the existence of God, a well disposed person will
admit the conclusion reached with moral certitude.

With Hugh of St. Victor a new chapter begins in the history of the proofs[89].
Hugh points out that God's invisible reality can only be known through what
is visible (this includes man's inner life). Hugh himself develops an argument
based upon the fact that the things we know don't have their being by themselves. For instance, man knows that he has not always existed and that his
being must depend on a source of being[90]. For Hugh the experience of one's
own being and the process of thinking is primary but in contrast to St. Anselm
he appeals at the same time to the experience of the outside world. It would
be wrong to read his argument as an anticipation of Descartes' proof. The
insistence on the argument starting from sensible things is even stronger in the
writings of Richard of St. Victor[91]. Richard puts forward the proof from the
degrees of being[92]. He adds an argument from the "possibility of being".
This possibility of being cannot but come from a power of being (*potentia
essendi*) so that ultimately there has to be a being which exists by itself[93]. This
proof apparently depends on the Neoplatonic theory that the road of the
emanation from the First Principle is also that of man's return to it[94].

Petrus Lombardus mentions four ways by which we come to the knowledge

(1975) 72-89. For an assembly of texts one may also consult R. Arnou, *De quinque viis sancti
Thomae ad demonstrandam Dei existentiam apud antiquos graecos et arabes et iudaeos praefor-
matis vel adumbratis textus selectos*, Roma 1932.

[86] *De consol. philos.* III, prose 10 and 12. On John Scot Eriugena see his *De divisione naturae*
II, 1: *PL* 122, 524. See also M.M. Davy, *Théologie et mystique de Guillaume de Saint-Thierry,
I. La connaissance de Dieu*, Paris 1954, 11.

[87] *Monologion*, c.1.

[88] *Theologia christiana* V 6.

[89] See M.-D. Philippe, *o.c.*, 347.

[90] *De sacramentis* III, c.31.

[91] *De Trinitate* V, c.6.

[92] *O.c.*, I, c.11.

[93] *O.c.*, I, c.12.

[94] Philippe, *o.c.*, 379.

of God's existence. He borrows them from St. Augustine and Ps.
Ambrosius[95]. Alexander of Hales attempted a systematic survey of all the
demonstrations he found in the writings of the Church Fathers and
theologians. He enumerates a class of proofs *"per intentionem esse"* and
others *"per intentionem causalitatis"*, *"per intentionem veritatis"*, *"per
intentionem bonitatis"*, etc.[96]. Although Alexander shows little originality in
his presentation of the proofs, his classification is an important development
and indicates that the Five Ways of St. Thomas are likely to be more than just
a random selection of arguments.

St. Bonaventure's position with regard to the demonstration of God's
existence has already been mentioned: God is immediately present to the
human mind as the source of all its understanding. When St. Bonaventure
speaks of "reasons" showing that God exists he means to provide an intellectual meditation which accompanies our faith in God. As Gilson observes strict
proofs of God's existence are inconceivable in Bonaventure's thought[97].

In general, however, the theologians and Christian philosophers of the 13th
century show a solid confidence in man's discursive power. They do not have
the slightest hesitation to affirm or demonstrate the existence of a being which
is not observed by the senses. This trust in illative reason is already found in
Platonism and Aristotelianism, but it was strengthened by the introduction
into the West of Aristotle's syllogistic (the *logica nova*). It is only in the last
quarter of the century that this confidence in the deductive power of natural
reason was shaken by the condemnation of the 219 Articles in 1277.

St. Albert the Great submitted the various questions concerning God's
existence to a careful examination: the knowability of God from different
points of view; the type of demonstration to be used; the nature of the certitude we can reach[98]. Subsequently he examines the arguments presented by
the philosophers[99]. St. Albert lists six ways of showing God's existence and
one argument concluding to the attributes of God. He then notes that these
are the ways of coming to the knowledge of God from created things. However, the arguments as he presents them are hardly demonstrations in the strict
sense of the term: rather, they help the faithful to grasp by reason the
existence of God they already admit in faith. Hence it is not unlikely that St.
Thomas similarly intended to summarize the possible philosophical proofs of

---

[95] *Sententiae* I, d.3, c.1.

[96] *Summa theologica*, pars I, tr.1, q.1.

[97] E. Gilson, *La philosophie de saint Bonaventure*, 93. Cf. A..C. Pegis, "The Bonaventurean
Way to God", in *Mediaeval Studies* 29 (1967) 206-242.

[98] *Summa theologica* I, tr.3, qq.13, 14, 15.

[99] *O.c.*, q.18. Philippe points to Albert's awareness of the fact that these proofs belong to the
natural order ("naturali ductu rationis"), *o.c.*, 448 n. Albert uses 'via' although he also has
'ratio' to name the demonstrations.

God's existence, as he saw them, in his Five Ways, and that the latter
primarily stand in a theological context.

Another attempt at the systematization of the proofs of God's existence is
found in the works of Henry of Ghent. We may proceed, he says, to the
knowledge of God's existence from causality (*per viam causalitatis*) or by
ascending above the limitations we encounter in the world (*per viam eminentiae*). In doing so we obtain respectively six and two arguments, which, Henry
thinks, belong more properly to the philosophy of nature[100]. This shows us
once more how much the 13th century theologians were concerned with the
epistemology of the proofs and how they attempted to bring the arguments
into a systematic order. In addition to those mentioned already Henry proposes a proof which is more metaphysical in character: through a process of
abstraction we can obtain concepts of forms such as goodness[101]. Without
recourse to the principle of causality man may discover God in the formal
contents (*intentiones*) which the mind conceives. According to A. C. Pegis,
with this argument Henry of Ghent prepared later *a priori* constructions
which aim at showing God's existence in an absolute way[102].

We encounter a somewhat similar concern in Scotus' works. Scotus has
reservations with regard to the proofs from motion and efficient causality in
the physical world and prefers to establish a metaphysical point of departure,
viz. the metaphysical properties of created being. Not the existence of things
but a metaphysical aspect such as the "productibility" or "effectibility" of
a thing should be considered. This requires as its correlative the "efficient"
cause. From there we ascend to a First Efficient: this First Efficient has not
been produced itself; it is possible and therefore it exists[103]. As M.-D. Philippe
notes[104], Scotus' demonstration is very complex and goes in the direction of
an extreme formalism. As a matter of fact, he employs a way of arguing introduced by Henry of Ghent[105]. Logical categories are at the centre of interest
and the possible overshadows the actually existent. The contingent existence
of the physical world does not allow a definite conclusion about the necessary
being (*esse*) of the First Principle.

Ockham criticizes Scotus' argument. He himself seems to attribute a certain
value to the proof from efficient causality. However, since he thinks that the
impossibility of infinite regress is not evident, he substitutes efficient causality

---

[100] *Summae questionum ordinariarum*, art. 22, q.3.
[101] *O.c.*, q.5.
[102] "Henry of Ghent and The New Way to God", in *Mediaeval Studies* 30 (1968) 226-246; 31 (1969) 93-110.
[103] *Ordinatio* I, d.2, pars 1, q.2. We do not consider Scotus' arguments in his *De primo prin-cipio*.
[104] *O.c.*, 652.
[105] Cf. C. Balič, in *Duns Scotus. Opera omnia* I 167*-168*.

in the conservation of things for efficient causality in their production: what is produced by something else, is conserved by it as long as it exists[106]. Ockham is convinced that in this way he is able to show that there must be a *Primum Conservans*: since the causes which may collaborate to keep a thing in existence work simultaneously, there is no infinite series. What is novel in Ockham's view is that God is seen as simultaneous with his effects. Relations take the place of substances. In this life man has no knowledge of God's essence and therefore the proposition "God exists" cannot be affirmed with metaphysical certitude.

The shift toward a logical approach as apparent in Henry of Ghent and Scotus as well as in Ockham's critical attitude suggests that there is no access to God from process or the actual existence of things in our world. This position resulted in a pervasive scepticism, as appears in the works of Adam Woodham and Robert Holcot. The classical exponent of this movement is Nicholas of Autrecourt who has been called the mediaeval Hume: he argues that it is impossible to affirm or to deny that God exists[107].

In the fifteenth century Gabriel Biel takes up several of Ockham's views and asserts that we cannot demonstrate in an evident way by natural reason that God is the final or efficient cause of all things. Luther went beyond these sceptical positions: man's reason itself is corrupt and a prey to the devil. Hence it cannot lead us to God. Those who attempt to prove God's existence from visible things become the slaves of these things.

At the end of the sixteenth century the influence of Suarez makes itself felt. This great Spanish philosopher thinks that the argument from movement does not allow us to reach certitude about God's existence (the principle 'whatever is moved, is moved by something else' is not certain). His preference is for a demonstration which is more metaphysical in nature, sc. whatever is has been made or has not been made. Now it is impossible that all things belong to the first category[108]. The reason is that an infinite regress is not possible. It follows that a being that has not been made exists. However, we must still show that this being is the one and only God. The order of the universe suggests that God is one, but this does not give us full certitude. An argument is required to demonstrate God's unity[109].

Descartes' main proof for God's existence, the so-called ontological argument, has already been mentioned. We may perhaps note in passing that in his *Third Meditation* Descartes indicates an argument from man's con-

---

[106] *In I Sent.*, d.2, q.10.
[107] Cf. P. Vignaux, "Nicolas d'Autrecourt", in *Dict. de théol. cath.*, XI, 567; H. Ley, *Studien zur Geschichte des Materialismus im Mittelalter*, Berlin 1959, I, 475ff.; L.A. Kennedy, *Peter of Ailly and the Harvest of Fourteenth Century Philosophy*, Queenston 1986, 47ff.
[108] *Disp. metaph.* XXIX, sectio 1, n.21.
[109] *O.c.*, sectio 2, n.2ff.

tingency (if we were ourselves the cause of being, we would have given ourselves the fullness of perfection and knowledge as well as permanent duration). But he does not seem to consider this an independent proof. Rather, he uses this insight to make clear that man himself cannot have produced the formal content of the idea of an infinitely perfect being. What is new in Descartes is his overruling preoccupation with certitude and his attempt to set up a chain of deductions based upon initial evidence and all this in the keynote of his own subjectivity. Although he admits and uses the traditional concept of God, his metaphysics no longer is an ascent to God but makes of God a noetic principle in man's spiritual universe. Descartes was also innovative in his refusal to go to God from the external world: his approach is intuitive and, in a sense, *a priori* rather then *a posteriori*; physics follows upon metaphysics.

Shortly after Descartes had published his works Pascal criticised the rationalistic approach of Descartes and Gassendi with regard to the problem of God's existence: God is hidden and the world hides him more than it reveals him[110]. Perhaps their demonstrations lead to the admission of a supreme Engineer, but not to the God of Christianity. The philosophical arguments are uncertain. Although they concern the true God they are quite useless for man's supernatural salvation. In his famous *Wager* Pascal advises unbelievers and sceptics to bet on the safer alternative, to admit provisionally God's existence and Christian revelation. Subsequent praxis of Christian life will lead them to conversion and true faith.

Spinoza was convinced that Descartes had not gone far enough in his rationalism since his idea of God is still dependent on Judaeo-Christian revelation. He asserts that God is the all-embracing reality (Nature) of which other things are modes or determinations. In this way it is possible to uphold both a fully deductive system and the perfect unity of all things. However, God is placed by him at the service of a system[111]. In Spinoza's pantheistic monism the world is absorbed into God and this prepared the way for God's absorption into the world in later philosophy.

British empiricism challenged the role Descartes had assigned to God as the guarantor of certitude in our knowledge of the world. John Locke rejects any innate idea of God. Moreover, he adds, the fact that we have an idea of something does not prove that it exists. We must demonstrate God's existence *a posteriori*[112]. Although Locke admits the proof from the order of the world, he clearly prefers the argument from the intuitive and, therefore, wholly cer-

---

[110] See J. Orcibal, "Le fragment Infini-Rien et ses sources", in *Blaise Pascal, l'homme et l'oeuvre. Cahiers de Royaumont. Philosophie* I, Paris 1956, 164-168; P. Magnard, *Nature et histoire dans l'apologétique de Pascal*, Paris 1975, 330-339.

[111] See J. Collins, *God in Modern Philosophy*, Chicago 1959, 72.

[112] See his *Essay concerning Human Understanding* IV, c.10. Locke does not make it very clear what the stages of his arguments are. He also resorts to the impossibility of infinite regress.

tain perception of one's own contingent existence. Our being requires a cause which is "an eternal, most powerful and most knowing Being". Locke calls this conclusion a "certain and evident truth". David Hume agrees with Locke on the fact that the idea of God is derived from experience, viz. from the perception of the activity and qualities of our own mind, which we enlarge limitlessly [113]. But Hume rejects any aposteriori demonstration for the simple reason that every argument drawn from effects to their causes is non-conclusive. We cannot know more than that which we experience in an effect. The existence of its cause is not perceived and is not certain. Hume's philosophy is dependent on the empirical postulate: deductions beyond immediate experience are unlawful, for our knowledge concerns only the phenomenal and not the essential nature of things and their properties. At best Hume is prepared to admit some principle of order in the universe but he did not attach much importance to it. He also rejects the moral argument in favour of God's existence as inhumane. One might as well argue from the presence of evil to the existence of an evil principle [114].

It is difficult to qualify Hume's positions with regard to the problem of God: it definitely approaches agnosticism although one may find some traces of a "threadbare deism" [115]. He probably did not want to remove this ambiguity. His writings became a powerful force in the neutralizing of theological thinking: religion was now placed outside the field of scientific thought and morality was completely liberated from theological attachment and became totally secularized.

While in England empiricism was on the rise, on the European continent rationalism still dominated. Christian Wolff is quite close to Descartes in several of his positions: because philosophically speaking the reality of material things is not entirely certain, the contingent existence of our own soul must become the starting point of the demonstration of God's existence. For this, however, we must first show that the notion of an infinitely perfect being is not self-contradictory [116]. In Wolff's philosophy existence is reduced to the status of a qualification of an essence.

The French Enlightenment was marked by naturalism and criticism of revealed religion. While Diderot's position shifted from deism to atheism, Voltaire remained a deist: there is order in the world and nature clearly shows the signs of having been made by an intelligent Creator. The presence of evil led Voltaire to consider God a non-voluntary cause of things.

---

[113] *An Enquiry concerning Human Understanding* II (edit. Selby-Bigge, 19).
[114] *A Treatise of Human Nature* I 3, 2-4. See also his *Dialogues on Natural Religion* II.
[115] Cf. J. Noxon, *Hume's Philosophical Development*, Oxford 1973, 170.
[116] See his *Theologia naturalis* II and J. Ecole, "Les preuves wolfiennes de l'existence de Dieu", in *Archives de philosophie* 42 (1979) 381-396.

At first Kant shared the deism of so many of his contemporaries, but after a careful study of the works of Hume he made a "Copernican revolution" and began to develop his transcendental philosophy: since there is an unbridgeable gap between the idea of a transcendent God and the empirical world experience of the latter cannot lead to the knowledge of God's existence. Recourse to causality to establish God's existence is in vain, since our experience of causality only applies to the phenomenal world. It follows that the arguments from the contingency of things[117] and from the order in the world[118] are devoid of conclusive value. Kant does admit, however, that man has an idea of God, but this is the product of human reason which seeks the unconditioned unity of all predicates. In doing so reason conceives a most perfect being which is personified. God is the third so-called transcendental idea of pure reason, an ideal toward which the mind tends[119]. Kant asserts that we do not know at all whether God, represented by this idea, is real or not: the ontological argument from the idea of a most perfect being to its existence is not possible. If we add being to the idea, all we can say is that an existent idea exists, which is a tautology.

For Kant, indeed, every existential proposition is synthetic and the only basis for an existential judgment is experience, not analysis. Whoever affirms that an idea exists, posits this idea in reality but he does not add a predicate to a subject. Kant concludes that the speculative intellect cannot reach definite knowledge concerning God's existence. But Kant's criticism of the traditional proofs is so dependent on his particular epistemology that it lacks validity. Despite his rejection of the traditional proofs Kant holds that belief in God is absolutely necessary in order to secure the moral order. We cannot conceive how man can reach happiness except on the supposition that God exists. Thus practical reason must establish the postulate of God's existence[120]. But practical reason depends on a choice of our will. In this way our free will becomes the source not only of the moral order, but even of God's existence. For speculative reason God is not more than a hypothesis[121]. Kant's criticism of the traditional proofs had a far reaching, devastating effect on their later use.

---

[117] Kant calls this the cosmological argument.

[118] *Kritik der reinen Vernunft* B620ff./A592ff.—Kant also expressed his criticism by means of this metaphor: one cannot erect a high-rise building on a foundation of loose stones.—This objection keeps coming back in later philosophical literature. Hegel says that proofs must be based on the primacy of the spirit, not on the contingency of material reality (*Logik* II 40 Meiner).

[119] Kant assigns an important function to this idea: it promotes a reduction of our knowledge into a systematic ensemble; our reason should regard all order in the world as if it had been caused by a supreme mind.

[120] *Kritik der reinen Vernunft* II, 2, V (A223ff.). On the postulate of God's existence see A. Winter, "Der Gottesbeweis aus praktischer Vernunft", in K. Kremer (hrsg), *Um Möglichkeit oder Unmöglichkeit natürlicher Gotteserkenntnis heute*, Leiden 1985, 109-178.

[121] We cannot here consider the question of an evolution of Kant's position in his last years, in particular as expressed in his *Opus postumum*

In his last writings Kant opposed the spreading idealism and romanticism and stressed that human reason does not reach God as he is in himself. God is unattainable and cannot be identified with Nature or a World Soul[122]. But the tide of idealism was too strong to be arrested by Kant's warnings.

About 1790 Fichte reached the conviction that the self is the centre of reality. In his view there are no proofs of God's existence; awareness of God has its roots in faith, the organ of our knowledge of the supra-sensible world. Faith is awareness of our own freedom[123]. While Fichte assigned a dominating role to the individual self and its awareness, Hegel set out to reconcile the individual and the whole, faith and reason. As a matter of fact Hegel attaches a paramount importance to the question of God. Aware of the hopeless state in which Kant had left metaphysics and philosophical theology Hegel sought a way to overcome the difficulties, to save from metaphysics and religion what he thought worthwhile saving and to re-assign to God his place in the totality of things. To do so he developed his monistic and dialectic idealism: God is the absolute spirit and the totality of being who by dialectical process is the source and core of the unfolding reality in history, thought, art, religion and social life. Using Christian terms Hegel often gave them a wholly new meaning, creating at the same time a certain ambiguity as to his own position.

In line with German fideism and in particular with F.-H. Jacobi Hegel felt that man can apprehend God immediately, although such an apprehension must be critically examined. The finite can only be an expression of the Infinite. The traditional proofs of God's existence, the cosmological as well as, more specifically, the ontological argument must be understood as attempts to formulate how the (human) spirit, which is part of the dialectical process of the Spirit, recognizes its own belonging and elevation to God[124]. Hegel's own arguments for God's existence are not intended to make his readers discover God. Rather they are a description of the process of thought taking place within the mind which transforms sensible contingent reality (by "thinking" it) into the universal[125]. The defect of the traditional proofs is that they do not make clear what God's essence is. Furthermore these arguments do not show that contingent being cannot coexist with the Necessary Being, but must return to it[126]. Hegel's own demonstration is based on the "dialectical identity of the finite and the Absolute"[127].

---

[122] *Opus Postumum* VII 4 (*Gesammelte Schriften*, 22, 57f.).

[123] See *J.G. Fichtes Werke. Auswahl in 6 Bänden*, (Medicus) Leipzig 1908ff., III 129. C. Fabro, "Genèse historique de l'athéisme contemporain", in J. Girardi et J.F. Six, *L'athéisme dans la philosophie contemporaine*, Tournai 1970, 23-96, 61.

[124] *Vorlesungen über die Beweise vom Dasein Gottes*, hrsg. G. Lasson, Leipzig 1930, 156f.

[125] I owe this remark to Dr. K. Hedwig. Cf. also B. Lakebrink, *Kommentar zu Hegels "Logik" in seiner "Enzyklopädie" von 1830*, Bd. 1, München 1979, 361ff.

[126] *O.c.*, 100-125. Cf. also *Enzyklopädie*, § 50.

[127] See B. Lakebrink, *Hegels dialektische Ontologie und die thomistische Analektik*, Ratingen 1968, 267ff.

It is obvious that in Hegel's system the traditional proofs cannot but lose their value. God's transcendence is denied and man is taken up in an impersonal dialectical process he does not control. Hence it is not so surprising that soon after Hegel's voice had become silent, elements of his system were used in an atheistic synthesis. Other thinkers such as Kierkegaard pointed out that it is not as important to demonstrate God's existence as to get to know oneself before God, who is present in Christ. Proofs are useless: either God does not exist and then any proof is impossible, or, if God exists, proofs are superfluous because we already assume that God is. For Kierkegaard, indeed, to exist is to be present; one does not prove existence, one accepts it. It is not hard to see that Kierkegaard's position is very much dependent on Kant's theory and that his idea of existence is much narrower than that employed by Aquinas[128].

Although he shared Kierkegaard's aversion to rationalism, J. H. Newman never called into question such philosophical demonstrations as the Five Ways of St. Thomas. But he felt that man is often not convinced by this type of argument. He even hesitated to use the proof from design, probably in order to avoid ending up in "physical theology". Instead he tried to develop a demonstration which would be a more concrete process starting from a personal experience[129].

At the end of the nineteenth century the question of the proofs of God's existence loses its actuality in European non-Christian philosophy as does philosophical theology itself. William James sums up the situation as he sees it: "The arguments for God's existence have stood for hundreds of years with the waves of unbelieving criticism breaking against them, never totally discrediting them in the ears of the faithful, but on the whole slowly and surely washing out the mortar from between their joints. If you have a God already whom you believe in, these arguments confirm you. If you are atheistic, they fail to set you right"[130]. James's view that arguments only serve to confirm pre-existent partialities is an application of the pragmatic principle. There are better explanations than that of James as to why the proofs fail to convince some people. The variety of opinions in philosophy does not prove that truth cannot be reached. It rather shows the ease with which factors alien to reason itself may warp its work[131].

---

[128] See C. Fabro, "L'existence de Dieu dans l'oeuvre de Kierkegaard", in *a.a.v.v., L'existence de Dieu*, Tournai 1961, 37-47.

[129] See below for some remarks on his argument from conscience. Cf. J. Boekraad, *The Personal Conquest of Truth according to J. H. Newman*, Louvain 1955; A.J. Boekraad and H. Tristram, *The Argument from Conscience to the Existence of God according to J. H. Newman*, Louvain 1961, 103ff.

[130] *The Varieties of Religious Experience*, Lecture XVIII.

[131] See St. Thomas, *S.C.G.* I 4 where he enumerates the following factors which may hamper a correct grasp of metaphysical truth: (a) a defective personal disposition and a lack of interest and application; (b) a lack of a solid philosophical preparation; (c) the occurrence of error on

According to Alfred North Whitehead "any proof which commences with the consideration of the character of the actual world cannot rise above the actuality of this world; ... it may discover an immanent God, but not a God wholly transcendent"[132]. Implicit in Whitehead's criticism is the positivist principle that causes are always homogeneous causes. He subscribes moreover, to the empiricist maxim that the analysis of a being whose existence has been established cannot teach us anything about its nature. When we consider Whitehead's previous scientific endeavours it is not so surprising that he uses the method of the sciences in metaphysics, but this does damage to the value of his work.

Karl Jaspers admits that transcendence exists[133]. It is revealed to us by our tendency toward it which we experience. If we deny it, we lose ourselves[134]. However, a rational proof of transcendence is not possible. Instead Jaspers stresses the importance of "philosophical faith" and also warns against recourse to wrong concepts of God (idols). Altogether he remains extremely vague and many critics consider his statements on transcendence devoid of any basis[135].

Heidegger observes that arguments for God's existence may be formally correct and yet not prove anything because a God whose existence must first be shown is a very ungodly God[136]. Unfortunately Heidegger does not tell us how he comes by his idea of "an ungodly God" nor what to make of demonstrations in the sciences.

A good number of the analytical philosophers are also sharply critical of demonstrations of God's existence. Their critique generally follows the line of Hume's empiricism: the principle of causality is of dubious validity and certainly does not have enough strength to bridge the gap between a wholly different Infinite Being and our physical universe. In other words, the principle

---

account of the weakness of the intellect and the ease with which representations of the imagination can lead it astray.

[132] *Religion in the Making*, Cambridge 1926, 77.

[133] *Philosophie* III, 6ff. God is formal transcendence (III, 66).

[134] *O.c.*, II, 196ff.

[135] See X. Tilliette, "La philosophie et le langage des chiffres selon K. Jaspers", in *a.a.v.v., L'existence de Dieu*, Tournai 1961, 77-94.

[136] *Nietzsche*, I, Pfullingen 1961, 336. What is really dangerous in Heidegger's assertion is that it makes truth subject to factors beyond the control of reason, *c.q.* even to the human will. Only what I want to be true is true. According to the so-called transcendental philosophy as it is taught by authors such as Karl Rahner, E. Coreth and J. de Vries, all proofs of God's existence must be inserted into a foundational free act by which man affirms his own contingency and so reaches the Absolute Being. But under these rhetorical clauses serious difficultes are hidden, not the least being that man's affirmation of God is made dependent upon a choice of the will. See B. Lakebrink, "Die metaphysischen Voraussetzungen der thomistischen Gottesbeweise und die moderne Philosophie", in L. Elders (edit.) *Quinque sunt viae*, Città del Vaticano 1980, 7-8 and H.M. Baumgartner, "Über das Gottesverständnis der Transzendentalphilosophie", in *Philos. Jahrb.* 73 (1965-1966) 303-321, 314.

.

of causality cannot carry us outside our world[137]. What is at issue in this objection is whether our mind is able to formulate laws of being and relations of cause and effect which are truly universal, that is, express structures which apply to all beings. In other terms, can the intellect deduce from the particular facts offered by the senses universal concepts and laws which hold true of all reality? Modern man distrusts the reasoning power of the intellect and is inclined to admit only what he can directly experience himself. Analytical philosophers will say that it is not possible to build a bridge between mere abstractions and concrete existence. Some argue that all statements about God are meaningless because no verification is possible[138]. But this position begs the question: why should verification be restricted to sense experience instead of including also the careful checking of one's starting point and reasoning? The empiricist's position itself is a universal position which cannot be verified[139].

---

[137] Cf. Austin Farrer, *Finite and Infinite*, Westminster 1943, 7.

[138] This is the position of A.J. Ayer, A. Flew and others. See Flew's "Theology and Falsification", in A. Flew and A. MacIntyre (edit.), *New Essays in Philosophical Theology*, London 1955, 106-108. See also J.N. Findlay, "Can God's Existence be disproved?" in *o.c.*, 47-56.

[139] P. Tillich writes in his *Systematic Theology* I, Chicago 1951, 205: "If we derive God from the world, he cannot be that which transcends the world infinitely. He is the "missing link" discovered by correct conclusions. He is the uniting force between the *res cogitans* and the *res extensa* (Descartes) or the end of the causal regression in answer to the question "Where from?" (Thomas Aquinas) or the theological intelligence directing the meaningful process of reality, if not identical with these processes (Whitehead). In each of these cases God is "world", a missing part of that from which he is derived in terms of conclusions. This contracts the idea of God as thoroughly as does the concept of existence. The arguments for the existence of God neither are arguments nor are they proofs of the existence of God. They are expressions of the question of God which is implied in human finitude. This question is their truth, every answer they give is untrue".—Tillich's remarks do perhaps apply to the physico-theology of the deists but lose their force in the case of St. Thomas' doctrine of the transcendence of God. Aquinas' theology is predominantly a negative theology.

CHAPTER THREE

THE FIVE WAYS OF THE *SUMMA THEOLOGIAE*

St. Thomas himself was convinced that it is of paramount importance in philosophy to demonstrate that God exists: without such proof any philosophical consideration of being is ultimately without a foundation, for philosophy is the study of reality and not a logic of the human mind[1]. But here we encounter a difficulty. The *Summa theologiae* is a treatise of sacred theology. Do we have the right to isolate the Five Ways in I 2, 3 from their theological context and consider this passus merely from a philosophical point of view? Some have doubted the very possibility of such an undertaking[2], but the answer is a clear 'yes'. For St. Thomas the demonstration of God's existence is a *praeambulum fidei* and cannot intrinsically belong to sacred theology[3]. Hence the arguments are part of philosophy and what holds true for the arguments also applies to their order (if there is a meaningful arrangement of the Five Ways), for this order is given with the different points of departure which are facts of observation. This, of course, is not to deny that the Five Ways do have a function in sacred theology, as will be explained in a later section of this chapter.

A first question is to which philosophical discipline the proofs of God's existence belong. Aristotle presents arguments for the existence of a First Unmoved Mover both in the *Physics* and in the *Metaphysics*. According to Avicenna the demonstration belongs to metaphysics[4], but Averroes defends the view that such a proof has its place in the philosophy of nature[5]. Suarez sides with Avicenna, but he does so for a reason St. Thomas would not admit, viz. that the argument from movement does not reach certitude[6].

---

[1] *S.C.G.* I 9: "... praemittendum est quasi totius operis necessarium fundamentum, consideratio qua demonstratur Deum esse. Quo non habito omnis consideratio de rebus divinis necessario tollitur". See Wayne J. Hankey, "The Place of the Proof for God's Existence", in *The Thomist* 46 (1982) 370-393.

[2] See A. Finili, "Is There a Philosophical Approach to God?". in *Dominican Studies* 4 (1951) 80-81.

[3] A statement to this effect is found in the *Expositio in Boetii De Trinitate*, q.2, a.3. In *S.C.G.* I 13 St. Thomas speaks of arguments the *philosophers* used.

[4] *Metaphysica* I, c.5. For Avicenna and Averroes the difficulty was caused by the question as to what is the precise subject of metaphysics. If God is thought to be its subject matter, his existence must be shown in another discipline, for no science proves the existence of its own subject. Averroes held this latter position as did Alexander of Aphrodisias before him (*In Metaphysicam* 668, 26ff.)

[5] *In Physicam* I, comm. 83; In Metaph. XII, comm. 5.

[6] He thinks that the principle "whatever is moved, is moved by something else" is not certain. See his *Disput metaph.* 29, sectio I, n.21.

St. Thomas clearly affirms that the demonstration of God's existence is part of metaphysics. In the Proem to the *Commentary on the Metaphysics* he writes that it belongs to the same science to study the proper causes of a class of being and to study that class of being itself[7]. Hence metaphysics which studies being, must also consider the causes of being. This does not mean that the study of movement, contingency and finality in the physical world (as required in the Five Ways) as such belongs to metaphysics. It does so in an accidental way (*quasi per accidens*) inasmuch as it allows us to come to the knowledge of God[8].

A second remark concerns the question of how to proceed in our arguments. In the preceding article St. Thomas indicated that when a being is unknown in itself, but produces some effects proper to it, we may deduce, from such effects, the existence of their proper cause; if the effect exists, the cause must pre-exist[9]. For this reason we demonstrate that God exists when we can show that things, activities and processes as we observe them, are the effects of a (hidden) transcendental cause, which we call God. However, at first sight it appears that things are effects of natural causes, so that recourse to God seems superfluous. St. Thomas himself raises this objection: "It seems that everything we see in the world can be accounted for by other principles, supposing God did not exist. For all natural things can be reduced to one principle, which is nature and all voluntary things can be reduced to one principle, which is human reason, or will". However, as will appear and as St. Thomas observes in his answer to this objection, natural causes and the human will alone are not sufficient to explain what exists and happens in the physical world. The becoming and being of things must be traced to a First Cause. This is done in the Five Ways.

It must be stressed that in the Five Ways Aquinas each time takes facts perceived by the senses as the starting points of his arguments. Such mediaeval doctors as Hugh of St. Victor preferred to use our inner experience (for instance, of the existence of our own soul) as the point of departure for a demonstration. St. Thomas by no means excludes such a procedure but wants to base his arguments on rock bottom facts which must be admitted by everyone.

---

[7] "Eiusdem autem scientiae est considerare causas proprias alicuius generis et genus ipsum".

[8] *Expos. in Boetii De Trinitate*, q.5, a.4 ad 1. In this work. q.5, a.1 ad 9 the question is discussed whether theology is prior to the philosophy of nature. Avicenna is quoted as holding that metaphysics uses many elements of the philosophy of nature such as the deduction of the existence of the First Mover from movement (*Metaph.* I, c.3, 71 ra: Van Riet 21, 81). St. Thomas, however, omits this last remark, replacing it by a "et alia huiusmodi". This means that he holds even more strongly than Avicenna had done that the demonstration of the First Mover belongs to metaphysics. In view of the above it is difficult to understand how M.-D. Philippe can write that the Five Ways, even if they employ metaphysical arguments, are not of the metaphysical but of the theological order" ("La troisième voie de S. Thomas", in *aa. vv., De Deo in philosophia S. Thomae et in hodierna philosophia*, I, Roma 1965, 41-47, 43.

[9] I 2, 2.

Unfortunately that which in reality is an asset and grounds the proofs on unshakeable evidence, has become for some an obstacle. The attitude of many scientists has changed with regard to sense data. They have become averse to a 'naive realism' and feel that they must take an 'active attitude' toward what is observed. Observation influences the facts. To this we answer that in St. Thomas' realism we are not at the level of the sciences, but at that of the metaphysics of common sense. This holds as evident that our senses and intellect can truly know real things as they are.

In one of his works G. K. Chesterton writes: "give me anything to start from, a flower if you want, and I can construct an argument for God's existence". Chesterton is right provided we consider such things as effects resulting from causes, i.e. we must consider them from the point of view of the four genera of causality[10]. The first genus is that of material causality. Its fundamental instance is primary matter which receives a form. By extension every potency to a new form is reduced to the genus of material causality. Because primary matter itself is not visible, its nature and existence must be deduced. Hence it cannot be a starting-point of an argument intended to be based on sense experience[11]. On the other hand, the gradual actualization of a potency in a continuous movement is a process which can be observed and in which material causality is involved[12]. The central question in the First Way is precisely the actualization of this potency. The Second Way, as St. Thomas himself writes, starts from the nature of efficient causes and their order[13]. The Fourth Way is taken from the gradation of formal perfections in things such as goodness or truth and the like. The question is raised why these perfections are sometimes realized in varying degrees. Now every actualization of a subject comes about by formal causality. The Fifth Way starts from the fact that things move toward an end. Acting in view of an end is dependent on final causality[14].

---

[10] On the division of causes see St. Thomas, *In II Phys.*, lectio 2, n.240.

[11] See below the commentary on the starting point of the First Way.

[12] Cf. *In II Metaph.*, 1.4, n.328: "In omni eo quod movetur, necesse est intelligere materiam. Omne enim quod movetur est in potentia; ens autem in potentia est materia ..." See also *Quodl.* III, q.8 (20): "... si materia dicatur omne illud quod est in potentia quocumque modo ..."; *De princ. naturae*, n.340: "Sicut autem omne quod est in potentia, potest dici materia ..." See also J. Gredt, *Elementa philosophiae aristotelico-thomisticae*, II[13], n.751: "Ad causam materialem reducuntur ... quodcumque subiectum potentiale suscipiens aliquem actum". W.A. Wallace points out in a remarkable study that the proof of the principle "whatever moved, is moved by another" is made not through efficient but rather through material causality. See *Proceedings of the American Catholic Philosophical Association*, vol. 46 (1972) 43-57, 44.

[13] Some authors avow that they do not see the difference between the First and the Second Way. Gilson speaks of a narrow relationship (*Le thomisme*[6], 77). In his *The Elements of Christian Philosophy* (Mentor Omega, New York 1963, 74) he writes: "The same proof can be read in the language of efficient causality". See also his remark in *AHDLMA* 1963, 53-70.—We trust that our distinction has cleared up the issue.

[14] The causality of the end consists precisely in being strived after (cf. *De veritate*, q.22, a.2).

These four ways apparently find their starting points in facts belonging to the four classes of causality. But what about the Third Way? St. Thomas writes that it is taken from possibility and necessity, by which he means the possibility of the being and non-being of corruptible things and the necessity of immaterial beings or celestial bodies[15]. The possibility of being is dependent on the essence of material things, that is on the presence of primary matter in it. When a being is a pure form, its existence follows necessarily upon its form[16]. The argument of the Third Way dwells on the fact that things do not have their being (*esse*) of themselves, that is on the contingent relationship between the *suppositum* and its being. This relationship can be expressed in terms of causality, viz. the *esse* exercises a quasi-formal and quasi-efficient causality. The causality of the *esse* lies at a deeper level than that of the four physical causes and is the root of all causality. In this way there are the four genera of causality and this metaphysical relationship[17] from which we may start to attempt to demonstrate God's existence[18].

This interpretation of St. Thomas' assertion that "the existence of God can be proved in five ways" contradicts such commentators as A. R. Motte and E. Gilson who do not attach any importance to these words[19]. But if, as Cajetanus says, St. Thomas always expresses himself formally[20], the "quinque viis probari potest" must signify what it says. Moreover contemporaries of Aquinas tried to place the demonstrations of God's existence in a systematic order[21]. It would be very surprising if the greatest systematic thinker of all times would just have presented a random non-exhaustive enumeration of the arguments. It is true that the great commentators Cajetanus, Johannes a Sancto Thoma and Billuart do not dwell upon this

---

[15] Aristotle and a good number of mediaeval philosophers held the celestial bodies to be incorruptible and, therefore, necessary beings.

[16] We must presuppose that God causes their being: I 104, 1.

[17] See our "Les cinq voies et leur place dans la philosophie dce saint Thomas". In L. Elders (edit.) *Quinque sunt viae*, Città del Vaticano 1980, 133-146.

[18] It should be noticed that in enumerating the four genera of causes Aquinas repeatedly uses the genetic order: on a subject (matter) the efficient cause impresses a form in view of an end. Cf. *De princ. nat.*, c.4; *Exp. in Boetii De Trin.* Proemium; *De pot.* q.3, a.16; *In II Phys.*, lectio 5; *In II Metaph.*, lectio 11.

[19] See Motte's note in *RScPhTh* 27 (1938) 578-582: "Saint Thomas a voulu tout bonnement démontrer que Dieu existe et non pas qu'il y a cinq manières spécifiquement distinctes ni plus ni moins de faire la démonstration" (*l.c.*, 582). In his Introduction à la philosophie chrétienne, Paris 1960, 161 Gilson speaks of "les controverses stériles sur le nombre et l'ordre des voies vers Dieu, sur la question de savoir si chacune d'elles est une preuve distincte des autres".

[20] Cf. Cajetanus' famous words: "... semper formaliter loquitur". Although the Five Ways stand in a theological context, they are arguments developed by man's reason and must be seen as philosophical proofs.

[21] Cf. what was said of Alexander of Hales and St. Albert the Great. In his *Summa quaestionum ordinariarum*, tom. I, art. 22, q.4 Henry of Ghent distinguishes between demonstrative and probable arguments. The former are divided into proofs from efficient, formal and final causality and from the *via eminentiae*.

question. Bañez, however, presents this explanation: the visible world refers us to God, in the first place inasmuch as by divine causality potency is reduced to actuality and, in the second place, insofar as there is a First Efficient Cause. Then it becomes evident that this Cause must exist necessarily and by itself. After that we show that this Being is the Supreme Being from whom the order of things descends[22]. In his explanation Bañez insists upon the result attained in each way and discerns a certain progression. His observation is correct, but what specifies the individual character of the Five Ways must be the point of departure rather than the conclusion reached[23].

Another attempt at an explanation is that of Santo Schiffini who suggests that one may take the facts from which the arguments start individually or collectively. In the first case one may consider change in itself (the First Way), in its cause (the Second Way), with regard to its subject (the Third Way). Taken collectively the physical things show unequal perfections and point to the Highest Being (the Fourth Way) and they work together for the good of the universe (the Fifth Way)[24]. But this explanation resorts to accidental and even arbitrary factors such as the division into "things taken individually" and "things taken collectively".

R. Garrigou-Lagrange proposes to start from the Third Way in order to explain the other four and thinks that the Fifth Way was given the last place on account of the methodological difficulties it entails[25]. The author gives no explanation why there are five ways. Joseph Gredt draws attention to the fact that God is the efficient, exemplary and final cause of created things. Inasmuch as he is an efficient cause his activity may be considered in a threefold way: his effects are either in the process of becoming (in an active or in a passive way: the first two arguments) or have been made (the third proof). The Fourth and Fifth Ways lead to God as the exemplary and final cause of the universe[26]. It should, however, be noted that not God's causality but facts of the created order are the basis and specifying elements of the Five Ways. A different attempt to explain the order of St. Thomas' arguments is made by L. de Raeymaeker[27]: man undergoes changes, acts, understands that he is a contingent being and partakes in values; he discovers finality in his own life and in nature. De Raeymaeker's description, however, is an application

[22] In I^am Partem, q.2, a.3.

[23] The Five Ways may also be considered in the light of the conclusions they allow us to attain. In fact, they present divine being each time from a different point of view: deity is free from potency; it works in all processes taking place in the world; God is the foundation and source of the being of things; all perfections share in divine being which is perfect in the highest degree; the divine intellect is the cause of the order in the world.

[24] Theologia naturalis, Torino 1894, n.387.

[25] Dieu, son existence et sa nature², Paris 1928, 227-231.

[26] J. Gredt, Elementa ... (n.12), II, n. 792.

[27] Philosophie de l'être. Essai de synthèse métaphysique, Louvain 1947, 345f.

of the order of the Five Ways to man's situation rather than an explanation.

Jacques Maritain also examined the problem. He observes that what brings about the distinction between the Five Ways are the starting points: the Five Ways rest upon facts of experience which differ from one another[28]. Maritain provided the elements for a solution but did not go any further. A. Kenny proposes to connect the Ways with the four genera of causality. The first two proofs would depend on efficient causality, the third would be related to material causality[29]. Kenny may be right in general, but is not in the details of his explanation. If two ways are connected with one type of causality, the equilibrium is disturbed[30]. Moreover, in the Third Way something deeper than material causality is envisaged, viz. contingent existence of which coming-into-being and passing-away are a sign. We must finally mention a suggestion by N. Hinske who believes that the theory of participation is the basis of the Five Ways[31].

The Five Ways are different proofs because of their different starting-points which involve different causal processes. Inasmuch, however, as the genera of causality occur together, the proofs form an organic whole and are complementary. It is a mistake to base the differences of the Five Ways on the (wrong) assumption that their conclusions do not coincide, i.e. do not terminate in the same God[32]. This question will be discussed later on in this chapter.

Turning now to the study in detail of each of the Five Ways we notice that the formulation St. Thomas gives is brief and simple. He was convinced that their strength lies in the evidence of the facts from which they start and in the unassailable principles used. For a correct understanding of the proofs one must adhere to realism, submit oneself to the inescapable evidence of the principles of being involved, practice metaphysical meditation and have the readiness to admit God's existence when reason demonstrates it[33]. A further

[28] *Approches de Dieu*, Paris 1958, 31f.

[29] *The Five Ways. St. Thomas Aquinas' Proofs of God's Existence*, London 1969.

[30] See C. Vansteenkiste in *Rassegna di Letteratura tomistica* IV (1972) 198. Cf. also *o.c.* III (1971) 193 where the solution proposed by L. Iammarrone is examined ("Il valore metafisico delle cinque vie tomistiche", in *Miscellanea Francescana* 68 (1968) 3-80; 278-315. Iammarrone connects the Ways with modes of causality.

[31] "Teilhabe und Distanz als Grundvoraussetzung der Gottesbeweise des hl. Thomas von Aquin", in *Philos. Jahrb.* 75 (1968) 279-293.

[32] E. Gilson, *The Christian Philosophy of St. Thomas Aquinas* (transl. by L. K. Shook) New York 1956, 67, points out the organic coherence of the Five Ways, but E.L. Mascall thinks that their conclusions differ. See his *Existence and Analogy*, Toronto 1949, 77f.

[33] See J. Walgrave, "De benadering van de godsvraag door Thomas van Aquino", in *Algemeen tijdschrift voor wijsbegeerte* 66 (1974) 279-286. This seems to have escaped a number of critics. Thus F. Van Steenberghen is struck by the contrast between Aquinas' profound doctrine and the cursory character of the Five Ways (*Le problème de l'existence de Dieu dans les écrits de S. Thomas d'Aquin*, Louvain-la-Neuve 1980, 353, n.30), W. N. Clarke ("What is most and least Relevant in the Metaphysics of St. Thomas Today?", in *Intern. Philos. Quarterly* 14 (1974)

difficulty is caused by St. Thomas' way of writing by means of terse and very general statements, in particular in the Fourth and Fifth Ways. His metaphysical reflection is at such heights that its linguistic expression is somewhat left behind and fits his thought only loosely. Hence it is not always easy to grasp right from the beginning the high degree of coherence of the arguments and their development. It is for this reason that the text has generated so much discussion.

This also affects the so-called efficacy of the proofs. It has been said that this is not very great because many readers of the text do not appear to be convinced by them. Gabriel Marcel once wrote that we get this paradox that the proofs are only efficacious for those who do not need them[34]. The answer to this difficulty is easy: man can choose to reject any mediated evidence. Furthermore, while *basically* each of the Five Ways takes up facts of experience and common sense arguments, it makes also explicit use of metaphysical principles. Those who cherish an empiricist attitude will be tempted to refuse the absolute and universal validity of these principles (which they do in fact admit in daily life), because of the influence of their particular philosophical position or an insufficient power of abstraction[35].

The First Way

I. The Text

The first and more manifest way is the argument from motion. It is certain, and evident to our senses, that in the world some things are in motion. Now whatever

---

411-434, 434) writes: "The famouw Five Ways of St. Thomas for proving the existence of God seem to me in their present textual form the least adequate part of his metaphysics and certainly the least relevant for the contemporary philosopher". When D. Dubarle writes in "Pensée scientifique et preuves traditionnelles de l'existence de Dieu", in (coll.) *De la connaissance de Dieu*, Tournai 1958, 35-112, that "les cinq voies ne répondent plus du tout aux exigences de l'esprit scientifique actuel", he obscures the issue. Does he admit the basic postulates of Comte's positivism and believe that modern science is the criterion for metaphysical truth? On modern science and God's existence see L. Elders, "Die Naturwissenschaften und die Existenz Gottes", in *Salzburger Jahrbuch für Philosophie* 1985/1986. Another voice in this choir of critics is G.A. Blair, "Another Look at St. Thomas' First Way", in *Intern. Philos. Quart.* 16 (1976) 301-314: "I think that it is time that Thomists stop taking the Five Ways as something sacred, especially the First Way".

[34] *Du refus à l'invocation*, 229.

[35] *S.C.G.* I 4; III 108. St. Thomas himself stresses the weakness of the intellect in its search for truth and for God. He lists various obstacles: few understand the praeambula for a philosophical demonstration of God's existence (*S.C.G.* I 4). Many do not have sufficient time or don't make the necessary effort. Cf. also *Expos. in Boetii De Trin.* 3, 1; *De veritate* 14, 10. In this connection J. Maritain writes, perhaps not without a certain disdain for his fellow philosophers: "Because of the fact that they are perceptions of sound common sense, they presuppose an integrity, an equilibrium and spontaneity of our faculties of knowledge which one finds more often among the illiterate than among philosophers and, above all, these proofs presuppose that one does not have with regard to common sense the preconceived disdain which characterises the doctors of modern science" (*La philosophie bergsonienne*[3], Paris 1948, 170).

is moved is moved by another, for nothing can be moved except it is in potentiality to that towards which it is moved; whereas a thing moves inasmuch as it
is in act. For motion is nothing else than the reduction of something from potentiality to actuality. But nothing can be reduced from potentiality to actuality,
except by something in a state of actuality. Thus that which is actually hot, as fire,
makes wood, which is potentially hot, to be actually hot, and thereby moves and
changes it. Now it is not possible that the same thing should be at once in actuality
and potentiality in the same respect, but only in different respects. For what is
actually hot cannot simultaneously be potentially hot; but it is simultaneously
potentially cold. It is therefore impossible that in the same respect and in the same
way a thing should be both mover amd moved, i.e., that it should move itself.
Therefore, whatever is moved must be moved by another. If that by which it is
moved be itself moved, then this also must needs be moved by another, and that
by another again. But this cannot go on to infinity, because then there would be
no first mover, and, consequently, no other mover, seeing that subsequent movers
move only inasmuch as they are moved by the first mover; as the staff moves only
because it is moved by the hand. Therefore it is necessary to arrive at a first
mover, moved by no other; and this everyone understands to be God.

II. Analysis

(a) St. Thomas calls this argument the first and more manifest way: movement
is a most widely observed phenomenon and everyone admits that when something is moving there must be a cause of its movement. The argument is firmly
anchored in experience. The "it is evident to our senses" emphasizes that all
our knowledge, even that of God, is based upon what we learn by the senses
about reality. In this way the words apply to the starting points of each of the
Five Ways. "Instead of stigmatizing this ... as naive realism, one should consider it an expression of a healthy philosophical appraisal of the value and
nature of human knowledge" [36].

Motion is the basic fact analysed in our proof. It must be pointed out that
'motion' is used as it is observed by man and analysed in the philosophy of
nature. The concept of motion of modern physics does not necessarily coincide with this. Ever since the early beginnings of philosophical speculation the
Greeks had been fascinated by the changes constantly taking place in the
world and tried to discover an underlying unchanging substance [37]. In the First

---

[36] See N. Luyten, "Der erste Weg: ex parte motus", in L. Elders (edit.), *Quinque sunt viae*,
Città del Vaticano 1980, 29-41, 34. One may also consult E. Gilson, "Prolégomènes à la prima
via", in *AHDLMA* 30 (1964) 53-70; R. Nasi, "De Prima via", in *De Deo* (n.8), I, 3-37.—One
should notice that in the clause "whatever is moved, is moved by another", the "is moved" is
not used twice in the passive voice (as F. Van Steenberghen seems to think, *o.c.*, 115), but signifies
first "is moving" (intransitive) and then "is moved" (passive voice). See G. Verbeke, "La structure logique ..." (note 65), 153. One may also compare J. Owens, "Actuality in the 'Prima Via'
of St. Thomas", in *Mediaeval Studies* 39 (1967) 26-46.
[37] Luyten, *o.c.*, p. 31.—This is the gist of Aristotle's account in *Phys.* 203 b 15ff. (the need
for an infinite substance); *Metaph.* 986 b 18ff. (it is intimated that the supreme God must reign
in unmoved omnipotence).

Way Aristotle's analysis of motion which St. Thomas himself fully endorses is used[38]. As the examples used by St. Thomas show, facts of experience such as local movement and alteration constitute the point of departure of this first proof[39]. Such movements are among the most obvious facts observed by man in the universe. A continuous movement is "the actualization of what exists potentially insofar as it exists potentially"[40]. As long as a movement lasts, the actualization is incomplete and continues toward further fulfilment. St. Thomas makes this definition his own and declares that movement cannot be defined in any other way[41].

(b) In the light of this analysis of movement it is obvious that the potency which is actualized cannot actualize itself, but requires a cause distinct from itself or at least from that part or organ in which this potency is present. The reason is that potency to something is to be potentially, but not actually this thing. Hence a potency cannot give itself a fulfilment it does not have[42]. By its efficient influence the agent actualizes this potency, that is, it brings about out of and in this potency a formal perfection similar to what it is itself. In other words, the thing which changes does so moved by something else.

In certain cases, as for example in living beings, it is not immediately clear which part moves which, but this does not undermine at all the inescapable self-evidence of the principle[43]. If one of the parts of a being is moved by another, this being is not moving itself *per se* and primarily. The principle "whatever moves is moved by something else" applies to self-movement *per se*[44]. This also provides us with the answer to another objection against the universal validity of the principle: a body which continues to move according to the law of inertia is not something moving itself *per se*[45]. The impulse com-

---

[38] See *In III Phys.*, lectio 2.

[39] Cf. n.8. See also E. Gilson, *o.c.* (n.36), 61: "Le problème de l'origine première du mouvement, même si les données en sont physiques, est essentiellement métaphysique. L'origine principale de l'expérience n'est pas dans l'expérience".

[40] *Phys.* III 1, 201 a 10-11. One may of course also take a more complex instance of movement such as cosmic processes. F. Brentano does so in his *Vom Dasein Gottes* (hrsg. von A. Kastil, Hamburg (Meiner) 1929, 387ff.).

[41] *In III Phys.*, 1.2, nn.284, 285 and 289.

[42] This is the so-called principle of causality. See vol. I, chapter 18. There is a considerable literature on this principle as it is used in the First Way. See J.A. Weisheipl, The Principle "omne quod movetur, ab alio movetur", in *Isis* 56 (1965) 26-45. In his article cited in n.36 Gilson makes the astonishing statement that there is nothing in Thomism which could be called the principle of causality and he refuses to admit that the First Way is based on it. Apparently he does so in order to be able to connect this Way with a special metaphysics of being as he sees it.

[43] This objection was already formulated by some Scholastics. Scotus has it in *Metaph.* IX, 14, 18-22 (Vivès VII, 599b) and Suarez repeate it after him in his *Disp. metaph.* 29, sectio 1, 7ff.

[44] In *Phys.* VII 1 Aristotle mentions this difficulty to solve it. Cf. the important commentary by St. Thomas, *In VII Phys.*, 1.2, nn.885-890.

[45] The objection is quoted by Maritain, *Approches de Dieu*, 41. It is treated extensively by W.A. Wallace, "Newtonian Antinomies Against the Prima Via", in *The Thomist* 19 (1956) 151-192. Wallace points to the fact that one cannot use the laws of inertia and gravitation against the

municated to it does not become an active moving power or quality of the moving body itself, for this continues to undergo a movement imposed upon it. Moreover, inertia is an unclear concept as modern physics has shown. It does not make sense when conceived as a quality of a single body in isolation from other forces and bodies. A body in continuous movement changes with regard to the rest of the universe. To this effect an active cause other than itself is required[46]. To explain the phenomenon of a certain inertia one may perhaps assume that the impulse is grafted on one or more of the basic forces of matter as, for instance, the gravitational field. In classical mechanics, on the other hand, the impetus communicated to a body becomes the latter's property and this body is from then on moving itself.

A major difficulty raised against the principle of causality is the conviction of some people that at the level of nuclear processes events occur which do not have a cause (the principle of indeterminism) or which are to be explained by a dialectical leap forward of matter (Marxism). Those who hold these positions will tend to consider the doctrine of causality of classical metaphysics a naive interpretation of reality. This difficulty is solved when we take into account the nature of modern physics: it studies reality with the help of a quantitative approach which allows one to understand certain events and to formulate relationships but which does not consider being inasmuch as it is being. The conclusions of modern science may have validity for a limited understanding of material reality, but it is wrong to deduce from the same that the metaphysics of common sense and the philosophy of being no longer hold true. Such a claim is not so much the result of scientific knowledge as the product of an underlying ideology.

Although in everyday life people would not dream of denying the principle of causality (of which the "whatever is moved is moved by another" is one formulation), some refuse to admit it as a general law of being since they are averse to using general propositions. Ironically basic laws and principles are used in the sciences so that their exclusion from philosophy is an anomaly. Empiricists, furthermore have argued that laws have their exceptions: what

First Way, because the concepts used are not clear: the real cause of gravity is unknown. Likewise the so-called impulse which causes a body to keep moving (inertia) cannot become a natural movement of this body but must be connected with a more encompassing cosmic carrier. Some critics argue against the First Way that scientific analysis shows that there is no need for an external source of motion.—Here we must recall that modern science has a different approach to reality. It only seeks homogeneous explanations which do not give an ultimate intelligibility.
[46] Cf. D. Bonnette, *Aquinas' Proofs for God's Existence*, The Hague 1972, 100ff.; W. Wallace, o.c. (n.45); id., "The Cosmological Argument: a Reappraisal", in *Proceedings of the American Catholic Philosophical Association* 46 (1972) 43-57. Some commentators overlook this and argue that the law of inertia refutes the universal validity of the principle "whatever is moved, is moved by another". See, for instance, J. Seiler, *Das Dasein Gottes als Denkaufgabe. Darlegung und Bewertung der Gottesbeweise*, Luzern-Stuttgart 1965, 36ff.; V. Preller, *Divine Science and the Science of God: A Reformulation of St. Thomas Aquinas*, Princeton N.J. 1967, 114f.; A. Kenny, o.c. (n.29) 12.

for some is unthinkable, is possible for others[47]. Why would not self-movement be possible in some cases? The answer to this objection is not difficult. We must distinguish between what is thinkable and what is imaginable. An infinite straight line is perhaps imaginable, but it does not follow that it can exist. Self-contradictory notions never exist. Potency passing by itself to actuality and giving itself a determination it does not have, is clearly unthinkable.

(c) In the next step of his argument St. Thomas points out that in a series of causes we cannot proceed *ad infinitum*. Therefore there must be a *first* mover who is not moved by anything else, but is himself the source of all movement. The principle that in a series of causes *per se* infinite regress is not possible is also used in the Second and Third Ways. The principle is not based upon the impossibility of an infinite multitude in act, but on that of an infinite chain of causes *per se*. Aristotle excludes infinite regress in such a chain of causes[48]: neither of material, efficient, final nor formal causes is there a series which is infinite in the upward direction. The reason is that in a chain of causes there is a first which is the cause of the rest, but in an infinite series all the causes are intermediate causes and there is no first cause from which movement would originate. It must be noted that the principle applies to causes *per se*, that is to causes which in the exercise of their causality depend on a prior cause. When the latter ceases to work there is no activity and no movement[49]. Causes *per se* are simultaneous with their effects: when a doctor cures, health results[50]. In a chain of such causes the first brings it about that the subsequent causes are actually causing their effects, for it brings them from a state of potential causality to the actual exercise of it[51].

In the Five Ways other chains of causes besides that of causes *per se* are not considered. An example of such a different chain is the series of successive generations descending from the same ancestors. At a given moment in time a man who engenders progeny is in this act of reproduction only *per accidens*, that is in a secondary way, dependent on his ancestors[52]. St. Thomas never says that an infinite series of causes, *per accidens* depending on one another, is impossible. His critics, however, often overlook the difference between the

---

[47] An example given by Kenny is that of the fourth dimension. Apparently Kenny is not hampered by metaphysical insight into the nature of potency and actuality when he writes: "It has never been shown that there cannot be a body which can initiate its own movement without external causal concurrence" (*o.c.*, 19).

[48] *Metaph.* II (a) 2, 994 a 1- b 31.

[49] *In V Metaph.*, 1.3, n.787.

[50] *In II Phys.*, 1.6, n.195.

[51] See J.M. Shea, "St. Thomas Aquinas on the Principle Anankè Stênai", in *The New Scholasticism* 55 (1981) 139-158

[52] *S.Th.* I 46, 2 ad 7.

two types of series[53]. In a series of causes *per se* dependent on the earlier cause in the series, the causal influence would never be actualized if the series were infinite[54].

A final objection against the use of the principle which excludes infinite regress is that it is too much tied to the outdated cosmology of concentric spheres[55]. It is certainly true that the argument can easily be visualized in this cosmological context. However, as his treatise on motion shows[56], Aristotle has in mind a general law of being which applies to the different types of movement. His favourite example is the series: hand, stick, object moved[57]. We must see the problem against the background of the question of the origin of movement. Plato had assumed that a principle which is essentially self-movement must be the source of all movement[58]. Aristotle corrected this Platonic position in the light of his theory of potency and actuality and concluded that the source of all movement is not a self-moving principle but an unmoved mover[59]. Although Aristotle applied his principle to the movements of the homocentric cosmic spheres, St. Thomas' argument in the *Summa theologiae* is not bound to any specific cosmology.

(d) The argument concludes that there must be an absolute origin of all movements and processes, that is a First Mover who is not moved by another mover. Everyone understands this to be God.—The First Way leads indeed to the conclusion that when moving others this First Mover cannot pass from potency to actuality and that for this reason it must be pure actuality[60].

[53] Cf. B. Russell who writes in his *History of Western Philosophy*, (1969) 453, that the Five Ways "depend on the supposed impossibility of a series having no first term. Every mathematician knows that there is no such impossibility: the series of negative integers ending with minus one is an instance to the contrary". C.J.F. Williams, "Hic autem non est procedere in infinitum", in *Mind*, 69 (1960) 403 thinks that St. Thomas wrongly starts from the assumption that there must be a first term (denying that an infinite series is possible). However, Aquinas' argument runs as follows: there must be a cause to reduce potency to actuality. There would not be such a cause if there were an infinite series.

[54] In his *S.C.G.* I 13 St. Thomas gives another argument to show that infinite regress *in causis per se* is impossible. See D. Bonnette, *o.c.* (n.46), 86-90.

[55] Kenny, *o.c.*, 12ff. See also Whitehead, *Science and the Modern World*, New York 1954, 250.

[56] *Physics* VII and VIII.

[57] St. Thomas points out that the immobility of the First Mover is deduced not so much from the eternity of the revolution of the heavens as from the occurrence of motion as such. See *In VIII Phys.*, 1.13, n.1083.—It is true that *Metaph.* XII, cc. 6, 7 and 8 stand in a cosmological context, but in chapter 7 the influence of the Unmoved Mover is described as final causality only. The problem of the origin of movement at the level of efficient causality is not here considered.

[58] *Phaedrus* 245 c. The question examined is that of the source and principle of movement. The same line of argument which led Plato to admit the existence of ideas, also made him postulate a principle of movement which possesses movement in a perfect form, sc. that is which is essentially self-movement.

[59] It is possible that the first lines of *Metaph.* XII 7 present traces of a stage in Aristotle's development intermediary between Plato's theory and Aristotle's more definite views. See my *Aristotle's Theology*, Assen 1972, 160ff.

[60] Cajetanus, *In I^{am}* 2, 3, III stresses that this is the conclusion "non curando utrum illud sit

This conclusion provides a basis for further development of a philosophical doctrine of God[61]. The concept of pure actuality (*actus purus*) will prove to be fundamental in the question of God's simplicity and throughout the entire treatise.

At the end of our study of the Five Ways the question will be answered how the identification of the First Unmoved Mover with God can be made. Provisionally one may say that God is considered by most people to be the origin of all movements and processes and that, therefore, they recognize God in the First Unmoved Mover.

III. The Sources of the First Way[62]

As we shall see in the course of our discussion, the Five Ways of St. Thomas are also a summary and transposition into a unified structure and stringent form of more than sixteen hundred years of philosophical efforts to prove God's existence. St. Thomas himself was very much aware of the fact that he was using materials from philosophical tradition. For in *S.C.G.* I 13, beginning his account of four proofs (which agree with four of the Five Ways), he calls them "arguments by which both philosophers and Catholic teachers have proved that God exists". One may also compare the penetrating survey of the *Commentary on the Gospel of St. John*[63] where the ways are listed by which in the course of time man has understood that God exists.

On the sources of the First Way we may be brief. Its remote origin is Plato's reduction of all movements to a being or form which is essentially movement[64]. But St. Thomas' argument is directly dependent on Aristotle's

---

anima caeli aut mundi". Those who think in a Whiteheadian framework will deny the need to exclude all potentiality from the First Mover. But the metaphysics of being shows the impossibility of such a view: there would have to be another First Mover to explain movement in Whitehead's mover and to cause the actualization of potentiality.

[61] J. Owens, "The Conclusion of the *Prima Via*", *The Modern Schoolman* 30 (1952) 33-53; 109-121; 203-215, argues that St. Thomas concludes to a pure act in the sense of the subsistent act of existing. "This conclusion is radically different from the conclusion of the Aristotelian argument which was a plurality of finite entities" (*o.c.*, 212). Owens' view calls for some comments. It is only later on in his text that St. Thomas shows the existentialist implication of the conclusion now reached, viz. that in God being is the same as his essence (I 3,4). St. Thomas' argument is not radically different from that of Aristotle; he uses the same principles, applying these more rigorously

[62] On the source of the First Way and the following proofs see G. Grunwald, *Geschichte der Gottesbeweise im Mittelalter bis zum Anfang der Hochscholastik.* BFPhMA 6, 3, Münster 1907; E. Rolfes, *Gottesbeweise bei Thomas von Aquin und Aristoteles*, Limburg a.d. Lahn 1927; R. Arnou, *De quinque viis sancti Thomae ad demonstrandam Dei existentia ... adumbratis ...*, Rome 1932.—According to J. Owens "The Five Ways ... are arguments taken from other thinkers but understood by Aquinas in the framework of his own metaphysics of existence" ("Aquinas and the Five Ways", in *The Monist* 58 (1974) 16-35, 25).

[63] *In Evangelium Ioannis Lectura*, edit. Marietti, 1-2.

[64] *Phaedrus* 245 d-e.

demonstration of the existence of the First Unmoved Mover.[65] It is surprising
to see that after Aristotle the argument is seldom used. The idea of a First
Mover at the outside of the universe may have held little attraction. The argument was perhaps disregarded by Christians because it was thought to be connected with the theory of an eternal world. However, it made its influence felt
inasmuch as it 'contributed to the general admission of God's total
immutability. A somewhat related argument runs: there must be a perfect
being; corporeal things are changeable and imperfect; hence a perfect
unchangeable being as distinguished from the material universe exists[66].

The First Way is used by the Arab philosophers. Wensinck thinks it is present in the argument *e novitate mundi* of the *Risalat al-Quddsiya* of Ghazali[67].
According to Averroes the argument from motion is the only decisive proof.
Other demonstrations such as that from finality only lead to a certain
probability[68]. In his zeal to return to pure Aristotelianism Averroes admits a
plurality of unmoved movers, but he also holds that there must be a First, for
in all different orders there is a first[69]. Maimonides also employs this
argument[70]. However, St. Thomas' main sources were the texts in Aristotle's
Physics and *Metaphysics*.

IV. The First Way in Other Works of St. Thomas[71]

We do not encounter the argument from movement in Aquinas's earlier
writings, at least not in an explicit form, but it occupies much space in the
Summa contra gentiles, viz. about seven times more than the three remaining
proofs taken together. Closely following Aristotle's texts in the *Physics* VII
and VIII. St. Thomas offers several proofs for each of the principles used in
the First Way. In the *Compendium theologiae*, c. 3 the argument from move-

[65] In particular *Phys.* VIII. Cf. *Phys.* VII, 1 and *Metaph.* XII, cc.6, 7 and 8. See G. Verbeke,
"La structure logique de la preuve du Premier Moteur chez Aristote", in *RPhL* 46 (1948) 137-
160; E. Betti, "La struttura logica della dimostrazione dell'atto puro in Aristotele", in *Scritti
in onore di Carlo Giacon*, Padova 1972, 41-62. According to W. Schadewaldt Eudoxus of Cnidos
would have been the first to develop the theory of a First Unmoved Mover. See his "Eudoxos
von Knidos und die Lehre vom Unbewegten Beweger", in *id., Hellas und Hesperien*, Stuttgart
1960, 451ff.
[66] See St. Augustine, *Conf.* II, 4; Joannes Damascenus, *De fide orthodoxa* I 3.
[67] A.J. Wensinck, "Les preuves de l'existence de Dieu dans la théologie musulmane", in
Mededelingen der Koninkl. Akademie der Wetenschappen, Afd. Letterkunde, 81, serie A,
Amsterdam 1936.
[68] *In XII Metaph.*, c.5; *In VIII Phys.*, comm. 3, etc.
[69] See E. Gilson, *La philosophie au moyen-âge*, Paris 1952, 365.
[70] *Guide for the Perplexed*, II, c.1.
[71] For the occurrence of the Five Ways in St. Thomas' other works see F. Van Steenberghen,
Le problème de l'existence de Dieu dans les écrits de S. Thomas d'Aquin, Louvain-la-Neuve 1980.
Cf. V. Décarie, "Les rédactions successives de la Secunda Via de Contra Gentiles I 13", in *De
Deo ...*, 138-144.

ment is the only one brought forward. Finally, the proof is discussed in
Aquinas' commentaries on the respective passages of the *Physics* and
Metaphysics.

The Second Way

I. The Text

> The second way is from the nature of efficient cause. In the world of sensible
> things we find there is an order of efficient causes. There is no case known
> (neither is it, indeed, possible) in which a thing is found to be the efficient cause
> of itself; for so it would be prior to itself, which is impossible. Now in efficient
> causes it is not possible to go on to infinity, because in all efficient causes follow-
> ing in order, the first is the cause of the intermediate cause, and the intermediate
> is the cause of the ultimate cause, whether the intermediate cause be several, or
> one only. Now to take away the cause is to take away the effect. Therefore, if
> there be no first cause among efficient causes, there will be no ultimate, nor any
> intermediate, cause. But if in efficient causes it is possible to go on to infinity,
> there will be no first efficient cause, neither will there be an ultimate effect, nor
> any intermediate efficient causes; all of which is plainly false. Therefore it is
> necessary to admit a first efficient cause, to which everyone gives the name of
> God.

II. Analysis

(a) The fact of experience from which this way starts is the existence of an
order of efficient causes. What is meant is that we observe agents in action
one of which is dependent on a prior agent: a hand moving a stick which
moves a stone. In such a series of subordinate causes all others beside the first
are like instruments inasmuch as they only act when acted upon by the first
efficient agent [72]. A rather widespread interpretation holds that St. Thomas is
here considering the *production* of being. "For St. Thomas, an efficient cause
is an active force; that is, it is a being which produces being" [73]. The Second
Way would thus consider the being (*esse*) of the effect, while the First dealt

---

[72] *Comp. Theol.*, c.3. To this understanding of the *Via Secunda* it has been objected that it
reduces all created causes to the status of instrumental causes (R. Lauer, "The Notion of the Efficient Cause in the *Secunda Via*", in *The Thomist* 38 (1974) 755-767, 763). We answer with a
distinction: with regard to the eliciting of actual causality all causes which begin to exercise their
causality, whether principal or instrumental, must be moved by another cause, but the principal
cause receives a causality which is richer and has the perfection to be communicated as belonging
to itself. In the concise text of the Second Way the notion of efficient cause and the objectivity
of the concept of causality are not furter explained. St. Thomas' general doctrine is presupposed.
See vol. I, cc.18 and 19 (Introd., n. 29).

[73] *The Christian Philosophy of St. Thomas Aquinas*, New York 1956, 178f.; *Le thomisme* [6],
Paris 1972, 78.

with the coming-into-being of such an effect[74]. However, a careful reading of the text shows that Aquinas does not speak of things produced but of the actual exercise of causality.

That he has in mind causes *in actu* can also be seen in the fact that he excludes here an infinite series of causes. If he would have envisaged the *production* of beings, such an infinite series is possible[75]. Cajetanus understood the text correctly[76]. The reason why this misunderstanding arose could be the desire to obtain an easy distinction between the First and Second Ways. However, the account which connects the Five Ways with the different genera of causality sufficiently establishes the proper character of each argument.

In other words, the starting-point of this proof is any activity in the universe which, being provoked by another agent, is part of a chain of efficient causes[77]. Causes *per se* are meant, that is agents which owe their very activity to another efficient cause: writing letters on a piece of paper depends on moving one's hand; this, again, depends on a command being carried to the muscles, etc. In the universe there are a great number of causal processes where an agent is dependent on another in the very exercise of its activity. Indeed, the universe shows a high degree of organization and unity[78]. A series, however, may be so short that it only comprizes two causes.

(b) St. Thomas next recalls the principle "nothing is the efficient cause of itself". By "of itself" is not only meant the existence of the cause but also its being a cause *in actu*. In order to make itself an agent the cause would already have to be active[79]. It is true that one part of a being can sometimes

---

[74] This is E.L. Mascall's position in *He Who Is*, London-New York-Toronto 1958, 49. It is also that of L. Charlier, "Les cinq voies de saint Thomas. Leur structure métaphysique", in *aa. vv.*, *L'existence de Dieu*, Tournai 1961, 181-227, 197. Charlier gives as an example the production of a new living being. We can use it inasmuch as we consider the actual causality of generation as dependent on the universal causality of the celestial bodies and this on God. But even so it is not a very good example of what is meant because Aquinas would never say that the celestial bodies make man exercise his generative capacity.

[75] The examples given by J. Maritain in his *Approches de Dieu*, 43, are unfortunate inasmuch as they concern causes *per accidens*. Obviously this mistake was triggered by the fact that he is thinking of the causes of being rather than of the causality of the cause itself. Gilson, on the other hand, understood the argument correctly (*o.c.*, 78).

[76] *In I^{am}* 2, 3, V: "... causa in actu, de qua est sermo...."

[77] A. Kenny is once more wrong in his flippant assertion that "the series of causes from which the Second Way starts is vouchsafed only by medieval astrology" (*o.c.*, 44). As we have seen any activity can be the starting point.

[78] This is not only so in medieval cosmology but also in modern physics and biology.

[79] The words "efficient cause of itself" mean what they say. One may compare the parallel text in *Comp. theol.*, c.3: not even illiterate people accept that instruments or tools begin to work all by themselves.—Some students of St. Thomas understood the argument to be concerned with the causes of being as such. See E. Gilson, *Le thomisme*⁶, 1972, 78: "Alors que la première (preuve) nous faisait atteindre Dieu comme origine du mouvement cosmique, la seconde nous le fait atteindre comme cause de l'existence même des choses". Cf. E.L. Mascall, *He Who Is. A Study in Traditional Theism*, Hamden, Conn. 1966, 46.

communicate an activity to another part but in such a case we say that this being is *per accidens* the cause of its activity. The question must still be answered how this active part begins to act. If it is always actively causing we have found a first activity which is the ground of all other causal action. If not, we must look for another agent which causes it to become and be active.

Against the principle that nothing is the cause of itself it is objected that two chemical elements or complexes may react when brought into contact just because of their chemical affinity. To this we answer that this explanation is perhaps satisfactory at the level of chemistry but that it is not adequate in philosophy. In reality there is a disposing cause which actuates the chemical properties so that a chemical process can result[80].

(c) The next step in the argument is the statement that in a series of causes one cannot go on *ad infinitum* in resorting each time to an earlier cause which makes the following one act. For in a series of causes *per se*, that is causes which in the very exercise of their causality depend on a prior cause[81], there must be a first. If the series were infinite, no causal influence would ever make its way to the activity we are now observing. For it is proper to the infinite that it cannot be traversed[82].

Characteristic of the intermediate causes of which Aquinas is speaking here is that they are principal, secondary or instrumental causes which are made to exercise their causality by a preceding cause and which in their turn bring the next (or last) cause in the series to exercise its causality[83]. This section of the argument runs parallel to the corresponding passus of the First Way.

(d) Taken together the intermediate causes are not sufficient because they cannot operate without a First Cause. Therefore the argument leads us to the conclusion that there is a First Cause which never begins to work but is always active or which is its own activity. This remarkable insight, when it is further analysed, implies that this always Acting Cause or Super-Activity is the cause

---

[80] *In V Metaph.*, 1.2, n.767.—On Spinoza's concept of *causa sui*, see vol. I, c.18.

[81] This has sometimes been overlooked. D. Bonnette, *o.c.*, 106, speaks not without some ambiguity of "a series of effects which constitute the *per accidens*" in the Second Way. He adds to the confusion by writing that the causality of every intermediate cause is in that intermediate cause *per accidens* (sic) since it is extrinsic to its nature and must be found in it by reason of an exterior cause" (*o.c.*, 122). It is not extrinsic to the nature of intermediate cause to be a cause but it may be extrinsic to it to be an intermediate.

[82] Bañez gives a second argument to show that in a series of causes the infinite cannot be traversed: "if there were an infinite number of subordinate causes, no end would be reached and the causal activity would not be determinate as it should be" (*Scholast. Comment. in Primam Partem Summae theologicae s. Thomae Aquinatis*, Valencia 1934, 116).

[83] On the notion of intermediate cause see *In II Metaph.*, 1.3, n.302. With regard to the function of the intermediate cause it makes no difference whether there is one intermediate cause or more.

of all process and of all things[84]. But at this stage we need not elaborate this point. St. Thomas tersely writes that there is a First Efficient Cause we all call God[85].

III. The Sources of the Second Way

If we take the Second Way in a broader sense (there is a supreme efficient cause of all cosmic processes and of all beings), we may say that it was prepared by Plato's doctrine of the Demiurge who framed the world. In *S.C.G.* I 13 Aquinas seems to ascribe the argument to Aristotle. However, upon closer inspection the text does not say more than that Aristotle shows that in a series of efficient causes infinite regress is not possible and that, therefore, there must be a first[86]. When in later ages the conviction that the world depends on God had become more widespread, the Second Way came to be used by several authors, at least in a less formal manner. Cicero mentions it[87] and Philo speaks of the all embracing causality of the First Cause[88]. Seneca also knows this type of argument[89] and we find traces of it in St. Augustine's works[90]. Avicenna proposes a demonstration of the existence of a first cause which comes close to the Second Way of Aquinas[91], although elements of the Third Way are mixed with it. Peter Lombard recalls that God can be known from the things he made[92]. St. Albert the Great mentions the

---

[84] At this stage the ways in wich respectively the First Cause and secondary causes exercise their causality need not be taken into consideration. Cf. *S.Th.* I 104, 1. J. Walgrave goes too far when he takes the conclusion of the Second Way to be that there is a First Cause which produces everything *sub ratione entis* and is the cause of being for all things ("De benadering van de godsvraag door Thomas van Aquino", in *Algemeen Tijdschrift voor Wijsbegeerte* 66 (1974) 279-286, 281).

[85] For the precise meaning of the identification of the First Efficient Cause with God see the concluding part of the chapter. Notice that the "aliquam" intimates that the nature of the First Cause is as yet unknown to us.

[86] Aristotle's text is found in *Metaph.* II (a) 2, 994 a 1ff., where he sets forth the principle that in a series of causes, whether material, formal efficient or final, there must be a first, but it is not used as a demonstration of God's existence. Aristotle could hardly have done so because God is neither a first material nor a first formal cause. In his commentary on the text Aquinas refrains from reading a demonstration of God's existence into these lines. Van Steenberghen's statement that the Second Way is entirely taken from Aristotle (*o.c.*, 187) must be qualified.

[87] *De natura deorum* II 6. The argument is attributed to Chrysippus.

[88] *De opif. mundi* II 7-9. Philo sees a confirmation in *Isaiah* 26, 12.

[89] *Epist. ad Luc.* 7, 64, 12: "Sed nos nunc primam et generalem quaerimus causam. Haec simplex esse debet nam et materia simplex est. Quaerimus quid sit causa? Ratio scilicet faciens, id est deus".

[90] *De civ. Dei* XI 25 and *Ennar. in Ps.* 74, 25, but it is almost always connected with arguments related to the Third and Fourth Ways,

[91] See *Metaphysica* II, VIII, c.3: (Van Riet), *Philosophia prima*, II, 395.

[92] *I Sent.*, dist. 3.

argument[93]. But unlike St. Thomas these authors do not distinguish between a cause of the activity of things and a cause of their being.

IV. The Second Way in Other Works of St. Thomas

S.C.G. I, 13 has a short but excellent formulation of the argument. The only difference: from the text of the *Summa theologiae* is that the latter puts more stress on the starting point, viz. the order of efficient causes we observe. This is, however, implicit in the *S.C.G.*[94]. The Second Way is perhaps also intimated in the first group of approaches to God given in the *Commentary on the Gospel of St. John*, although the text itself mentions in an explicit manner only the proof from finality[95].

The Third Way

I. The Text

> The third way is taken from possibility and necessity, and runs thus. We find in nature things that are possible to be and not to be, since they are found to be generated, and to be corrupted, and consequently, it is possible for them to be and not to be. But it is impossible for these always to exist, for that which can not-be at some time is not. Therefore, if everything can not-be, then at one time there was nothing in existence. Now if this were true, even now there would be nothing in existence, because that which does not exist begins to exist only through something already existing. Therefore, if at one time nothing was in existence, it would have been impossible for anything to have begun to exist; and thus even now nothing would be in existence—which is absurd. Therefore, not all beings are merely possible, but there must exist something the existence of which is necessary. But every necessary thing either has its necessity caused by another, or not. Now it is impossible to go on to infinity in necessary things which have their necessity caused by another, as has been already proved in regard to efficient causes. Therefore we cannot but admit the existence of some being having of itself its own necessity, and not receiving it from another, but rather causing in others their necessity. This all men speak of as God.

The text contains a major difficulty. In line four the *Leonina* has "Impossibile est autem omnia quae sunt talia, semper esse" which is the text of the English translation printed here. However, several editions of the text omit the *semper*, printing a comma before *talia* ("It is impossible that all things which exist are of such a nature"). This correction was vigorously defended by P. Gény[96]. From the point of view of textual criticism, the principle of the *lectio*

---

[93] *Summa theol.*, I, tr.3, q.18, m.1.

[94] "Sed si procedatur in causis efficientibus in infinitum, nulla causarum erit prima".

[95] Prologus, n.3. In his *In I Sent.*, d.35, q.1, a.1 Aquinas calls the proof based on finality in the world the *via causalitatis*.

[96] "A propos des preuves thomistes de l'existence de Dieu", in *Revue de philosophie* 31 (1924) 575-601, 581. Gény is followed by a number of others, as, for instance, F. Van Steenberghen,

difficilior, however, it is easier to explain the disappearance of *semper* in a number of codices than its later introduction into other ones[97]. Moreover, "omnia quae sunt, talia esse" does not run very smoothly. It is our conviction that the *semper* must be retained, even if the argument does not become impossible by its excision. That a contemporary of Aquinas, who allegedly reproduced the Third Way almost textually, ignored the *semper*, does not prove that it was not in St. Thomas' text[98]; countless formulae of the argument were current in the 13th century. We are here concerned with the form St. Thomas himself gave it. Our analysis will show, as we hope, that maintaining the *semper* is by far the best solution.

At the end of the Third Way the *Leonina* has "quod omnes dicunt Deum" ("this all men speak of as God") although this clause is absent from the vast majority of codices. It is not unlikely that the words were later introduced because of the parallelism with the conclusions of the other Ways. St. Thomas may have omitted them because it is already sufficiently clear that the Being which has of itself necessity and which causes the being of others is God.

II. Analysis

(a) The fact which is the point of departure of the Third Way is the existence of the possible, that is of things able both to exist and not to exist. We recognize this possibility when in our physical world things come into being or cease to exist[99]. Compared to the starting points of the first two Ways we now have not only an observed fact but also the implication that what we see involves the possibility of being and of not being. St. Thomas deals with the possibility of being and of not being of *material* things, not with the general contingency of all created beings. He makes this clear when he writes that the possibility of being and of not being belongs to things on account of matter[100].

Le problème de l'existence ... 189; Th.C. O'Brien, *Metaphysics and the Existence of God*, Washington 1960, 226-227, n.83.

[97] M.-V. Leroy, "La troisième voie de saint Thomas et ses sources", in *Recherches d'islamologie. Recueil d'articles offerts à Georges C. Anawati et Louis Gardet par leurs collègues et amis*, Louvain-la-Neuve 1977, 171-200, 174n. See also M. Durant, "St. Thomas' Third Way", in *Religious Studies* 4 (1968-1969) 229-243 and the excellent study by A. Pattin "La structure de la tertia via" in *De Deo*, I, 253-258, 254.

[98] Van Steenberghen, *o.c.*, 189 n.

[99] In *In I De caelo et mundo*, 1.24, n.240 Aquinas explains what generation (coming-into-being) implies: an element or aspect common to all beginning (viz. to begin to be) and a particular way of doing so, viz. to be through a transformation of a previous thing.

[100] Cf. *De pot.*, q.5, a.3: "potentia enim ad esse et non esse non convenit uni nisi ratione materiae". As Pattin points out (*o.c.*, 255) St. Thomas does not take metaphysical contingence as his starting point (as he did in *S.C.G.* II 15). Moreover, contrary to Avicenna, St. Thomas does not hold that all essences outside God are indifferent with regard to being; there never is a positive orientation to not-being in created things. Material things have mutability, which is given with the non-necessary connection between their essence and existence. See also *In I De*

(b) Reflection shows that it is not possible for these things always to exist, for that which can not-be, at some time (*aliquando*) is not. This statement is the very core of the argument as presented in the *Leonina* text. Some commentators object: why must possible things necessarily perish? [101]. In their view the *semper* is to be deleted and the argument jumps right away to a metaphysical consideration: viz. contingent being does not explain itself, a consideration we find also in *S.C.G.* I 13 and II 15 [102].

However, the "it is impossible that these things always exist" is a principle given by Aristotle in the *De caelo* I cc. 10-12 and accepted by St. Thomas who even explains it in the subsequent line: "for that which can not-be, at some time is not". As A. Pattin notes, this statement is the central point of the argument: a corruptible thing which would never cease to exist, would have the possibility of not being corrupted, while at the same time it is corruptible. But this is impossible [103]. One may also express this by saying that these possibles have a limited life-span [104]. It appears therefore that Aquinas means the reasoning of the Third Way to consider duration in time rather than the general metaphysical contingence of created things.

It is objected by some "that there is no good reason why there cannot be something which has the power not to exist, but as a matter of fact always does exist" [105]. But such a criticism is short-sighted: there is finality in nature and the natural structure of things makes sense. Nature may sometimes be obstructed in what it seeks to carry out, but it does not contradict itself in the very structure of the various beings [106]. If the contrary were to happen, science would no longer be possible because then such laws as that of gravity or of the maximum velocity of light would for no reason whatsoever no longer apply in a number of cases.

---

caelo et mundo, 1.25, n.248: the term 'possible' can be used: (a) absolutely (what is intrinsically possible because of the terms which are related the one with the other); (b) as what is possible for something (*alicui*), viz. what can be with regard to active or passive potency. In this sense the possible belongs mostly to the things in the physical world.

[101] This is the view of P. Gény, *o.c.* (n.96).

[102] *O.c.* (n.97), 254.

[103] See *In I De caelo*, 1.29, n.283 and 1.26, n.257.

[104] In this interpretation *quandoque* (at some time) signifies not only the corruption of things at a given moment in the future but the possibility to not be (*possibile non esse*) which implies that the existence of a thing is limited in duration and therefore followed and preceded by not-being. On this point we agree with Van Steenberghen (*o.c.*, 192) against U. Degl'Innocenti, "La validità della 'terza via' ", in *Doctor communis* 7 (1954) 41-70, 48ff.

[105] A. Kenny, *The Five Ways* ..., 56, J.F.X. Knasas, "*Making Sense of the tertia via*", in *The New Scholasticism* 54 (1980) 476-511, 483 also thinks that those possibles are programmed for corruption, but that they need not corrupt in fact. He refers to *De pot.* 5, 7 ad 16, assuming that it says that the elements will last for ever. However, St. Thomas only says that in the universe (but not in their present individual occurrence) they will last as long as cosmic process lasts.

[106] It is a constantly recurring theme in Aristotle. Cf. *De caelo* 271 a 32: "the god and nature do nothing in vain". See also *De part. anim.* 658 a 9. The axiom is a conclusion from the principle that every worker works in view of an end (See vol. I, chapter 19, under 'final cause').

(c) The next step in the argument is: If everything can not-be, then at one time (*aliquando*) there was nothing in existence[107]. The text itself indicates that a nothingness in the remote past is meant. With regard to the future one might indeed argue that existing possible things in our universe, when passing away, are replaced by other things so that for an indefinite time there will be being. But this does not hold true when we go backward to the past. A series of finite spans of existence cannot add up to an infinite length of time[108]. Since we must assume that there always was being (else there would be nothing now), it is evident that the whole of reality cannot from all eternity have consisted of these perishable things[109].

Against the criticism of some we note that in the argument there is no confusion between logical and physical possibility. Only the latter is envisaged. Nor is there confusion between all things considered individually and such things considered collectively, for the question at issue is how to explain that there always, that is from all eternity, was being. Even less is there a quantifier shift from "each thing is not at a certain time" to "at some time everything is not", for there is a medium term in the argument, viz. that the multiplication of limited spans of duration cannot fill infinite time.

(d) But if at one time there was nothing, even now there would be nothing in existence, because that which does not exist, begins to exist only through something already existing[110]. Therefore there must be necessary being in

---

[107] Van Steenberghen gives a fair survey of the various interpretations of the "aliquando nihil fuit in rebus". He thinks that the text becomes altogether "puzzling" (194). Some believe there is question here of the nothingness which would follow the total disappearance of possible things. Others hold that a previous nothingness is meant. Van Steenberghen lists among the defenders of the first view P. Gény, E. Gilson (*Le thomisme*, (1948) 104), U. Degl'Innocenti (1951), L. Caprile, W.Dunphy. We may add F. C. Copleston (*Aquinas*, London 1961, 121). The second interpretation is defended by R. Garrigou-Lagrange, *o.c.*, 270; L. Charlier; M. González; L. Iammarrone, etc.

[108] On this point our interpretation fully agrees with that of M.-V. Leroy, *o.c.*, 195: "Ajouter du temporel au temporel ne peut faire de l'éternel".

[109] Some think the Third Way proceeds from the assumption of the eternity of the world. See Ch.J. Kelly, "The Third Way and the Possible Eternity of the World", in *The New Scholasticism* 56 (1982) 273-291, 282. However, this is wrong. The assumption is that there always is being, otherwise nothing would exist today. The question of an eternal world or an eternal time is not considered, not even as a hypothesis. This has been overlooked by some interpreters. Even Gilson writes that St. Thomas argues within the hypothesis that time is of infinite duration (*Le thomisme*[6], Paris 1972, 81). Maritain says the same in his *Approches de Dieu*, Paris 1953, 54 ("Let us imagine a time without beginning or end").

[110] See Volume I, chapter 18 (The Principle of Causality).—From this part of the argument it becomes evident that the question in the background is: "From where do things ultimately originate?". It is remarkable that some modern philosophers refuse to tackle this question and argue that we must admit precisely such a groundless contingence without any reason or cause. See J.-P. Sartre, *L'être et le néant*, 713. Several Marxist philosophers hold that the world exists and that this is enough. According to Merleau-Ponty explaining contingent existence by reducing it to a necessary Being is doing away with contingence (*Eloge de la philosophie*, 61). St. Thomas' argument, however, answers these objections.

addition to the things which are possible. St. Thomas' argument is generally admitted by spontaneous reflection inasmuch as it is commonly thought that there is an eternal substance which would itself lie outside the chain of corruptible things. Lacking the possibility not to be, it is given the properties of necessary being.

Aquinas does not further determine here the nature of this necessary being unless in the sense that it must be necessary of itself. It follows from our presentation of the argument that St. Thomas' recourse to necessary being in the Third Way is not dictated by the ancient division of the world into the spheres of incorruptible planets and stars and the sublunar zone of perishable things. The argument abstracts from any concrete class of necessary being.

(e) The question where being comes from is paramount all through the Third Way and so St. Thomas introduces the further distinction between a necessary thing which has its existence caused by another and that which has its necessity of itself and therefore has no further cause.

In things which have their necessity from another cause, we cannot go on to infinity, that is we cannot explain their coming-into-being by means of an infinite series of causes, for the causality of the first would never arrive at the last[111]. As in the First and Second Ways causality *per se* is meant, not the accidental way in which a son's existence today depends on that of his father or grandfather. A necessary being which has its existence from another is intrinsically and permanently depending on this other cause: the (necessary) existence it received never becomes so much its own that it henceforth possesses it of itself. St. Thomas deliberately does not say which beings he has in mind with the necessary beings which do not have their necessity of themselves. They are a stage in the argument which is a dialectical possibility. Ontologically they can be dispensed with[112].

As we have seen in our analysis of the First and Second Ways, in a series of causes *per se* we cannot proceed to infinity. Hence we must conclude that the ground and cause of perishable things ultimately is a being which has of itself its own necessity. This all men speak of as God.

(f) From our discussion it appears that the Third Way is not exactly the same type of metaphysical proof as those of *S.C.G.* I 15 and II 15. In these texts St. Thomas argues that whatever has the possibility of being or of not being, must have a determining cause which makes it be. For of itself it is indifferent with regard to its being or not being. That argument raises the

---

[111] See above the commentary on the First Way, II c.

[112] D.J. Hawkins suggests that St. Thomas is arguing hypothetically on behalf of those who admit with Avicenna pure intelligences between God and the material world (*The Essentials of Theism*, London and New York 1949, 54ff.). This explanation seems better than that of Gilson according to whom an aspect of reality is meant: being is necessary to the extent that it is (*The Elements of Christian Philosophy*, New York 1960, 80).

question of by what cause perishable things exist since they do not explain themselves. Such a type of proof seems clearer and is shorter than that of the *Summa theologiae*. Hence several commentators interpret the *Tertia Via* with the help of the demonstration of the *Summa contra gentiles*.

Why did St. Thomas change his argument when he wrote the *Summa theologiae*? Van Steenberghen lists a number of reasons advanced to explain this innovation[113]; to distinguish the argument better from the Second Way; to remain at the level of physics; to be closer to Maimonides' text. His own preference goes to Pattin's explanation who suggests that St. Thomas now sides with Averroes: certain things have no possibility whatsoever not to be but are necessary and there is no positive indifference with regard to existence.

The real answer to the question of the why of this change seems to be that St. Thomas wanted to present a more concrete argument and to avoid a metaphysical analysis at the very beginning of his proof. So he shuns the formulation of the proof inspired by Avicenna[114]. Moreover, against the formulation of the argument in the *Summa contra gentiles* one could object that an endless series *a parte ante*[115] of generations of perishable things seems possible[116], in which the prior explains the existence of the subsequent being. To counter this objection one would have to argue that if the causes are only possible beings, they do not ultimately explain why there is being at all, because they themselves do not really account for their own existence. This argument is subtle and in order to be valid it must be connected with the question of the real distinction in created things between essence and existence. For this reason as well as in order to ground his proof more extensively in experience St. Thomas bypassed the difficulty by introducing the perspective of limited durations which together never make up eternal duration. He also made use of the principle that there always must be being[117].

With these comments we hope to have answered the criticism of those who feel that the Third Way is not conclusive or who explain its assumed lack of clarity by the not so fortunate attempt (as they say) of St. Thomas to present his proof in isolation from a theological perspective[118]. But these adventurous

---

[113] *O.c.*, 203ff.

[114] We do not mean by this that in the *S.C.G.* he upheld Avicenna's essentialism.

[115] We mean the series which we conceive as extending backwards from now to infinity.

[116] Cf. *S.Th.* I 46,2 and 5 and 6.—If it is objected against the reasoning of the Third Way as we presented it that an endless succession of limited durations can fill infinite 'time', the answer is that it may give an endless succession of limited durations but no real limitless eternity.

[117] Cf. *Metaph.* XII, 6, 1071 b 35: ἀλλὰ δεῖ τι ἀεὶ ὑπάρχειν. St. Thomas comments: "Sed semper oportet aliquid existere quod est causa motus" (*In XII Metaph.*, 1.6, n.2505).—Heidegger's assertion that the first question to face in metaphysics is why there is something and not nothing, does not make sense. Total nothingness is not thinkable.

[118] This latter view is that of Gilson and some members of the Toronto Institute. See Knasas, *o.c.*, 500f. It may even lead those who follow this line of thought to remarks such as "Since Aquinas is writing for believers, he need no linger over arguments for God's existence".

interpretations are the result of a failure to understand correctly the starting point and the development of the Third Way, and a preconceived metaphysical view warps this entire approach.

III. The Sources of the Third Way

A remarkable number of sources have been proposed from which St. Thomas might have borrowed his argument. One could perhaps say that in a general way Plato's philosophy provides the background for the Third Way. Plato sharply distinguished between the necessary being of the World of ideas on the one hand and the transitory existence of sensible things which have their cause (at least partly) in the first type of being[119]. In keeping with Platonic thought Plotinus ascribes being of itself to soul and makes it the principle of other things[120]. St. Augustine takes up this Platonic argument: whatever changes, does not exist of itself but is made by another[121]. Likewise St. John Damascene argues that the various elements continuously submitted to process would not remain in existence if not sustained by an infinite supporting power[122].

Leaving the Platonic tradition we must now consider Aristotle's influence on the Third Way. Some have pointed to *Metaph.* XII 6, 1071 b 22-27 as the source of the argument: What is possible, does not have existence of itself but depends on something in act; of itself a possible being remains in potency; from the point of view of possibility alone at some time nothing is[123]. More recently scholars have drawn attention to the *De caelo* I 12[124], where the statement is found: "What can not be, at a certain time is not". With this insight Aristotle provided an essential element for the argument as we find it in the *Summa theologiae.*

Of the Arab philosophers Alfarabi developed an argument quite close to

[119] There is, however, a strand of dualism in Plato's theory: the shadowy realities of the physical world also depend on a second principle "the Great and (the) Small" or the Receptacle (also called the Indeterminate Dyad).

[120] *Enn.* I 1, 9.

[121] Cf. *Conf.* XI 4, 6; *Ennar. in* 154, 13).

[122] *De fide orthodoxa* I 3. This argument has a Stoic flavour. See below the chapter on the conservation of the world.

[123] Thus L. Chambat, "La 'Tertia via' dans saint Thomas et Aristote", in *Revue thomiste* 10 (1927) 334-338 and above all H. Holstein, "L'origine aristotélicienne de la 'tertia via' de saint Thomas", in *RPhL* 48 (1950) 354-370, who reads the "quandoque non est" as having an ontological rather than a temporal sense.

[124] Dermot O'Donoghue, "An Analysis of the Tertia Via of St. Thomas", in *The Irish Theological Quarterly* 20 (1952) 129-151; T.K. Connoly, "The Basis of the Third Proof for the Existence of God", in *The Thomist* The Thomist 17 (1954) 281-249 17 (1954) 281-349.—With regard to a preparation for the argument in Aristotle's works one must also consider *Peri hermeneias* 22 a 17ff., especially in the translation of Boethius who uses *aliquando.*

that of Aquinas[125]. Avicenna followed him and made the contingence of beings the starting point of his proof. On account of some resemblances in vocabulary and contents it has been suggested that St. Thomas took over his Third Way from Avicenna[126]. But as M.-V. Leroy shows there are important differences[127]. According to Avicenna any created being is possible, because its essence does not include existence. For Aquinas, however, only the corruptible things are possibles[128]. On this point St. Thomas rather follows Averroes' criticism of Avicenna's position. As a matter of fact, the text of the argument in *S.C.G.* I 15 and II 15 is quite close to the formulation Averroes gave of the proof, but which at the time he wrote the *Summa contra gentiles*, St. Thomas did not yet know[129].

The Third Way also shows a certain correspondence with a text of Maimonides in the *Dux perplexorum*[130]. The Jewish philosopher notes that in beings composed of matter and form their being (*esse*) depends on the union of these two principles. Only things which are composite in this way have the possibility of not existing. Other created things such as spiritual substances have a non-necessary existence, but there is no possibility in them of perishing. Maimonides also brings in the alternative that reality would only consist of things which have a beginning and an end. In this case "all things would come to an end and nothing would ever be in existence". P. Gény and E. Gilson were so impressed by the resemblances of the Third Way with Maimonides' text that they concluded that St. Thomas followed the Jewish

---

[125] See J. Wensinck, *o.c.* (n.67), 16-17.

[126] The texts are found in his *Metaphysics* II, 1, cc.2 and 3 and in other works. Cf. A. M. Goichon, *La philosophie d'Avicenne et son influence en Europe médiévale*, Paris 1944, 126.

[127] *O.c.* (n.97), 179ff.

[128] *De pot.* 5, 3; *S.C.G.* II 30.

[129] Another important difference has been brought out by M. E. Marmura, "Avicenna's Proof from Contingency for God's Existence in the *Metaphysics of the Shifa*", in *Mediaeval Studies* 42 (1980) 337-352: Avicenna's proofs do not argue from our observation of the existence of the world but from an analysis of the concept of existence. For Avicenna it is not doubtful that there is existence. In *Metaph.* I, c.3 he even writes that one may prove the existence of the First Principle not by way of inference from the sensible things, but through universal rational premises. Concepts such as 'existent' and 'necessary' are received directly by the soul from the active intellect without the help of sensation. According to A. existence is not included in the quiddity of the contingent. The contingent is the thing the existence of which, considered in itself, is not necessary. But it is rendered necessary by its cause. Necessarily connected effects and causes coexist. On the other hand, St. Thomas starts from an experience of material things; his concept of the contingent is different; he has a different view of divine causality. See furthermore, Leroy, *o.c.*, 182; M. Bouyges, "Exégèse de la Tertia Via de saint Thomas d'Aquin", in *Revue de philosophie* 32 (1932) 126-128. A reformulation of Avicenna's proof is found in Averroes' *Destructio destructionum* (transl. S. Van Den Bergh, *Averroes' Tahafut al-Tahafut*, London 1969, I, 169).

[130] In addition to the already quoted paper of M.-V. Leroy, 183ff. one should also consult M. González, *El problema de las fuentes de la "Tercera Via" de santo Tomás de Aquino*, Madrid 1961, 69ff. and G. Jalbert, *Nécessité et contigence chez saint Thomas d'Aquin et chez ses prédécesseurs*, Ottawa 1961, 43-53.

philosophei quite closely. Howevei, on close inspection impoitant differences come to light and an essential part of Maimonides' argument is not taken up by St. Thomas[131].

We must therefore conclude that while composing the text of the Third Way Aquinas availed himself of the insights and formulae of his predecessors, but that he used them in a novel and original way to construct an argument which is his own.

Besides the non-Christian authors we have referred to some medieval theologians also developed a proof of the existence of God from the mutability of things. In this connection we must mention Hugh and Richard of St. Victor[132].

IV. The Third Way in St. Thomas' Other Works

In *In I Sent.*, d. 3, *divisio textus* St. Thomas, while rendering more explicit an argument advanced by Peter Lombard writes: "Whatever has its being (*esse*) out of nothing must be from someone, from whom its being flows forth. As appears from their imperfection and potentiality all creatures have their being out of nothing. Hence they must be from some one thing and this is God". This proof appears to be based on the fact that (created) things do not have their being from themselves, so they must have it from another. Several obscure points are nor further explained as, for instance, the question as to how we know that things do not have their being of themselves. Aquinas may have had in mind the argument of Avicenna[133].

In the *De ente et essentia*, c.4 St. Thomas proceeds to show that being (*esse*) does not belong to the essence of things[134]. Hence it must be caused by a cause which has being by itself and this is the cause of the being of all other things. While this text corresponds quite well with the last lines of the Third Way, its first part is quite different. The arguments of *S.C.G.* I 15 and II 15 differ in that the *aliquando non est* is omitted. In these texts Aquinas insists from the outset that a thing which can both be or not be must have a cause. The proof is metaphysically valid but does not use the same middle term as in the *Summa theologiae*.

---

[131] Whatever is predicated as possible for a species must happen necessarily. See L. Chambat, *o.c.* (n.123), 334-338; Leroy, *o.c.*, 186.

[132] See, for instance Hugh of St. Victor, *De sacramentis* III, 10: "omne autem quod mutabile est, aliquando non fuisse necesse est, quia quod stare non potuit cum praesens fuit, indicat se aliquando non fuisse priusquam fuit". Cf. *De Trinitate*, I, c.4. On William of Auvergne see Jalbert, *o.c.* (n.130).

[133] Cf. *In I Sent.*, d.3, q.1, a.2, obi.4.

[134] On the value of this argument (we can conceive an essence without considering whether it exists) see volume I, chapter 11. In his *De ente et essentia* Aquinas uses the logical method.

V. Surprisingly the Third Way returns in modern philosophy. Voltaire brings the following argument: "I exist, therefore something exists. If something exists, something has existed from all eternity"[135]. Despite Kant's criticism Brentano considers the Third Way a valid demonstration[136]. Hegel also used a proof from the contingent to the necessary[137], but for him the terms have a dialectical rather than an ontological meaning: the contingent disappears and the necessary results. Hence the necessary is that which is mediated; it is not the foundation but the end; the mind gives up the "ground-less contingent" to transpose it into the universal.

F. C. Copleston tried to use the Third Way in a debate with Bertrand Russel[138]: there are at least some beings in the world which do not contain in themselves the reason for their existence[139]. Russell replied by asserting that the words "necessary" and "contingent" are useless except insofar as they are applied to analogical propositions. The idea of a contingent or a necessary being is meaningless. Russell's assertions, however, proceed from his preconceived ideological position.

The Fourth Way

I. The Text

> The fourth way is taken from the gradation to be found in things. Among beings there are some more and some less good, true, noble, and the like. But *more* and *less* are predicated of different things according as they resemble in their different ways something which is the maximum, as a thing is said to be hotter according as it more nearly resembles that which is hottest; so that there is something which is truest, something best, something noblest, and, consequently, something which is most being, for those things that are greatest in truth are greatest in being, as it is written in *Metaph.* ii. Now the maximum in any genus is the cause of all in that genus, as fire, which is the maximum of heat, is the cause of all hot things, as is said in the same book. Therefore there must also be something which is to all beings the cause of their being, goodness, and every other perfection, and this we call God.

(As will be indicated below, at some points we shall change the wording of this translation.)

---

[135] *Traité de métaphysique* (1734), ch.2. See also A. Altmann, "Moses Mendelsohn und die Beweise der Existenz Gottes", in *Mendelsohn Studien*, vol. 2 (1975) 9-29.

[136] See his *Vom Dasein Gottes*, Hamburg (Meiner) 1929. I owe this reference as well as the note on Hegel's use of the terms contingent and necessary to Prof. K. Hedwig.

[137] *Enzyklopädie*, § 50; *Vorlesungen über die Beweise vom Dasein Gottes*, 10. Vorlesung (Suhrkamp, 17, 412ff.).

[138] Quoted from B. Russell, *Why I am not a Christian*, London 1957, ch. 13.

[139] This fact alone is not an adequate basis for the argument. One has to give a metaphysical ground.

II. Analysis

The Fourth Way is not without its difficulties. Its validity as an argument has been rejected by a number of commentators. E. LeRoy thinks that it is only a modified form of the ontological argument since it would pass from the *concept* of a greatest to a greatest *being*[140]. F. Van Steenberghen rejects the general validity of the principle of the more and less requiring a greatest[141]. Others pass over the Fourth Way in silence. Finally, as Gilson observes, those who do admit its validity, often propose diverging explanations[142].

(a) Although for some critics the Fourth Way evokes an argument in the style of those of St. Anselm or Hegel, it is nevertheless firmly rooted in experience. The observed facts which give the starting point for this proof are the gradations occuring in things. St. Thomas explains that he means a more and less of goodness, truth, nobility and the like. Now these terms attributed to things signify so-called pure or transcendental perfections, i.e. perfections which are not limited in their signification to a particular class of being (say, angel or man)[143]. That this is Aquinas' intention appears from the terms he uses and from the parallel texts as well as from the fact that no other qualities are mentioned[144]. It is true that St. Thomas uses the example of a sensible quality (heat) to illustrate his text, but this is only a comparison and not an instance of such a perfection.

"More" and "less", therefore, do not have a quantitative sense in this context nor is the intensification of sensible qualities meant. Nevertheless, although Aquinas has in mind transcendental perfections he means things which are perceived by the senses and known by the intellect[145]. From this it follows that the "true" of the text refers to the ontological truth of things rather than to the logical truth of the intellect[146]. Elsewhere St. Thomas

[140] *Le problème de Dieu*, Paris 1929, 46.

[141] *O.c.*, 213.

[142] *Le thomisme*[6], 82: "De toutes les preuves thomistes aucune n'a suscité autant d'interprétations différentes".

[143] Cf. *S.Th.* I 13, 3 ad 1.

[144] See J.-P. Planty-Bonjour, "Die Struktur des Gottesbeweises aus den Seinsstufen", in *Philos. Jahrb.* 69 (1961-1962) 282-297, 289.

[145] This is connoted by the "invenitur in rebus" as well as by the parallelism with the other ways. The insistence on observed facts is also initmated by the expression "secundum quod magis appropinquant". St. Thomas avoids "secundum quod participant". See P.M. Bordoy-Torrents, "Estudios sobre la 'cuarta via' de santo Tomás de Aquino", in *Ciencia Tomista* 63 (1942) 30-43, 38. For the sake of comparison one may mention that Henry of Ghent sought to establish a proof of God's existence for which he would not have to start from the physical world (so that the argument would not be contaminated by the 'dangerous' Aristotelian view of the world). He believed he had found it in Avicenna's demonstration from universal propositions concerning the transcendental concepts (ens, bonum, verum), viz. man can perceive being or goodness just in themselves. See A.C. Pegis, "A New Way to God: Henry of Ghent", II, in *Mediaeval Studies* 31 (1969) 93-116, 97. Cf. *ibidem*, 30 (1968) 226-246 and 33 (1971) 158-179. From a Thomistic point of view this argument can be reduced to the Fourth Way.

[146] This is the more so because logical truth is indivisible. A judgment is true or is not true.

explains what he means by "more true" or "greatest in truth": of those things about which there is science some are causes of other things and for that reason carry more knowability, certitude and truth (in the sense of causing their knowledge in the intellect)[147].

Aquinas also lists *nobile* as one of the transcendental perfections. Some have called it a vague term or a metaphor[148]. An examination of its use in the writings of St. Thomas reveals that the term signifies the perfection of things either in their being or according to a certain aspect, in particular insofar as they are compared to other things[149]. Man spontaneously compares things with one another and distinguishes better and 'higher' in them. St. Thomas most frequently uses the term in an ontological sense: a substance is nobler than its accidents, a cause than its effects, the intellect than the other faculties of the soul[150].

The facts Aquinas refers to do not leave room for any doubt: there are differences in transcendental perfections which things possess: we observe that animals have more perfection or content than plants and minerals. The problem is that some will place themselves at the level of the sciences and speak of the greater complexity of a chemical compound or of a biological organization, but refuse to acknowledge such a thing as 'goodness' or 'perfection'. Aquinas' answer to this difficulty is that goodness and perfection must not be conceived as special forms added to these things, but as signifying these things themselves. While a biochemist deals with the quantitatively expressible structure of things, the metaphysician considers the underlying being itself in its unity. The transcendental concepts express what is really contained in these essences.

(b) "But more and less are predicated of different things according as they resemble in their different ways something which is the maximum"[151]. This maxim is found sixteen times in Aquinas' works[152]. The validity of the princi-

---

In another sense, however, one may compare different statements concerning the same reality and find that one gets closer to the truth than the others (or is less wrong). Aristotle does so in *Metaph.* IV, c.4, 1008 b 31ff. in order to refute the opinion that an affirmation and a negation are equally close to truth. His example is used in *S.C.G.* I 13 in the argument from the degrees. Van Steenberghen (*Le problème ...*, 208) thinks that logical truth is meant (whereas in the *S.Th.* I 2, 3 *verum* patently signifies ontological truth). However, Aquinas' commentary *In IV Metaph.*, 1.9, n.659 underlines that the reference is to ontological structures: "... sed tamen in natura entium oportet quod aliquid sit magis et minus verum".

[147] *In II Metaph.*, 1.2, n.294.295.297 (primae causae ... sunt ea quae sunt maxime vera).

[148] Van Steenberghen, *o.c.*, 209.

[149] *In I Sent.*, d 17, 9.1, a.1 ad 6.

[150] The term is very frequently used by St. Thomas. See the *Index thomisticus*, sectio 2, vol. 15, 6-24. Approximately nine tenths of its use is in the comparative or superlative form.

[151] The translation 'resemble' is not so fortunate. The 'appropinquant' of the text means a drawing closer at the ontological level. Aquinas uses this verb, instead of 'to partake' because at this stage of the proof we are still at the level of the observation of differences.

[152] V. de Couesnongle, "La causalité du maximum", in *RScPhTh* 38 (1954) 433-444, 435.

ple has been denied by some[153], so that we must carefully examine it. How can we proceed from the existence of limited perfections to that of an unlimited being? St. Thomas has taken over from Aristotle or rather from the *Corpus aristotelicum* the principle: "That which gives other things a certain form or perfection has itself this perfection to the highest degree". He also borrowed the example of fire[154]. However, Aquinas uses the maxim in a different way and states that where a perfection is found according to more or less there must be something which has it most.

The reason is indicated very clearly in another text dating from approximately the same time as this question of the *Summa theologiae*: "When there is something that is participated in by several things in different ways, it must be bestowed by that in which it is found most perfectly upon all those in which it is found more imperfectly. For those things which are positively said according to more or less, are said to be so because of their closeness to or remoteness from some one thing: for if that (this perfection) would belong to each of them by itself, there would be no reason why it is found more perfectly in the one than in the other"[155].

With this principle we are at the centre of metaphysics. If a being is or has of itself a certain perfection, this perfection will fully unfold itself. If the perfection appears to be limited, this is because it has been received by the subject which possesses it and sets a limit to it by its potentiality[156]. This principle imposes itself upon the mind as evidently true. Precisely because the argument is metaphysical, i.e., abstracts from the material conditions of being, and all material things are necessarily limited, it follows that with our senses we cannot observe a transcendental maximum. 'Fire' is only an example.

Now this "unfolding" of a formal perfection, to a lesser or greater degree, belongs to formal causality. It is this fact which is the starting point of the Fourth Way. This must be distinguished from the question how such a perfection comes to be present in its limited participations. This takes place by exemplary and efficient causality. See the explanation under (d).

(c) The conclusion from what was said above is that "there is something which is truest, best and noblest and consequently which is most being, for

---

[153] For instance, Van Steenberghen, *o.c.*, 215ff. Cl. Bäumker found the argument difficult. Cf. P.M. Bordoy-Torrents, (n.145) 38.
[154] *Metaph.*II (a) 993 b 24-25.
[155] *De pot.*, 3, 5.
[156] The principle is that an act is not limited by itself, but by a potency which receives it. See vol. One, chapter ten. It has been objected to the contrary that things are only themselves in their differences and share in nothing common. See Bauer' "Glossen über den gemässigten Realismus", in *Salzb. Jahrb.* 1 (1957) 49-71. However, this is the nominalist position and in opposition to the philosophy of common sense which admits classes and species. It fails to acknowledge formal causality and is unable to explain the occurrence of multiplicity.

the things which are truest are also most being''. A first question is: is St. Thomas speaking here of one and the same thing which is at the same time truest, best and noblest, or of different things? The translation of the English Dominicans chooses the second solution, but the grammar of the sentence as well as the identification of truest with being and the conclusion of the argument require the first translation just stated. 'Noble', 'good' and 'true' do in fact go together in things since they are all based on perfection and are the same being[157]. The things which are truest, that is, which cause most certain knowledge, are the principles and causes, as Aristotle writes[158]. Now causes are more being than their effects are. Hence the truest thing is also that which is most being[159].

Why does Aquinas resort to this somewhat difficult detour in his argument? The answer is that he places himself at the level of everyday experience: nobility, goodness and knowability can be directly ascertained, while the degree of being as such cannot. The transcendental perfections coincide with being in the identity of one reality. For it is impossible to add anything to being (*ens*) from the outside: being contains everything[160]. The transcendentals are modes of being rendering explicit what is already contained in things. Being shows itself in the perfections it exhibits. For this reason St. Thomas can pass from the transcendental concepts to a conclusion about being. He does so with the help of an argument borrowed from *Metaphysics* II 1: "Things which are truest, are also most being". In this chapter Aristotle shows that the highest things, viz. principles and causes, are truest because they are the ground of our knowledge and certitude. St. Thomas changes the order somewhat and argues from truth to being. The argument is valid, for 'truest' is that being which also communicates its truth to others. This is what causes do.

St. Thomas uses this 'detour' through 'goodness' and 'truth' to being to strengthen the traditional proofs proposed by St. Augustine who argued from the degrees of goodness and truth to the existence of Goodness and Truth itself[161]. Aquinas avoids creating the impression that there is a plurality of subsistent pure ideas, as there was for Plato, and thus he brings the various perfections to unity, associating them with and reducing them to being.

---

[157] With regard to 'true' we notice that the more perfect a thing is, the greater is its knowability. Cf. *S.Th.* I 16, 3; *In I Sent.*, d.19, q.5, a.1: in order to be known a thing must exist; that which is more perfect, is 'more' and is better knowable.

[158] *Metaph.* II (a) 2.

[159] St. Thomas has 'maxime ens' and not 'maximum ens'. He means being in its most intensive and fullest way. One may evoke here the discussion on the meaning of the Platonic expression τὸ παντελῶς ὄν (*Soph.* 248e). See A. Diès, *La définition de l'être et la nature des idées dans le Sophiste de Platon*, Paris 1932, 86-88. Cornford translates the expression as "the perfectly real" (*Plato's Theory of Knowledge*, London 1935, 241).

[160] *De veritate* 21, 1.

[161] *De civ. Dei* VIII, 6 and the texts quoted in n.10 and following of chapter two.

Although the Fourth Way is based upon the metaphysics of participation, as C. Fabro has clearly shown[162], St. Thomas nevertheless makes some corrections to the traditional way of setting up this demonstration of God's existence by showing that the transcendental perfections are properties of being[163].

(d) This takes us to the conclusion of the argument: "Now the maximum in any genus is the cause of all in that genus as fire, which is the maximum of heat, is the cause of all hot things.... Therefore there must be something which is to all beings the cause of their being, goodness and every other perfection and this we call God".—Having demonstrated that there is a greatest among beings Aquinas now argues that this greatest being is the cause of being (esse), goodness etc. to other beings.

Contrary to what happened in the other Ways this concluding section gives a further development. Some commentators believe that it is superfluous and that St. Thomas should have terminated his proof with the previous section. For instance, Gilson[164], Fabro[165] and L. Charlier[166] hold that the first part as such is sufficient to show the existence of God. Others, however, are of the opinion that this second part is necessary[167]. Connected to this question of the function of our passus is that of the sense of the term cause in both the first and the second part of the Fourth Way.

The passus opens with the formulation of a principle: "The maximum in any genus is the cause of all in that genus". This formula, as we have seen, occurs sixteen times in St. Thomas' works[168]. Once Aquinas has "What is greatest, is the cause", a formula closer to Aristotle's text[169]. The principle is central in the metaphysics of participation. The limited occurrence of a form, as we have seen, cannot be explained unless there is also a pure and

---

[162] Cf. C. Fabro. "Sviluppo, significato e valore della IVª Via" in *Doctor communis* 7 (1954) 71-109; *id.*, "Il fondamento metafisico della quarta via", in *Doctor Communis* 18 (1965) 49-70.

[163] Significantly Aquinas refers to Aristotle (and not to Plato), perhaps intimating herewith that his text is closer to Aristotle's philosophy than to Plato's. Our interpretation of the structure of the Fourth Way is confirmed by the *Expos. in librum de causis*, 1.3, n.84, where St. Thomas recalls that the various perfections, in their highest realisation, do not exist juxtaposed to one another but are one and the same divine being, from which they descend to created things.

[164] *Le thomisme*¹, 85: "La conclusion est dès ce moment acquise".

[165] *O.c.* (n.163). Fabro thinks so because he reads the text solely through the spectacles of the doctrine of participation.

[166] "Les cinq voies de saint Thomas d'Aquin", in *aa. vv., L'existence de Dieu*, Tournai 1961, 181-227, 210ff. (The second part of the proof is not superfluous). The same position is also defended by R. Lavatori, "La Quarta Via di S.Tommaso" in *Divinitas* 8 (1974).

[167] Cf. M.L. Guérard des Lauriers, *La preuve de Dieu et les cinq voies*, Rome 1966, 115; A.L. González, *Ser y participación*, Pamplona 1979, 169.

[168] See V. de Couesnongle, *o.c.*, (n.152) 443; compare also *idem*, "La causalité du maximum. Saint Thomas a-t-il mal cité Aristote?", in *RScPhTh*38 (1954) 658-680.

[169] *Metaph.* 993 b 24-25; cf. the study by Couesnongle.

unlimited instance of it[170]. This purest and greatest must at the same time be the source of the things which share in it, that is, it must be a cause. Without it there would be no occurrence of limited participations. Things would possess this perfection of themselves, but then they would have it in a limitless way. For instance, if one would be the only cause of one's love, this love would be unlimited. A perfection which is only partially realized, must therefore be caused by an outside agent[171].

But what type of cause is this limitless perfection shared in by other things? In Platonism participation in the ideas is explained either by means of the presence of the ideas or by imitation[172]. But for St. Thomas (a) the formal cause does not act without the efficient cause[173]; (b) the example of fire serves the purpose of stressing that *efficient* causality of the maximum is meant. Aquinas repeatedly recalls that fire is the most *active* of the four elements[174]; (c) finally, God can in no way be a formal cause of created things[175]. After the first part of the Fourth Way has proposed an ascending dialectic, St. Thomas now completes it by passing from the maximum as such to its causality, thereby finishing his transposition of Plato's metaphysics. A first transposition was from a plurality of forms to unity and from transcendental concepts to being[175a]. The second transposition is that this participation is brought about by the exercise of *efficient* causality by the maximum. It is understood that this efficient causality is not a blind influence but that it is determined by form[176]. The being, then, which is most being, is the source and cause of being and perfection to all things and this we call God[177].

---

[170] The "of all in that genus" does not mean a univocal genus since we are dealing with transcendental properties, but a collection of things which analogically share a perfection with a first member in this group.

[171] Cf. *S.C.G.* II 15: "Omne enim quod alicui convenit non secundum quod ipsum est, per aliquam causam convenitei, ...; nam quod causam non habet primum et immediatum est. Unde necesse est ut sit per se et secundum quod ipsum".

[172] See volume I, c.14 on participation. Plato's own theory of the presence of ideas in participating things was not without a certain ambiguity: in certain texts he speaks of a presence of the forms in these things, but in other passages the forms remain extrincic and are imitated. Cf. W.D. Ross, *Plato's Theory of Ideas*, Oxford 1951, 228.

[173] See *In V Metaph.*, 1.2, n.763ff. The efficient cause is the absolute beginning in bringing something about. Cf. *In II Phys.*, 1.2, n.240.

[174] See *In II Sent.*, d.6, q. unic., a.3 ad 2 and *In II Sent.*, d.16, q. unic., a.2 ad 5; *S.C.G.* III 69.

[175] See below the commentary on I 3, 8.

[175a] Our interpretation of the structure of the Fourth Way is confirmed by the *Exp. in libr. de causis*, 1.3, n.84, where Aquinas recalls that in God the highest perfections do not exist juxtaposed to one another, but are one; from God they are derived and communicated in diversity to created beings.

[176] Cf. *S.Th.* I 44, 3: "Ad productionem alicuius rei ideo necessarium est exemplar ut effectus determinatam formam consequatur". This is perhaps the reason why Cajetanus writes in his commentary: "Esse causam contingit in proposito dupliciter, scilicet effectivam proprie vel exemplarem. Hoc in loco confuse assumitur esse causam" (*In I^am* 2, 3, VIII). See also R. Garrigou-Lagrange, *Dieu* ..., 285 and Fr. Muñoz, "La 'quarta via' de Santo Tomás para demonstrar la existencia de Dios", in *Revista de filosofía* 3 (1944) 385-433; 4 (1945) 49-101.

From our discussion it has become clear that this last section of the argument is necessary. The first part of the Fourth Way is at the level of formal causality and concludes that an occurrence of a perfection in a limited degree shows that there is a maximum. This does not yet make clear, without further analysis, in which way this maximum is the cause of the limited occurrences we observe. St. Thomas himself ascribes the first part of the argument to Plato, whereas he bases the second part more explicitly on Aristotelian principles (and/or on Avicenna)[178].

From what we have seen the Fourth Way as St. Thomas proposes it in the *Summa theologiae* is not just repeating Platonic metaphysics, but is a very subtle transposition of the latter into St. Thomas' own doctrine of being and of divine causality. It is in keeping with his transposition of Plato's theory of participation as has been shown in Volume One, chapter fourteen.

III. The Sources of the Fourth Way

If the heart of the argument is the limited participation in a purest and greatest perfection, the ultimate source of the Fourth Way is Plato, who first developed the theory of formal causality and of participation. There is, in fact, an outline of the argument in the *Symposium*[179] where Plato describes the ascent from imperfect instances of beauty to Absolute and Separate Beauty itself, in which all beautiful things are sharing in some fashion. St. Thomas acknowledges this attachment of the argument to Plato[180]. However, it is remarkable that both in the *Summa contra gentiles* I 13 and in the *Summa theologiae* I 2, 3 as well as in the *Quaestio disputata de potentia*, q.3, a.5 he refers to Aristotle. The texts of the *Corpus* quoted are *Metaph.* II 993 b 24f. and IV 1004 b 2 ff. (there are degrees in falsehood, therefore also in truth). The principle formulated by Aristotle has already been discussed in our analysis.

Although the doctrine of participation is hardly Aristotelian, Aristotle nevertheless admits that at the level of efficient causality there is a first and

---

Muñoz convincingly argues that no perfection realized according to different degrees in different subjects can be the essence of these subjects nor their property. Hence it must be caused *ab extrinseco*.—Others believe that the exemplary cause is meant. Cf. Lemaître, "La preuve de l'existence de Dieu par les degrées des êtres", in *Nouvelle Revue théologique* 54 (1927) 321-339; 436-468 and L. Chambat, "La Quarta Via de Saint Thomas", in *Revue thomiste* 33 (1928) 412-422.

[177] On this identification with God see our remarks at the end of this chapter.
[178] *De pot.*, 3. 5.
[179] 210e-211d.
[180] *De pot.* 3, 5. Plato already acknowledged that before all multiplicity there must be unity. Aquinas does not ascribe to Plato that form of the proof which starts from the degrees of a perfection. On the other hand, the Stoic philosopher Cleanthes insisted on the degrees we see in the world: man with his mind-body structure cannot be the highest being (*SVF* I 529).

a maximum with regard to qualities. He uses the example of fire as an illustration[181]. Above all Aristotle teaches the unity of being, which to St. Thomas is of paramount importance: the transcendentals coalesce in the unity of the concrete thing and do not constitute juxtaposed distinct formal realities.

St. Thomas also uses the argument in a form which goes back to Proclus[182]. He furthermore repeatedly refers to Avicenna for a certain formulation of the proof or for part of the demonstration, in particular with regard to its application to *being*: there must be a First Being from which all other beings receive their *esse*[183]. St. Augustine has the argument in the following form: the different degrees of perfection and beauty in things are changeable; this suggests that there must be a being in which they are in an immutable way and to which they belong first[184]. St. Anselm likewise argues that the diversity of goodness we observe in a multiplicity of things, makes us understand that these things are good by *one* goodness[185].

IV. The Fourth Way in St. Thomas' Other Writings

The central argument of the Fourth Way occurs repeatedly in Aquinas' works and this is a clear sign of the importance he attached to it. However, the form in which the argument is presented varies. In our short survey we can only mention a few texts[186]. In the *Commentary on the Sentences* it is argued that each formal content (*natura*) which is found with the connotation of earlier and later ("secundum prius et posterius") must descend from a first which has this content in a perfect way[187]. The proof is shorter than that of the *Summa theologiae* but the essential elements are present. The demonstration of God's existence from the degrees of perfection is also found in other texts of the *Scriptum in libros Sententiarum*[188].

---

[181] *Metaph.* II (a) 1, 993 b 25: fire is hottest and so it is to other things the cause of their heat. Aristotle presents an argument from the degrees of being in the *De philosophia*, fr.16. Cf. *De ideis*, fr.3. One may also compare *Met.* 1055a 3ff.

[182] *In II Sent.*, d.1, q.1, a.1, Sed contra: "Omnem multitudinem praecedit unitas ..." Cf. Proclus, *Elem. Theol.*, prop. 5.

[183] *In II Sent.*, d.1, q.1, a.1 and *De pot.* 3, 5. The reference is to Avicenna, *Metaphysica* VIII, c.7;

[184] *De civ. Dei* VIII, c.6. Cf. *De Trin.* 4, 6. The argument is also found in Dionysius, *De div. nom.* VII 3. Cf. Boethius, *De consol. philos.* III, c.10: "Omne enim quod imperfecte esse dicitur, id imminutione perfecti imperfectum esse perhibetur. Quo fit ut si in quolibet genere imperfectum quid esse videatur, in eo perfectum aliquid esse necesse est".

[185] *Monologion*, c.1.

[186] For a more complete survey we refer to Fabro's studies (n.162), and the articles of Planty-Bonjour (n.144) and of González (n.167).

[187] *In I Sent.*, d.2, q.1, a.1, Sed contra.

[188] See, for instance, *In I Sent., d.2, q.1, a.2; d.3, div. primae partis textus, 3ª ratio.*

In *S.C.G.* I 13 the wording of the argument is extremely concise. More explicit is a text of the Second Book[189] which argues that that which belongs to something in a lesser degree than that in which it belongs to other things, does not belong to it only because of its nature but by another cause. That which is the greatest in a class is the cause of all the things in that class. God is most being ("maxime ens") and hence he is the cause of being to other things.

In a modified form the argument is used further on in the *Summa theologiae* to show that things have been created by God[190]. The demonstration from the degrees as it occurs in the *De potentia* was already mentioned in II b. Actually St. Thomas presents it in three forms: multiplicity demands unity (Plato); degrees of perfection require a most perfect which is the cause of being (Aristotle); what exists by another must be reduced to that which exists by itself (Avicenna)[191].

In the Prologue of the *Commentary on the Gospel of St. John* St. Thomas observes that some (viz. the Platonists) came to the knowledge of God because they understood that whatever is by participation must be reduced to what is *per se*. Now all things which are, participate in being. Therefore there must be a being which is being (*esse*) by itself[192]. This presentation of the argument lacks the clear basis in sense experience the Fourth Way has. In the *De substantiis separatis* St. Thomas describes Plato's doctrine of participation and explains to what extent it agrees with Aristotle's view[193]. This text is not intended to provide a proof of God's existence. In his *Commentary on the Apostolic Creed* St. Thomas writes that the existence of various degrees of heat and beauty, which increase the higher we ascend, suggest ("credendum est") that they all come forth from one Good Being which gives existence and rank to all things[194]. Finally the *Compendium theologiae* also insists on the presence of degrees in things which allows us to ascend to a most perfect being which is the cause of the things which share in it in a lesser way[195].

Our conclusion is that despite Fabro's insistence on participation, in almost all the texts quoted St. Thomas speaks of degrees rather than of participation. The reason clearly is that he considered this starting point more accessible to sense experience and more obvious than that of the reference of multiplicity to unity or of participated being to the Being it participates in. St. Thomas furthermore wants to go from the various transcendental perfections to the

---

[189] *Cf. S.C.G.* II 15.
[190] *S.Th.* I 44, 1.
[191] *De pot.* 3, 5.
[192] *Lectura super Evang. Ioannis*, Prologus, n.5.
[193] *O.c.*, c.3.
[194] *In symb. apost. expos.*, n.878 (edit. Marietti).
[195] *Compendium theol.*, n.68. Throughout his works Aquinas applies the principle of the maximum to being (*esse*).

unity of the being (*ens*) of which they are properties. On this point his use of the argument fundamentally differs from Plato's view of participation. Finally he passes from a consideration of formal causality in the starting point to that of efficient causality in the conclusion.

The Fourth Way can also be formulated in terms of awareness of moral duties, or of our experience of freedom or of thought. We shall come back to this later[196].

The Fifth Way

I. The Text

> The fifth way is taken from the governance of the world. We see that things which lack knowledge, such as natural bodies, act for an end, and this is evident from their acting always, or nearly always, in the same way, so as to obtain the best result. Hence it is plain that they achieve their end, not fortuitously, but designedly. Now whatever lacks knowledge cannot move towards an end, unless it be directed by some being endowed with knowledge and intelligence; as the arrow is directed by the archer. Therefore some intelligent being exists by whom all natural things are directed to their end; and this being we call God.

The text does not present major difficulties. The title of the Fifth Way says "from the governance (*ex gubernatione*) of the world". For St. Thomas "governance" means the directing of things toward an end which is good[197]. In modern times the proof has been called the teleological argument.

II. Analysis

(a) The fact which is the point of departure for the demonstration is the purpositive activity of physical bodies and plants. St. Thomas does not consider here finality in the activities of living beings endowed with cognition because an opponent might say that their purposive actions are dependent on their knowledge. On the other hand, it is obvious that if things without knowledge act consistently in view of a purpose, viz. their own good and that of other things, they must be directed to that purpose by someone else[198]. St. Thomas speaks of the activity of things toward an end rather than of the order of

---

[196] See M. Corvez, "La preuve de l'existence de Dieu par les degrées des êtres", in *RPhL* 72 (1974) 19-52, 42ff. Contrary to what fr. Corvez writes, we think that the natural desire of happiness, which demands the existence of an infinite Good in order to be satiated, if it can be the basis of an argument, must be reduced to the Fifth Way (see below under "proofs of the Practical Intellect").

[197] *S.Th.* I 103, 1.

[198] The Latin text says "acting always or in most cases" (the 'nearly always' of the translation is somewhat strong).

things or of their collaboration, as he does in other works[199]. Not that there
is any opposition between these two approaches. The text of the *Summa
theologiae* proposes the elements or basic constituents of such a world order
and restricts itself to something which is simpler and can be observed more
easily.

Natural things without knowledge act for an end. St. Thomas means by
natural things the elementary and the celestial bodies, compounds, etc. Some
modern interpreters reject this starting point and assert that if one wants to
obtain a satisfactory demonstration, one should start from design in the
biosphere[200]. It is impossible, they feel, to speak of finality in inanimate
bodies. St. Thomas nevertheless maintains that such bodies do act for an end,
because they always act in the same way so as to obtain the best result ("id
quod est optimum"). What does Aquinas mean by his statement that these
natural things are always or almost always acting in the same way and reach
what is best? When we read this text against the background of the commentary on Aristotle's *Physics* II, lesson 13 which explicitly studies this question,
we notice that to act for an end is distinguished from chance events. What
happens by chance is not directed towards a certain purpose. The classic
example is that of a tile falling from a roof which hits a pedestrian who happens to be passing. It is impossible that things which happen always or in most
cases in the same way, come about by chance[201]. The reason is that in chance
events there is no intended connection between an action and the result
obtained. Therefore this result comes about in a capricious manner.

In the activity of natural things where there is a final term, there is an
intended connection between the action itself and its result. St. Thomas
explains this in his already quoted commentary: when something is done
naturally in a certain way, it has a natural disposition and apitude ("aptum
natum est") to be done in this way[202]. This is precisely what Aristotle writes
himself: "and as they are by nature such as to be, so they are done, if there

[199] In *S.C.G.* I 13 St. Thomas writes: "In mundo videmus res diversarum naturarum in unum
ordinem concordare". In the Prologue of his *Lectura super evang. Ioannis* he likewise speaks not
only of individual bodies but of a "totus cursus naturae" toward an end.—In an excellent article,
"Establishment of the Basic Principle of the Fifth Way", in *The New Scholasticism* 31 (1957)
189-208 R.L. Faricy points out that many commentators of the Fifth Way do not sufficiently
distinguish between this concurrence of several agents and the acting of an individual thing in
view of the good.
[200] Van Steenberghen, *o.c.*, 234. As M. Duquesne observed ("De quinta via", in *De Deo ...*,
I 71-92, 73) Aquinas himself writes (in perfect agreement with Aristotle) that finality in nature
shows most in animals (*In II Phys.*, l.13, n.259).
[201] The wording of the first lines of the Fifth Way is very close to Aristotle's text (*Phys.* II,
c.8) and that of St. Thomas commentary (*ibid.*, n.256).
[202] *L.c.*, n.257. The text uses (as in the Latin translation) the passive voice "made by nature"
so as to compare it with "made by art". "Aptum natum est" renders the Greek πέφυκεν.

is no impediment"[203]. What Aristotle writes is obvious: every year in spring the sun climbs higher in the ecliptic, it warms the atmosphere and the higher temperature melts the snow; the chemical elements react with one another according to a set affinity; in the course of the seasons of the year plants act always or almost always in a regular pattern to reach certain ends. They do so according to their natural aptitude. Nature has fitted them out in such a way that these activities follow conveniently and easily[204].

Some modern authors speak here of determinism and refuse to apply the term finality. They argue that the course of these actions as well as their regularity is pre-set and fully explicable by the forces acting on such a body, by the genetic code and other similarly determining mechanisms. St. Thomas does not deny the role of such determining influences[205], but in his more encompassing approach he gives a different assessment: when in their actions natural things are determined so as to attain something, that which they attain must be convenient to them. In fact it is a certain perfection which is their good and their end. Hence they act in view of an end[206]. As a matter of fact, all agents act in view of an end ("ex intentione finis"): to produce a determinate effect they must be determined to something precise, else there would be no reason why they act in this way rather than in another. The determination by which a thing acts in a particular way, explains its activity at the level of an efficient causality, but from the fact that this determination is such as to lead to a specific effect which is a good for the agent it follows that this efficient causality, causing the determination, is contained in a more embracing final causality[207].

Now there is a certain parallelism between the agents which act with intellectual knowledge and natural agents. The former determine themselves in view of an end, the latter move toward the end determined by nature[208]. They do so with purposiveness: a growing tree spreads its roots, builds up its stem

---

[203] *Phys.* 199 a 10 (transl. by W. Charlton). In the last analysis all activity tends to reach the fulness of perfection which agrees with a certain being. Activity as such is the expression of the substantial form and not an attribute attached to it without any deeper ontological connection.

[204] Cf. *In II Phys.*, 1.12, n.252.

[205] See *S.C.G.* III 2: "Sicut autem in intellectu praeconcipiente existit tota similitudo effectus ad quem per actiones intelligentis pervenitur, ita in agente naturali praeexistit similitudo naturalis effectus ex qua actio ad hunc effectum determinatur: nam ignis generat ignem et oliva olivam".

[206] One may compare *S.C.G.* III 3 and 16.

[207] *S.Th.* I-II, 1, 2. On the principle "omne agens agit propter finem" see volume I, ch. 19 (under 'The Final Cause'); *S.C.G.* III 2: "Si agens non tenderet ad aliquem effectum determinatum, omnes effectus essent ei indifferentes. Quod autem indifferenter se habet ad multa, non magis unum eorum operatur quam aliud". Cf. also *S.Th.* I 44, 4. If one objects that there is indeterminism in microphysics, the answer is that this is an indeterminism of our knowledge (which cannot precisely know certain facts at a given moment), but not an indeterminism in nature.

[208] St. Thomas insists on this parallelism in *S.C.G.* III 3; *S.Th.* I-II 1, 2 and *In II Phys.*, 1.13, n.257. He even elaborates on the comparison of the building of a house with a growing tree.

and unfolds its leaves to produce fruits, much as building contractors first lay the foundations of a house in order to erect the walls and finally to cover it with a roof.

(b) This point being clear we now pass to the next step of the argument: "Whatever lacks knowledge cannot move toward an end unless it is directed by some being endowed with knowledge and intelligence, as the arrow is directed by the archer". When we find "determination" in a thing, which is a matter of certain factors due to which it always or almost always attains a particular end by its activity, we say that an intellect must be its cause. The reason is that in order to attain precisely this end the factors involved, which dispose to such an activity, must have been made or arranged in such a way that the effect to be attained was taken into prior account. Since it is the intellect which compares and connects things, this particular disposition and arrangement must be the work of an intellect. Sensitive knowledge only grasps individual facts[209]. It does not have a comprehensive view of the end to be attained and the means necessary to reach it. Only the intellect understands this connection[210].

(c) Apparently all natural processes have been organized by an intellect[211]. Is this intellect one or many? In the text of the Fifth Way St. Thomas writes "some being endowed with knowledge and intelligence". On purpose he leaves his conclusion rather vague: there must be some intellect which comprehends all things and their actions and disposes them in such a way that they act for their good. Implicitly contained in this conclusion is the insight that ultimately the intellect must be one (in order to explain the interdependence and cooperation of untold things) and be the author of nature, for only one who makes things can dispose their being to act as they do. However, in his conclusion St. Thomas does not formally say more than that there must be an intellect which encompasses and disposes all natural things and their actions. In this intellect the believing Christian recognizes the Creator of the world. For the philosopher the nature of this intellect must still further be determined and in particular the question of its immanence or transcendence as well as that of its unity or plurality must be dealt with.—Our analysis has

---

[209] Since in nature the highest of a lower order approach the lowest of a higher order. it is not surprising to find in some higher animals a certain capacity to reflect and to combine, but this is to be explained by their sensitive faculties and instinct. Cf. I-II 13, 2 ad 3: Animals can have an imperfect knowledge of the end to be attained and of a means to be used, but this is not a knowledge of how the means is related to the end (I-II 6, 2).

[210] One may compare the *Q.d. de pot.* 3, 15: "Natura enim cum non cognoscat nec finem nec rationem finis nec habitudinem eius, quod est ad finem, in finem, non potest sibi praestituere finem nec se in finem movere aut ordinare vel dirigere". The undeniable finality in nature is due to a mind. Hence St. Thomas can sum up his account in the maxim "opus naturae est opus intelligentiae".

[211] See *S.Th.* I 103, 1 ad 3.

also made plain why in the Fifth Way St. Thomas does not have to resort to a series of intellects and why regress to infinity is not mentioned.

III. The Sources of the Fifth Way

The teleological argument is that proof of God's existence which is most widely found in religious and philosophical tradition. The reason is that it is obvious to man that order does not come from nothing but requires someone who arranges things[212]. Xenophon gives a version of this proof of God in the *Memorabilia*[213]. Plato presents the argument in the *Timaeus* and the *Laws*[214] and Aristotle in the *De philosophia*[215]. Cosmic religion as it developed in the second half of the fourth century B.C. attached much importance to this proof[216]. In Stoic philosophy the teleological argument occupied a central place[217]: chance cannot be the cause of the marvellous order we observe in the cosmos: a haphazard mixture of letters does not produce a meaningful text[218].

The argument is found in the *De mundo*[219], in Plutarchus[220] and in the *Corpus hermeticum*[221]. Plotinus writes: "To ascribe to spontaneity and chance the existence and formation of the physical world is a mark of absurdity of him who does not understand and look"[222]. Maximus of Tyre[223] and Marcus Aurelius[224] also know the proof from the order in the world. The Fathers of the Church frequently use the argument[225]. St. Thomas quotes a text to this effect of St. John Damascenus[226]. The Arab philosophers resort to it as do the Christian Medieval Authors. St. Thomas himself also refers the argument to Averroes[227].

---

[212] In the Prologue to the *Lectura super Evang. Ioannis* St. Thomas calls this the most efficacious way.

[213] I 4; IV 3.

[214] *Tim.* 90a-e; *Laws* 886 a. Cf. *Philebus* 28d: "This world of things all about us, Protarchus, this universe, as they call it,—shall we say it is administered by the power of unreason, chance and haphazard, or rather, as our precursors have taught, that its course is set for it by some marvellous intelligence and thought?"

[215] Fr. 10 R; In *Metaph.* XII 10, 1076 a 3 Aristotle attributes to Homer the thesis that there must be one principle which governs the cosmos.

[216] Cf. A.-J. Festugière, *La révélation d'Hermès trismégiste*, II. Paris 1949, 75.

[217] *SVF* I 528; II 1010-1015; Cicero, *De nat. deorum* II 37, 95; *Tusc. Disp.* I 27, 67; 28, 70.

[218] M. Pohlenz, *Die Stoa*, I, Göttingen 1948, 94.

[219] VI, 399 a 30-b 22.

[220] *De sera numinis vindicta.*

[221] V 2.

[222] *Enn.* II 2, 1, 15-19. See also Porphyrius, *De abstinentia* IV 20.

[223] XVII 5.

[224] V 16.

[225] Cf. St. Augustine, *Sermo* 141, 2: "Haec et philosophi nobiles quaesierunt et ex arte artificem cognoverunt"; *Sermo* 241, 1: "Nec potuerunt in animum inducere ... caelum et terram sine auctore constare".

[226] *De fide orthodoxa* I 3.

[227] In *S.C.G.* I 13.

IV. The Teleological Argument In St. Thomas' Other Works

We have already had the opportunity to note that the argument as found in St. Thomas' works exhibits two different forms: in the *Summa theologiae* Aquinas insists on the principle of finality "every agent acts in view of a purpose", but as we have seen (n. 199) elsewhere he dwells upon the order of things which work together. This second presentation of the argument is found in most texts of Aquinas and it is the form the argument has in the entire philosophical tradition. St. Thomas' departure from the usual form of the argument must be explained by his desire to choose rock-bottom facts as his starting point which, at the same time, are most apparent to simple experience and hence unassailable. But this presentation of the argument requires more metaphysical reflection to understand the implications of the observed facts although the argument itself is basically the same as in the other texts using the marvellous conspiracy of things in one world order [228] and pursuing the insight of an age old and almost unanimous philosophical tradition: to make a great number of different things and forces work together consistently to obtain complex and well-ordered effects an intelligent being must have imposed the plan. Hence St. Thomas repeats after St. Albert that "opus naturae est opus intelligentiae" [229]. This version of the argument applies in particular to living beings, in whose organism so many factors faultlessly collaborate in a most astonishing way. A number of animals moreover such as bees and ants show a high degree of purposive action which for its organization requires an intellect [230].

V. The Fifth Way and Its Critics

Design in nature has been bitterly attacked by the Atomists and Epicurus [231]. Since there is some similarity between their views and those of modern science we must examine the reasons why they reject finality.—Leucippus' and Democritus' atoms have a free, irregular motion in all directions; the collisions leading to the formation of bodies are the result of random encounters [232]. When an atomist spoke of chance he did not mean to do away with determinism: for each atom its movement is necessary and of invariable

[228] On this point we agree with L. Vicente-Burgoa, "Los problemas de la 'quinta via' para demonstrar la existencia de Dios", in *Divus Thomas* 84 (1981) 3-37, 28. See also S. Kowalczyk, "L'argument de la finalité chez Thomas d'Aquin", *ibid.* 78 (1975) 47-48.

[229] See note 210.

[230] Hence St. Thomas agrees with Aristotle that this teleological organization shows most in animal life (*In II Phys.*, l.13, n.259).

[231] With regard to their theory one may compare C. Bailey, *The Greek Atomists and Epicurus*, Oxford 1928, 476. The author speaks of "a striking instance of anticipation of the attitude of modern science".

[232] In *Metaph.* 985 b 19 Aristotle notes that the atomists fail to indicate the cause of motion.

direction, but collisions with other particles are unpredictable by man and are therefore said to be due to chance[233]. But there is no design whatsoever since whatever reality there is it consists of atoms and their local movement.

As we have seen[234] Plato was sharply critical of this attack on purposiveness in nature by the atomists whom he held responsible for the spread of atheism[235]. In his *Physics* II c.8, Aristotle convincingly argues against the enemies of design in the world[236]. Shortly after his death, however, Epicureanism renewed the denial of purposiveness in nature and excluded a foreseeing mind from cosmic process: there are only motions and collisions which result in the formation of our world[237]. The Epicureans launched a vehement attack against the admission of finality in the formation of bodily organs: the organs were not made so that we can use them the way we do, but what comes into being creates its own use[238].

Finality in nature was nevertheless widely admitted in the following ages[239]. Even David Hume yielded to the evidence although he felt that the argument from finality only admits the limited conclusion that some ordering mind exists. No inference from it is possible as to the nature and unity of God[240]. Kant notes that the teleological argument is the oldest and most seductive proof of God's existence but he thinks that it does not produce certitude. It already presupposes the idea of a perfect being and therefore it is to be reduced to the ontological argument[241].

In the nineteenth century philosophers waver with regard to the question of finality. Kierkegaard thinks that the teleological argument does not succeed unless one has already admitted divine providence. Newman was afraid that

---

[233] Cf. the balanced review of the problem in W.K.C. Guthrie, *A History of Greek philosophy*, II, 414-419; G. Vlastos, "Ethics and Physics in Democritus", in *Philosophical Review* 55 (1946) 53-64.

[234] Cf. n.214.

[235] Cf. *Laws*, Book X. See H. Görgemans, *Beiträge zur Interpretation von Platons Nomoi*, München 1960, 193ff.

[236] See. W. Theiler, *Zur Geschichte der teleologischen Naturbetrachtung bis auf Aristoteles*[2], Berlin 1965. Theiler assigns a preparatory role to Diogenes of Apolonia.

[237] See Lucretius, *De natura deorum* I, 1021ff.

[238] Lucretius, *o.c.*, IV 823-842.

[239] Ockham voiced his doubt as to whether beings without knowledge act for an end (*Summulae in libros Physicorum*). Descartes and Bacon excluded the study of the final cause from the new natural science.

[240] J. Noxon, *Hume's Philosophical Development*, Oxford 1973, 168ff.; P. Bayle, *Dictionnaire historique et critique*, concedes that the teleological proof moves our heart and witnesses to the existence of "the Great Clockmaker" but it is not a scientific proof.

[241] *Kritik der reinen Vernunft* A 623ff/B 651ff. In his *Kritik der Urteilskraft* Kant further developed his thinking on the principle and now said it stands beside a mechanistic interpretation of nature which alone has scientific value. Finality derives from subjective needs. F. Brentano criticizes Kant for restricting the appearance of finality to the organic world. Those who admire atomism, he writes, will with Maxwell consider it astonishing that billions of atoms are exactly the same as if produced by the same mould (*Vom Dasein Gottes*, 471).

the proof might lead to a deistic view of God. Moreover he himself does not
see the force of the argument: he believes in design because he believes in
God[242]. His position is ambiguous: design is not denied, yet in view of the
presence of evil and the explanation provided by modern science design was
thought by many to be a religious notion[243].

Just as in the past religious belief has facilitated the admission of design,
so nowadays an evolutionist ideology makes it more difficult to admit the
unassailable evidence of its presence. As appears from the above, St. Thomas'
sober presentation of the argument is not affected at all by the criticisms
which we have mentioned. Nevertheless A. Kenny rejects the Fifth Way
because, he says, it simply is not true that every agent acts in view of an end.
Moreover it is not clear whether the "for an end" ("ad finem") of the text
means "its goal" or "a single goal". Kenny finally thinks that the connection
between intelligence on the one hand and the adaptation of means to an end
on the other does not seem to be a simple empirical correlation at all[244]. Our
analysis has already sufficiently answered these objections, but it will be of
little help against prejudice.

The two objections mentioned by Saint Thomas

The existence of evil in the world is often alleged as contradicting the
teleological argument and as a good enough reason to deny God's
existence[245]. Despite its beauty, orderliness and efficient organization nature
offers a spectacle of evanescence, struggle, monstrosities, cruelty, natural
disasters and untold suffering. Man who is a part of the world not only
undergoes evil but also has an uncanny capacity for doing evil and inflicting
suffering. Often God does not seem to come to the rescue of the faithful but
rather lets the innocent suffer. One of the reasons why Darwin so readily
resorted to the hypothesis of spontaneous variation of living beings was that
in this way "we need not marvel at certain things being abhorrent to our ideas
of fitness". John Stuart Mill rhetorically exclaims: "In sober truth, nearly all
the things which men are hanged or imprisoned for doing to one another are

---

[242] J.H. Newman, *The Letters and Diaries of John Henry Newman* (edit. with notes by C.S.
Dessain and T. Gornall), vol. 25, Oxford 1973, 97.

[243] St. George Jackson Mivart, *On the Origin of Species*, London 1871, although admitting
that the exclusion of design means accumulating improbabilities nevertheless felt that religious
conviction is the seat of the opinion that there is design. Charles Darwin denied design because
he felt that God cannot be the author of the cruelty, violence and waste we see in nature.

[244] *The Five Ways*, London 1969, 97-119.

[245] Boethius formulated the question in his *De consol. philos.* I (*PL* 63, 625A): if God exists,
where does evil come from? To answer the question one must first analyse what evil is. See vol.
I, chapter 7.

nature's everyday performance... If the Creator of the world can all that he
wills, he wills misery"[246].

In his answer to this objection St. Thomas succinctly solves the problem.
He does not deny at all the existence of evil[247], but there are limits to it: the
natural goodness of things must be admitted; nature exhibits an astonishing
beauty and efficacy. Sometimes evil is a road to another good so that we can
see its use and a certain finality. For example, the passing away of things
serves the succession of generations, adaptability and innovation. Suffering
encountered in the course of our life may contribute to spiritual enrichment
and moral progress. But there are many instances of evil where we do not see
any usefulness. Given the existence of God who as "the most being" and the
greatest good is the origin of things and their order one must assume that he
would not allow evil to exist, if it were not in order to produce a greater good
out of it. St. Thomas quotes the well-known saying of St. Augustine to this
effect[248]. Elsewhere he even reverses the argument of the opponents of God's
existence: if there is evil, there is also an order of good things of which the
evil is a privation. But if there is an order of good things, God exists[249].

A second objection often raised against the validity of the proofs of God's
existence argues that the explanation of natural process given by the sciences
is adequate or will be so in the near future; to leave behind the empirical world
to resort to a mysterious being no one can experience or conceive is an aberra-
tion. Aquinas' reply to the second objection concerns this difficulty: the Five
Ways precisely show that observed causes can provide no *ultimate* explanation
and the existence of changeable, contingent, limited but well-arranged things
must be traced back to an unmoved Mover, a Being necessarily existing of
itself and a supreme First Principle.

Looking back at this celebrated page of St. Thomas we notice that the Five
Ways are constructed according to a regular pattern: (a) a fact of sense
experience is each time the starting point. In contrast with St. Augustine, the
defenders of the ontological argument, Hugh of St. Victor, St. Bonaventure
and others St. Thomas does not argue from man's inner experience (although
this can be done) but from facts observed by the senses and perceived by the
intellect. This places his proofs at the level of objective scientific investigation
and is in keeping with his conviction that all knowledge comes to us through
our senses. According to Aquinas the formal object of our intellect in this life

[246] *Nature and Utility of Religion.* For Darwin see C. Gillispie, *Genesis and Religion*, Cambridge Mass., 1951, 32ff. Cf. also this text of Schopenhauer: "If a god has created this world,
I would not care to be this god: its misery would break my heart". See H. Spierling (edit.),
Schopenhauer im Denken der Gegenwart, München 1987, 295.
[247] One may compare what he writes on death as the greatest of evils.
[248] *Enchiridion*, XI.
[249] *S.C.G.* III 71.

is the quiddity of material things[250]. Some critics argue that no knowledge of God is possible for us unless we start from our relation with our fellowmen[251]. To this we answer that in order to establish God's existence with certitude we must go deeper into the very core of things as beings. In this respect intersubjective relations are secondary, even if we may use our experiences in a human community in order to develop our attitude with regard to God.

(b) this fact of experience is analysed in the light of a general principle which establishes the need of an adequate causal explanation. In some proofs the principle is added that infinite regress in a series of causes *per se* is not possible.

(c) the conclusion follows that a First Cause, a Being which exists of itself and is "most Being" must exist.

The various steps in the arguments are presented in a logically unassailable form. Even Anthony Kenny, generally sharply critical of Aquinas and whose competence is certainly greater in the field of logic than in metaphysics, cannot help writing: "It is unwise, therefore, for a critic of the Five Ways, to attack their formal structure"[252].

The Place of the Five Ways in St. Thomas' Philosophy

At the beginning of our commentary on the Five Ways we pointed out the relationship of the facts of experience, analysed in each of them, with the genera of causality. Here we must add that the starting points of the proof concern most important sectors of St. Thomas' philosophy of being.

The distinction between act and potency in the background of the First Way is fundamental in Aquinas' thought. Apparently an analysis of movement in terms of act and potency leads to the acknowledgement of the existence of a Being who is pure actuality without any potency. Hence wherever there is question of act and potency God is within reach. The *First Way* is a road we must daily walk.

Furthermore throughout his writings St. Thomas vigorously affirms the causality of created things. Those who deny it derogate from God's greatness and goodness[253]. St. Thomas' world is a universe in which things act the one upon the other. Wherever there is created activity, the First Cause is involved.

With regard to the *Third Way* we recall the paramount importance of the real distinction between being and essence: created things are not their own being (*esse*). The Third Way precisely uses this insight.

---

[250] For this reason Aquinas refrains from starting from what is produced by man.

[251] See E. Levinas, *Totalité et infini*, 51: "Autrui est le lieu même de la métaphysique et indispensable à mon rapport avec Dieu".

[252] *The Five Ways*, 39.

[253] *S.C.G.* III 69.

The important doctrine of participation which in the last decades has come to be considered the hall mark of Aquinas' thought, is the mainstay of the *Fourth Way*, which shows that the entire universe is a reflection of God's perfection. Even man's truth and love participate in God's being.

It is, lastly, St. Thomas' conviction that final causes provide the ultimate explanation of all process. Aquinas' view of the universe is marked by its stress on order and finality. In all their actions things strive to attain an end; all things imitate God[254]. Thus the *Fifth Way* which has its point of departure in this finality, accompanies us in our study of the physical world and of man.

The Conclusion of the Five Ways

Each of the Five Ways ends with the statement that the being whose existence has been demonstrated is that which all men call God or understand by 'God'. This concise and stereotypical identification is not without its problems. Some critics observe that it is by no means evident that the Five Ways really all end up at the same God[255] or that a good deal of analysis (in fact that given in questions three to eleven) is required before such an identification is legitimate[256]. It has even been argued that in I 2, 3 St. Thomas does not show at all that God exists[257]. Others again assert that God as known in the conclusion of the Five Ways has nothing to do with the God of religious worship[258], that Aquinas' proofs are traps of a "causalistic interpretation"[259] or present us with a profane God. Recently J.-L. Marion surpassed all these critics with his phantastic and ridiculous assertion that the Five Ways end in blasphemy since they would reduce God to a concept[260].

In view of so much dissent we must consider the meaning of the closing sentences such as "this all men speak of as God". This formula is already found in Aristotle: the attributes popular thinking assigns to deity must be assigned to the First Mover, the existence of which was established[261]. The identification is found in Diogenes of Apollonia B 5 and may even go back as far as Anaximander[262]: the attributes which tradition ascribes to the gods must be assigned to the Infinite or to the First Principle philosophical analysis

---

[254] *Ibid.*, III 19.

[255] E.L. Mascall, *Existence and Analogy*, London, New York, Toronto 1949, 78.

[256] F. Van Steenberghen, *Le problème* ..., 235ff., 287.

[257] E. Sillem, *Ways of Thinking About God*, New York 1962, 72.

[258] H. Bergson, *Les deux sources de la morale et de la religion*, 256.

[259] G. Marcel, "Dieu et la causalité", in *aa. vv., De la connaissance de Dieu*, Paris 1958, 28-29. Marcel even calls St. Thomas' proofs "materializing".

[260] "La double idolâtrie. Remarques sur la différence ontologique et la pensée de Dieu", in J.S. O'Leary and R. Kearney, *Heidegger et la question de Dieu*, Paris 1980, 46-74.

[261] Cf. *Metaph.* 1072 b 30; *Phys.* 203 b 10-15.

[262] See D. Bahut, "Le divin et les dieux dans la pensée d'Anaximandre", in *Revue des Etudes grecques* 85 (1972) 1-32.

has shown to exist. In other words the identification formula serves the purpose of pointing out that philosophical conclusions about God's existence intend to say the same as what the wisdom of common sense holds about the gods.

Turning now to the *Summa theologiae* there are, it would seem, two levels at which the text may be read. (a) At a purely philosophical level is says that what people commonly understand by the term 'God' coincides with the "First Unmoved Mover", "the First Efficient Cause", etc. St. Thomas indicates that man spontaneously reaches the insight that there exists a common Cause of all things, a Being which exercises a universal providence[263]. Obviously at this level such an idea of God is most imperfect and the identification provisional, so that further analysis is required (questions 3 to 11): our thinking about God must be "corrected" so that we realize that we only know what God is not. At this level of provisional philosophical identification we should not use our Christian idea of God, but rather the pre-Christian notion of the divine[264].

(b) But since the Five Ways are set in a theological context as the *Sed contra* argument, taken from *Exodus* 3, 14, reminds us[265], we should mainly see this identification against a theological background: God, as we know him through revelation, is recognized by us in the conclusions, viz. in the Being which is the Unmoved Source of all motion and activity, which is self-subsistent, necessary Being, supreme Goodness and governing Wisdom. When one asks what a philosophical conclusion has to do with the God of revelation[266], the answer is: Aquinas by no means reduces the God of the Christian faith to philosophy. Rather philosophy serves as a preparation for the faith; philosophical theology may also help us to understand certain aspects of what revelation tells us about God[267]; finally, it has an apologetic

---

[263] Cf. I 13, 10: "Intelligit nomine Dei rem omnipotentem et super omnia venerandam et hoc idem intelligit gentilis cum dicit idolum esse Deum"; I 13, 8: "Omnes enim loquendo de Deo hoc intendunt nominare Deum quod habet providentiam universalem de rebus". See also II-II 85, 1; *In III Phys,*, lectio 6, n.335 and J. de Finance, "Le sujet et l'attribut. A propos d'un texte de Feuerbach", in *De deo*, 149-153.

[264] This provisional character has often been noticed. Cajetanus writes: "Ergo datur primum movens immobile non curando utrum illud sit anima caeli aut mundi; hoc enim quaeretur in sequenti quaestione" (*In I^{am}* 2, 3, III). Some missed the subtlety of Aquinas' composition and reproached him on account of "the lack of a rigorous method, for instance, less rigorous than that of St. Ansselm" (S. Vanni Rovighi, "La 'prima via' tomistica per dimostrare l'esistenza di Dio", in *De deo*, II, 345-350, 347). See also F. Van Steenberghen, (*l.c.*) and J. Owens, "The Conclusion of the Prima Via", in *The Modern Schoolman* 30 (1952) 33-53.

[265] See L. Elders, "Structure et fonction de l'argument "Sed contra" dans la *Somme théologique* de saint Thomas', in *Divus Thomas* 80 (1977) 245-260.

[266] Pascal and others assert that it has nothing to do with the faith.

[267] It shows, for instance, something of the meaning of St. Paul's words "In him we live, we move and we exist". See I, 1, 8 ad 2 and *Quodl.* IV 18. What faith holds about God's existence by far exceeds what reason can show. See *De ver.* 10, 12 ad 5 and *In III Sent.*, d.25, q.1, a.2 ad 2.

function[268]. In short under the guiding light of revelation reason becomes subservient to and harmonized with what God reveals, although it remains at its own level.

The Five Ways and the Three Ways of Dionysius

A further question concerns the relationship of the Five Ways with the *via remotionis* (or *negationis*), *via affirmationis* (or *causalitatis*) and *via eminentiae* of the Platonic tradition. The term *via* itself, in this particular sense, occurs in Dionysius[269]. Plato himself already uses it in the sense of man's approach to supreme being[270]. The scheme of the Three Ways seems to have been elaborated first in Middle Platonism. Albinus teaches that if we want to know God, we must first use negations, proceed next with the help of analogy and finally ascend from the goodness and beauty of things here below until we arrive at the immense ocean of divine being[271].

The choice of the term *via* in the *Summa theologiae*[272] suggests that St. Thomas saw some connection between his five arguments and the Three Ways of Dionysius[273]. That there is such a connection becomes clear in the commentary on the *Sententiae*[274]. The First Way leads to the conclusion that God is devoid of any potentiality. This implies that he is incorporeal, immaterial, incomposite and has no parts. In the *Scriptum super libros Sententiarum* the ascent from bodies to what is beyond corporeal things and from what is changeable to immutable reality is said to be the *via remotionis*. Under this heading Peter Lombard has two proofs which in the *Summa theologiae* are welded into one. For the author of the *Sententiae* the *via causalitatis* is the argument from the contingency of things which do not have being of themselves. Elsewhere St. Thomas distinguishes between the causality of God in the production and in the being of things. The former is more easily recognizable than the latter[275]. The Second and the Third Way describe God as the First Cause of all activity and as the Cause of the being of things. It would, therefore, seem that they are both an ascent through causality.

The two final arguments of Dionysius are those of the *via eminentiae*, viz. in being (*esse*) and in knowledge. The first agrees with the Fourth Way of the

---

[268] See the *Exp. In Boetii De Trinitate*, q.2, a.3 and L. Elders, *Faith and Science. An Introduction to St. Thomas Expositio in Boethii De Trinitate*, Rome 1974, 52.

[269] *De div. nom.* VII, c.3. See *In I Sent.*, d.3, exp. primae partis textus.

[270] *Rep.* 508e-509b.

[271] *Didaskalikos* (edit. Hermann) 165ff.

[272] *S,C.G.* I 13 has *rationes*.

[273] St. Thomas mentions the Dionysian ways in I 84, 7 ad 3. See also *S.C.G.* I 14.

[274] See n.269.

[275] *In De div. nom., c.l*, lectio 3, n.93: "Ipsa Deitas per suum esse est causa productionis et existentiae rerum".

Summa theologiae, whereas it is not so clear just what the second argument is. Dionysius probably means degrees in knowledge, such as sensitive and intellectual knowledge, degrees which require a most perfect knowledge in which they share to a certain extent. As such this second proof is hardly different from the first, but we may perhaps assume that the Fifth Way is to be connected with the *via eminentiae* at the level of knowledge inasmuch as design and purposive activity in the world point to a transcendent intellect which established this order. The Fifth Way moreover leads us to the admission of a Divine Intellect which far surpasses man's knowledge. As Dionysius writes, we must unite ourselves to its light [276]. The terminus of the Fifth Way is God's Intellect as the author of the order in the world and so it implicitly refers to the supernatural order which surpasses whatever man may conceive.

It is superfluous to say that the Five Ways are also related to the discovery of the divine attributes as we shall see in our discussion of the following questions of Aquinas' text.

Are There Other Arguments besides the Five Ways?

As we have seen, the formulation of the Five Ways varies in the works of St. Thomas. The Third and Fifth Ways are each found in two different types of demonstration. On the other hand, we also observe a certain continuity: the Five Ways take up arguments found in the *Summa contra gentiles*. It would seem that St. Thomas considered his Five Ways a synthesis of the proofs of God's existence brought forward by philosophical tradition.

However, in his works Aquinas also mentions an ascent to God from man's quest for happiness [277]. It appears though that wherever he speaks of man's happiness, God's existence is presupposed. R. Garrigou-Lagrange, however, and others thought that the quest for happiness does allow one to develop a new argument for God's existence: every man has an innate desire for happiness which cannot find its full satisfaction in any limited good nor in the sum of such goods. Hence there must exist a supreme good. If not, there would be a basic error in nature [278]. Against this argument of Garrigou one may object with G. Manser, W. Kluxen and J. Malik [279] that in our life on

---

[276] *In De div. nom.*, c.7, lectio 4, n.732.

[277] The argument was first used by St. Augustine in his *De lib. arb.* II, 19. St. Bonaventure also quotes it. For a survey of the immense literature see J. Malik, "Gibt es einen eigenen Gottesbeweis, der ausgeht vom Streben des Menschen nach Erkenntnis und Glück?", in L. Elders (edit.) *Quinque sunt viae*, Città del Vaticano 1980, 109-133.

[278] "Le désir naturel du bonheur prouve-t-il l'existence de Dieu?", in *Angelicum* (1931) 145ff. The argument takes up Augustine's words at the beginning of the *Confessiones*: "Fecisti nos ad te et inquietum est cor nostrum donec quiescat in te".—J. Gredt, *Elementa* ..., II [13], n.790, also defends the argument.

[279] *Das Wesen des Thomismus*[3], Friburg 1949, 390ff.; W. Kluxen, *Philosophische Ethik bei Thomas von Aquin*, Mainz 1964, 129; J. Malik, *o.c.*, 130.

earth, God is not the specifying object of our striving. If the opposite would
obtain, all men would, of necessity, explicitly direct themselves to God. However, God is sought under the aspect of the good in general (*bonum in communi*)[280]. Only after God's existence has been demonstrated may we conclude
that God is the true source of our happiness since he is our origin and the
infinite good. A similar observation applies to the argument from the desire
to know the cause of what we see: when we observe an effect we continue to
search until we reach the First Cause[281].

One might moreover speculate which type of argument the above mentioned 'proof' would be. It would conclude from a natural desire of the will
and the intellect to the existence of the object corresponding to such a desire.
The latter must exist because otherwise there would be a basic fault in the way
nature has arranged things. It would seem that the starting point alleged by
the partisans of these arguments, can be reduced to that of the Fifth Way,
which has its basis in design and finality. However the actual reasoning of the
alleged new arguments differs from that of the Fifth Way and is open to
critique.

Another attempt to formulate a new proof was made by J. Maritain[282]: the
act of thinking is supra-temporal. It issues from a subject which apparently
has existed always, if not in itself then at least in another. Hence an Eternal
Thinking Subject must exist[283]. We may or even must go along with the argument insofar as it asserts the immateriality of thought. To pass from this to
the existence of God as an eternal thinking subject is possible, but takes us,
it would seem, to the Fourth Way. Maritain's Sixth Way is not really a new
proof.

Related to Maritain's own approach to God is an argument proposed by J.
Bobik, which he claims to be Aquinas' own in the *Summa theologiae* I 79,
4[284]. It runs as follows: man's soul is not entirely intellectual, but it is only
so in one of its parts. Hence it is intellectual by participation. Thus there is
a superior intellect by which our soul is aided in its activity of understanding.—Aquinas uses a reasoning close to this to prove the existence of the
agent intellect; it would seem that it could also be used to demonstrate God's
existence, but if so, it comes in under the Fourth Way (viz. a less perfect form
of intellect demands a perfect form) or, in a sense, also under the First Way

---

[280] Cf. *In IV Sent.*, d.49, q.1, a.3 ad 2; *S.Th.* I 44, 4.

[281] *S.Th.* I 12, 1.

[282] See his *Approches de Dieu*, 81-93.

[283] For a good analysis of the argument see S. Kowalczyk, "Le rôle de la sixième voie de J.
Maritain dans la philosophie moderne de Dieu", in *Divus Thomas* 83 (1980) 381-393. K. stresses
the role of experience and intuition in this argument and a certain connection with St. Augustine
(truth requires eternal truth). The author also points out a relationship with Descartes' thesis
(thought is existing thought).

[284] J. Bobik, "The Sixth Way of St. Thomas Aquinas", in *The Thomist* 48 (1978) 373-399.

(in order to be reduced from potential thinking to actual thinking our intellect needs the causal influence of a First Unmoved Mover who is himself always in act). But the point of departure of this type of argument lacks the immediateness of the facts of sense experience Aquinas uses.

In so-called transcendental philosophy a 'new' argument is proposed which starts from the fact that man's existence is immediately given; through his own being man perceives the reality of the world. When he experiences himself as real, man may proceed with the help of a *reditio completa* to acknowledge God's being in which he exists. This returning to the depth of one's being corresponds to what Heidegger called the passing from being (*Seiendes*) to Being (*Sein*). God manifests himself as the innermost ground of man's being. In opposition to the Five Ways, which are too 'ontic' and use facts and principles extrinsical to man's deepest experience, this 'new' argument would be deeply religious and show at the same time God's immanence and transcendence[285]. Lotz's reasoning is a prolongation of Heidegger's thought, in particular of the "ontological difference". Heidegger refuses to consider man as a reality which belongs to the physical universe in the manner of a thing. From man's being there is a road to an immanent transcendence. However, Heidegger consistently refuses to see God in this transcendence[286]. This makes Lotz' argument problematic, for how can he see a proof of God's existence in the "ontological difference" very much against the intention of its author? On closer inspection Lotz's reasoning stumbles on other formidable obstacles. There is, in the first place, his assumption of an almost total opposition between man and the world. Against Lotz we hold that our sense experience of the physical world is immediate and certain, for our external senses are only receptive and do not construct their objects. The intellect can know with certainty this immediate perception of reality by the senses. On the other hand, the so-called "Selbstvollzug" (awareness of one's own being in the world) as such is not clearly perceived, but connotatively experienced inasmuch as the intellect becomes aware of itself, of its ground (the soul and its being (*esse*)) while it thinks the reality of the world. To gain a clear knowledge of itself and its being further reflection and analysis are required[287]. Moreover, Lotz unwarrantably restricts man's being to its intellectual aspect, whereas it encompasses man's entire reality as a body and a living being. If one can show the contingence of one's being (*esse*) in this wider sense, one has found a road to God. But this road coincides with St. Thomas' Third Way. Some critics furthermore note that the use of the terms being

---

[285] J.B. Lotz, "Zur Struktur des Gottesbeweises", in *Theol. u. Philos.* 56 (1981) 481-506. We may perhaps reduce B. Welte's reasoning to the position of Lotz (*Religionsphilosophie*, Freiburg-Basel-Wien 1978, 47-67): man experiences nothingness and looks for meaning.

[286] See the account of Heidegger's view of the proofs in the previous chapter.

[287] *De ver.* 10, 8: "Nullus autem percipit se intelligere nisi ex hoc quod aliquid intelligit".

(*Seiendes*) and Being (*Sein*) by Lotz is confusing and a sort of mystification which must first be cleared up. Finally, Lotz's argument fails to bring out that God's being is not being-in-general but is wholly other than created being[288]. From the point of view of Aquinas' metaphysics this "new way" looks like a regress rather thàn progress.

Desirous to avoid the difficulties sometimes raised against the Five Ways, insofar as they have their starting points in the physical world, J.-D. Robert elaborated a new demonstration based upon the implications of scientific knowledge[289]: there is a connection between things and the laws concerning them formulated by physics or chemistry. If true, these laws are necessarily true. However, their truth cannot rest upon the individual material things which are contingent nor does our intellect create it. We must look elsewhere for a Being which is the ground of this truth. This is God[290]. Robert's assumption that changing, individual things cannot be the bearers of universally valid propositions is not true. For the sciences intend to explain reality as it is; laws state objective structures present in things[291]. We do, however, concede to Robert that it is possible to use our imperfect scientific knowledge as a starting point in a demonstration of God's existence, but such an argument must be reduced to the Fourth Way.

Another group of arguments are sometimes called proofs of the practical intellect inasmuch as their reasoning is closer to everyday experience and does not resort to the scientific formulations of the theoretical intellect[292]. At the beginning of our modern era Pascal had already stressed the need of more practical ways of convincing unbelievers of God's existence[293]. Kant played a leading role in the introduction of an approach to God dependent on the practical intellect. In agreement with Kant it was often argued that God's existence is necessary in order to guarantee moral values.

As foremost among these proofs of the practical intellect one may consider the fact that most people admit the existence of the Divine, the Holy or God. This yields, the argument from common consent, which is found in Aristotle[294], the Stoa, whose view is echoed by Cicero[295], and the Christian

---

[288] This may well be a remnant of Suarezian thinking.
[289] See his *Essai d'approches contemporaines de Dieu*, Paris 1982, 46.
[290] *Id., Approche contemporaine d'une affirmation de Dieu*, Paris 1962, 186ff.
[291] See *Exp. in Boetii De Trin,*, q.5, a.2.
[292] For the distinction between the speculative and practical intellect see Aristotle, *De anima* III 10, 433 a 14 (when the intellect applies itself to something to be done it becomes practical). For this reason we should not speak of proofs of the practical intellect in the strict sense of the term.
[293] See L. Elders, "Intelletto pratico e ricerca di Dio", in V. Possenti (edit.) *Jacques Maritain Oggi*, Milano 1983, 456-462.
[294] *De caelo* 270 b 5ff.
[295] *De nat. deorum* I 17; *De leg.* I 24.

authors[296]: What is the unanimous opinion of mankind must be considered true[297].

Next we must mention the argument from conscience or the moral order. We understand that there are fundamental laws which we have established ourselves but which appear as sacred obligations[298]. We do know, at a given moment, that a certain choice or type of conduct is wrong and we experience this insight as coming to us from Another[299]. Hence one can easily conceive this moral obligation as a command given us by a supreme Person ("the voice of conscience")[300].

The demonstration of God's existence from the moral order is intimately related to the development of philosophical thought in the late 18th and the 19th centuries. According to Kant practical reason gives an answer to certain questions (such as the existence of God) which theoretical reason cannot solve. But the verdict of practical reason ("God must exist so that man's happiness is secured") is only admitted by those who live virtuously. Fichte even went beyond Kant and made conscience the source of all truth[301]: it is a beam of light which reaches us from an eternal world[302]. The argument from conscience also was J. H. Newman's favourite proof. The great English thinker points out that in our conscience we dimly discern a sanction higher than ourselves[303]. An analysis of and a reflection on this awareness are necessary for us in order to acknowledge a divine Being[304]. This reflection is embedded in and carried along by the general movement of the mind which seeks to make explicit the truth of its own ontological dependence[305]. In this way

---

[296] Cf. Clement of Alexandria, *Strom.* V 14.

[297] See K. Oehler, "Der consensus omnium als Kriterium der Wahrheit in der antiken Philosophie und der Patristik", in *id., Antike Philosophie und Byzantinisches Mittelalter*, München 1969, 234-271.

[298] Sophocles, *Antigone* 454ff. In Plato and in the Stoa the same line of thought recurs. Cf. also Cicero, *Pro Milone* 4, 10. See R. Pizzorni, *Il Diritto Naturale dalle origini a S. Tommasso d'Aquino*, Roma 1978.

[299] Cicero is quite clear about this, but see also St. Thomas, *De ver.* 17, 3 ad 1: conscience does not itself make the law, but makes us acknowledge the law made by another. For Kant conscience implies the idea of an 'imperans': *Opus postum. Ges. Schriften* Bd 22, Berlin 1938, 120ff.

[300] It is asserted by a number of modern authors that our moral judgments are the product of education, enlightened self interest, taste or character, or are even the result of arbitrary choices. J. Piaget, *The Moral Judgment of the Child*, New York 1962, 84-108, considers education to be their source. Against this view see J.G. McKenzie, *Guilt. Its Meaning and Significance*, London 1962, 52.

[301] *Die Bestimmung des Menschen. Fichtes Werke* (hrsg Fr. Medicus) III, 351.

[302] *O.c.*, 394. For Kant God is a personalization of practical reason.

[303] *Grammar of Assent*, 101 (104).

[304] See E. Sillem, *The Philosophical Notebooks of J.H. Newman*, vol. II, Louvain 1970, 63.

[305] Cf. A.J. Boekraad and H. Tristam, *The Argument from Conscience to the Existence of God according to J.H. Newman*, Louvain 1961.

Newman discovered a presence, a personal Reality rather than a mere moral Imperative [306].

It would seem that the argument from conscience, if it is to be valid, must be completed by the doctrine of participation: a certain moral goodness and moral rules require an absolute source. We are back again to the Fourth Way [307]. In his analysis of the argument Maritain points to the dynamism of the choice of what is morally good, which is directed to the Infinite Good, God, without man being always aware of it [308]. In its choice of the good the will brings about this conformity and this choice creates the dispositions in the soul required to reach the truth which agrees with it. In this way the argument is subservient to the philosophical proofs of speculative reason.

A new approach to God is given with the experience of beauty. We use building materials to construct houses and churches. When the product of our hands is a work of art, it goes beyond the immediately useful and expresses beauty [309]. The artist and those who enjoy his art feel and grasp something more than a plain thing for daily use. Many artists experience their art as an attempt to catch a glimpse of transcendent beauty, of divinity or something transcendental they wrestle to express in words [310]. Some say that in artistic creation the artist listens to something which lies beyond the world of immediate experience [311]. There is in art and beauty a tendency to lift man up above the fleeting instant of material reality and to reach Beauty itself. Apparently this is the reason why art has always played such an important role in religious worship [312]. But this movement toward Beauty and God is not conceptual knowledge, but an intuition or feeling in darkness. Some artists even declare themselves atheists, although actually their works of art possess this capacity to carry people to what is transcendental, as long, at least, as they

[306] J. Walgrave, "La preuve de l'existence de Dieu par la conscience morale et l'expérience des valeurs", in aa. vv., L'existence de Dieu, Tournai 1961, 109-132, 114. Cf. M. Scheler, Vom Ewigen im Menschen [5], Bern 1954, 55: "Wenn es nichts anderes in der Welt gäbe, woraus wir die Idee Gottes schöpfen: die Reue allein könnte uns auf Gottes Dasein aufmerksam machen. Die Reue beginnt mit einer Anklage! Aber vor wem klagen wir uns an? Gehört nicht zum Wesen einer Anklage auch wesensnotwendig eine Person, die sie vernimmt und vor der die Anklage stattfindet?"

[307] See R. Garrigou-Lagrange, Dieu ..., 308ff. Sertillanges, on the other hand, wants to reduce it to the Fifth Way (Les sources de la croyance en Dieu, I, Paris 1933, 278ff.)

[308] Approches de Dieu, Paris 1953, 95-103; Raison et raisons, Paris 1947, c.6. On this tendency toward the supreme Good see St. Augustine, De vera religione 30, 56; De lib. arb. II 9, 26.

[309] Ch. de Moré-Pontgibaud, Du fini à l'infini, Paris 1957, 100-107.

[310] Cf. Baudelaire's experience as quoted by Maritain, Approches de Dieu, 96ff; S. Fumas, La poésie à travers les arts, Paris 1954, 83, recalls Matisse's convinction. Paul Klee called art the attempt to make visible the essence hidden behind the contingent (Creative Credo, quoted after W. Grohmann, Paul Klee, New York 1954, 99).

[311] Cf. J.-D. Robert, Essai d'approches contemporaines de Dieu, Paris 1982, 328ff.

[312] For some texts see L. Elders, "La place de la philosophie de l'art dans la formation des futurs prêtres", in Seminarium (Rome) 33 (1981) 436-452, 446.

are not maimed in their beauty on account of a pessimistic ideology of the ugliness or absurdity of life.

Related to this approach by means of an experience of beauty is the way of access to God through love. Not unlike truth and beauty goodness and love, encountered in our contact with our fellowmen, also refer to a transcendent goodness and love[313]. Saintliness in particular witnesses to God's existence.

Since the metaphysical arguments for God's existence meet with obstacles on account of the lack of the proper philosophical attitude (see notes 31ff.) the approaches of the practical intellect are helpful as a general preparation. By their persuasive force they facilitate the admission of the metaphysical arguments which are implied by them.

[313] See J. Maritain, *Science et sagesse*, 50-52 on the so-called law of transgression. Cf. also volume I, c.14, on transcendental participation.

CHAPTER FOUR

THE *VIA NEGATIONIS*

I. *Negative Theology*

Having established that God exists we must now consider what he is. The methodical distinction between the questions whether something is and what it is goes back to Aristotle[1]. Even if the two questions must be kept separate Aristotle observes that when we know that a thing exists, we also know something of what it is[2]. This distinction between two steps in our process of knowledge was applied by Cicero to the enquiry concerning the gods[3]. Philo likewise uses it[4]. It was accepted by the Arab philosophers.

Following Avicenna Maimonides declares that we only understand that God is, but not what he is: negative attributes alone are true attributes[5]. Avicebron further distinghuishes between the *quale est* and the *quare est*[6]. In the Neo-platonic tradition as well as in Jewish philosophy all knowledge of what God is was excluded. In the Christian West the Augustinian tradition was not so pronounced in its denial of the possibility of knowledge of God's being. Alexander of Hales lists various aspects of the problem such as knowing that God is, knowing what he is not, knowing what he is according to his being, knowing how he is and how great he is[7]. St. Albert the Great is more precise: knowledge of what God is requires comprehension which is the grasping by the intellect of God, his being and properties[8]. However, of God we cannot know what he is. but only that he is and even this not very clearly[9]. St. Albert is strongly influenced by the negative theology of Dionysius.

---

[1] *Anal. Post.* II 1, 89 b 24ff. Cf. W. Kullmann, *Wissenschaft und Methode. Interpretationen zur aristotelischen Theorie der Naturwissenschaft*, Berlin 1974, 205-255.

[2] *O.c.*, II 8, 93 a 20-26. Cf. St. Thomas, *In II Post Analyt.*, l.7, n.475: "Oportet autem quod qui cognoscit aliquam rem esse, per aliquid rei illud cognoscat: et hoc vel est aliquid praeter essentiam rei vel aliquid de essentia ipsius".

[3] *De nat. deorum* I 23, 65: "concedo esse deos; doce me igitur unde sint, quales sint ..." See also II 1, 3: "Omnino dividunt nostri totam istam de diis immortalibus questionem in partes quattuor, primum docent esse deos, deinde quales sunt..."

[4] *L.A.* I 91; *Spec.* I 35; *De post. Caini* 15 (distinction between the essence of God and his existence).

[5] *Guide* I, c.58.

[6] Cf. *Fons vitae*, edit. Bäumker, *BGPhMA* I, Münster 1892-1895, 301-303..

[7] *Summa fratris Alexandri* I, n.14 (Q.I, 24).

[8] *Summa theologiae* II, q.89, m.2 ad 3 (Borgnet 33, 168). On this question one may compare H. F. Dondaine, "Cognoscere de Deo 'quid est' ", in *RScPhTh* 22 (1955) 72-78

[9] *In De div. nom.* VII (Simon 356, 42f.). Cf. *In I Sent.*, d.9, a.12 ad 1 (B.25, 291).

Negative theology has its roots in Hellenistic philosophy as well as in religious tradition. In Plato's works a number of statements occur which indicate that we can only approach the Supreme Principle by means of negative propositions[10]. The One (the Good) is said to transcend all our knowledge. Aristotle, on the other hand, hardly mentions God's unknowability. He does, however, speak of things which to us are not spontaneously known although most knowable in themselves[11]. In the second century A.D. the theme of God's unknowability was taken up in Hermetism and by Numenius as well as Albinus[12].

Christian tradition had always taught the transcendence of God, yet the theme of God's unknowability gained in importance through Neoplatonic influences[13]. Origenes shows that God is not in a genus; he does not participate in anything, but rather is participated in. Nevertheless Origines maintains against Celsus (who held that God is beyond human reason) that man can know something about God[14].—In a similar way St. Basil asserted against the heresy of Eunomius (who taught a radical agnosticism with regard to our knowledge of God) that we can know that God exists and also certain of his attributes, although not his substance[15]. St. Gregory of Nyssa develops the theme of the hidden God: by a mystical ascent we may penetrate into the cloud surrounding God[16]. The closer we come to God, the more we find ourselves in darkness[17]. St. Gregory here expresses a common experience of religious man: the more one becomes aware of God's transcendence, the more one will resort to negations. St. Gregory's mystical theology had a profound influence on Dionysius. Another Greek Church Father, St. John Chrysostomus insisted no less on God's radical incomprehensibility for all

---

[10] See *Parmenides* 137 d ff.; *Symp.* 211 a. See A. Festugière, *La révélation d'Hermès Trismégiste, II: Le dieu inconnu et la gnose*, Paris 1954. This study is of fundamental importance for the understanding of the place of negative theology in the Platonic tradition.

[11] H.A. Wolfson, "The Knowability and Describability of God in Plato and Aristotle", in *Harvard Studies in Classical Philology* 56-57 (1947) 233-249, asserts that neither Plato nor Aristotle knew the theme of the incomprehensibility of God. Plotinus would have borrowed it from Philo. But this thesis is biassed. Although it is true that Philo makes the important statement that our greatest good is that God cannot be comprehended according to his essence (*De post.* 15). See also J. Whittaker, "Neopythagoreanism and Negative Theology", in *Symbolae Osloenses* 44 (1969) 109-125, 123.

[12] See Albinus, *Didask.* 10. Cf. A. Norden, *Agnostos Theos*[4], Darmstadt 1956, 80. The author thinks that the notion of the unknown God came from Eastern religious tradition and is distinct from the notion behind Plato's reference to the difficulties of speaking about God. Norden's view is far from certain.

[13] See Justinus, *Dial.* 127, 2; Clemens Alex., *Strom.* II 2.

[14] *Contra Celsum* VI 64-65. Cf. VII 38; 42.

[15] *Letter* 234. The Christian authors point out in particular that God has made himself known to man through his Word. See St. Basil's *Contra Eunomium* and St. Gregory of Nyssa's *Contra Eunomium*.

[16] *Vita Moysis* II 163-164.

[17] *In cant. hom.* XI.

created beings[18], although his account is of a more popular nature than that of St. Gregory[19]. We possess true knowledge of God when we acknowledge that we do not know him[20].

Dionysius absorbed this heritage. It is his central theory that God is above being and unity[21]. We can make affirmative statements about God because he is the cause of all things, but at a higher level we must deny the predicates we affirmed of God because God is above everything[22].

St. Augustine admits and uses this negative theology[23]. He speaks of a *docta ignorantia*[24] and says that we must learn what God is not[25], but this Augustinian ignorance never excludes all knowledge with regard to God[26]. In the earlier period of the Middle Ages negative theology was widespread under the influence of the works of Dionysius. John Scotus Eriugena, among others, asserts that nothing can be said of God in the proper sense of the terms[27]. Something of this negative theology survived in the mysticism of the Later middle ages as well as in idealism[28].

St. Thomas is the heir to this ancient tradition of negative theology. In several of his texts he reproduces the thought of Origines, St. Gregory of Nyssa and Dionysius on the unknowability of God. In the *Commentary on the Sententiae* he writes that when we progress in the knowledge of God we first deny that he is material, then we realize that such attributes as wise and good are wholly different when predicated of God; lastly we deny of God that

---

[18] *De incomprehensibilitate Dei* IV 309.

[19] *Ibidem*. See the edition of *Sources chrétiennes*, n.28bis with the valuable introduction by J. Daniélou. As D. points out (*o.c.*, 23) it was not unfrequent that in those days theologians dwelt upon the limits of human knowledge.

[20] *Ibid.*, V 371-372..

[21] *De div. nom., passim*. In particular see c.13, *PG* 3, 977B. Cf. O. Semmelroth, "Gottes überwesentliche Einheit in der Gotteslehre des Ps. Dionysius Areopagita", in *Gregorianum* 25 (1950) 209-234.

[22] *Myst. Theol.* I 2 (*PG* 3, 1000B). In this light we must understand the well-known statement which was so often repeated by the Scholastics, "negationes de divinis verae, affirmationes vero incompactae" (*De cael. hier.* 2, 3: *PG* 3, 141 A). 'Incompactae' is Eriugena's translation of ἀνάρμοστοι, the sense of which is 'not fitting', 'discordant' or 'incongruous'. On Dionysius' negative theology see also H.Ch. Puech, "La ténèbre mystique chez le Ps. Denys l'Aréopagite et dans la tradition patristique", in *Etudes carmélitaines* 23, vol. 2.

[23] Cf. his *De ordine* II 16, 44 (*PL* 32, 1017) where he says of God: "cuius nulla scientia est in anima nisi scire quomodo eum nesciat".

[24] *Epist.* 130 (*PL* 33, 505).

[25] *De Trin.* 8, 2 (*PL* 42, 984).

[26] V. Lossky, "Les éléments de 'Théologie négative' dans la pensée de saint Augustin", in *Augustinus Magister* I, Paris 1954, 575-581.

[27] On his position see also W. Beierwaltes, "Das Problem des absoluten Selbstbewusstseins bei Johannes Scotus Eriugena", in *Philos. Jahrb*, 73 (1965-1966) 264-284.

[28] Cf. the following text of Fichte: "Was ich begreife, wird durch mein blosses Begreifen zum Endlichen; und dieses lässt auch durch unendliche Steigerung und Erhöhung sich nie ins Unendliche verwandeln" (J.G. Fichte, *Werke. Auswahl in sechs Bänden*, hrsg. von F. Medicus, Leipzig. III 400).

he is in the manner that creatures are. Thus we are left in a certain confusion[29]. In St. Thomas' other works further statements of the same import may be found: "The mind has progressed most in its knowledge of God when it understands that God's essence is above what can be known about him in this life on earth"[30].

As this text suggests we must distinguish between the present state in which our intellect carries out its task and a more fundamental inclination of the mind to know the ultimate cause. St. Thomas emphatically teaches that in the created intellect there is a natural desire to see God and that this desire cannot be in vain, although the created intellect is not able to attain God by its own force, as he will point out in Question 12, article 4. Aquinas also argues that God in himself is that which is most knowable because he is real in the highest degree[31]. In this life, on the other hand, man cannot see God because his intellectual horizon is restricted to the knowledge of material things[32]. Knowledge of God can only be obtained through the mediation of material things inasmuch as these are effects of God and as such bear a remote similarity to him[33]. The comprehension of God's essence is altogether excluded. This conclusion is presupposed in the Prologue to the Third Question. Our knowledge of God, obtained from created things, will nevertheless indicate something of God's being, viz. it will show how he is (*quomodo sit*), or rather, as Aquinas immediately adds how he is not. The *quomodo sit* (*non sit*) replaces the *quid sit*. Elsewhere St. Thomas also uses the *quomodo* after having first established the fact of the existence of something[34]. In the *Commentary of the Metaphysics* he writes that Aristotle, having established the existence of the Unmoved Immaterial and Eternal Substance, inquires about its condition[35]. The "how God is not" is a warning to the effect that the conclusions of the following arguments are in the last analysis negative. Even if we say that God is perfect, good or eternal, we must realize that we do not know what these terms mean when predicated of God.

According to Ferrariensis, in the *SCG* Aquinas would first establish *that* God is, then *what* he is (or is not) and finally *how* he is[36]. Even if this division applies to the *SCG*, it does not to the *STh*. We cannot say what God is.

---

[29] *In I Sent.*, d.8, q.1, a.1 ad 4. On this text one may compare J. Owens, "Aquinas-"Darkness of Ignorance" in the Most Refined Notion of God", in R.W. Shahan and F.J. Vovach (edit.) *Bonaventure and Aquinas, Enquiring Philosophers*, Oklahoma 1976, 69-86.

[30] *Exp. in Boetii De Trinitate*, q.1, a.2 ad 1. See also *S.G.G.* III 49: the highest state of knowledge we can attain is that we know what God is not.

[31] *S.Th.* I 12, 1; *S,C.G.* III 50 and ñ1.

[32] *Q.d. de anima*, a.8; *S.Th.* I 12, 12; *Exp. in Boetii De Trin.* q.1, a.2.

[33] *S.C.G.* I 30.

[34] In *S.C.G.* III 18 (cf. also 51) Aquinas after having established that man has God as his end, explains how man can see God.

[35] *In XII Metaph.*, l.7, n.2519. In *In III Phys.*, lectio 11, n.382 St. Thomas writes that Aristotle first studies the *quomodo est*, then the *quid sit* of the infinite.

[36] *In I S.C.G.*, c.10, circa primum. He makes the following division: I 13, I 14 ff.; I 28 ff.

II. *Attributes of God*

The questions in the *STh*. following the exposition of the Five Ways present what has been called a treatise of God's attributes. Aquinas first studies God's entitative attributes and, after his treatise on divine names, the so-called operative attributes. The Neo-Scholastics define an attribute as "an absolutely simply perfection which exists necessarily and formally in God and which according to our imperfect way of knowledge is deduced from what we conceive to be constitutive of divine essence" [37].

Parmenides ascribed certain predicates to the One as did Plato to the Good and the One. Aristotle also attributed a number of properties to his First Unmoved Mover [38]. In the Hellenistic Age philosophers customarily assigned goodness, self-sufficiency and immutability to God [39]. The Middle Platonists added some negative predicates such as invisible, incomprehensible, unspeakable, etc. According to Philo the attributes assigned to God signify that God is the cause of these perfections [40].

In mediaeval Islamic thought the question of whether God's attributes must be distinguished from his being received different answers. Some authors refused to ascribe any reality to the attributes while they accepted attributes such as science and omnipotence. An important group of philosophers in their concern to remove any multiplicity from God considered the attributes as having a negative value. Others, however, admitted their reality [41].

Maimonides is of the opinion that one cannot say that God is one and at the same time assign a multiplicity of attributes to him. Attributes must either signify God's unique being or a quality added to him. This second meaning must be excluded. Because we cannot define God or make him a subject of accidental determinations, we cannot predicate any accidental attribute of God. Surprisingly Maimonides admits the predication of operative attributes of God [42]. We shall return to his theory of the attributes in chapter VII. One characteristic of his discussion of divine attributes deserves to be mentioned here. In his treatise the Jewish philosopher rigorously applies the Aristotelian scheme of the predicaments whereas Aquinas follows a different order: he gives a list of five main attributes, three of which are followed by

---

[37] R. Garrigou-Lagrange, *Dieu, son existence et sa nature*, 370. G. closely follows Billuart.

[38] See *Metaph*. XII 7 and 9 and our *Aristotle's Theology*, Assen 1972, 165ff.

[39] See, for instance, C. Moreschini, "La posizione di Apuleio e della scuola di Gaio nell'ambito del medio platonismo", in *Annali della Scuola Normale Superiore di Pisa*, Lettere, Storia e Filosofia II 53 (1964) 17-56.

[40] See H.A. Wolfson, "Albinus and Plotinus on Divine Attributes", in *Harvard Theological Review* 45 (1952) 115-130.

[41] See L. Gardet, *Etudes de philosophie et de mystique comparées*, Paris 1972, 82-86. Averroes' doctrine of divine attributes is close to that of St. Thomas. See A. Garcia Marques, 'Averroes, una fuente tomista de la noción metafísica de Dios", *Sapientia* 37 (1982) 87-106. 94f.

[42] *Guide for the Perplexed* I 50ff.

a related attribute, but his attributes are not taken from the list of predicaments.

In the Christian Middle Ages the question of divine attributes is usually considered under the heading "the Names of God". It would seem that the term attribute came into use quite late. St. Thomas knew it, but refrained from using it except on a few occasions to distinguish what is said of divine essence from what is proper to each of the divine Persons. A distinction was made between names expressing a mixed perfection and those names which do not signify any limitation[43].

In the fourteenth century Ockham as innovator formulated the problem in all its clarity: are the divine attributes identical with God's essence and also identical with one another? Ockham rejects Scotus' formal distinction but also St. Thomas' *distinctio rationis* (between the attributes). For him the plurality of attributes is only a plurality of concepts or of symbols. In this way our discourse about God loses its importance. Ockham also opposes himself to those who want to deduce the attributes the one from the other and introduce a certain hierarchy of perfections in God[44]. Particularly from the fifteenth century onward the problem was raised of the mutual connection of the attributes. An attempt was made to deduce all of them from one fundamental property of God. Capreolus and Bañez considered God's aseity to be the first and most basic attribute (God's metaphysical essence)[45].

Descartes wrestled with the problem of how to relate the characteristics of the three types of substances (infinitude, thought, corporeality) to their respective substances. He concludes that there must be a distinction in reason only between a substance and its attribute. In reality both coincide so that substance cannot exist in separation from any of these basic attributes[46]. With regard to our other statements about God (apart from the affirmation of his infinity) Descartes seems to hold that they depend on God's will, as do the metaphysical principles. It is within God's power to refrain from affirming these principles so that our utterances are not necessary. In his pantheistic monism Spinoza reduced Descartes' three genera of substance to unity. God is the entirely infinite being which "consists of infinite attributes"[47], each of which expresses his essence which is one and incomposite. However, it is not clear how these attributes are one without either fusion or juxtaposition[48].

---

[43] See St. Anselm, *Monologion*, c.15.

[44] *In I Sent.* d.2, q.2. See P. Vignaux, "Nominalisme", in *DThC* XI A, 755-758.

[45] Aseity is already used by Dionysius (αὐτουσία). Anselm has the term in *Monol.*, c.6.

[46] *Principia philos.* I 62 (Adam et Tannerie VII 30);

[47] *Ethica* I, def. 6: "... constantem infinitis attributis". Spinoza means that each attribute is infinite in its own genus (*Epist.* II, Van Vloten-Land III 5).

[48] M. Guéroult, *Spinoza, I: Dieu*, Paris 1969, 237; H.A. Wolfson, *The Philosophy of Spinoza* (Meridian Edition) 1958, 140, suggests that for Spinoza the term 'attribute' has the meaning of *proprium*.

Spinoza needed this theory of divine attributes in order to be able to explain multiplicity in the world, a multiplicity which was basically excluded by his monism which admitted only one unique substance present to itself. The constituents of God's essence, Spinoza felt, are infinite in number[49]. However, we only know two of them, viz. thought and extension. From each of these attributes flows a series of modes making up respectively minds and bodies. Modes and divine substance are the *natura naturans*, the totality of modes the *natura naturata*. If we approach reality in the light of these modes, we see it as it truly is[50]. Spinoza's theory of attributes is, to say the least, unclear. Some historians consider it contradictory. He seems to have conceived God as an infinite formless being in which an endless number of attributes are floating.

According to Hegel the treatise on divine attributes of the classical theodicea belongs to man's way of representing God. Kant is right when he writes that we cannot know God. Hegel thinks that the use of attributes is contradictory: on the one hand the attributes are held to be finite determinations, but on the other hand they are infinite[51]. Hegel's criticism may be right with regard to eighteenth century deism, but, as we shall see in the chapter on speaking about God, it does not apply at all to St. Thomas' doctrine of divine names.

Schleiermacher shows his allegiance to idealism when he asserts that none of the attributes of God tell us anything about God himself. Rather, they signify that man is aware of being the object of a certain divine activity[52]. Divine omnipotence, however, has a special place, since it is what answers to our most basic experience of such a divine activity embracing ourselves and the world.—L. Feuerbach also insisted on the distinction between God as a subject and his attributes. The latter are the result of man projecting his own properties on God. These attributes, he says, are the real object of religious worship[53].

William James was one of the last leading philosophers of the modern age to discuss the question of divine attributes. Examining whether current Scholastic natural theology is logically consistent he applies the principle of pragmatism to the metaphysics of the entitative attributes to conclude that

---

[49] The *distinctio rationis* between the attributes (*Cogitata metaphysica* II, c.V) seems to be a distinction without any foundation *in re* (*distinctio rationis ratiocinantis*). See K. Heckler, *Spinozas allgemeine Ontologie*, Darmstadt 1978, 120; O. Proietti, "Distinzione formale e teoria degli attributi in Baruch Spinoza", in *Rivista di filos. neoscolastica* 76 (1984) 374-384. Certain scholars attempt to explain the distinction between the attributes by means of Scotus' *distinctio formalis*, but this goes beyond what Spinoza meant.

[50] *Tract. theol. pol.*, c.13: "... quatenus cum relatione ad res creatas consideratur". Cf. J. Collins, *o.c.*, 74 and K. Hedwig, "Natura naturans/naturata", in *Hist. Wörterbuch der Philosophie* VI, 504-509. See also Wolfsen, *o.c.*, 152.

[51] *Enzykl.* § 36.

[52] *Der christl. Glaube nach den Grundsätzen der evangelischen Kirche*[5], Berlin 1861, 261.

[53] *Das Wesen des Christentums*, Frankfurt 2976, 37-38.

"even were we forced by a coercive logic to believe them, we still should have to confess them destitute of all intelligible significance; ... these attributes do not make any definite connection with our life and they do not call for distinctive adaptations of our conduct". Their deduction is only "a shifting and matching of pedantic dictionary adjectives" [54]. James distinguishes between God's metaphysical and moral attributes, a distinction which goes back to the eighteenth century philosophers. James finds better use for the moral attributes.

In the twentieth century philosophical theology left the scene and so the question of divine attributes also disappeared from view.

As we have seen St. Thomas divides his study of God's being into (a) the question of God's existence; (b) the question of how he is, or, rather, is not, and (c) finally the study of God's operation (his science, will and power) [55]. As we shall see, under (b) he successively discusses entitative attributes, five of which are main attributes and three secondary, connected each time with one of the first group, viz. goodness is connected with perfection, existence in things with infinity and eternity with immutability. What is remarkable is that Aquinas does not deduce these main attributes the one from the other, at least not directly. He rather sets out in each case from the conclusions of the Five Ways as well as from experience. He certainly does not favour a metaphysics of the attributes which consists only in logical deduction. His philosophical theology remains always close to experience. This also explains why Aquinas avoids the term "attribute" to designate God's properties [56]. For the term attribute presupposes that one already knows the nature of the thing of which the attribute is predicated [57]. It also suggests some composition between a subject and its properties. Nevertheless St. Thomas does not exclude all deduction: God's eternity is deduced from his mutability and his unity can also be concluded from divine omniperfection.

Philosophically speaking the five main ways of how God is (or is not) are implied in the conclusions of the Five Ways; theologically they are contained in Revelation.

III. *Simplicity of God (I 3)*

The First Way leads to the conclusion that there exists a First Unmoved Mover whose being does not contain any potentiality [57A]. Because in all composition

---

[54] *The Varieties of Religious Experience*, Lecture XVIII.

[55] Prologue to *S. Th.* I 2. The distinction between (b) and (c) is also called that between divine substance and God's operation. Cf. Prologue to I 14.

[56] Only once or twice in trinitarian theology Aquinas uses the terms *essentialia attributa*.

[57] See M.-D. Philippe, *De l'être à Dieu*, Paris 1977, 381ff.

[57a] In *S.C.G.* I 14 we read: "Ad procedendum igitur circa Dei cognitionem per viam remotionis accipiamus principium ... quod Deus sit omnino immobilis".

potentiality is involved, this Unmoved Mover is necessarily incomposite. Hence God's being is simple. This implies that God is not a body and does not enter into composition with other things. Throughout its eight articles the third question is also an exercise in negative theology telling us how God is not. Thus it helps us to correct our thinking about God. Since language follows thought we can also say that Aquinas "is engaged in the metalinguistic project of mapping out the grammar appropriate *in divinis*"[58].

When we call a thing simple, we intend to say that it is not composite or is less so than are other things. 'Simple' evokes that which is not diluted nor adulterated but is itself in purity and strength. Although the term is sometimes used to denote persons who are simple-minded and naive, it often has a moral sense: a simple person is devoid of sly intentions and mental reservations. He is transparent. We speak of the simplicity of the child and of the wise man, but also of that of the saint or mystic.

Already some of the early Greek philosophers held that the divine must be simple (ἁπλοῦς). Anaxagoras' *nous* is explicitly said to be so[59]. Even the atomist considered the atoms as simple entities[60]. In Plato's theory of being the term seldom occurs for the probable reason that he considered even the ideas to be compounded of the One and the Indefinite Dyad. Nevertheless he does write that God is simple[61]. The Supreme Principle, the One, is simple and those beings which are closest to it share in its simplicity[62]. Aristotle also assigns simplicity to what is first, both to the absolutely first and to the first in each genus. Thus 'simple' is also predicated of the First Unmoved Mover[63].

The Church Fathers attribute simplicity to God[64]. St. Cyril of Alexandria writes that all men confess that God is simple and without composition[65]. St. Augustine strongly emphasised God's simplicity: in God there is no distinction between his nature and his properties, between his substance and qualities[66].

Turning now to St. Thomas' Third Question we notice that its eight articles show a good deal of agreement with the corresponding chapters of the *S.C.G.*[67]. However, there are a number of noticeable differences. For

---

[58] D.B. Burrell, *Aquinas. God and Action*, London 1979, 17.

[59] See Aristotle, *De anima* 405 a 16; Diels-Kranz, *FV* II, Democritus A 135.

[60] See M.-D. Philippe, "La simplicité de Dieu", in *aa. vv., Hommage aux catholiques suisses*, Fribourg 1954, 304-315.

[61] *Rep.* 380 d; 382 e; Democritus, *FV* II, A 135.

[62] *Metaph.* 989 b 16; 1059 b 35.

[63] Cf. our *Aristotle's Theology*, 170.

[64] Origines, *In Ioannis Evang.* I, 20; *De principiis* II 4, 1.

[65] *Thesaurus* 31: *PL* 75, 452 D.

[66] *De civ. Dei* XI, c.10. See R.R. La Croix, "Augustine on the Simplicity of God", in *The New Scholasticism* 51 (1977) 453-469.

[67] *S.C.G.* I 16-27.

instance, the *STh*. first examines the question whether God is a body, which in the *S.C.G.* is treated much later; that in God there is no composition whatsoever follows upon the other denials of the different ways of composition in God, but in the *S.C.G.* it comes quite close to the beginning of the treatise. This means that in the *STh*. Aquinas follows an inductive method and proceeds along the *via remotionis* starting with the denial of cruder misconceptions about God.

God is not a Body (I 3, 1)

The view that the divine is a body or has a coporeal nature is often found among religious people. Our senses perceive things belonging to the material world and the representations of the senses accompany our thinking. In materialistic philosophies such as atomism and Stoicism being is declared to be corporeal only. Even some early Christian authors considered God to be a body (to secure the reality of his being), calling him at the same time a spirit[68]. In this connection we must also mention later theories which 'spatialized' God. According to the Cambridge Platonist and adversary of Descartes Henry More, God is an infinite, extended entity (although he is distinct from matter). God is to be identified with absolute space and intelligible extension[69].

St. Thomas proposes three arguments arranged in a cogent order. (a) The first is taken from the primary property of corporeal reality, viz. its mutability. No body moves without being moved, as one can see by a simple induction[70]. Even modern physics acknowledges the principle in its law of action and reaction; for any action energy is needed and thus a change is introduced into the acting body.—However, as the First Way has shown, God is the Unmoved First Mover without any potentiality. Hence, he cannot be a body. (b) Aquinas' second proof argues from the fact that a body is extended and therefore infinitely divisible. The divisibility involves potentiality. In God, however, there is no potentiality whatsoever. (c) The third argument compares a body as such to other realities such as life which do add something to a body. An animal is by all considered to be nobler than an inanimate body. But God is the noblest being, as was shown in the Fourth Way. Therefore,

---

[68] Tertullianus, *Adv. Prax.* 7: "Quis negabit Deum corpus esse, etsi Deus spiritus est?". For further texts (e.g. of Lactantius) see G. Verbeke, *The Presence of Stoicism in Medieval Thought*, Washington 1983, 21-44.

[69] Cf. A. Koyré, *From the Closed World to the Infinite Universe* (edit. Harper), New York 1958, 151ff.

[70] "Movens" (moving) must be understood in an active sense. It applies in the first place to the agent causing a local movement, but the principle holds true universally: causing a change in a body always implies that the acting body itself changes.

he cannot be a body.—All three arguments start from facts of experience which are easily accessible to all.

Is there in God Composition of Form and Matter? (I 3, 2)

Why does St. Thomas devote a special article to this point afer he has already excluded that God is a body, which implies that there is no matter in him? The reasons are in the first place to discuss those texts of Holy Scripture which intimate that there is in God a composition of form and matter; in the second place to answer those who place matter in God to explain his individuality; furthermore to reject the view according to which all beings are composed of contraries[71]. In this connection we may recall that St. Bonaventure and others held that angels are composed of form and matter[72]. Aquinas presents three arguments to exclude any composition of matter and form in God: (a) matter means (passive) potency but in God there cannot be any such potency, as has been shown in the conclusion of the First Way; (b) a being composed of matter and form has its goodness by its form. It is good by participation inasmuch as its matter is a substrate participating in a form. But God is the first and highest good(the Fourth Way) and therefore he is good by his own essence and not by participation; (c) the third argument is based upon the principle that every agent acts by its form. It has the same proportion to its form as it has to its activity. Now God is the first agent, acting by himself (*per se agens*). Hence he must also be form by himself. Any composition with matter in his being would limit and hamper his activity.—These arguments show that God transcends the material universe[73].

God is the Same as his Essence (I 3, 3)

The third article is concerned with the relation of God as a being to his essence or nature. This topic naturally follows the foregoing one: material things share each in some specific nature, but as individuals they are not entirely identical with it. Individual matter, with the accidents which make up the characteristics of the individual, is not contained in the definition of a species. On the other hand, beings without matter are distinguished from one another by themselves. Their specific essence is identical with what they are. Therefore, God, in whom there is no matter, exists by himself and is his deity and life.

---

[71] Cf. *Metaph.* IV 2, 1004 b 27ff. and *In IV Metaph.*, l.4, n.581.

[72] In his treatise on the angels (I 50, 1 and 2) St. Thomas likewise distinguishes between the two questions.

[73] Plutarchus shows that to safeguard God's transcendence one must hold that he is remote from matter. Cf. *De E apud Delphos* 393 C.

This one argument takes the place of six proofs or considerations in *S.C.G.* I 21. It shows that what we call individuality or personality is not absent from God, but it realised in him in a higher way[73A]. The conclusion of the article that God is his own essence, or in other words that he is a form existing of itself whose essence is to be God, is common to Christian theological tradition[74]. From the above it also follows that God is a person, for we define a person as an individual substance of a rational nature[75]. We must omit what is limitative in this concept or what is typically human, which leaves us with the idea of a subsistent, intellectual being. In this way we obtain what is most perfect in reality[76]. We say that God is Subsistent Being rather than a substance, intellect rather than gifted with reason, incommunicable rather than individual[77]. This takes us to the following article.

God's Essence and Being (*esse*) are the Same (I 3, 4)

One of the main theses of St. Thomas' metaphysics is that all created beings are characterized by a composition more profound than that of form and matter or even of specific essence and individuality[78]. As becomes apparent from the arguments he uses in this article the thesis of the real distinction between being and essence in created things is presupposed by Aquinas here and the exception to it, i.e. God's total simplicity, must be proved. Incidentally, the gist of this article's reasoning shows that Gilson's thesis on the real distinction is not quite correct. He assumes that the insight that in (created) beings essence and existence are really distinct depends on the *prior* acknowledgement of God as subsistent being itself. However, it is by denial of what is proper to created things that we must gain some inkling of how God is.

Almost all other philosophers rejected Aquinas' position with regard to the real distinction. Scotus and Suarez hold that a thing is not made real except by what it is itself[79]. But this view does not take into account that the union of act and potency (as Aquinas asserts that of essence and being to be) is entirely different from that of two *things*: being (*esse*) is not something dif-

---

[73a] Cf. *S.C.G.* IV 11: "In Deo est quidquid pertinet ad rationem vel essentiae vel subsistentis vel ipsius esse. Convenit enim ei non esse in aliquo inquantum est subsistens, esse quid inquantum est essentia et esse in actu ratione ipsius esse". In I 11, 3 Aquinas writes: "Idem est Deus et hic Deus".

[74] See E. Gilson, *The Elements of Christian Philosophy* (Mentor edit.), 128.

[75] See Boethius, *De duabus naturis*, c.3: *PL* 64, 1343.

[76] *S.Th.* I 29, 3: "id quod est perfectissimum in tota natura".

[77] See *Concilium*, 1977, n. 23: *A Personal God?* Most essays of this issue apparently intend to consider the question from a theological point of view. H. Vorgrimler, "Recent Criticisms of Theism", discusses a number of modern Protestant views of the problem. Interesting is G. Wildmann's study of the relevance of the idea of a personal God for religious and political life.

[78] See volume I, chapter eleven.

[79] Cf. Suarez, *Disp. metaph.* 31, sectio 1, 13.

ferent (an *aliud*) from the essence. Nor does this opinion explain the multiplicity and contingency of things. Suarez' opinion fails in addition to consider that "to be real" is understood by us in separation from the quidditative contents of things.

By means of three arguments St. Thomas shows that in God essence and being (*esse*) are·identical: (a) In the first argument he reasons from what is implied in the fact that a being's essence is not its existence.—Whatever is in a thing outside its essence must be caused either by the thing itself or by an outside cause. However, being (*esse*) cannot be caused by the essence (which does not exist prior to receiving its being). Hence it must be caused by an outside cause. But God is the First Being (Second and Fourth Ways) and so he cannot depend on an outside cause. (b) When we consider what the being (*esse*) of a thing brings about, it becomes obvious that in God it cannot be different from his essence. For the (*esse*) is the actualization and actuality of each form (*actualitas omnis formae*). It follows that with regard to essence it has the function of an act, to which the essence is related as potency[80]. In God, however, there is no potentiality (the First Way). Hence his essence cannot be distinguished from his being (*esse*). In these lines the famous formulation occurs "esse est actualitas omnis formae" which means that the *esse* is the being real of the form. This implies that at the same time it gives actual existence and realizes a certain perfection of essential content[81]. This doctrine of Aquinas is so subtle that it was not always correctly understood in later Scholasticism. (c) If God would not be but have his *esse*, he would be a being by participation and not be essentially being. Consequently God would no longer be the First Being.—In this third argument St. Thomas takes the *result* of the assumed composition of essence and existence as his starting point to show that it leads to a contradiction in God so that the assumption must be abandoned.

In I 2, 3 Aquinas describes God as "the most being" (maxime ens) and, in I 3, 1, as "the first being" (priminum ens), whereas in this article God is said to be *esse*. *Ens* may be said of God inasmuch as God is a subject who exists, but insofar as *ens* connotes a composition of a subject and the act of being, it does not apply to God, who is prior to *ens* (I 5, 2).

The answers to the two objections are important: being as it is said of God, is not that predicated of created things. For, as we have seen, God's being is entirely unique. We reach our knowledge of his being in a negative way, viz.

---

[80] On act and potency as key concepts of St. Thomas' philosophy see vol. I, c.10.
[81] Cf. volume I, c.12. See in particular *In I Peri herm.*, l.5, n.73: "Hoc verbum *est* ... significat enim primo illud quod cadit in intellectu per modum actualitatis absolute". The causality of being (*esse*) with regard to formal perfection is consequent on its first causality, viz. of actuality. See *Q.d. de pot.*, 7, 2 ad 9: (esse est) "actualitas omnium actuum et *propter hoc* est perfectio omnium perfectionum".

when we understand that God's *esse* is entirely different from that of the beings around us. Because God transcends our knowledge, we cannot attain a proper concept of his *esse*[82], but only affirm that he is; that is, we know that our conclusion "God exists" is true, but we do not grasp God's innermost being itself. The distinction made between "this is" in the sense of the affirmation of the truth of a proposition and "this is" in the sense of the concept of the reality of a thing, also occurs elsewhere in St. Thomas' writings[83]. It is essential to his negative theology of God.

If God *is* his being, he exists of himself. This insight was expressed by some philosophers in a somewhat unfortunate way, viz. they said that God is the origin and cause of himself. The expression "Deus causa sui" probably goes back to Plotinus who applies the term to the *nous* and its activity, but also to the One, although he adds that it has a metaphorical sense[84]. It is not unlikely that Plotinus influenced St. Hieronymus and St. Augustine *via* Marius Victorinus[85]. The expression is found again in Suarez' works[86]. Descartes uses it to denote the *esse a se* of God, although he conceives God as an infinite power which gives itself that which an efficient cause gives to its effects[87]. Spinoza understands by *causa sui* that being of which the essence implies existence. For Hegel *causa sui* expresses the life of the Absolute Spirit. We find the terms also in some modern authors[88]. Whitehead makes God the cause of himself by introducing the theory of the consequential nature of God which grows with the developing cosmos[89].

St. Thomas vigorously rejects the notion that something can be said to be the cause of its own being. This would involve a contradiction for it is conceived as acting (existing) before it exists[90]. This article is the climax of the entire question because it shows how God's essence is not. In doing so it cor-

---

[82] St. Thomas explicitly says that "we cannot know God's *esse* just as we do not know his essence". This sufficiently answers the incredibly shortsighted remark by which H. Duméry ridicules those theologians who, while admitting the identity of essence and existence in God, declare that we cannot know his essence, whereas they claim to be sure about his existence (*Le problème de Dieu dans la philosophie de la religion*, Paris 1957, chapter 2).

[83] See *Q.d. de pot.*, 7, 2 ad 1 where St. Thomas says that "sicut eius substantia est ignota, ita et esse".

[84] Cf. *Enn.* VI 8, 14.

[85] St. Jerome, *In Eph.* 3: "Deus sui origo est suaeque causa substantiae"; Lactantius, *Liber I de falsa religione*, c.7: "Deum seipsum fecisse ..."; St. Augustine, *Liber de LXXXIII quaest.*, q.15 and 16: "Deum esse causam sapientiae suae". St. Anselm uses aseity in such a sense that he makes God the formal cause of himself (*Monologion*, c.6). A similar view may be found in Henry of Ghent, *Summa*, art. 20, q.5: "Deus habet esse a seipso; ... a se dicit causam formalem".

[86] *Disp. metaph.* 28, 1, 7.

[87] *Meditationes de Prima philosophia*, 3. meditation.

[88] Cf. L. Lavelle, *De L'acte*, 3, 7 and J. Ecole, "La notion de "Deus causa sui" dans la philosophie française contemporaine", in *Revue thomiste* 54 (1954) 374-384.

[89] *Process and Reality*, 523ff.

[90] *S.C.G.* I 22.

responds to the revelation of God's name to Moses. Aquinas cautions us that if God is subsistent being itself, we should not say that he has no essence. In his *De ente et essentia*[90a] he mentions "certain philosophers" who assert that God has no essence. Avicenna is one of them[90b]. But such a view deprives God of what in this world is a perfection. God is not, of course, marked by the imperfections of essence (such as its limiting function and potentiality) but possesses in an eminent way the positive contents of essence. The philosophers who unilaterally stress God's *esse* to the exclusion of what constitutes the perfection of essence, risk reducing their concept of God to pure spontaneity.

God is not in a Genus (I 3, 5)

In the preceding articles real composition, whether physical or metaphysical, was excluded from God. Aquinas now argues that the logical composition of specific difference and generic nature cannot apply to God and must also be denied of him. St. Thomas makes a distinction between two ways of being in a genus, viz. in the proper sense of the term and, secondly, by reduction. Both are to be excluded from God.

If God would be a species within a genus, this would have to be the genus "being" and he would then be distinguished from other things by his own particular way of being, viz. infinity. However, such a composition is impossible in God for it would suppose some potentiality. Although a genus as such is an *ens rationis*, a generic community with other beings would imply that there is composition in God of what he has in common with others and of what is proper to himself.

Moreover, if God would be in a genus, the genus would be that of being (*ens*) for his essence is being (*esse*). But being cannot be a genus, for formal differences are not conceivable outside being (even such differences must be real)[91]. In a third argument Aquinas points out that when several specific essences share in the same genus, they must be composed of essence and existence. The reason is that if their essence would also be their being, each would be a universe of its own and there would be no possibility of multiplication within a community[92].

Likewise God cannot belong to a genus by reduction in such a way that he would be the principle of a genus such as being (*ens*) or substance. St. Thomas means a principle in the manner in which a point is the principle of the line, or a component (such as matter and form) of a substance. God is not an

---

[90a] Edition by Roland Gosselin, Le Saulchoir 1926, 37.
[90b] *Metaphysica* VIII 4: "omne habens quidditatem causatum est".
[91] Scotus did not accept this argument, since he thinks that the specific differences are not formally included in being. See volume I, chapter one.
[92] See volume I, chapter eleven, the third argument.

imperfect component, but the universal cause containing all perfections in himself[93].

The upshot of this article is that we need a radical re-thinking of the concepts we use of God. We cannot help use terms such as being, principle, cause, substance, etc. to signify God. But God is beyond any class or term we predicate of him. He simply does not belong to our world and is beyond our horizon and our concepts cannot express his transcendent greatness. In this way this article is the culmination of negative theology. However, some find fault with Aquinas' conclusion. J. Bauer advances this criticism[94]: (a) it is not correct to speak of genus and species in terms of act and potency, for genus and species apply only to our concepts, not to things.—The solution of this objection is obvious: 'genus' and 'species' are *entia rationis* but do have a basis in reality. This basis is a community caused by matter and its different degrees of actualization or (in spiritual beings) by the various ways in which a spiritual form is realised by the act of being (*esse*). Hence there always is potentiality and act wherever there is a genus and its species.

(b) Against the second proof Bauer objects that the concept of being is so vast that it also comprizes God, for it is either being *ab alio* or being *a se*.—We answer that the concept of being is analogous (for instance, it applies to substance and accidents, to potential and actual being). Because God is not composed of being (*esse*) and essence he is being in an entirely different way. Our concept of being (*esse*) no longer applies to him, unless we correct it, by writing into it that God's being is totally different from other beings.

God's Simplicity. There are no accidents in God (I 3, 6)

After having excluded any composition from God's essence Aquinas now deals with the question whether there are accidents in God. Our way of speaking about God would suggest that there are, for we attribute predicates to him which in our world are accidental determinations. How can what is an accident in us be a substantial reality in God? How can totally different classes of accidents be one and the same being in God? Despite these difficulties a careful analysis of the question shows that there cannot be any accidents in God. The reason is that accidents presuppose a certain potentiality in the subject they determine, but in God there is no such potentiality. In the second

---

[93] In certain texts St. Thomas seems to say that God belongs to substance by reduction (cf. *De pot.* 7, 3 ad 7). In these texts he means that God is the non-homogeneous cause of substances. God is connected with substance rather than with accidents because substance, in contrast to accidents, says "being of itself" (*per se esse*). See *In I Sent.*, d.7, q.4, a.2 ad 3 and Cajetanus, *In I^{am}*, 3, 5 IX.

[94] "Fällt Gott unter einem Gattungsbegriff?", in *Salzburger Jahrb. f. Philos.* 23/24 (1978-1979) 89-98.

place, God is pure being (*esse*): being cannot have any accidents added to it. Finally, if there were accidents in God they would be subsequent upon God's substance and God would no longer be the absolutely first being. Similarly God cannot have any accidents *per se* in the sense of properties which flow forth from his essence. For such accidents *per se* are caused by the essence. But in God there cannot be anything which is caused.

In his reply to the objections Aquinas concludes that qualities such as wisdom and goodness are said of God in a wholly unique way. God is the source of all substances and accidents, but he himself is outside the genus of substance and the genera of accidents. Our way of predicating attributes of God is nevertheless valid, if we keep these restrictions in mind. Aquinas returns to this question in his treatise of the names of God[95].

God is entirely simple (I 3, 7)

In *S.C.G.* I 18 St. Thomas first excludes in general any composition in God before rejecting particular sorts of composition in the following chapters. But in the *S.Th.* he reverses this order and concludes with an article on the total simplicity of God. First he remarks that, as the previous arguments have shown, none of the compositions found in (created) beings is present in God. Aquinas then sets forth four proofs of God's total simplicity: (a) What is composed is posterior to its components (at least in the order of generation and material causality). But God is the First Being so that there is no 'posterior' in him.

(b) What is composed has a cause. God has no cause.

(c) In every composition there is actuality and potency. However, in God there is no potency.

(d) In every composed being there is something which does not belong to one or the other of its parts. In other words, there is something in it which it is not itself. But because God is pure being (*esse*) itself, this cannot apply to God.

In *S.C.G.* I 18 the same arguments are given, but (c) comes first. Their order in the *S.Th.* is more formal. "Composite" means "composed of elements". To bring these parts together a cause is needed. If one being is to result, the components must be mutually related as act and potency. A final consideration shows that in every composite reality there is something which is not or not adequately this reality itself.

Thus we conclude that the admirable quality of simplicity is found eminently in God who is without the possibility of contrast or opposition and lives in total self-identity, transparency and unity of purpose.

---

[95] See below chapter seven on the names of God. cf. the *Guide for the Perplexed* I, c. 50.

Can we say that the higher a thing is in the hierarchy of being, the more simple it becomes?[96]. In his answer to this question Aquinas observes that in our world (*apud nos*) composed things are better than simple beings for a compound of the elements surpasses the particular elements taken separately. In divine reality this is different. We must therefore make a distinction between the simplicity of bodies and formal simplicity of more perfect beings[97].

God does not enter into composition with other things (I 3, 8)

In the preceeding articles all composition within God was excluded. Here the question is raised whether God can be a component in a greater whole. In the *S.C.G.* Aquinas first excludes that God can be primary matter of things[98] to argue in a following chapter that he is not the formal being (*esse*) of things. In this article of the *S.Th.* both questions are treated together. The opposite view implies a form of pantheism. From his earliest works onwards St. Thomas always fought this pantheism. In the *Scriptum super libros Sententiarum*[98a] he quotes the *Liber de causis*, prop. 20 (the text of which is still attributed here to Aristotle) to argue that God is not essentially but causally the *esse* of things. Aquinas distinguishes here between three positions: God is the world soul; he is the formal principle (being, *esse*) of things; he is primary matter.

(a) St. Thomas does not give the names of those who defenders the first position but certain Platonists might be meant. According to Plato the world soul is a spiritual being which is the source of all moving forces and directs the organization of the world. Although it is a divine reality, it remains at a lower level than the world of ideas[99]. In Stoic thought it becomes a principle no longer distinct from the material world it permeates[100]. In the monism of the Stoa God and man's spirit are basically the same. This view was still widespread in St. Augustine's day[101]. According to the Gnostics the human soul is a spark of the divine substance, an opinion which was vigorously rejected by such Christian authors as Tertullian[102]. Stoic monism was, indeed, very influential in the first centuries.

---

[96] *S.C.G.* I 18 (Item) affirms this without more ado: "In quolibet genere tanto aliquid est nobilius quanto simplicius".

[97] Ferrariensis, *In S.C.G.* I, c.18, VIII.

[98] *S.C.G.* I 17. See further I 26.

[98a] *In I Sent.*, d.8, q.1, a.2.

[99] J. Moreau, *L'âme du monde. De Platon aux Stoïciens*, Paris 1939.

[100] See *SVF* I 530.

[101] Cf. *Epist.* 166, 2, 3.

[102] *De anima*, 8 & 9.

God was often conceived of as fully immanent to the material universe where he exercizes his activity[103]. In the Middle Ages the rise of Platonism contributed if not to the spreading of a form of pantheism, at least to the formulation of a number of confusing statements. Authors such as Theodoric of Chartres, Arnaldus of Bonneval and William of Conches identified the world soul with the Holy Spirit[104].

Cajetanus, referring to a remark by Averroes[105], thinks the text may contain an allusion to Sabeism, a syncretistic religion or ideology in Southern Arabia and Mesopotamia, which taught that there are intermediary levels between God and lower beings.

(b) The second group considers God the *esse* of things. This view is ascribed to the Ammariani, the School of Amaury of Bène. We must distinguish between Amaury himself and some of his followers who went beyond their master's positions[106]. To understand the rise of this brand of pantheism in the Middle Ages we must keep in mind that Neoplatonic influence was still very strong up to the middle of the thirteenth century. John Scotus Eriugena and Thierry of Chartres used expressions which when literally understood simply pantheism, although these authors themselves were no pantheists[106a]. Amaury was perhaps also influenced by certain currents of mysticism and doxographies of Greek philosophical opinions such as Aristotle presents at the beginning of his *Physics* and *Metaphysics*[107].

In *S.C.G.* I 26 Aquinas shows the impossible consequence of this view: everything would be one; the universal would only exist in the intellect; God would be the end of a process of coming-into-being and, therefore, he would no longer be eternal; divine transcendence is destroyed[108].

(c) The third error is that of David of Dinant (who lived from approximately 1150 to 1208). David used Aristotelian texts, placing them in a pan-

---

[103] According to Aristotle of Mytilene (2nd century A.D.) God is present in material things as substance. See P. Moraux, *Der Aristotelismus bei den Griechen, II: Von Andronikos bis Alexander von Aphrodisias*, Berlin 1984, 417f.

[104] Cf. Ph. Delhaye, *Une controverse sur l'âme universelle au XI° siècle*, Namur 1950; T. Gregory, *Anima mundi*, Firenze 1955.

[105] In *I^am*, 3, 8 II; Averroes, *In XII Metaph.*, comm. 41.

[106] See G.C. Capelle, *Autour du décret de 1210: Amaury de Bène. Etude sur son panthéisme formel*, Paris 1932.

[106a] Cf. John Scotus Eriugena, *De div. nat.* 1, 13: PL 122, 455B: "Ipse (Deus) essentia omnium est". Eriugena was apparently misled by a statement of Dionysius to the effect that God is the "esse superstantiale omnium". See *De cael. hier.* IV, 1: "esse omnium est super esse divinitatis"; *De div. nom.* 5, 4: "Ipse Deus est esse existentibus". See also Gilbert of La Porrée, *In I Boethii De Trinit.* (edit. Häring) 52 and Thierry of Chartres, *In Boethii De Trinit.* II 56. On Thierry see also J.M. Parent, *La doctrine de la création dans l'école de Chartres*, Paris-Ottawa 1938, 86. Cf. Also *Librum hunc. Der Kommentar des Clarenbaldus von Arras zu Boethius De Trinitate* (edit. Jansen), 10.

[107] Capelle, *o.c.*, 86ff.

[108] For the text of the condemnation of 1210 see Denifle and Chatelain, *Chartularium universitatis Parisiensis*, I, Paris 1881, 71.

theistic framework, and thereby discrediting Aristotle's doctrine. David made primary matter the element common to God, souls and material things. God is without a form and is wholly the same as primary matter[109].

The views which we have mentioned under (a), (b) and (c) are shown to be wrong by means of three arguments. (a) As the first efficient cause God must be distinguished, at least numerically, from the effects he produces. God is, indeed, an efficient cause and not an agent exercising an unknown new type of causality. Hence he must be different from his effects, as every efficient cause is. (b) God works immediately by himself since he is pure activity. This would not be possible if he would be a component of a composite whole, for in that case his activity would be proper to the whole. (c) No constitutive part of a whole can be absolutely first because as a part it depends on the whole. However, God is absolutely first.

Pantheistic theories were taken up again in the Age of the Renaissance by Giordano Bruno[110]. In the seventeenth century Henry More sympathised with them inasmuch as he identified God with space[111]. Theistic interpretations of Newton's theory of gravitational force were also proposed[112]. Closer to us A. N. Whitehead partially identified God and the universe. His view will be discussed in greater detail in chapter six. A shift seems to have taken place from the concept of the transcendent God of Christian tradition to a view which makes God a factor in the physical universe, so that he serves the creative advance of the world. "If God has a reality beyond that of an abstraction, then God is in some sense concretely actual. As an actuality or a group of actualities God is then to be identified either with a point or the totality of the concrete actual world, including its possibilities"[113]. In Aquinas' philosophical theology God's total transcendence is affirmed. Nevertheless, as we shall see in the next chapter, God is also intimately present to things, so that God's transcendence cannot be separated from his immanence[114].

In denying any composition in God we drew the conclusion that God is his being (*esse*). In their imperfect knowledge of God philosophers and theologians alike have been attempting to define the most fundamental characteristic of God by which he is distinguished from all other things and from which other attributes can be deduced. A solid tradition considers aseity

---

[109] Cf. G. Théry, *Autour du décret de 1210, I: David de Dinant. Etude sur son panthéisme matérialiste*, Paris 1925.

[110] See his *De la causa, principio et uno Dialogo primo*. In this work he sometimes wavers between the affirmation of God's transcendence and his partial identification with cosmic reality.

[111] *Enchiridium metaphysicum*, c.8, 8 (Quoted after A. Koyré, *From the Closed World ...*, 137).

[112] Cf. M. Jammer, *Concepts of Force. A Study in the Foundations of Dynamics*, N.Y. 1962 (Harper edit., 156).

[113] B.M. Loomer, *The Size of God*, 2.

[114] See chapter five below on God's existence in things.

(being of itself) God's metaphysical essence. Greek religion and Aristotle assigned autarchy to God[115]. Proclus calls the Eternal self subsistent[116]. In the Thomistic School many consider aseity of God's metaphysical essence and some identify it with "self subsistent being" (*ipsum esse per se subsistens*). This is also our position. Some authors, however, see a distinction between the two expressions[117].

In later philosophy aseity is sometimes differently understood. To Descartes it is tantamount to *causa sui*. In Hegelianism it is given a dynamic function: the Absolute creates itself; essence produces existence. Marx applied this view to man: the authentic socialist constitutes and causes himself; he refers nature only to himself and his ideal is no longer to live for another or by the grace of another. In this way Marx attributes a sort of aseity to man[118].

In Scotus' philosophy the theme of God's metaphysical essence is of great importance for being is viewed by him as univocal[119], so that the question arises by which characteristic God is to be distinguished from created things. As is known, Scotus makes infinity this metaphysical constituent.

In St. Thomas' natural theology the question of God's metaphysical essence is to a certain extent out of place: God is altogether different from created things and is beyond our thinking. Even a statement that his being (*esse*) differs from ours in that he is of himself and we are from another risks seducing us into the error of univocity, if our statement is not duly accompanied by some negative theology. Furthermore, although St. Thomas knows a limited deduction of some divine attributes from others, he never develops a cogent *a priori* deduction of all divine attributes from a first, but tries each time to construct an argument from a concrete experience of the physical world. Hence the concept of God's metaphysical essence as such has little importance in the *S.Th.*, although the insight that God is self-subsistent being itself is central.

Aquinas does however acknowledge that among the names of God certain are more proper than others. He prefers, as we shall see in chapter seven, the name *ipsum esse* (*per se subsistens*) as belonging most properly to God[120].

---

[115] Cf. our *Aristotle's Theology*, Assen 1972, 233: all things aspire their good, that is their self-sufficiency. Cf. *Metaph.* 1074 a 20; *Polit.* 1331 b 39f.; *E.N.* 1094 a 3.

[116] *Elem. theol.* 51 (αὐθυπόστατος).

[117] Cf. J. Gredt, *o.c.*, II, n.799; J. Maritain, "Sur la doctrine de l'aséité divine", in *Nova et Vetera* 42 (1967) 189-206.

[118] See G.M.M. Cottier, *L'athéisme du jeune Marx. Ses origines hégéliennes*, Paris 1959, 342f.

[119] See volume I, chapter one.

[120] *S.Th.* I 13, 11.

CHAPTER FIVE

THE *VIA CAUSALITATIS*[1]

In his Introduction to Question Four Aquinas rather abruptly announces that after the study of divine simplicity we must now deal with God's perfection. In the *S.C.G.* he follows the same order: after a number of chapters which study the fact that there is no composition in God the question of God's perfection is raised to be followed by the treatise on divine names and after that, by six chapters on God's goodness.

When we consider the argument given by St. Thomas to prove God's perfection, we notice that he leaves out the first three proofs from the corresponding chapter of the *S.C.G.* to insist only on the fact that God is the first active Principle. Hence we must assume that the *via causalitatis* is now being used. We shall go on to suggest that the consideration of God's infinity comes in under a consideration of his causality. This explains the title we have chosen. It should be kept in mind that the *via negativa* remains present inasmuch as we must be constantly aware of the negative aspects of our knowledge of God.

I. *The Perfection of God (I 4, 1-3)*

The original meaning of the term 'perfect' is 'finished', 'achieved'. Something which is achieved has all the properties and qualifications belonging to its nature; it is complete.

In Greek philosophy 'perfect' describes the virtuous man. Parmenides applies the term to being: the homogeneous, immutable and solid being he acknowledges is perfect, that is, complete, whole and full in content[2]. Plato sporadically predicates τέλειος of the One, of God or of the Whole[3]. Perfect and good are synonyms. The Good is the most perfect among beings[4]. Aristotle lists three senses of the term[5]. (a) that of which no part is outside it; (b) that which is not exceeded in its kind in respect of excellence; (c) that which possesses its end.

---

[1] This title must not be understood in a restrictive sense, but as having a broader meaning which covers the contents of divine perfection, goodness, infinity and existence in things.
[2] See G. Calogero, *Studi sull'eleatismo*, Roma 1932, 28.
[3] *Parm.* 157e; *Tim.* 30d; 68e.
[4] *Rep.* 532e.
[5] *Metaph.* V, 16.

In *Metaph*. XII, chapter seven Aristotle, while affirming God's actuality and eternal life, recalls the view of some Pythagoreans and of Speusippus who hold that the First Principle is imperfect. In their view the One is not even a being[6]. According to Speusippus reality evolves from the One through successive stages of concretization[7]. But Aristotle firmly rejects this view: the real and the perfect must precede the imperfect[8].

Philo calls God the first Good and most perfect[9]. In the *New Testament* 'perfect' is seldom used, *Matthew* 5, 48 being the important exception. The Fathers use the term to signify perfect conduct rather than to to describe God.

In his *Commentary on the Metaphysics* St. Thomas establishes that 'perfect' in its most proper sense means "not lacking anything which is necessary to a thing"[10] or "which does not lack anything according to the manner of its perfection" (that is, according to the way in which its nature must unfold itself). Perfection, therefore, is directly related to actuality. Aristotle makes this clear by using the term ἐντελέχεια to signify a thing's actuality and form. Hence St. Thomas writes that everything is perfect insofar as it is actual (*in actu*); a thing is perfect if proportionate to its state of actuality[11].

To show that God is perfect Aquinas uses this argument: the First Efficient Principle is perfect; God is the First Efficient Principle (as has been shown in the Second Way); hence he is perfect. The major of this syllogism is considered to be self-evident: a cause must be as perfect as or more so than its effects, because it produces the latter. It cannot give what it does not somehow possess itself[12]. St. Thomas' doctrine is also admitted by such philosophers as Descartes[13] and Spinoza. The latter even writes that the degree of perfection is the degree of reality[14].

An apparent exception is the growth of living beings from 'imperfect' beginnings so that the imperfect seems to be prior to the perfect. Some Pythagoreans and Speusippus felt that this was the case. We also encounter this opinion in modern philosophical literature, in particular in Whitehead's process theology. However, those who argue along this line consider material causality. In the order of becoming the imperfect does indeed precede the per-

---

[6] Cf. *Metaph*. 1091 b 30-35.
[7] See our *Aristotle's Theology*, 201ff.
[8] *Metaph*. 1072 b 30ff.
[9] *Spec. leg.* I 277.
[10] *In V Metaph.*, l.18. n.1040. Cf. *In De div. nom.* XIII, l.1, n.967.
[11] I 5, 1 and I 4, 1.
[12] The principle is self-evident and has been acknowledged as such. Cf. Plato, *Philebus* 27a; Cicero, *De nat. deorum* II, 33, 86; Proclus, *Elementatio*, prop. 7-11; A.C. Lloyd, "The Principle that the Cause is Greater Than Its Effects", in *Phronesis* 21 (1976) 146.
[13] *Princ. philos.* (Adam et Tannery IX 2, 34).
[14] *Ethica* II, def. 6: "per realitatem et perfectionem idem intelligo".

fect. They seem to overlook that in the order of being and of efficient causality the perfect is prior.

Another objection one might raise against the thesis of God's perfection runs as follows: God is being (*esse*). But being is imperfect and must be further determined to "being a body", "being man", etc. St. Thomas' answer to this difficulty is one of the most important statements of the *S. Th.*: "Being is the most perfect of all things, for it is compared to all things as that by which they are made actual; for nothing has actuality except insofar as it is. Hence being itself is that which actuates all things, even their forms". Precisely because being (*esse*) realizes things it is the source and cause of reality and perfection. One should not consider being a substrate to which a certain modality (e.g., being man) is added. Being is ultimate. Nothing is added to it but being itself brings other things to reality[15].

The next question is whether the perfections of all things are in God. The answer is affirmative: God is the First Efficient Cause and therefore the perfections of the effects must all be found in God, for an effect pre-exists virtually in its efficient cause. Hence all things pre-exist in God. They do so in the simplicity and unity of God's being, that is, in a more eminent way than the manner in which they exist in the physical universe.

St. Thomas adds a second argument: God is being (*esse*) itself and thus he is whatever is real and contains within himself the whole perfection of being.

The third article considers the question whether any creature can be like God, in other words, whether it can possess God's perfections. The theme of "being like God" or "being akin to God" occupies a central place in religious tradition[16]. We must distinguish between the more general relationship of all things with God and man's especial kinship. Man must consciously develop his likeness with God and return to his origin in his intellectual and moral life. In order to understand better what is meant by the question which introduces the third article an analysis of the meaning of "to be like" will be helpful. Likeness is communication or sharing in the same form. This can be with regard either to its formal nature or to the manner of its being realised (according to the degree of its realisation). When things are alike in each of these ways we speak of equality. For instance, two individuals of the same species are equal. When they share in a form in different degrees we speak of likeness. Thus two white things in different shades of white are alike. When things communicate in the same form but do not have it according to the same essential content (*ratio*) their likeness is rather remote. This relationship

---

[15] On what being (esse) means to St. Thomas see vol. I, chapter twelve.

[16] Cf. *Genesis* I 26 and 1 John III 2. See H. Merki, *ΟΜΟΙΩΣΙΣ ΘΕΩΙ, Von der platonischen Angleichung an Gott zur Gottähnlichkeit bei Gregor von Nyssa*, Fribourg 1952; E. Des Places, *Syngeneia. La parenté de l'homme avec Dieu d'Homère à la patristique*, Paris 1964; D. Roloff, *Gottähnlichkeit, Vergöttlichung und Erhöhung zum Seligen Leben*, Berlin 1970.

obtains between God and creatures: every agent insofar as it is an agent produces an effect similar to itself (for an agent works according to its form).
Since God is not contained in a genus or species, his effects, which are limited
beings, will resemble him only remotely.

Moreover God so much exceeds all classes and species of things that one
cannot say that he resembles his creatures although it may be admitted that
creatures are in some sort like God, "for we say that a statue is like a man,
but not conversely".

Summing up the doctrinal content of this question we notice in the first
place the insistence on God's causality: God is the first efficient cause. This
is the conclusion reached in the Second Way, even if in the latter the problem
at issue is to show that all efficient activity has its source in an Agent who is
actuality itself. Implicitly this means that God is the cause of all being. In the
question on God's perfection St. Thomas draws his conclusion from the
insight reached in the Second Way and is moving toward the formulation of
the doctrine of creation.

A second major point to be noted is that because every agent works effects
similar to itself, the things which God makes must resemble him. This conclusion is the foundation of the doctrine of the analogy between God and the
world; it provides the basis for the statements we are to make about God. For
this reason in the *S.C.G.* the chapters on God's names follow immediately on
those which study God's perfection and the similitude between created beings
and God. In the *S.Th.*, however, Aquinas chose a somewhat different order.
He first determines more precisely how God is (is not), before dealing with
the issue of how we know God and speak of him.

A third observation to be made is that while we are using the *via
causalitatis*, we are nevertheless reminded of the limits of our knowledge
about God. Although we resemble him in some way, he escapes our
knowledge in the transcendence of his being. God does not resemble us. This
conclusion is a stepping stone for the question of God's goodness.

II. *The Goodness of God (I 6)*

In his early dialogues Plato expressed his conviction that God is good and
does not envy man. In the *Republic* he criticizes the way in which Greek poets
describe the gods and argues that the gods must of necessity be just and cannot do harm to anyone. Aristotle, for his part, calls the First Unmoved Mover
the noblest being [16a] and 'most excellent'[16b]. The Christian authors all affirm

---

[16a] *Metaph.* 1072 b 18.
[16b] *Metaph.* 1075 a 9-11.

God's goodness, identifying his being and goodness, whereas Neoplatonism distinguished between them placing goodness above being[16c].

St. Thomas argues that goodness is based upon perfection and therefore God's goodness is studied after the question on divine perfection. In a similar way God's presence in things and his eternity are said to follow upon his infinity and immutability.

In the text 'good' is being used formally: "Good is what all desire and a thing is desirable only insofar as it is perfect, for all desire their own perfection"[17]. Hence in the text the secondary sense of 'good', viz. kind, loving, generous, is not primarily meant. In fact, St. Thomas does not argue from the love of God some people cherish nor from an experience of God's goodness such as Israel claimed to have had, but he uses a more formal and ontological consideration which at the same time shows the profound unity of all strivings and all activities in the universe. The argument runs: being desired is most eminently proper to God, "for everything seeks after its own perfection and the perfection and form of an effect consist in a certain likeness to the agent, since every agent makes his like; and hence the agent itself is desirable and has the nature of good"[18].

It must be noticed that this argument is intimately connected with the third article of the preceding question: God makes things which have some likeness to him. Things always strive to attain their own perfection, i.e. the completion of their form, and therefore they strive after God. From this it follows that in all activity in the universe God is sought and striven after. Nothing can escape from this seeking to become more similar to God because all things work for their perfection[19]. This conclusion shows once more how far Aquinas' metaphysics is removed from deism which makes God extrinsic to the universe.

The Second Article asks the question whether God is the highest good, a theme which in the *S.C.G.* comes after the thesis that God is good by his essence. Among all goods that we strive to attain God is the highest, for he is the source of all perfections and therefore himself the highest perfection. While affirming this Aquinas points out that God is not a univocal agent: he possesses in the highest way what he effects in created beings[20].

In the Neoplatonic tradition God's goodness is affirmed but at the same time the gulf separating his greatness from the things derived from him is brought out: all other beings outside the First are good by participation. In

---

[16c] St. Augustine, *De lib. arb.* II 15, 39.

[17] I 5, 1.

[18] I 6, 1.

[19] This is elaborated in detail in *S.C.G.* III, cc. 17-20.

[20] Cf. St. Thomas' remarks on Dionysius' metaphysics of divine goodness in his *In De div. nom.*, c.4, 1.1-3, esp. nn.306ff.: the image of light is only metaphorical.

Christian Platonism the question was debated whether created things are good
by themselves, i.e., by their own essence or only by participation. While the
Biblical revelation clearly teaches the goodness of all things, Neoplatonic philosophy holds that things are not good by themselves but by participating in
the form of goodness. Boethius devoted a treatise to this problem: he affirms
the goodness of things, but placed the ground of their goodness in their
dependence on God[21]. St. Thomas rejects this view and shows that things can
themselves be something essentially while they still possess it through
participation[22].

In the Third Article Aquinas shows that God alone is good essentially, arguing his point not with the help of a metaphysics of participation, but formally,
i.e., by means of an analysis of what 'good' means. The goodness of things
is achieved in three stages: (a) according to the constitution of their being; (b)
in respect of accidents added as necessary for their perfect operation; (c) by
attaining something else as their end. To illustrate this we can use an example:
man possesses a basic goodness and value inasmuch as he exists as a human
being. When his bodily and mental powers are well developed he is called
'good' in a more particular sense. When he always seeks the good and reaches
truth he is called good in the most encompassing way. However, this triple
perfection belongs to no creature by its own essence. It is proper to God alone,
whose essence is his being(*esse*), and in whom there are no accidents, since
whatever belongs to other things accidentally belongs to him essentially. Furthermore, God is not directed to anything else as to his end, but he is himself
the last end of all things.

This implies that things are good by participating in God's goodness, as
they are beings by participating in God's being (*esse*), although this participation does not exclude that created things are also formally their own
goodness[23].

III. *The Infinity of God (I 7)*

As will become clear in the following pages the question of the infinity of God
must also be connected with the *via causalitatis*.—In some ancient
cosmological myths the cosmos is said to have its origin in an infinite principle
or substance. Anaximander of Miletus called the original substance, out of
which all things are formed, the Infinite. The early Pythagoreans also

---

[21] See his *De hebdomadibus*.

[22] *Expos. in Boetii De hebdomadibus*, 1.3, nn.44-45.

[23] In the fourth article of question six St. Thomas points out that which is "absolutely true"
in Plato's theory of ideas and participation, viz. that there is something first which is essentially
being and essentially good. He also writes that on this point Aristotle agrees with Plato. See vol.
I, ch. 14

acknowledged an infinite Principle surrounding the cosmos and from which the cosmos is produced by a process of determination[24]. The Atomists assume that the atoms are infinite in number and move eternally through a void which is infinite in extent. If space would be finite, it would have to be so because limited by something external to it. But there is nothing external that can be a limit[25].

In his later theory Plato admits two principles, the One and the Indeterminate Dyad. The latter principle was also sometimes called the Infinite. These two principles make their influence felt at all levels of being. The One is furthest from infinity. Aristotle attributes indetermination to primary matter, whereas the First Unmoved Mover is determination in the highest degree. Nevertheless he speaks of an infinite power and duration of this Unmoved Mover[26]. Aristotle denies that there can be a body of infinite size, but Epicurus teaches that both the universe itself and the number of atoms are infinite[27].

Plotinus distinguishes between infinitude in power which characterizes the One[28] and the infinity of matter which is pure indetermination[29]. Noûs and soul are both finite and infinite: infinite when they set out on the journey of return to the One, finite when they reach their goal. The One itself is above determinations. Plotinus' view may have contributed to the rise of Christian speculations on God's infinity[30].

Since Holy Scripture does not explicitly mention divine infinity it is not surprising that the Fathers speak of it with a certain hesitation. St. Gregory of Nazianze calls God an "infinite sea of being"[31]. St. John Damascene notes that infinity transcends any measure one can take. God is infinite inasmuch as he is incomprehensible and eternal. He is infinite in power and is above all created things. We cannot say what is he is, but only what he is not. It appears that Damascene's concept of God's infinity is rather vague and quite different from that of St. Thomas[32]. St. Hilary uses 'infinite' mainly to signify the eter-

---

[24] On the infinite in Greek thought see R. Mondolfo, *L'infinito nel pensiero dell' antichità classica*, Firenze 1956 and L. Sweeney, *Infinity in the Pre-socratics*, The Hague 1972.

[25] I. Avotins, "On Some Epicurean and Lucretian Arguments for the Infinity of the Universe", in *The Class. Quart.* 33 (1983) 421-427.

[26] *Metaph.* 1073 a 7-11.

[27] *Epist. ad Herod.* X 41.

[28] *Enn.* VI 7, 14.

[29] *Enn.* VI 6, 1.

[30] L. Sweeney, "Infinity in Plotinus", in *Gregorianum* 38 (1957) 515-535; 713-732.

[31] *Orat. theol.* 38, 7; 45, 3 (see Damascene, *De fide orth.* 2, 9). For St. Gregory of Nyssa one may compare E. Mühlenberg, *Die Unendlichkeit Gottes bei Gregor von Nyssa*, Göttingen 1966. From Gregory the expression was taken over by St. John Damascene. See L. Sweeney, "John Damascene's 'Infinite Sea of Essence' ", in *Studia Patristica* VI, edit. by F.L. Cross, *Texte und Untersuchungen zur Geschichte der altchristlichen Literatur* 81 (1962) 76-106.

[32] See L. Sweeney, "John Damascene and Divine Infinity, in *The New Scholasticism* 35 (1961) 76-106.

nity of God[33]. With regard to St. Augustine's view we notice that in his earlier years when he was still close to Manicheism, he conceived the world as a huge sponge floating in an infinite sea of divinity, but soon he realised that God cannot be infinite in the way in which a body might be[34]. God is infinite, but not extended in space. Thus St. Augustine began to connect infinity with spirituality.

Until about 1150 the Christian theologians were quite reserved with regard to God's infinity but in the following 150 years a much greater importance began to be attached to this attribute of God. St. Albert used the distinction between infinite by privation and infinite by negation, which he borrowed from John Damascene[35]. According to Albert the Great no created intellect is able to form a determinate notion of the essence or attributes of God. Hence God cannot be circumscribed by the intellect; his being is not contracted to a particular form, genus or species[36].

By this insight St. Albert prepared the way for Aquinas' doctrine of divine infinity. But before we deal with this, it is useful to consider some of the efforts of later theologians to explain God's infinity. Henry of Ghent is the great promotor of a theory of infinity which makes it God's central attribute. Infinity is connected with divine spirituality. Scotus follows him on this point as on so many others. His argument insists on the fact that God is being gifted with intellect and will; his thinking extends to an infinite number of objects. This thinking is God's very essence[37]. Following Scotus later theologians often considered infinity the primary characteristic of God.

A text of the 12th century, the *Liber Hermetis*, calls God an intelligible sphere, the centre of which is everywhere, the circumference nowhere. This formula was used by several authors (Pascal, Giordano Bruno, etc.) and was instrumental in promoting less fortunate views of infinity and even certain forms of pantheism.

In *S.C.G.* I 43 St. Thomas begins his account of the problem with the analysis of spiritual magnitude, which is great by its plenitude and power. In this connection he recalls the distinction between the infinite by privation and the negatively infinite. A magnitude which would be infinite, is deprived of the limitations it otherwise has. Hence we would have to say that it is infinite

---

[33] J.M. Dermott, "Hilary of Poitiers: The Infinite Nature of God", in *Vig. Christ.* 27 (1973) 172-202.

[34] *Conf.* VII 14, 20: "Et evigilavi in te et vidi te infinitum aliter ...". Cf. E. Gilson, "L'infinité divine chez saint Augustin", in *Augustinus Magister* I, Paris 1954, 569-574.

[35] *In I Sent.*, d.1, B, a.15 (Borgnet 25, 37). See also F.J. Catania, "Albert the Great, Boethius and Divine Infinitude", in *RThAM* 28 (1961) 97-114; L. Sweeney, "Divine Infinity", in *The Modern Schoolman* 35 (1957-1958) 38-51.

[36] Catania, *o.c.*, 111-114.

[37] See E. Gilson, *Jean Duns Scot. Introduction à ses positions fondamentales*, Paris 1952, 149ff.

by privation. This type of infinity does not apply to God, in whom there is no privation of anything whatever. God is what he is. If he is infinite, he is so negatively, that is by the absence of any limit. Aquinas then recalls that God's spiritual magnitude is not in a genus, so that it is not limited. He finally offers a different argument which is based on the fact that God is first act without any potency.''

In *S.Th.* I 7, 1 the entire problem is viewed in the light of the theory of act and potency: matter is in a way made finite by form and form by matter inasmuch as form is determined by matter to this particular thing. A form which is not limited by matter is not contracted. Now, as has been shown, being is what is most formal of all things[38]. God is self subsistent being and therefore infinite and perfect. This argument is directly connected with the Third Way which concluded that there must be a Being which has of itself its own necessity to be and which is the cause of the being of other things. The contingence of created things which shows in generation and corruption, requires that the ultimate cause is a being which has the ground of its necessity in itself. It follows that the study of God's infinity comes in under the *via causalitatis.*

St. Thomas' argument is new insofar as it is based on the strict application of the concepts of act and potency and gives a central place to being (*esse*). The idea of infinity means the unlimited realisation of reality and perfection and so it is entirely free from any such spatial, magnitudinal or numerical considerations as Scotus proposes (who deduces divine infinity from the infinite number of intelligibles known by God). Aquinas' treatment of divine infinity is an intellectual accomplishment of the first order.

In the answer to the third objection St. Thomas recalls that God is not one particular thing standing over and against other beings. God cannot be compared with other things but transcends them in his otherness and divine eminence. This reply shows that the Negative Way must act as a corrective to whatever knowledge we acquire of God.

In the second article St. Thomas discusses whether there can be infinity in created things. A relative infinity is possible: matter has a certain infinity in its capacity to receive new forms. Furthermore, a form not received in matter has a relative infinity. In the third article infinite magnitude is excluded as is in the fourth an actually existing infinite number. The conclusion of the fourth article of the question gives rise to some difficulties when we compare it to certain statements in other works of Aquinas, but a discussion of the subject does not properly belong to philosophical theology.

In modern philosophy God's infinity continued at first to be affirmed. For Descartes infinity is God's essential characteristic. According to Spinoza every

---

[38] I, 4, 1.

substance is necessarily infinite (there is only one monistic substance). He holds that we have an adequate idea of infinity, but does not explain how we acquire it[39]. Kant made an important innovation by arguing that the cosmological proof only leads to the conclusion that there is a limited being who is the architect of the world[40]. As one would expect, in Hegel's dialectical idealism God is at the same time finite and infinite[41].

In the second half of the nineteenth century a tendency appeared in England and in the United States to overcome deism and to tie God more intimately to man and to the universe by presenting him as a finite being. This so-called finitism is perhaps also a reaction against the theory which conceived God as infinite homogeneous space (Henry More) or as possessing infinite spiritual extension. Thus J. Stuart Mill argues that God's power is finite because his design is often baffled[42]. William James likewise holds that God cannot be omnipotent but must be finite: man can more readily consider himself a collaborator of God when he conceives God as a finite being which is also developing further[43]. Similar views are found in the works of S. Alexander[44] and A. N. Whitehead[45]. According to Alexander deity is just a degree above the human mind and as the world grows, God grows with it.

Some theologians now seem to prefer the concept of God as a finite being to the transcendent God of Semitic-Christian tradition. For instance, John Cobb thinks that a finite God makes the best companion to man in his advance toward perfection[46]. But considered in the light of St. Thomas' metaphysics these views are the result of a mistaken concept of infinity and of less than philosophical thinking. They do away with God's transcendence and so with God himself[47].

IV. *The Existence of God in Things (I 8)*

In Aquinas' view the study of God's infinity should be followed by that of his existence in things. He sees this connection between the two themes: "Since it evidently belongs to the infinite to be present everywhere and in all things, we now consider whether this belongs to God". As we shall see, it is

---

[39] See *Ethica*, Def. 6 and propositio 8.
[40] *Kritik der reinen Vernunft* B650/A622.
[41] *Enzykl.* § 386 Zusatz.
[42] *Three Essays on Religion*, London 1874, 37-38.
[43] *The Will to Believe* (Dover Edit., 141); *A Pluralistic Universe*, (1909) 124ff.
[44] *Space, Time and Deity* II 347.
[45] *Religion in the Making* (New York 1926,) 71.
[46] See his *A Christian Natural Theology*, Philadelphia 1965.
[47] On finitism see Thomas McTighe and Lottie H. Kendziersky, "The Finite God in Contemporary Philosophy", in *Proceed. Amer. Cath. Philos. Assoc.* 28 (1954) 212-236; Vernon J. Bourke, "Recent Approaches to a Finite God", in *De Deo ...* I, 165-168.

not spatial magnitude which is the ground for God's omnipresence but his being the source of all existence. In this way God's presence in things prolongates God's infinity, that is, the unlimited plenitude of his subsistent being.

Before examining St. Thomas' arguments we must first analyse the concept of 'presence'[48]. Some consider presence a relation, viz. the togetherness of two substances, accompanied by some form of communication. A relation, however, requires a foundation[49]. Presence requires contact which can be contact of magnitude or ontological contact[50].

God's presence can only be based upon the ontological contact of causality. God is, indeed, causally working in things, since their being participates in God's being, that is, is continuously coming forth from God and supported by him. "God causes this effect (being) in things, not only when they first begin to exist, but as long as they are preserved in being, as light is caused in the air by the sun as long as the air remains illuminated"[51]. St. Thomas adds that this presence of God is most intimate, for being (*esse*) is innermost in each thing since it is formal in respect of everything found in a thing[52]. God is present in the deepest core of created being. One may therefore conclude that created things are in direct contact with God's reality, a contact so intimate and fundamental that it surpasses any type of contact between things in the physical universe[53]. At this point St. Thomas rejoins the theological and mystical tradition which holds that God is most intimately present in the deepest recesses of our being. St. Augustine even called God "the life of my life" and felt that he is "more interior than my own innermost"[54]. On the other hand, as Gilson pointedly remarks, Aristotle's First Mover is not only separate from the cosmos, he is also ontologically absent from it[55]. This presence of God is not contrary to his transcendence as the author of the *De mundo* thought[56]. Furthermore, his presence does not absorb things as

---

[48] We follow H. Stirnimann, "Zum Begriff der Gegenwart", in *Divus Thomas* (Freib.) 29 (1951) 65-80.

[49] In *In I Sent.*, d.14, q.2, a.1, sol. 1 and 2 Aquinas expresses presence in terms of a relationship. Ferrariensis developed this view (*In III S.C.G.*, c.68, I 3; XXII, 2).

[50] This seems to be the doctrine of Cajetanus, *In I^am*, q.8, a.1, n.VIII: "Coniunctio Dei cum rebus potest sumi dupliciter: uno modo pro ipso contactu quo Deus ipse rem per seipsum tangit. Alio modo pro relatione praesentiae qua, denominatione relativa, dicitur praesens secundum se alicui". This relation is consequent upon contact and is real only in created things. Cf. *In I Sent.*, d.14, q.2, a.1, sol. 1 ad 1: "... quae quiden realiter non est in ipso, sed in creatura".

[51] I 8, 1. The comparison of God's Presence sustaining things in being with the sun which illuminates the air is used by John Scot Eriugena (*De divisione naturae* I 10: PL 122, 450f.) who borrowed it from Maximus Confessor. In I 104, 1 St. Thomas refers to St. Augustine, *De Gen. ad litt.* 8, 12. See also *Q.d. de pot.* 3, 3 ad 6.

[52] Cf. I 7, 1.

[53] Joannes a Sancto Thoma, *Cursus theol., In I^am*, q.8, disp. 8, a.3, n.11.

[54] *Conf.* VII 1, 2 and III 6, 11 ("interior intimo meo et superior summo meo"). See also St. Teresa of Avila, *Las moradas (Castillo interior del alma)*.

[55] *Le thomisme*[6], 118.

[56] Ps. Aristotles, *De mundo* 6, 397 b 24-27.

John Scot Eriugena seemed to hold[57]. "God is above all things by the excellence of his nature; nevertheless he is in all things as the cause of the being (*esse*) of all things"[58].

St. Thomas' doctrine of God's existence in things is a transposition of Plato's theory of participation to the level of his own philosophy of being. It admirably keeps the middle between divergent and often opposing views, bringing into a synthesis God's transcendence and immanence.

Later Scholastics did not always understand it well. According to Scotus activity in a place already presupposes presence. Suarez follows him trying to deduce God's omnipresence from his immensity[59]. As Stirnimann observes, for us activity in a place requires that we are present there. With regard to God, however, we must say that his very activity is the cause why there are things in which he is present[60]. In this way God's action and presence sustain and contain created things[61].

In his reply to the second and third objections St. Thomas adds some observations taken from negative theology: God's presence in the innermost of things is at the same time a presence which contains these things; there is no distance between created things and God inasmuch as God gives being without using any intermediary. Yet he is above all things by the excellence of his nature. Finally Aquinas observes that God is not present in the deformity which is sin, because sin is a privation and a lack of being.

In the remaining articles of this question St. Thomas further explains the manner in which God is present and in doing so he solves a number of difficulties. A first problem is whether God as an immaterial being can be present in a place. In his *De hebdomadibus* Boethius asserts that incoporeal things are not in a place. A further difficulty is that a thing in a place is contained in that place and cannot be elsewhere without losing its coherence and unity, so that it would seem that God cannot be present everywhere in the physical universe. In his solution St. Thomas points out that place is a thing (*res quaedam*). Therefore God, who gives being to all things, is also in each place as the cause of its reality and of its locative power. The accidental being which is place is the determination accruing to a body by reason of its belonging to the physical universe; it is given with its distance from other bodies[62].

We must also say that God fills every place inasmuch as he gives being to

---

[57] *De div. nat.* II 2: *PL* 122, 528 AB.

[58] I. 8, 1 ad 1. Cf. Cajetanus, *In I^{am}*, 8, 4: "Nihil potest esse sine Deo in eo".

[59] *Disp. metaph.*, disp. 30, sectio 7, nn. 18-19; 32; 49. Scotus refuses to admit that the *esse* in the proper effect of God: if fire produces fire, it produces a particular thing. The deepest meaning of being is to be a particular thing. Cf. *Reportata parisiensia* (Wadding XI) I, d.37, q.2, n.3. For St. Thomas, on the other hand, the basic meaning of *esse* is to be real.

[60] *L.c.*, 73ff.

[61] I 8, 1 ad 2.

[62] For St. Thomas' theory of place see his *Commentary on the Physics IV*, c.4.

the bodies which occupy place. The difficulties raised against God's presence in place are solved when we keep in mind that incorporeal things are in a place not by means of contact of dimensive quantity but by the contact of their power. Furthermore, God is indivisible not in the manner of continuous quantity or a continuous successive duration. He is outside the whole class of continuous things and is indivisible by his own inner coherence, concentration of being and unity. His power nevertheless extends to all things and so God is whole in every place and in every part of it, as the soul is whole in every part of the body. The objections and the answers serve the purpose of bringing out what is proper to God's presence and correcting a materialistic understanding of it.

In mediaeval theological tradition[63] God was said to be everywhere by his essence, presence and power. These three modes are not separtate ways of presence but aspects or moments of God's indivisible reality. "God is in all things by his power inasmuch as all things are subject to his power; he is by his presence in all things as all things are bare and open to his eyes; he is in all things by his essence inasmuch as he is present to all as the cause of their being". St. Thomas completes this traditional division by pointing out that there is another way of presence, viz. that of a thing known in the one who knows it and the object loved in the rational creature who loves.

Having demonstrated God's ontological presence in created things as the ground of their being Aquinas adds that there is no direct contact with God in knowledge and love. Only grace, that is God giving himself to man, makes God to be present in this way[64]. Once more we notice that St. Thomas' philosophical theology does not give man any possession of God.

There is a noticeable difference between St. Thomas' doctrine here and Ockham's view. Ockham asserts that the presence of an object is possible without its existing outside us[65]. Apparently the presence of something is reduced to man's experience of it. In Thomism a distinction is made: we can represent a thing in our imagination or intellect even when it is not present, but this is not the presence of a thing, but only of an image.

In the fourth article of this question Aquinas argues that God is everywhere in an absolute sense and that this belongs to God alone, for nothing can exist except by God's causality; God is present not by a part of his being but by his very self.

---

[63] Cf. *In I Sent.*, d.37, q.1, a.2, Sed contra est "Quod in littera dicitur et auctoritatibus confirmatur". For St. Thomas the division is complementary for a better understanding but not essential. Alexander of Hales and St. Bonaventure attach more importance to it. The latter explains the *potentialiter, praesentialiter* and *essentialiter* with the help of the Neoplatonic scheme of *exitus, reditus, unio.* See Quar. I 648. The editors refer to St. Anselm, *De fide Trin.*, c.4 and to Richard of St. Victor, *De Trin.* II, c.23.

[64] I 8, 3 ad 4.

[65] *Ordinato*, prol. q.1 (edit. SB I 5-6; A.L. González, "Intuición y escepticismo en Ockham", in *Anuario filosófico* 10 (1977) 105-129.

CHAPTER SIX

THE *VIA EMINENTIAE*

After the discussion of God's infinity and existence in things St. Thomas quite abruptly introduces the following two questions: "We must next consider God's immutability and his eternity following on his immutability".

I. *The Immutability of God (I 9)*

It has nowadays almost become the fashion to point out that the Bible does not know the term 'immutable' except in this sense that God is always faithful[1]. Inspired by some texts of Luther certain Protestant theologians developed a theology centered on *kenosis*: in the Incarnation God deprived himself of his divinity and ceased to be God. This way of thinking influenced Hegel who reformulated this *Kenosis* as a stage in a process of evolutionistic monism. God is negated and becomes (or yields his place to) the Spirit, conscious of itself, in the mind of the philosopher[2]. Hegel admits, indeed, an evolution in the Absolute Idea which unfolds itself in time to return again to itself. All constituent parts of reality are intrinsically connected with one another and relative to this dialectical process. God is the entire totality.

H. Bergson considers God a "duration in movement"; God has nothing finished[3]. The thesis of God's mutability found even stronger supporters in the partisans of the so-called process-theology. God is infinitely actual but he can nevertheless be enriched. According to classical logic it is impossible to be infinitely actual and to become more complete at the same time, but this logic is one-sided. In A. N. Whitehead's view the ultimate metaphysical principle is "the creative advance into novelty"[4]. Within this process-theology further developments took place. In particular Charles Hartshorne's brand of it is now widespread in the United States[5]. According to Hartshorne God is

---

[1] W. Pannenberg, *Was ist der Mensch?*, Göttingen 1961, 54.

[2] See *Enzykl.* § 36 and P. Henry, "Kénose", in *Supplément du Dictionnaire de la Bible*, fasc. 24, 7-161.

[3] *Evolution créatrice*, 270.

[4] *Proces and Reality*, 59. In Whitehead's philosophy not God but this creative advance is the Ultimate Principle. See A. Cloots, "De vraag naar het ultieme in de Process-filosofie", in *Tijdschrift voor Filosofie* 42 (1980) 48-73. See also L. Gillon, "Dieu immobile et Dieu en mouvement", in *Doctor communis* 1976, 135.

[5] Ch. Hartshorne, *A Natural Theology for Our Time*, La Salle Ill. 1967. See also E.E. Creel, *Divine Impassibility*, Cambridge 1985. According to Creel we should distinguish between four aspects of passibility in God in process theology: nature, will, knowledge, feeling.

co-constituted by the universe. He is not so much the universal *agens* as the universal and the all comprising *locus*. Without the world God is not God. On a more popular level it is argued that God, being a person, cannot lack emotional response, receptiveness and femaleness. He is bound to change with the spirit of each respective age of history.

A somewhat related view is found in Teilhard de Chardin's work: God only exists by unifying himself. He is the ultimate unity of cosmic stuff[6].

Given the wide response these views have found it is perhaps useful to consider the question of God's immutability in the history of philosophy. While the Ionians assumed ceaseless change of one underlying principle, Parmenides asserted a total immutability of Being: since being is already being, it cannot acquire anything real. Plato called goodness and immutability the main characteristics of God: God cannot be moved from the outside, because the more perfect something is the less it is moved by agents outside itself. Likewise it is not moved by itself for it lacks nothing and nobody makes himself willingly worse. Hence "every God remains simply and forever in his own form"[7]. Plato also attributes immutability to the ideas which always have their being in the same way[8]. Immutability goes together with the absence of composition and parts.

Aristotle's First Unmoved Mover is likewise an eternal, immutable and indivisible substance[9]. While Plato based his argument in favour of immutability on perfection and simplicity, Aristotle bases his on the absence of potentiality. He even writes that the science of theology has unmoved, separately existing substances as its subject matter[10]. The immutability of God is affirmed by Plutarchus, Albinus and Numenius[11]. Philo of Alexandria wrote a treatise on the topic[12] observing that Biblical texts which seem to admit changes in God must be understood metaphorically[13].

The early Christian authors and the Church Fathers all affirm God's immutability with great vigour[14]. Origenes even argues against Celsus that God's immutability is a fundamental part of the Christian doctrine of God[15]. St. Cyrillus of Jerusalem teaches it in his catechetical courses[16]. St. Augustine at first considered immutability the primary characteristic of God: all things

---

[6] "Esquisse d'un univers personnel", in *Oeuvres* VI, 88-209.
[7] *Rep.* 380c-381c. A similar argument is found in Aristotle, *De philosophia*, fr. 16 R.
[8] *Phaedo* 78c (cf. *Symp.* 211b; *Soph.* 248a).
[9] *Metaph.* 1073 a 4. Cf. *De caelo* 279 a 18ff.: that which is outside the first heaven is necessarily immutable. See also Simplicius, *In De caelo* 288, 30.
[10] *Metaph.* 1026 a 10ff.
[11] See respectively *De E apud Delphos* 392 a 18ff; *Didask.* 164, 22 (Hermann); fr. 17 Leemans.
[12] *Quod Deus sit immutabilis*.
[13] *Ibidem, passim.*
[14] Aristides, *Apol.* 4; Justinus, *I Apol.* 13, 4.
[15] *Contra Celsum* 1, 21. See also Clemens Alex., *Strom.* I 163, 6.
[16] *Orat. cat.* 4, 4.

change; only that which remains unchanged, truly is [17]. In his later works however, he makes immutability dependent on God's being [18]. According to St. Augustine the notion of a God whose essence is immutability, because he is, gives access to a dialectic of time and of eternity. It concerns man himself whose existence is carried away by the flux of time, gnawed away from the inside by its lack of being and who seeks to escape from the predicament by passionately cleaving to the *Ego sum et non mutor* (*Malach.* 3, 6). The words of St. Augustine are engraved in the memory of us all: "Quando solidabor in te?"[19].

This idea of God's immutability kept its central place in Christian tradition. Boethius expressed it in his rhyme "... stabilisque manens dat cuncta moveri"[20]. St. Bonaventure affirmed divine immutability and the Fourth Council of the Lateran defined it as of faith, as did the First Vatican Council. It is not a Greek idea alien to Christian revelation, but it is a consequence implied by God's perfection and transcendence [21].

St. Thomas demonstrates God's total immutability by three arguments: (a) What changes is in some way in potentiality. But God is pure act without the admixture of any potentiality. (b) Everything which changes remains partly as it was, and partly passes away. But in God there is no composition and hence he cannot change. (c) Change seeks to acquire something. But God is infinite, comprehending in himself the plenitude of the perfections of all things. Hence he cannot acquire anything new.

In his reply to the first objections St. Thomas intimates that this immutability is not the immobility of a crystal: God is full of intellectual life and love. His immutability transcends our capacity for understanding. God is life in an infinitely eminent way. The question of God's immutability belongs to the Way of Eminence.

The Second Article examines whether immutability belongs to God alone. It is a masterful survey of the various ways in which created things are changeable [22]: (a) All things outside God share in God's being as the Third Way has shown. Their continued existence depends on God and so they are mutable by the power of another. (b) All things are also mutable by a power

---

[17] *Conf.* VII 11, 27: "Id enim vere est quod incommutabiliter manet". Cf. *De civ. Dei* VII 6, 1; *De div. quaest.* 73, 2. Mutability is a characteristic of what has been created. See A. Trapé, "S. Agostino, dal mutabile all' immutabile o la filosofia dell'*Ipsum esse*", in aa. vv., *Cinquant'anni di Magistero teologico. Scritti in onore di Mons. Antonio Piolanti*, Città del Vaticano 1985, 46-58.

[18] *De civ. Dei* XII 2: "Cum Deus summe sit et ideo immutabilis".

[19] See E. Gilson, *Introduction à la philosophie chrétienne*, Paris 1960, 92.

[20] *De consol. philos.* III 9. For St. Bonaventure see *In I Sent.*, d.8, 1, a.2, 1.1.

[21] The opinion to the contrary of W. Maas, *Unveränderlichkeit Gottes*, Paderborn-Wien 1974, is inadmissible.

[22] In this article St. Thomas uses conclusions he has demonstrated elsewhere.

In themselves, which is active or passive. Passive mutability can be with regard to being (incorruptible things do not have this mutability) and with regard to accidental perfections. Furthermore, some creatures can apply their active powers to diverse objects. God is in none of these ways mutable and so he alone is immutable[23].

In a Platonic and Avicennean view forms, being forever their own formal contents, are immutable. However, in his reply to the fourth objection Aquinas recalls that forms are not beings themselves but factors through which a mutable subject is a certain being.

II. *The Eternity of God (I 10)*

In virtue of its immutability God's being is alien to "having been" and "will be", whereas created being is characterized by a certain mixture with "having been" or "going to be"[24]. Thus the study of God's immutability takes us to that of his eternity. The insight that there is a Being outside time, which does not have any succession in its duration but only togetherness and simultaneity, is one of the greatest discoveries of man. The question of God's eternity, therefore, stresses the all-surpassing eminence of God's being. Parmenides is the first philosopher to attribute everlasting changeless duration to real being[25]. Plato also teaches that eternity is the ever present concentration of being in one moment without past or future[26]. Neoplatonic philosophers continue to teach this "remaining in an eternal *now*"[27]. Plato uses the term αἰών in the sense of timeless eternity and ascribes life to it. He is followed by Aristotle in *De caelo* I 9 and in *Metaphysics* XII 7. Αἰών denotes being always alive outside the flow of time[28].

---

[23] On the question whether all movement is to be excluded from the world of ideas Plato is not so clear. He feels that it would be absurd to remove from it life, knowledge and love. Some process theologians (Ch. Hartshorne and Leonard J. Eslich) capitalized on this and depicted Plato as a "Dipolar Theist". The solution of the problem obviously lies in the transcendent eminence of God. For the interpretation of Plato see A. Diès, *La définition de l'être et la nature des idées dans le Sophiste de Platon*, Paris 1932, 39-63: "Le mouvement de l'οὐσία".

[24] *De ver.* 21, 4 ad 7.

[25] *Fragm. der Vorsokratiker*, B 8, 5. The term αἰών is rich in meaning: in Homer it signifies vitality, living stuff and its persistency, span of life. It is not very clear how it acquired the sense of a certain period of time which it has in Pindar. See A.J. Festugière, in *La parola del passato* 9 (1948) 173ff.; E. Degani, *ΑΙΩΝ da Omero ad Aristotele*, Padova 1961; W. von Leyden, "Time, Number and Eternity in Plato and Aristotle", in *The Philos. Quart.* 14 (1964) 35-42.

[26] *Tim.* 37d.

[27] See Plotinus, *Enn.* 3, 7, 35 and Proclus, *In Platonis Timaeum* 28bc (Diehl I 291, 8): πάντα ἐν τῷ νυν. See also IV 33 where Proclus quotes Jamblichus (ἤδη ὄν and ὁμοῦ πᾶν), *l.c.*, 14, 16ff. on the unification of eternity. See also *Elem. theol.*, prop. 52. However, for Proclus eternity is not an attribute of the One (the One is above all attributes) but its creative power (*In Tim.* III 14, 16).

[28] *Metaph.* 1072 b 26ff.

St. Thomas begins his account with Boethius' definition of eternity: "Eternity is the simultaneously-whole and perfect possession of interminable life". Analysing the meaning of the terms Aquinas defines more precisely the concept of eternity[29]. A first observation he makes is that we must acquire knowledge of simple things by way of compound things and so we must obtain knowledge of eternity by means of time. Time, which is the numbering of movement by before and after, is marked by succession. In a thing bereft of movement, which is always the same, there is no before and after. From the apprehension of such a being results the idea of eternity. St. Thomas adds a further argument: what is wholly immutable has no succession and so it has no beginning and no end. It is eternal.

Summing up: we must signify what eternity is by means of two essential characteristics. What is eternal is without beginning and end; it has no succession but is in its entirety simultaneous. In the replies to the objections certain points are made clearer: with "life" in the definition of eternity is meant the highest form of being. What is eternal is 'whole' because it is wanting in nothing and it is perfect because it has its own eternal 'now' so that it exists entirely within itself.

In the second article Aquinas further explains the characteristics of God's eternity: God alone is his being (*esse*). This means that he is his own duration and so he is his own eternity. The concluding section of this article discloses a being wholly foreign to our experience, viz. which is its own duration and which is in a 'now' or, rather, which is a 'now' which does not flow along in succession but is in its entirety actualized and present. To denote this we use the terms "nunc stans" (the now that stands still)[30]. That in this question we are proceeding along the *via eminentiae* is also apparent from the twice repeated "according to our apprehension", in the reply to the first and the third objection. We must start from our experience of time to proceed to the idea of eternity, but the eternity of God is far beyond our understanding and surpasses whatever we can conceive.

In the remaining articles of this question time is compared to eternity and to the duration of spiritual beings.

With the decline of metaphysics the proper concept of eternity was lost. 'Eternal' was now understood as being without beginning and end[31], whereas

---

[29] *De consol. philos.* V, prose 6.

[30] Plato had already pointed out that eternity is the always present and permanent concentration of being in one moment without past or future (*Tim.* 37 d). Plotinus and Proclus subscribed to this view (*Enn.* 3, 7, 35; *In Plat. Tim.* I, 291, 8 Diehl). Boethius uses the expression 'nunc permanens' (*De consol. philos.* V 6, 4). St. Albert the Great speaks of a 'simplex mora nunc stans' (*Summa de creaturis* I , tr. II, q.3, art. 2: Borgnet 34, 341). On this term see H. Schnarr in *Hist. Wörterb. d. Phil.* VI 981-991.

[31] See Thomas Hobbes, *Leviathan* IV 46.

this absence of beginning and end is not the main characteristic of eternity[32]. Eternal is that which is entirely simultaneous and together. When one loses the eminence of God's being and eternity out of sight, one risks thinking with Paul Tillich that "if we call God a living God, we affirm that he includes temporality"[33].

III. *Unity of God (I 11)*

To conclude his series of questions on how God is or, rather, is not Aquinas treats the theme of God's unity. The unity of God is a basic truth of Biblical revelation but outside the monotheism of Israel and Christianity this unity was far from being clearly perceived or fully acknowledged by philosophers. In a sense it is surprising that God's unity is treated as the last of the entitative attributes. One of the reasons for this particular position might be that this unity was only acknowledged with great difficulty, if at all, by the philosophers. St. Thomas himself sometimes mentions the question of God's unity as being more important than the study of the other attributes[33a]. Even if it can be demonstrated by reason , the fact that God alone is to be adored is a conclusion philosophers did not in fact reach[33b]. The question of God's unity is a fitting conclusion to the treatise of God's being and prepares the way for the study of the mystery of Holy Trinity.

The search for unity had marked Greek philosophy from its very beginnings. The earlier cosmologists attempted to find one *arche* (principle and common material) from which all beings come forth. Heraclitus believed he had discovered that the many contrary things are really one. For Parmenides there exists only one corporeal reality. The world of change and multiplicity is not real. Parmenides' monism dominated the Greek philosophical scene for more than a century.

Plato upheld the unity of the world[34]. Moreover he established a theory according to which all of reality and even the ideas originated from two first principles, the One and the Indefinite Dyad. When Plato adopted the term 'one' as a primary philosophical concept, it had a dual meaning: it denoted the smallest point or unit but also the whole of reality; it was a measure but

---

[32] I 10, 5: "sed haec differentia est per accidens"; 10, 4: "sed tamen istae differentiae consequuntur eam quae est per se et primo differentia, per hoc quod aeternitas est tota simul, non autem tempus".

[33] See his *Systematic Theology*, London 1978, I 305. Cf. also K. Barth, *Church Dogmatics* II (transl. by G.W. Bromiley and T.F. Torrance, 1956, 620): "Without God's complete temporality the content of the Christian message has no shape".

[33a] *Expos. in Boetii De Trinitate*, q.2, a.3: "... ea quae naturalibus rationibus de Deo probantur ut Deum esse, Deum esse unum".

[33b] *I-II* 1, 8 ad 1. See also *Comp. Theol.* I, cap. ult.

[34] cf. H. Diels, *Doxographi Graeci*, Berlin 1929, 291 a 19ff.

also signified a plentitude[35]. As the supreme principle the One is (a) the element and essence of everything[36]; (b) it is a measure not unlike the 'Limit' in the *Philebus*[37]; (c) it must be identified with the supreme Good of the *Republic*[38].

In his treatise on the First Unmoved Mover Aristotle quotes the words of Homer that the government of the universe must be in the hands of one[39]. Nevertheless in some texts Aristotle asserts that there is a plurality of unmoved movers[40]. This discrepancy places the interpreter of Aristotle's theology before considerable difficulties.

In Neoplatonism the ineffable supreme principle is called the One. The reason for this name is likely to be partly historcal and partly metaphysical: the one is not divisible and is not further to be determined but determines other things[41]. Unity precedes multiplicity and all multiplicity must be reduced to unity. More important in this philosophy of the One may have been a latent choice in favour of monism: unity is the source of all perfection and development takes place within the very origin of things. In Neoplatonism the One is before (πρό) and above (ὑπέρ) being. What is correct in this view is that in order to be, something has to have unity and that unity is also the principle of knowledge[42].

St. Augustine teaches that since God is one, Being in its highest form is unity[43]. Nevertheless, he always substitutes Trinity for the Platonic supreme principle, the One, and he also passes from the neuter (*unum*) to the masculine form (*unus*)[44]. Dionysius considers divine unity a primary and absolute value and calls God super-one and super-unity[45]. He stresses unity in God so much that it is not always clear how much room there is left for the Christian doctrine of divine Trinity[46]. The influence of Dionysius made itself felt in the

---

[35] Theon of Smyrna mentions two different conceptions of the nature of the One held by the Pythagoreans: (a) it is the first odd number; (b) it embraces both the odd and the even numbers (21, 20 Hiller). This latter view may have led to later theories of the all-embracing power of the One. See also H.J. Krämer, *Der Ursprung der Geistmetaphysik*, Amsterdam, 1964, 363.

[36] *Metaph.* 1080 b 6; 1084 b 18; 987 b 22; 988 b 2; 1001 a 11.

[37] *Metaph.*1072 a 33; 1090 b 5; *Polit.* 1257 b 23.

[38] Aristoxenus, *Harm. Elem.* II, 30 (Meibom); *Metaph.* 1091 b 14; *Ethica Eud.* 1218 a 30. See E. R. Dodds, "The *Parmenides* of Plato and the Origin of the Neoplatonic 'One' ", in *Class. Quart.* 1928, 1ff.

[39] *Metaph.* 1076 a 3 (*Iliad* II 204).

[40] *Metaph.* XII, ch. 8; *Phys.* VIII, ch. 6. See L. Elders, *Aristotle's Theology*, 57-68.

[41] See J. Trouillard, *La mystagogie de Proclos*, Paris 1982, 84.

[42] See volume I, chapter four.

[43] *De mor. manich.* II 6, 8.

[44] Cf. *Conf.* X, cc. 10ff; *De vera relig.*, chapters 29-36.

[45] *De div. nom.*, c. 2, 11; c. 13.

[46] See J. Koch, "Augustinischer und dionysischer Neuplatonismus und das Mittelalter", in *Kantstudien* 48 (1956/1957) 117-133, 126f.; O. Semmelroth, "Gottes überwesentliche Einheit. Zur Gotteslehre des Ps.-Dionysius Areopagita", in *Scholastik* 25 (1950) 209-234.

Middle Ages. For Thierry of Chartres God's unity is the absolutely primary attribute. It is presupposed by all other properties, for unity is that by which all other forms have their being[47].

Over and against this Neoplatonic tradition St. Thomas affirms the priority of being over unity. Being is first to enter the intellect. To being all other concepts are reduced. Unity does not add something positive to being, but only the negation of division[48]. Aquinas demonstrates God's unity by means of three arguments:

(a) That which makes a man or a thing *this particular man* or *thing* is communicable only to one. "If Socrates were a man by what makes him to be this particular man, as there cannot be many Socrateses, so there could not in that way be many men. Now this applies to God alone: for God himself is his own nature as was shown above[49]. Therefore in the very same way God is God and this God. It is impossible therefore that there should be many Gods".

This profound and beautiful argument is found in a more rudimentary form in Aristotle's *Metaphysics*[50]. St. Thomas shows that multiplication simply does not apply to God, because he is of a different order and above division and multiplicity (We are following the *via eminentiae*!). But Aquinas also very subtly suggests here that God is a person, an 'individual' in a unique sense of the term, because his nature (essence) is his incommunicable self. This also gives a positive content to what as such is a negative term (unity is the denial of division).

Against this argument it is objected that unity or plurality only belongs to concepts. What exists is always itself and unique. To speak of unity or multiplicity is to make only a "second order" assertion[51]. This Nominalist position, however, is not correct. Every being does possess a certain unity and beings do not constitute a sheer plurality of unrelated individuals, but they exist in a real specific and generic community, as common experience shows and as is confirmed by the fact that living and inanimate beings alike show the same sharply marked and constant set of characteristics in various individuals belonging to the same species. This occurrence of fixed characteristics requires a cause. However, such a community does not and cannot occur in God, because in him his 'nature' is absorbed by his unicity and individuality.

---

[47] Koch, *o.c.*, 130ff.

[48] I 11, 1. For a discussion of the contents of the first two articles of question 11 see volume I, chapter 4.

[49] I 3, 3.

[50] *Metaph.* XII 8, 1074 a 31-38: there is only one heaven. If there were more, their formal Principle (the First Mover) would have to be many. But this is not possible because there is no matter in God and hence no possibility of multiplication. See Aquinas, *In XII Metaph.*, 1.10, n.2596.

[51] See G. Frege, *Grundlagen der Arithmetik* IV, § 46.

(b) God comprehends in himself the whole perfection of being. If many Gods existed, they would differ and one of them would not have something proper to the other. In that case God would not have the whole perfection of being. This argument is already used by Parmenides who excludes multiplicity in being: being is being and cannot be different from another being because a real difference would also be being.—This second argument recalls the all-surpassing plenitude and perfection of God.

(c) The third argument is based on the contemplation of the unity of the world. In the universe things are ordered to one another. They would not have this order unless some one being is the *per se* cause of it. The unity of a design in which many components are involved, cannot consistently be explained by many different agents, but must have a cause *per se* which is one. The argument partly coincides with the Fifth Way and is based on an insight proper to the metaphysics of common sense. Some have objected that the existence of more worlds is possible, each of which would have its own god[52], but entirely unrelated worlds are unthinkable. Where there is a relation, a supreme Mind must bring about this order.

In his reply to two objections Aquinas notes that it is true that people some-times use the plural 'gods', but this is an error. They have not sufficiently realised how much God is above everything[53]. The name 'God' is itself not communicable. It is so only in the opinion of those who have not understood the transcendent greatness and otherness of God.

The answer to the second objection is important. It is a rebuttal of the Neoplatonic identification of the numerical one with the one as a transcendental property of being[54]. Aquinas apparently felt that the Neoplatonic insistence on participation in the One was contaminated by a certain confusion with the function of 'one' as a number. St. Thomas also refrains from assigning an active role to the One as Dionysius did. The last lines of the text recall how limited our knowledge of God is: we must use negative terms such as infinite, incorporeal and one to determine God's being.

Unity means being undivided. In order to be one in the highest degree a thing must be being in the highest degree as well as undivided. Both conditions obtain in the case of God for he is subsistent being itself and supremely undivided. God's unity is given with his subsistent being, which surpasses infinitely whatever being there is in our world.

Spinoza questioned the value of the affirmation of God's unity. He holds that we can only call God one in an improper sense, viz. after we conceive

[52] This is the argument of Crescas against Aristotle. See H.A. Wolfson, *Crescas' Critique of Aristotle*, Cambridge Mass. 1929, 217. 472ff.

[53] In *S.C.G.* I 42 Aquinas notes that even when people admit a plurality of gods, they often posit one supreme god as the master of the others.

[54] He comes back to it in I 11, 4 ad 2.

something else to compare with God. But then we already start with the assumption that there is plurality[55]. To this we may reply that the proofs of St. Thomas are wholly different: far from submitting God to a class or comparing him to others, we discover that God is his own being and cannot but be one. One may so far agree with Spinoza that a plurality perceived by the senses is prior to our concept of unity, but this concept precedes that of multiplicity. Spinoza conceives unity too much in terms of the one as a number, which as such is a unit in a series.

When contemporary philosophers speak of the problem of God, they generally think along the lines of Christian monotheism. An exception is William James who presented his own theology as a pluralistic finitism[56]. As St. Thomas' arguments intimate, unity is absolutely prior to multiplicity and composition, although for the senses multiplicity is more accessible than unity[57]. However, from the point of view of a certain materialism the multiplicity of matter comes first and the unity of the 'spirit' is the term of all process in the world[58].

IV. *The Order of the Attributes in the Treatise on How God is not*

Having arrived at the end of the study of how God is not, we are now in a position to see what is peculiar to St. Thomas' treatise of 'divine attributes': the attributes are not determinations added to God's substance in the manner of the attributes mentioned by Spinoza. The treatise serves the purpose of showing somewhat better *how* God is or, rather, how he is not. A first step in this study is predominantly negative: we successively deny all forms of composition in God's being. In the second place we consider the implications of the fact that he is the cause of all things: he is omni-perfect and infinite in his being (and this implies that he is good and exists in things). Reflecting further on God's being we notice that he transcends whatever being we know because he is above all process and change in total immutability and in the simultaneity and togetherness of his eternal 'now'. His divine nature is identical with his self so that God is unique.

When we conceive the attributes in this way, we understand better why Aquinas chose among the many names of God these eight attributes. Considered together they help us understand somewhat the all surpassing uni-

---

[55] *Cogit. metaph.* I, c.6: "Deum nonnisi improprie unum et unicum vocari". S. Breton surprisingly declares his agreement with this view in *Unicité et monothéisme*, Paris 1981, 86. A philosophical affirmation of God's unity, he argues, is only possible if we subject God to the straitjacket of a logical class which alone can have number.

[56] *A Pluralistic Universe*, New York 1909, 25ff.

[57] See volume I, ch. 4 and ch. 11 (third argument).

[58] See P. Teilhard de Chardin, "Centrologie", in *Oeuvres* VII, 131.

queness and eminence of God's being. These so-called attributes are no
determination of God's being but the negation of the characteristics of created
being and of a human way of thinking. For this reason the treatise on God's
entitative attributes places us before the transcendent mystery of God's
greatness.

The order of the attributes in the *S. Th.* is quite different from that in the
S.C.G. In the latter work St. Thomas first gives four arguments for God's
existence and then points out that in order to proceed in our inquiry about
God along the *Via Negativa* we must accept as our starting point that God is
entirely immutable[59]. God's immutability is not especially treated and the first
attribute to be examined is eternity[60]. Chapters 16 to 27 study the different
aspects of God's simplicity (the order of the themes is not quite the same as
that of the *S. Th.*). After these chapters Aquinas considers God's perfection
and subsequently offers seven chapters on our way of speaking about God.
He then returns to the study of other attributes: goodness, unity and
infinity[61]. The different order of themes to be studied in the *S. Th.* was
deliberately chosen as the short introductions to each question indicate. This
order is as follows:

simplicity	*via remotionis*
perfection, upon which goodness is consequent infinity, upon which existence in things is consequent }	*via causalitatis*
immutability, upon which eternity is consequent unity }	*via eminentiae*

When we connect the study of these attributes with the three ways of the
Neoplatonic tradition, this must not be understood exclusively. The *via
negativa* remains present throughout.

One may also consider the relationship of the questions concerning the
attributes with the Five Ways of St. Thomas. It then appears that the proofs
of God's simplicity are in the first place but not exclusively connected with
the First Way, the demonstration of God's perfection with the Second and
that of God's infinity with the Third Way. God's immutability is demonstrated with the help of insights reached in the First, Second and Fourth
Ways. To show God's unity St. Thomas uses an argument related to the Fifth
Way. This shows that there is a certain correspondence between the order of
the attributes and the Five Ways.

---

[59] *S.C.G.* I 14.
[60] *Ibid.* I 15.
[61] In chapters 37, 42 and 53.

Finally, the arguments used to demonstrate the successive attributes often presuppose the results of what was argued in a previous question. This constitutes an additional reason for their present order[62].

[62] See L. Elders, "L'ordre des attributs divins dans la *Somme théologique*", *Divus Thomas* (Piac.) 82 (1979) 225-232.

CHAPTER SEVEN

ON HOW GOD IS KNOWN BY US AND THE NAMES
WE APPLY TO HIM (I 12 & 13)

The study of God's being ends with questions 12 and 13 which at the same time prepare the treatise on divine knowledge will and power. In the *S.C.G.* there is no special chapter on how God is known by us and the chapters on the meaning of the names of God are placed in the centre of the treatise on God's being, after chapters 28 and 29 on God's perfection and the similarity of created things with God, but before the study of God's goodness, unity and infinitude. There is good reason for such an arrangement inasmuch as our speaking about God is based on the fact that he possesses in an eminent way the perfections found in created things.

In the *S.Th.* this order is changed and Aquinas gives this explanation: "As hitherto we have considered God as he is in himself we now go on to consider how he is in our knowledge, that is, how he is known by creatures". Question 13 is presented as follows: "After the consideration of those things which belong to the knowledge of divine reality, we must now proceed to the consideration of the divine names. For everything is named by us according to our knowledge of it". The order chosen in the *S.Th.* becomes even better understandable when we consider the treatise of the entitative attributes a unity, i.e., not so much as the study of different attributes, but as a consideration of how God is or, rather, is not. In particular, when we take into account that our knowledge of God, even when we speak of him affirmatively, is negative and that God is above whatever we predicate of him then we must face the question what exactly we do know of him. In this way question 12 gives an evaluation and synthesis of the results reached in the preceding treatise on God's attributes, of which it forms part[1].

I. *How God is Known by Us: Can any Created Intellect See the Essence of*
God? (I 12, 1)

According to a widely held conviction which found its inspiration in the negative theology of Dionysius, the knowledge of God's essence is not possible to man. John Scotus Eriugena asserted that "we shall not see God through

---

[1] See the Introduction to Question 14: "Having considered what belongs to divine substance, we have now to treat of what belongs to God's operation". Cf. also J. Gervais, "La place et le sens des Q. 12-13 de la Somme théologique", in *Revue de l'Université d'Ottawa* 19 (1949) 80-85.

himself because not even the angels see him: for this is impossible for any creature"[2]. Amaury of Bene likewise excluded the possibility of man's knowing God's essence[3]. St. Albert the Great, who opposed a type of onto-theology according to which God is the first thing to come to our knowledge, taught that man, illuminated by God himself, can see God in the sense of reaching God's substance (*quia est*) and that *ratio* of God's being God will deign to show[4], but not in the sense that he will know what God is (the *quid* of God)[5].

This negative view of the possibility to see God's essence found support in the noetics of Avicenna, whose influence was quite strong between 1230 and 1250. Avicenna refused to admit Aristotle's doctrine that the intellect, the intelligible and the act of understanding are one. Rather he sees knowledge as the acquisition of a likeness[6]. From this it follows that the created intellect cannot enter into contact with God himself and that God will only be seen in a likeness[7].

Against some too restrictive interpretations of the beautific vision of God by the blessed in heaven Chancellor Odon of the University of Paris issued a doctrinal decision in 1241 which stated that the blessed in heaven see God's essence in itself[8].

St. Thomas raises four impressive objections against the possibility of seeing God and then recalls *1 John* 3, 2: "We shall see him as he is". In his reply he first argues that God is most knowable in himself because he is supremely being: That which is in potency has no actual contents and therefore cannot be known. What is actual, on the other hand, is knowable and the more so, the more actuality it has. This appears from experience, but it is also implicitly contained in the principle that every being is true and agrees with the intellect[9]. However, "what is supremely knowable in itself may not be

---

[2] *De div. naturae* I, c. 8 John Scotus may, however, be thinking of a *comprehensive* knowledge. See *o.c.*, c.3.

[3] See G.C. Capelle, *Amaury de Bène. Etude sur son panthéisme formel*, Paris 1932, 105.

[4] For the meaning of *ratio* see below the commentary on I 13, 4.—Mediaeval commentators tried to discern a certain order in God's perfections. St. Albert did so by arranging God's names according to the law of growing complexity of their 'rationes', e.g. he proposed the series: being, life, intellect. See P. Ruello, *Les noms divins et leurs raisons selon Albert le Grand, Commentateur du De divinis nominibus*, Paris 1963, 113.

[5] *In Dionysii De divinis nominibus* I (Simon 10, 64; 11, 28-35). See also E. Weber, "Langage et méthode négatifs chez Albert le Grand", in *RScPhTh* 65 (1981) 75-99.

[6] See his *Liber De anima* V, c.6 (*Avicenna Latinus*, 134f): "... quod ipsa anima fit ipsae res impossibile est secundum me".

[7] Cf. P.-M. de Contenson, "Avicennisme Latin et vision de Dieu au début du 13e siècle", in *AHLDMA* 34 (1959) 29-97.

[8] Denifle and Chatelain, *Chartularium Universitatis Parisiensis* I, 170. Cf. H.F. Dondaine, "La vision béatifique au XIIIe siècle", in *RThAM* 19 (1952) 60-99 and *idem*, "Cognoscere de Deo quid est", *ibid.* 22 (1955) 72-78.

[9] See volume I, chapter five.

knowable to a particular intellect because of the excess of the intelligible object above the intellect". The distinction between what is better knowable to us and what is better known in itself is frequently mentioned by Aristotle [10]. The saying can be understood in the terms of Plato's philosophy, but also against the background of Aristotle's epistemology. Plato holds that we first start knowing sensible things, but that only the intelligible things such as mathematical objects and the ideas are really knowable. Some argue that the Aristotelian understanding of the distinction is that we must move forward by analysis from sensitive experience and existential certitude to the apprehension of the intelligibility of things [11]. This understanding of the saying is possible but even in Aristotle's works the Platonic sense is never entirely absent: the causes and principles as well as the pure forms (of which Aristotle sometimes speaks as landmarks beyond our world of change) and, at a lower level, the fifth element are more knowable because they are closer to the purity and actuality of the First Mover. St. Thomas undoubtedly uses the saying in this sense.

St. Thomas then mentions the example of the bat who, being accustomed to darkness, cannot see the bright sunlight because of its excess of light. The example occurs in the *Metaphysics* [12]: just as the eyes of bats accustomed as they are to the darkness are blinded by daylight, so it is with man whose intellect is dazzled by the very brightness of the object. But this comparison creates a special difficulty, because in Aristotle's psychology the intellect is not blinded by its object [13]. Moreover bats appear to be able to see quite well in daylight, a fact which probably had not escaped Aristotle's attention. We need not discuss here the authenticity of the passus but only notice that in his *Commentary on the Metaphysics* St. Thomas observes that the simile is not adequate. In our text he even omits the "being dazzled by the very brightness of the object" to write only that God is intelligible in excess of the power of the human intellect. Man's intellectual activity is an expression of his being and hence there is a proportion between his own being and what he knows.

Despite this difficulty St. Thomas nevertheless holds that the created intellect has an aptitude to be elevated to the contemplation of God himself. A philosophical proof is presented: "There resides in every man a natural desire to know the cause of any effects he sees. Thence wonder arises in men.

---

[10] See *Anal.* 68 b 35; 72 b 26ff; *Phys.* 184 a 16ff; 193 a 4ff.; *De anima* 413 a 11; *Metaph.* 1018 b 30ff.; 1029 b 3-12; *E.N.* 1095 b 2ff.

[11] This is the interpretation proposed by S. Mansion in "Plus connu en soi, plus connu pour nous. Une distinction épistémologique importante chez Aristote", in *Pensamiento* 35 (1979) 161-170.

[12] Book II 993 b 9-11. See the Discussion Note by C. Mitcham, "A Non-Aristotelian Simile in Metaphysics II 1", in *Classical Philology* 65 (1970) 44-46.

[13] See *De anima* 429 b 2-3: an object that is highly intelligible renders the intellect more and not less able to think.

But if the intellect of the rational creature could not attain to the first cause of things, the natural desire would remain vain. Hence it must be granted absolutely that the blessed see the essence of God''. This text has given tise to a great number of different interpretations[14]. Two facts made its interpretation particularly difficult:

(a) a strong and wide spread Augustinian tradition insisted on the unrest of man's heart and warped the understanding of the text, so that it was thought to speak of a desire of the will.

(b) the supernatural order (and the vision of God) are totally gratuitous and surpass any desire of man who simply cannot have a natural tendency to his supernatural fulfilment. The condemnation (in 1567) of a tenet of Baius (before the fall man had a right to the beatific vision) made theologians even more careful to uphold the distinction between both orders (which our text seems to bridge).

In the framework of our study on Aquinas' philosophical theology we cannot present an exhaustive survey of the question, but must limit ourselves to a few pertinent remarks. In keeping with a profound intuition of St. Augustine ("amor meus pondus meum") Scotus, who knew St. Thomas' text, spoke of an internal "pressure" in man, viz. of man being attracted by God: just like the heavy bodies are drawn to the centre of the universe, man's will (prior to any free choice) is inclined to happiness by God. This natural desire of the will, Scotus goes on to say, does not concern the *beatitudo in communi* but is ordered to the particular object by which we are perfected. However, for a conscious act of the will (and for distinct knowledge) revelation and grace are necessary[15]. Apparently Scotus shifts the problem from the intellect to the will and its basic inclination. Thus he was instrumental in making many leading Thomists, including Capreolus, Sylvester of Ferrara and Toletus, interpret the text as dealing with an inclination of the will. The greatest drawback of Scotus' theory is probably not even that it impairs the distinction between the natural and the supernatural order[16], but its lack of clarity. Philosophically speaking it is impossible to deduce from man's insatiable desire of happiness that his specific happiness lies in the possession of God, if it is not shown first that the intellect has a natural desire to see God's being.

Turning now to the Thomist tradition we shall only mention some of the more outstanding interpretations. Cajetanus, who was very much concerned to uphold the gratuity of the supernatural order, makes a distinction: from the point of view of his nature man does not have a desire of what he cannot

---

[14] See Salmanticenses, *Cursus theol.* I, tr. 2, d.1 and B. Meijer, *De eerste levensvraag in het intellectualisme van St. Thomas en het integraal realisme van Maurice Blondel*, Roermond 1940.

[15] Cf. *Opus oxon., In IV Sent.*, d.49, q.10, schol. 1, n.2; n.4.

[16] This point was argued by P. Dumont in *Eph. theol. lovan.* 8 (1931) 205-224; 571-591; 9 (1932) 5-27.

reach by his own forces[17], but inasmuch as he knows about God's offer of supernatural grace, he does have such a desire[18]. However, Franciscus Sylvester of Ferrara rejected this explanation because of its minimalistic interpretation of St. Thomas' text and its tendency to deprive man from a capacity for or opening to the supernatural order. According to the commentator of the *S.C.G.* the desire to see God, of which St. Thomas speaks, is an act of the will, but it concerns seeing God inasmuch as he is the First Cause, not, however, inasmuch as he is the object of man's happiness[19]. This solution suffers from two major defects: (a) St. Thomas speaks of a desire of the *intellect*[20]; (b) man is to know God's essence. As the Salmanticenses pointed out, the distinction between God's essence and God as the cause of things does not help us[21].

Dominicus Soto takes up Scotus' expression of *pondus naturae* which he understands not as an elicited act but as a natural propensity[22]. Bañez, on the other hand, argues that in *S.Th.* I 12, 1 St. Thomas cannot have in mind a demonstration of the possibility of the beatific vision of God by means of an argument pertaining to natural reason (because this vision is strictly supernatural). Hence by "a natural desire of the vision of God" is meant a merely natural act of the will, which remains conditional and is not efficacious. "Conditional" inasmuch as it is not clear that this vision of God can be attained: if it were possible, one would want it. Other theologians such as Suarez, Vasquez and, as it seems, the Salmanticenses, sympathize with this solution. In our century they were followed by A. Gardeil and R. Garrigou-Lagrange. Gardeil is of the opinion that the desire of which St. Thomas speaks, cannot be inborn but is elicited, that is, springs from the normal use of our faculties[23]. Gardeil seems to think so because, if it were inborn, there would have to be in man an active natural potency to realize it. He nevertheless calls it a *natural* desire.

John of St. Thomas, on the other hand, concludes that the question must concern the appetite of the *intellect* and not of the will. St. Thomas means an elicited desire of the intellect to know the cause when it knows the effects (which can be either natural or supernatural). There is no inborn tendency to the vision of God resulting from the determinate nature of the intellect as human intellect, but a capacity or possibility, i.e., a non-repugnancy to see God. The mean of the demonstration is that it is conformable to man's intel-

---

[17] *In I^am* 12, 1, IX: "Naturale eius desiderium non se extendit ultra naturae facultatem ".
[18] *In I^am-II^ae* 3, 8, I.
[19] *In S.C.G.* III, c.51.
[20] I 12, 1. Cf. *S.C.G.* III, c.54.
[21] *Curs. Theol.* I, tr. 2, disp. 1, dubium 5.
[22] *In IV Sent.*, d.49, q.2, a.1.
[23] "L'âme, sujet récepteur de la grâce", in *Revue thom.* 31 (1926) 104ff. 391.

lectual nature to know the proper and *per se* cause of the effects he perceives. Now this desire, this tendency would be in vain if there would not be a capacity to be elevated to the vision of God[24].

Having surveyed some of the more important interpretations of this text we must now attempt to reach a definite conclusion with regard to St. Thomas' doctrine on this point. Aquinas argues that, contrary to what some theologians asserted, the possibility of the vision of God's essence cannot in principle be excluded from the human intellect. For, if this would be the case, man would not be able to reach his Cause with his intellect and find his happiness in God. This, however, would be against the faith and against reason, for when man sees an effect, there is a natural desire the know its cause. If we were not able to see God, a natural desire in us would not be fulfilled. This would contradict the order of nature.

St. Thomas clearly speaks of a desire of the intellect to see the cause, scil. the First Cause. The basic tendency of the intellect is accompanied by a corresponding desire of the will. The first seventeen questions of the *Prima Secundae* are constructed on this assumption. In some of his earlier works Aquinas insisted perhaps more on the will's natural desire of happiness[25], but in our text the desire or tendency of the intellect is meant in the first place. This desire is the very nature of the intellect as it tends to its proper operation and it shows itself in any pursuit of knowledge[26]. This inclination cannot be in vain; its fulfilment cannot be impossible. Otherwise there would be a contradiction in nature. The desire is the intellect's radical capacity and not something already realised[27]. Once we keep this in mind, the difficulties so often associated with the text can be resolved. (a) Those passages where St. Thomas denies that seeing God falls within the natural range of man's intellect and will[28] exclude an elicited, efficacious desire of the will or the determinate positive order of the intellect toward the vision of God and the active power to reach it[29]. (b) When Aquinas writes that there is no natural desire for anything, unless it can be reached by nature[30], he refers to such an elicited desire or to a positive, determinate order of a faculty to this object. (c) When

[24] *Cursus theol.*, In P.I, Q.12, a.3, n.3-13.

[25] Cf. P. Engelhardt, "Desiderium naturale", in *Hist. Wörterbuch d. Philos.* II, 117-130.

[26] It can, of course, be accompanied by the inclination of the will to the *bonum in communi*, which, in a sense, is a conditional, non-efficacious desire of the vision of God.

[27] See L. Gillon, "Du désir naturel de connaître au désir de voir Dieu" in *Atti dell' VIII Congresso tomistico internazionale*, vol. IV, Città del Vaticano 1981, 243-248, p. 247.

[28] See I-II, 114, 3: "Visio Dei cognitionem et desiderium nostrum excedit"; *De verit.* 14, 2; *S.C.G.* III, c.52: "Videre Dei substantiam transcendit limites omnis substantiae creatae".

[29] It has been suggested by L. Charlier, "Puissance passive et désir naturel selon saint Thomas", in *Eph. theol. lovan.* 7 (1930) 5-28; 639-662, that we must sharply distinguish between *appetitus naturalis* and *desiderium naturale* (the former is found in any being, the latter only in the will). This is hardly correct. Cf. I 62, 1 and I-II 41, 3.

[30] *In III Sent.*, d.27, q.2, a.2 ad 4.

he argues that an active potency must always correspond to a passive one, St. Thomas does not contradict what he says about the "desiderium naturale Dei videndi", because to a passive potency which is only a capacity in the sense of a non-repugnancy corresponds a disposition to become an actively engaged potency (that is, a capacity to be elevated by the *lumen gloriae*)[31]. (d) In this way the distinction between the order of nature and of grace is maintained[32]. (e) The passsus of I 12, 1 is in full agreement with other texts such as *S.C.G.* III 50 where six arguments are brought forward to show that there is a natural desire to see God[33]. (f) God is above the created intellect but "divine being is not in such a way outside the faculty of the created intellect as if it were something entirely foreign to it. For God's being is the first intelligible and the principle of all knowledge"[34]. (g) Thus we also understand better how the supernatural order is the fulfilment of man's deepest yearning, viz. for perfect knowledge. It also follows from the above that there is not a dual final end for man, viz. a natural and a supernatural end, but only one, the vision of God and beatitude in God[35].

In his reply to the objections St. Thomas writes twice that the *comprehension* of God's being by a created intellect is not possible. The capacity to see God is given with the intellect as such which has being as its subject matter and, therefore, is a passive potency to be satiated in the beatific vision of God's. This potency is a potency of the intellect to its own perfection as intellect and should therefore not be called a *potentia oboedientialis*[36].

How God is Known by Us: How or by What Means will the Created Intellect See God? (I 12, 2-13)

Aquinas first lays down that in order to see God the intellect must be reinforced and elevated so as to be able to reach God. Furthermore God must come to the created intellect and give himself to it. For no created likeness of God can represent God since God is above the order of created things. Moreover, God's essence is his being, whereas all created things differ from their

---

[31] *In IV Sent.*, d.43, q.1, a.1. ql.3.

[32] *Expos. in Boetii De Trin.*, q.6, a.4 ad 5: "Quamvis enim homo naturaliter inclinetur in finem ultimum, non tamen potest naturaliter illum consequi sed solum per gratiam et hoc est propter eminentiam illius finis".

[33] See also I-II 3, 8; *In I Metaph.*, l.1, 4; *Comp. theol.*, c.104.

[34] *S.C.G.* III, c.54.

[35] Cf. L. Laporta, *La destinée de la nature humaine selon saint Thomas d'Aquin*, Paris 1965. See also I 62, 1: "haec beatitudo non est aliquid naturae sed naturae finis". On the entire question see also the somewhat simplifying yet basically right study by Q. Turiel, "El deseo natural de ver a Dios", in *Atti dell'VIII Congresso tomistico internazionale*, vol. IV, Città del Vaticano 1981, 243-248. One may also compare E. Gilson, "Sur la problématique thomiste de la vision béatifique", in *AHLDMA* 31 (1934) 67-88.

[36] Gilson, *o.c.* (n.35), 87.

being and can never adequately represent God. Finally God's being is infinite and contains in itself supereminently whatever can be signified or understood by a created intellect. Since all created forms are determined according to some aspect, they cannot communicate divine essence to us. Hence God can only be seen by the intellect when he himself is present in it. The divine essence is united to the created intellect as the object seen and understood, making through itself the intellect in act[37].

In the fourth article Aquinas elaborates on the question whether any created intellect can by its own power see God's essence. This question provides the occasion for some important considerations on the way in which we know things. At the same time it adds a further restriction to the range of the conclusion reached in the first article. Aquinas sets forth that the mode of knowledge agrees with the mode of being (*agere sequitur esse*). In knowledge the object known is present and is adapted to the mode of being of the knower. This mode of being is manifold: angels exist as forms without matter; man is a spiritual soul existing in some particular matter. Insofar as our knowledge belongs to our bodily being it will use corporeal organs and know the singular. This is the level of sensitive knowledge. Intellectual knowledge which is proper to the immaterial soul alone, knows the material things in a higher way, using universal concepts. The angelic intellect knows natures that are not in matter.

It follows that to know God, who is self-subsistent being itself, is beyond the natural power of any created intellect. It cannot see God's essence unless God unites himself to it by his grace. In his answer to the third objection Aquinas further explains why, contrary to the senses which are altogether material, the intellect inasmuch as it is above matter, can be raised up to a higher level of knowledge by divine grace. St. Thomas sees an indication of this capacity to be elevated in the fact that the intellect by itself can move from the level of the knowledge of concrete things to abstract knowledge and thus consider forms by themselves separate from matter. Likewise the angelic intellect which naturally knows being (*esse*) as it is realised in a particular nature (itself), can nevertheless separate that being (*esse*) and consider it by itself since it knows that this nature itself is one thing and its being another. St. Thomas calls this process which takes place within the intellect a certain 'resolution' (*resolutio*). As he explains this *resolutio* is a process of analytical thinking by means of which we go from what is composed to what is simple, from the whole to its parts and from the less universal to the more universal. Also the movement from things to their extrinsic causes belongs to the *modus*

---

[37] In *In IV Sent.*, d.49, q.2, a.1 St. Thomas connects his doctrine of the direct union of the soul with God in the beatific vision with the noetics of Averroes, who himself refers to Alexander (*In De anima* III, c.36, Crawford 481): "... ipse copulatur nobiscum copulatione adeo quod sit forma nobis per quam intelligimus entia".

resolutionis[38]. For St. Thomas this *resolutio* expresses the fundamental structure of thought, viz. the tendency toward greater intelligibility, a more encompassing universality and the knowledge of ultimate causes.

However, the intellect must be raised up to the capacity to see God. This
is further explained in the fifth article. Although God is infinitely knowable,
no finite intellect, elevated by divine grace, will be able to *comprehend* God.
This does not mean that there is something in God that will not be seen but
that he will not be seen as perfectly as he is capable of being seen[39]. This also
implies that the created intellect will not see all God does or can do: if this
were the case, it would have to comprehend God[40]. The created intellect will
know other things in and through God's essence in which the likenesses of all
things pre-exist. It will see them not successively but all at once, because all
things are seen in the same eternal essence of God[41].

Concluding this question St. Thomas once more points out why in this life
God cannot be known by natural reason: our natural knowledge can reach so
far as it can be led by sensible things: since these sensible things are effects
of God which do not equal his power, they cannot give us knowledge of God's
essence, but only of his existence; they also show what must necessarily belong
to him as the first cause of all things exceeding whatever is caused by him.
Thus Aquinas soberly affirms the dependence of human knowledge on the
experience of material things by the senses. Not Descartes' *cogito* but sense-
knowledge is the origin and basis of our certitude, and even of our natural
certitude of God's existence. St. Thomas firmly refuses the thesis that we can
know God's essence in this life, which was defended among others by Siger
of Brabant[42]. It was the ninth thesis condemned by Etienne Tempier, bishop
of Paris, in 1277.

However, contrary to what empiricism and positivism hold, man is not
wholly imprisoned in the material world. There is an opening toward the
Transcendent Cause of the world, which all men can and must acknowledge[43],
even if only grace can give us real knowledge of God[44]. St. Thomas does not
side with those authors who hold that there is "a compelling touch of God"
or an intuition of God[45], unless one understands these expressions to mean

---

[38] See the *Expos. in Boetii De Trin.*, q.6, a.1; *In II Metaph.*, 1.1, n.278 and L.-M. Régis,
"Analyse et synthèse dans l'oeuvre de Saint Thomas", in *Studia Mediaevalia in honorem R.J.
Martin*, Brugge 1940, 303-330.
[39] I 12, 7.
[40] I 12, 8.
[41] I 12, 9 and 10.
[42] See F. van Steenberghen, *Maître Siger de Brabant*, Louvain-Paris 1977, 301
[43] I 12, 12 ad 3.
[44] I 12, 13.
[45] Cf. H.H. Farmer, *The World and God*, London 1935; J. Bailly, *The Interpretation of
Religion: An Introductory Study of Theological Principles*, New York 1928; R. Otto, *The Holy*
(1917).

an awareness of the conclusion of an argument (perhaps often not clearly perceived) which shows that there is a transcendent Cause. As such this intuition and feeling or this "sixth sense" are no sufficient basis for certitude about God's existence and scientifically responsible knowledge of his being. The varying positions taken by contemporary philosophers with regard to the question of our knowledge of God show once more the urgent need of a solid philosophical theology.

II. *The Names of God (I 13)*

Having considered how we know God St. Thomas now studies how we speak of him, asking what the precise meaning and bearings of the various predicates we apply to God are and how we can bring the multiplicity of divine names to a certain unity. The place of this theme after question thirteen is justified by the observation that "everything is named by us according to our knowledge of it". This statement implies that there is a parallelism between intellectual knowledge and its expression in language: some knowledge about God is possible and hence we can, to a certain extent, speak about God.

The various languages can differ considerably in the way in which doing or undergoing, time, modality, etc. are expressed. But languages are always translatable into each other, although one language may not have all the linguistic means at its disposal for expressing reality which other languages have. Thought precedes language although without the words of a language we cannot even express and know what we think.

The Aristotelian-Thomistic view of the nature and status of language is based on the perception of the natural function of speech as well as on the epistemology of realism. One might also call it the common sense view of language. As such it is entirely different from attempts by some philosophers of religion to explain religious language by means of the Wittgensteinian concept of a 'language game', by which they mean an autonomous use of language which has its own rules and can only be understood from within by those who play the game in question. However, this theory destroys the objective value of religious language, makes a scientific evaluation of it impossible and excludes any meaningful dialogue with those outside the group of players of a particular game. Language games are undoubtedly possible according to rules chosen by convention, exactly as non-Euclidian geometrics are. But in philosophical theology we want to reach reality and to know with scientific precision and certitude what the objective contents of our assertions about God consist of.

The Names of God: Whether a Name can be given to God? (I 13, 1)

In the first article of our question Aquinas summarizes in outline his theory
of language which is that of Aristotle: words are signs of ideas and ideas are
the similitudes of things and, therefore, words are referred to things through
the intermediary of the concept the intellect has acquires from reality. It
follows that we can give a name to anything insofar as we understand it[46]. In
the previous questions it was shown that a certain knowledge of God is possible inasmuch as God is the cause of things. although we must at the same time
qualify this knowledge by removing from God whatever is imperfect and
limited and by adding that God surpasses whatever we think of him. Since we
do not know God's essence, our names do not express his essence in itself,
contrary to what is the case when we use the name 'man' of Socrates.

By this answer St. Thomas rejects the theory which holds that no names
apply to God. In his *Seventh Letter* Plato notes that he has not written
anything on the true object of his research because it cannot be expressed in
words[47]. According to Philo God is unspeakable and unnamable[48]. Similar
expressions occur in Albinus[49], Apuleius[50] and Plotinus who goes so far as to
say that we want to remove everything from 'him' and not assert anything[51].
As we have seen St. Thomas is profoundly convinced of the negative character
of our knowledge of God, but he nevertheless affirms the possibility of
predicating certain names of him. In the reply to the second and third objection certain difficulties are solved, the first of which is: names are either concrete or abstract. Concrete names do not belong to God since he is simple;
abstract names do not belong to him since they do not signify a complete, subsistent being. In his reply Aquinas admits that in our knowledge of creatures
the names by means of which we signify complete, subsisting things (which
are always composite) must have a concrete meaning. Other names signify
simple forms but these are that by which a thing is something, e.g. whiteness
signifies that by which a thing is white. "Since God is both simple and subsisting, we attribute to him simple and abstract names to signify his simplicity
and concrete names to signify his subsistence and perfection although both
these names fail to express his mode of being, because our intellect does not
know him in this life as he is".

In the reply to the third objection Aquinas shows that among the words we

---

[46] In all his works Aquinas proposes the same theory of language. An important text is *De pot.*
7, 6: "Sunt enim voces notae earum quae sunt in anima passionum et ipsae intellectus concep-
tiones sunt rerum similitudines". One should notice the priority of thought over language.
[47] 341 b-d.
[48] Philo, *Post.* 48, 167. Cf. H.A. Wolfson, *Philo II*, Cambridge MA 1948, 94ff.
[49] Albinus, *Didask.* X (164-165).
[50] *Apologia*, 64, 7: "Paucis cogitabilis, nemini effabilis".
[51] *Enn.* V 3, 4.

use to signify God, there are nouns signifying substance or quality (for by these names we intend to denote God's subsistence and perfection), verbs (which signify with time) because God's eternity includes all time, and also demonstrative and relative pronouns. Hence religious language such as it is used in the symbola, in theology as well as in prayer and in the liturgy of the Church is justified. St. Thomas' explanations hold true for both cognitive and non-cognitive religious language, i.e. both propositions in the indicative mood which purport to express who God is and to impart knowledge and propositions which are invocations, prayers, blessings, etc. [52].

Aquinas' view of the use of religious language is more positive than that of the Platonic tradition. However, it comes into conflict with the position hold by a considerable number of analytical philosophers. According to Alfred Ayer all utterances about the nature of God are nonsensical. With regard to God's existence Ayer is agnostic or feels inclined to deny it outright. However, other authors who also consider that religious language is nonsensical feel that this conclusion need not be anti-religious [53]. But this position is hardly defensible for it subscribes to a distorted view of man who would have a religious life going against the grain of reason or, at least, outside the control of reason.

These authors describe cognitive religious language as nonsensical because it has no empirical content and cannot be verified. To 'save' God-language certain analytical philosophers tried to introduce some verification by resorting to Popper's falsification principle. However, A. Flew opposes these attempts and holds that religious language is not falsifiable at all because of its lack of an empirical basis [54]. R. M. Hare argues that religious propositions do not assert anything at all but are a *blik*, that is a particular attitude toward the world. Others want to give up all religious language and retreat into silence about God [55] or suggest that talk about God should be replaced by talking to God [56]. Other authors while admitting that religious statements are not empirical and not testable, assign an ethical use to them [57]. J. Wisdom insists on the aesthetic impact of religious language. There are, however, it would

---

[52] This distinction is based upon the fact that on the one hand the human mind must attain truth, but on the other direct man's activity and establish relations with others by calling for their attention or asking them something. See *In I Periherm.*, lectio 7, 5.

[53] See, for instance, Paul van Buren, *The Secular Meaning of the Gospel*, New York 1966; Th.J. Altizer, *The Gospel of Christian Atheism*, Philadelphia 1966.

[54] In A. Flew and A. MacIntyre (edit.), *New Essays in Philosophical Theology*, London 1955, 99. Popper's falsification principle says that in order to have some empirical content, a statement does not have to say something which can be verified positively by observation. It is enough if it is possible to refute it.

[55] See W.T. Blackstone, *The Problem of Religious Knowledge*, Englewood Cliffs 1963, 134ff.

[56] R.F. Holland, "Religious Discourse and Theological Discourse", in *The Australian Journal of Philosophy* 34 (1956) 148.

[57] R.B. Braithwaite, *An Empiricist's View of the Nature of Religious Belief*, Cambridge 1955, 10.

seem some philosophers of the empiricist or analytical school who have a
more positive view of cognitive religious language. Ian T. Ramsey points to
the fact that man knows that he is more than his body alone to show the
possibility of real though unclear language about God[58]. He thinks that the
main function of religious language is to evoke a *disclosure* situation in which
the universe comes alive in a personal way.

The problem belaboured by all these authors is that man cannot know at
all things of which there is no (sense) experience and hence he cannot meaningfully speak about God. But it is precisely this empiricist assumption which
is questionable. St. Thomas does hold, as we have seen, that all natural
knowledge of God cannot but come from the senses. Sense experience provides the facts which give the starting points of each of the Five Ways: each
of these proofs is based on a particular experience and developed within it,
for we reach God only insofar as he works and is present in the processes of
created causality[59]. This appeal to experience also dominates in the subsequent questions of natural theology in our text. As far as possible St. Thomas
bases his account each time on what is immediately given rather than deducing
the divine attributes from a previously reached insight concerning God's being
(a procedure often used in Neo-Scholasticism).

The difference between the position of Aquinas and that of the positivist
philosophers obviously is that St. Thomas holds that he is allowed to argue
from the basis of observed facts with the help of some general principles to
reach certain conclusions about the existence and the properties of God. Let
us explain this in detail. Aquinas does not think that in this way he betrays
experience or loses contact with reality. For he holds that intellectual activity
when it proceeds with care and follows a scientific method, does not imagine
things or work in complete separation from the senses. Rather the intellect
penetrates deeper into that which sensative knowledge presents to it remaining
nevertheless with the same reality. Thus the intellect does not add something
of its own to the sense data when it distinguishes the concept of cause and
effect, of substance and accidents, but it distinguishes what is already present
in the sense data, although the senses cannot perceive it as such. This also
holds true of the the so-called principles: the principle of contradiction, of
causality etc. are not subjective laws of our mind, but express objective facts,
structures and connections between things. For example, the principle of contradiction states that this being, because of its ontological contents, is not

---

[58] See the *Religious Language*, London 1957. Besides the works already mentioned one may
also compare F. Ferré, *Language, Logic and God*, New York 1961; W.A. de Pater, *Theologische
Sprachlogik*, München 1971; Peter J. Etges, *Kritik der analytische Theologie*, Hamburg 1973; A.
Dumas, *Nommer Dieu*, Paris 1980.
[59] By 'created causality' we also mean the causality of the intrinsic components of created
being.

another being. The principles we use in the Five Ways express objective laws of being, which we acquire from our experience and which manifest themselves as universally valid. They are admitted as such by everybody in the metaphysics of common sense.

Now the deduction of God's existence from sense data with the help of the principles of being, is not intended to provide us with an object of intellectual contemplation in isolation from sensitive knowledge. Rather our knowledge of God remains within the compass of the observed, insofar as we only know God in his effects. St. Thomas repeatedly points out that a cause must be present in its effects: each efficient is united with what it effects immediately; it touches it through its power [60]. Aquinas frequently compares the causality of God with regard to created things with that of the sun: only when the sun is shining, things can be recognised and seen. Likewise only through the action of God can beings exist and be knowable [61].

Here we encounter the term *repraesentatio*: each effect represents, also in the sense of making present, its cause. It shows that the cause must exist and it shows something of the form of the cause [62]. Of course, no creature perfectly represents God's being [63], but nevertheless something can be known about God. In the view of St. Thomas God is present in created things and is touched by us when we get to know the world. In all our doings, even when we are far from realizing it, we approach God and fulfil the purpose God set us [64]. For this reason St. Thomas writes "Every knower knows God implicitly in whatever thing he knows" [65]. Likewise in seeking to attain their own perfection all things seek to attain God's goodness [66]. But this experience of God or, rather, this touching of God should not be called a direct experience because it needs the mediation of created things [67].

In order to bring out even better the role St. Thomas assigns to experience in our knowledge of God we may compare the result of our account with the impact of Ayer's distinction between analytical and synthetic statements. Ayer uses this Kantian distinction to argue that propositions about God fall outside this division and are meaningless. For Ayer analytic propositions are statements in which the predicate brings out what is already contained in the subject (e.g., "my sister is a female"). Synthetic propositions state a fact of experience which can be verified. In a Thomistic perspective this division may

---

[60] *S.Th.* I 8, 1.
[61] *Expos. in librum de causis*, 1.6, n.168.
[62] *S.Th.* I 45, 7.
[63] *S.Th.* I 12; 42, 5 ad 1; 56, 3 ad 2; II-II 175, 4.
[64] *S.C.G.* III 42.
[65] *De ver.* 22, 2 ad 1.
[66] *S.Th.* I 6, 1.
[67] Cf. C.M. Martin in A. Flew and A. MacIntyre, *o.c.*, 79.

be maintained provided its limited scope is kept in mind[68] and some corrections are added: (a) The analysis of the subject sometimes give valid *new*
knowledge about it, viz. when we stringently deduce certain properties.
Examples are the properties of knowledge such as its immateriality, which are
deduced from an analysis of the phenomenon of knowledge itsself, and the
immortality of the human soul which is deduced from its nature as we know
it through an analysis of its proper activity. (b) Synthetic propositions also
comprise deductions from observed realities (with the help of principles) even
if the conclusions are not subject to verification by observation. Examples are
statements on the far geological past of our planet, the calculation of the
existence of a new planet on the basis of certain observed phenomena, conclusions about the existence of certain subatomic particles, about the initial state
of the universe before its present expansion, etc. If one insists that the conclusions of the arguments about God's existence must first be submitted to
verification in the sense of observation, before being valid, one applies a certain *a priori* restriction which in fact makes knowledge of the supra-sensitive
world impossible. But the very generality of this claim already exceeds the
concrete existence of material things. On countless occasions in life we resort
in all tranquility to these sorts of arguments, so that their *a priori* exclusion
is hardly consistent.

St. Thomas would also observe that philosophical theology is not a wholly
independent sector of thought but that it presupposes serious study of the
material universe and of man. Now in natural philosophy as well as in science
time and again valid conclusions are drawn for which there is not yet any
verification by observation possible or available. The difference with
statements about God in philosophical theology is that in the latter case no
observation will confirm our deductions. But this does not mean that there is
no verification. The validity of the deductions is verified by a careful checking
of the point of departure, the principles used and the process of reasoning
itself. One might even say that a falsification test can be applied insofar as
we must examine the precise meaning of our deductions about God. A Christian has a supernatural experience of God and in this way he has a certain
verification in the obscurity of faith. A definite and overwhelming verification
will only be had by him in the *eschaton*.

Continuing our study of Question 13 we must now analyse the following
articles which systematically deal with the study of our language about God.
The order of these articles is superb: Aquinas gradually and systematically
analyzes what the precise meaning is of the names we apply to God.

---

[68] The division concerns the *origin* of propositions.

The names of God: Can names be applied to God substantially? (I 13, 2)

A first problem is whether our language reaches God as a substance, that is, as a subsistent reality. In the Middle Ages as well as more recently it has been argued that what we say about God does not really express anything about his being. Maimonides claims that all the names we apply to God have a totally different meaning than when used to signify created things. The reason is that God is altogether different[69]. Nevertheless it is not useless to use these names to denote God, for when we predicate them of God we remove the opposite from him. For example, we say that he is a living God, we mean to say that he is not like things which are not alive. In this view naming God is tantamount to successively removing him from various classes of created beings.

St. Thomas mentions a second view somewhat similar to the first: these names attributed to God signify a relationship of God with created things. When we say that he is good, we intend to say that he is the cause of goodness in things[70]. As we have seen, in the perspective of analytical philosophy the use of names to signify God and what is proper to divine being is devoid of meaning for we have no direct experience of God and hence we do not know what it means when we make him the subject of theological statements[71]. Another voice in this choir of critics is the Protestant theologian Karl Barth who holds that our words do not signify anything at all of God's being and properties. God is not known by man but man by God. When God gives man certain words to express his being, he requisitions them but their signification remains totally alien to God[72]. There is no *analogia entis*. Human language about God has no value.

St. Thomas solves the problem by showing first that these positions cannot reasonably be defended. He admits that names which are said of God negatively or which signify a relation to creatures do not express at all his substance but the distance of created things from him or their relation to God. St. Thomas means negative sentences such as "God is not corporeal" and the Dionysian expression "God is not-life" as well as such statements as "God is greater than...", "God is the Maker of..." This leaves us with a limited number of names. (a) People consistently speak about God in certain ways. They call him wise and good, but not gold or silver, although he is the cause of wisdom as well as of all the physical elements. There must be a reason

---

[69] *Guide for the Perplexed* I, 58. Cf. *ibid.*, I, 42 (for 'good'). See also H.A. Wolfson, "St. Thomas on Divine Attributes", in *Mélanges offerts à Etienne Gilson*, Toronto-Paris 1959, 673-700. Wolfson thinks that Alfarabi and Avicenna are meant by the *quidam.* of St. Thomas (*o.c.*, 677).

[70] This view was defended by Alain of Lille, *Theol. Reg.* XXI; XXVI (PL 210, 631 and 633).

[71] I.M. Crombie, "The Possibility of Theological Statements", in Basil Mitchell (edit.), *The Philosophy of Religion*, London 1971, 28-32.

[72] Barth writes that the use of these terms is "von Gott her, nicht vom Menschen her". See J. Hamer, *Karl Barth*, Paris 1949, 60f.

behind this use of theological language. (b) The views mentioned above imply that no real knowledge of God is possible because all names primarily signify created things so that they do not express anything of divine being. However, as the previous questions on God's attributes have shown, some knowledge of God is possible. St. Thomas explains what he means: According to the views mentioned our statements about God would not go beyond the attribution of 'healthy' to medicine. Medicine is the cause of health in an animal but formally it does not possess the perfection it causes[73]. (c) Finally, the opinions we are now dealing with are also against the intention of those who speak of God. For when saying that God lives, they assuredly mean more than to say that God is the cause of life or that he differs from inanimate things.

Aquinas then lays down the principle on which our speaking of God rests: we know God from creatures in as far as creatures represent him. But God pre-possesses in himself all the perfections of created things, since he is himself absolutely and universally perfect[74]. Creatures represent God but not as something of the same species or genus but as the source of their perfection in whom it pre-exists in a higher way. St. Thomas, then, is convinced that some of our statements about God really concern God himself inasmuch as he is intimately present in things and is represented by them, just as the light of the sun is present in the atmosphere illuminated by it[75]. This is his answer to the difficulties raised by some analytical philosophers.

It is true that these names are in the first place given to created things. When we apply them to God we *intend* to signify God as the source of these perfections in whom they pre-exist in a more eminent way. This observation of St. Thomas in his reply to the second objection intimates that in his opinion we ourselves make our words analogous: we gain the insight that God is the source of all these perfections possessing them in a higher way. We then discern in which way we can ascribe them to God. The *intentio loquentium* is decisive in the analogical use of terms. The distinction between "that from which the name is taken" and "that which it is intended to signify" is not quite the same as the distinction between the *modus significandi* and the *res significata*[76]. This second distinction is used in the following article. The "id

---

[73] At first sight the fifth article seems to contradict this text. See our commentary.

[74] See I 4, 2 and 3.

[75] I 13, 2 ad 3: "... secundum quod repraesentatur in perfectionibus creaturarum". The comparison of God's presence with that of light in the atmosphere is found in I 8, 1.

[76] St. Thomas further explains the "id a quo imponitur" and "illud quod significatur" in *In I Sent.*, d.22, a.1 and in I 13, 8. One should notice the careful wording in I 13, 2 ad 2 which indicates the *intention* of the philosopher who applies certain terms to God. The correct application of names to God, transferring them from the level of created being, rests on a previously acquired insight into God's eminence.—On the distinction between the *id a quo* and the *id ad quod* see R. McInerny, *The Logic of Analogy*, The Hague 1971, 54-57. The author points out a second sense of the *id a quo* we are not now concerned with (viz. from the point of view of the thing itself; the expression then signifies the specific differences. Cf. *De ver*. 4, 1 ad 8).

a quo" and the "id ad quod" are further explained in article eight where St. Thomas also indicates the background to this distinction. Names are mostly imposed from what is perceived by the senses (e.g., sensible properties) from which we proceed to signify the underlying reality of the substance. To explain this better Aquinas uses the example of the word 'stone': we are first struck by its property of being an obstacle to our feet which is (St. Thomas believed) expressed by the etymology of the word, but then we mainly use it to signify the substantial being of this object. Sometimes the *id a quo* and the *id ad quod* are the same, viz. when we signify sensible qualities.

The Names of God: Whether any Name can be Applied to God Properly? (I 13, 3)

Having excluded from our discussion negative and relative names we are left with those names we use to signify divine being and God's properties.

St. Thomas justifies their use as follows: God is the source of all perfections present in created things and possesses them in an eminent way. Although the names by means of which we signify such perfections, indicate the mode in which these perfections exist in created things and as such signify created perfections rather than God's being, we must nevertheless say that with regard to the *thing* itself they signify (e.g., goodness) this is found more properly in God than in creatures. For this reason these names are properly (and even more properly) said of God (than they are of created things)[77].

In his reply to the first objection Aquinas further elaborates what is meant by the *modus significandi*: we sometimes use terms of God which not only signify what in creatures is an accident (e.g. 'good'), but also terms which have an imperfection in their own essential contents. An example is 'stone' which signifies a material thing. Because the restrictive *modus significandi* is inherent in the name, this class of names is only metaphorically used of God. In later Scholastic terminology these terms, signifying 'impure perfections' are sometimes called 'closed names'[78]. Terms expressing substances and their generic or specific essences as well as terms signifying material accidents such as colours, temperature etc. are 'closed' while names not signifying particular substances (and their essence) nor qualities belonging to material reality, are 'open' names.

Closed terms are not properly said of God but can only be used metaphorically. This does not mean that metaphors are without value: they may evoke a rich human experience. When God is called a rock and a shelter,

---

[77] The distinction between *res significata* and *modus significandi* was current among grammarians in the Middle Ages. See St. Albert, *In De div. nom.* I: Simon 32, 44.

[78] In his reply to the first objection Aquinas writes that in the names expressing a pure perfection a particular, limited *modus significandi* is not enclosed in their signification.

the ideas of protection, permanence and safety are co-signified. Besides this metaphorical language a properly scientific language about God is possible as we shall see in the following articles. But first a difficulty must be solved.

Metaphorical names are not properly said of God. Their meaning (the *ratio* or contents signified) is something limited and closed and so it does not properly belong to God. But how do metaphorical terms relate to analogous names? What is metaphorically said of God is not at all formally present but is applied to him by a proportion (e.g. as an effect similar to what the metaphorical term indicates)[79]. But is not the *ratio* also different in analogous names so that the difference between metaphorical and analogous terms vanishes?[80] "How can a thing be named *proprie* by a term whose *ratio propria* it does nor save?"[81]. Cajetanus tried to solve the problem by suggesting that in univocity and analogy of proportionality the same *ratio* is present, while it is not in analogy of attribution and metaphors[82]. R. McInerny points our that we must distinguish between the *ratio propria* and the *res significata*. "Every name involves a mode of signifying, a way in which the denominating form is meant"[83]. This comprizes the *res significata* and the mode of signifying it. In analogous names the same *res significata* is meant (although in different proportions or relationships). Sometimes this is called the *ratio communis*. In metaphorical terms, however, the *res significata* is different. In our commentary on the fifth article we shall come back to this question.

The names of God: Are the Names we Apply to God Synonymous? (I 13, 4)

If the names we apply to God signify his substance and some of them are said properly of him, it would seem that they are synonyms for God's being is simple without any composition whatsoever. In the Moslem world of the 12th century a lively debate took place on the precise meaning of divine attributes. Certain theologians upheld both God's simplicity and the multiplicity of attributes. They were the so-called Ash'arites (the quasi-official theologians of the Islam) who admitted literally what the Koran said. The Mu'tazalites, on the other hand, rejected this multiplicity to safeguard God's simplicity[84].

[79] *In I Sent.*, d.45, q.1, a.4.

[80] See I 13, 5: "... non secundum eandem rationem hoc nomen sapiens de Deo et de homine dicitur"; *In I Eth.*, 1.6, n.81: "non est una ratio communis"; I 16, 6: "Quando aliquid dicitur analogice de multis illud invenitur secundum propriam rationem in uno eorum tantum, a quo alia denominantur".

[81] R. McInerny, *Studies in Analogy*, The Hague 1968, 73: on this point we are indebted to McInerny's chapter "Metaphor and Analogy".

[82] *In Iᵃᵐ*, 16, 6, IV.

[83] McInerny, *o.c.*, 75. The author quotes an important text of *In I Sent.*, d.22, q.1, a.3 ad 2: "Aequivocum enim dividitur secundum res significatas, univocum vero dividitur secundum diversas differentias, sed analogum dividitur secundum diversos modos".

[84] See G.C. Anawati, "La notion de création dans l'Islam", in *Studia missionalia* 18 (1969) 271-295, 287.

Multiplicity was placed by some in the First Intellect which issued from God. Averroes rejects this Neoplatonic solution arguing that it is not against divine simplicity to be an intellect containing a plurality of ideas[85]. In the Latin West the discussion gained momentum with St. Albert the Great who reacted sharply against Petrus Lombardus and Gilbert of La Porrée. Gilbert insisted on God's unity and simplicity and denied that formally speaking the *ratio* of certain predicates is found in God[86]. In God himself there is no basis for a variety of names: the different names we apply to him express a causal relationship of God to what comes forth from him. Against this view St. Albert tried to justify our use of a variety of names to signify God's perfection. He argues that these names as such have a different sense, but their meaning becomes the same when they are applied to God. The names do not place a determination in God, but only in our way of understanding[87]. St. Albert does not make it very clear what precisely is the basis for our applying so many names to God nor how we can avoid considering these names synonyms and how the different perfections we encounter in created things are really present in God[88].

Even St. Thomas wrestled to find the best formulation of his solution of the problem. An important text is *In I Sent.*, d. 2, q. 1, a. 3 of which, it would seem, a later redaction was added by St. Thomas himself to his *Scriptum in libros Sententiarum*, after he had been asked to review the position of Peter of Tarentaise (who had followed the earlier version of the text by St. Thomas)[89]. Aquinas' solution is: our intellect cannot grasp God in a single concept because God transcends our knowledge. Hence we must use a plurality of concepts to express his perfection (as we also do to express being or the functions of the human soul). The immediate cause of this multiplicity of concepts is our imperfect understanding, but it is also dependent on God's being which is so all-embracing and perfect that it provides the foundation for our applying different names to him. In his simple and unified perfection God pre-contains what we predicate of him. All these perfections pre-exist in God in unity[90].

---

[85] See. L. Gauthier, *Ibn Rochd (Averroès)*, Paris 1948, 14ff.

[86] See his commentary on the *De Trinitate* of Boethius (*PL* 64, 1283A-1285C): "... neque enim aliud est Deus quod est, aliud quod justus est, sed idem est esse Deo quod justo" (*l.c., 1331D*).

[87] See his *In I Sent.*, d.8, A, a.3: "Nullum horum nominum quae etiam dicunt quid est, facit nobis determinatam notionem suae significationis in Deo, ita quod nihil sit extra intellectum de re eiusdem significati". Cf. F. Ruello, *Les "Noms divins" selon Saint Albert le Grand, commentateur du "De divinis nominibus"*, Paris 1963, 64f.

[88] See also below our commentary on the next article. St. Albert seems to favor the view that in God's intellect there is a plurality of *rationes* by which he knows the fulness of his being. These *rationes* are absolute, i.e. independent of any relation to creatures. The names we give agree with these *rationes*.

[89] See B.-M. Lemaigre, "Perfection de Dieu et multiplicité des attributs divins", in *RScPhTh* 50 (1966) 198-227.

[90] I 13, 4: "In Deo praeexistunt unite et simpliciter".

In his reply to the objections St. Thomas explains his solution in greater detail and seems to answer difficulties resulting from St. Albert's theory. The names we give to God cannot be synonymous because they express our concepts (which have different contents) and only mediately God's being which is one and simple. Because created things present God in a variety of ways and we know God from created things, we use several names to signify God's being. These names are not in vain because they represent each time something of the all-surpassing wealth of God's being. Thus God is one by his being and many according to our way of naming him[91].

St. Thomas' solution was criticized by William de la Mare and Scotus who insisted that there is no plurality in God but only in created things. A careful reading of the fourth article provides the answer to this criticism. St. Thomas' intention is to explain in the first place our theological language and to assess its value. The terms we apply to God are not synonyms because they signify different contents. In the eminence of his being God pre-contains in unity whatever perfections are found in created things. Cajetanus observes in his commentary on this article that in God the *ratio* of the names we apply to him, is a *super ratio* which is at the same time wisdom and love and all the other perfections[92].

The Names of God: are the Names said of God and of Creatures Univocally Predicated? (I 13, 5)

Having reached the conclusion that the names applied to God are not synonyms we must now face a new problem: when the names we apply to God signify perfections as we know them in created things and express also what is in an eminent way and in unity present in God, are they univocally predicated of God and of created things? By univocal predication is meant that a certain content (*ratio*) is said in the same way of different things. An example is 'man' which is said of the different human individuals. Diametrically opposed to univocal predication is the equivocal use of terms: a word is used in different and unrelated meanings. Equivocation applies to things not as things but as named by us. The same sound (*vox*) happens to have different meanings[93].

Between univocal and equivocal predication lies the analogous use of words

---

[91] I 13, 4 ad 3: "Et ex hoc contingit quod est unus re et plures secundum rationem". St. Thomas' theory was not always correctly understood and some mediaeval doctors placed a plurality of *rationes* in God, distinguished from one another by a formal distinction which would hold the mean between a real distinction and a distinction of thought only. See F. Ruello, "La notion thomiste de *ratio in divinis* dans la *Disputatio* de François de Meyronnes et Pierre Roger (1320-1321)", in *RThAM* 32 (1965) 54-75.

[92] *In I^{am}* 13, 4: "Sapientia in Deo est ipsa et aliae, imo nec ipsa nec aliae sed altior quaedam ratio".

[93] See R. McInerny, *The Logic of Analogy*, 67-70.

with which we are now concerned. St. Thomas first shows that it is impossible to predicate any name univocally of God and of created things before excluding secondly that names expressing a pure perfection are said equivocally of God and of creatures. The reason is that there must be some similarity of things to God, for God is their cause and every agent works what is similar to it. Univocal predication, on the other hand, is excluded because God is altogether different in the simplicity and eminence of his divine being (*esse*). God's effects cannot be on the same level as God. They fall short of his perfection and what is divided and multiple in created things pre-exists in God in unity. When we ascribe the term 'wise' to a man, "we signify some perfection distinct from a man's essence, and distinct from his power and being and from all similar things. But when we apply 'wise' to God, we do not mean to signify anything distinct from his essence or power or being. And thus when this term 'wise' is applied to man, in some degree it circumscribes and comprehends the thing signified; whereas this is not the case when it is applied to God, but it leaves the thing signified as uncomprehended and as exceeding the signification of the name. Hence it is evident that this term 'wise' is not applied with the same contents (*ratio*) to God and to man. The same applies to other terms. Hence, no name is predicated univocally of God and of creatures"[94].

This text prepares in a masterly way the conclusion: we know that in God wisdom must be present, because he is the First Cause of everything; we know that he is subsistent being itself and, therefore, when applying these names to God, we abstract from the mode of signifying proper to them when applied to created things. Apparently *we make* our concepts analogous[95]. The text also reminds us of the meaning of *ratio*, viz. the way of use of such a predicate when attributed to creatures and to God respectively. In man, 'wise' is an accident pertaining to a subject[96], but in God it signifies subsistent being itself. This is of importance in answering the question whether in the analogous use of names the same *ratio* is present or not.

One could object against St. Thomas' explanation, as Scotus did, that if in analogy we strip our idea of wisdom of its mode of signifying, we are left with the same *ratio* in the sense of notional contents. In other words, the same term is univocally predicated of God and of creatures[97]. The answer to this objec-

---

[94] I 13, 5.

[95] This is also explicitly stated in the *De potentia* 7, 6 where St. Thomas points out that the analogous use of names to signify created perfections and attributes of God is based on the fact that the human intellect knows that God is altogether different.

[96] The Latin text has: "Unde patet quod non secundum eandem rationem hoc nomen sapiens de Deo et de homine dicitur".

[97] The problem is presented with great clarity by K. Nielson, "Talk of God and the Doctrine of Analogy", in *The Thomist* 40 (1976) 32-60 and P. Lee, "Language about God and the Theory of Analogy", *The New Scholasticism* 58 (1984) 40-66.

tion is not difficult in the light of the text we have quoted. In the analogous use of terms we cannot and do not abstract from their mode of signifying, but we are clearly aware of the fact that the terms have a different mode of signifying in God, because the mode of signifying proper to created things is limited and defective. We also know that this mode of signifying co-determines the very contents of wisdom both in man (in whom wisdom is an accidental perfection of the intellect) and in God (in whom it is the simplicity and infinitude of·divine being). Without this previous knowledge about man and God there is no true analogous use of names. It is for this reason that in the *Summa theologiae* St. Thomas studies the question of analogy after the treatise on God's being.

In univocal predication, on the other hand, the mode of signifying is the same. For instance, 'man' when applied to Socrates and Plato has the same notional contents but also signifies what is essential to two substances which both possess it in the same way. Hence analogy is no random game of loose talk and guessing but rests on a previously acquired insight that there exists a similar proportion and correspondence which constitute the basis for predicating the same term of things belonging to different genera or levels of beings. We resort to analogy because our intellect seeks to establish coherence and unity.

Returning now to the text of the fifth article we see that St. Thomas argues that these names are not applied to God and to creatures in a purely equivocal way. If this were the case, nothing at all could be known from creatures about God. However, as effects of God they must have some similarity with him and hence there is analogy[98].

The term analogy was first used in mathematics and from there it entered into philosophy. Aristotle applies the proportionality $a:b = c:d$ as a heuristic principle. It allows him to indicate correspondences between certain classes of animals (wings are to birds what fins are to fishes; primary matter is to its substantial form as clay to the shape kneaded into it). In his *Metaphysics* Aristotle calls the causes and principles of things analogous and he mentions the analogous use of the word 'one'[99]. Aristotle also suggests that the term 'good' is used analogically[100]. With regard to being (*ens*) he repeatedly

---

[98] On analogy see volume I, chapter one. Some important works are Thomas de Vio Cajetanus, *De nominum analogia. De conceptu entis*, (edit. Zammit) Rome 1934; H. Lyttkens, *The Analogy between God and the World. An Investigation of Its background and an Interpretation of Its Use*, Uppsala 1952; G.P. Klubertanz, *St. Thomas Aquinas on Analogy. A Textual Analysis and Systematic Synthesis*, Chicago 1969; B. Montagnes, *La doctrine de l'analogie de l'être d'après Saint Thomas d'Aquin*, Louvain-Paris 1963. See also the studies by R. McInerny quoted in notes 76 and 93.

[99] *Metaph.* 1070 a 31; 1016 b 31.

[100] *Eth. Nic.* 1096 b 26.

declares his basic intuition that "it is said in many ways"[101], but nowhere does he call it an analogous term. But he does compare the various meanings the term may have with those of 'healthy' and he points out that the different types of being have each a different relation to a first being, substance, in which being is fully realised[102]. The Greek commentators brought analogy and this last kind of "equivocal" use of a term together into one group which received the name *aequivoca a consilio*, which were distinguished from pure equivocals (*aequivoca a casu*)[103]. These types of analogy were connected with the Neoplatonic metaphysics of emanation: the further things get removed from their origin the less like to it they become[104].

Turning now to the study of analogy in St. Thomas' works the following must be kept in mind: (a) Aquinas makes it very clear that whichever type of analogy we use, there is *one thing* with regard to which the analogous name is predicated of other things: "In names predicated of many in an analogical sense, all are predicated through a relation to some one thing; and this one thing must be placed in the definition of them all"[105]. R. McInerny correctly observes that this not only applies to the analogy of attribution (healthy), but is an absolutely universal rule of things named analogically[106]. (b) A second point no less important but often overlooked is that we ourselves make our concepts and words analogous. This follows from the fact that we give a name to some one definite thing and then extend its meaning and use to signify other things. 'To see' is first used for the proper operation of the human eye but its meaning may be extended to denote the "intellectual seeing" of the human mind and even, more remotely, the function of a radarscope.—St. Thomas repeatedly intimates that we ourselves make our words (and concepts) analogous. In the fifth article of the question we are now studying he writes: when we apply the term 'wise' to God, we do not *intend* to signify something distinct from God's essence to his being (as is the case when we apply the term to a man). This means that we operate a subtle change in the term while we are applying it to God. But this is always the case in any type of analogy. One might even say that analogous predication is an expression of the activity of the spiritual mind which establishes connections and unity between things. There are more texts of St. Thomas to the same effect. As we shall see in this

---

[101] See H. Wagner, in *Kantstudien* 53 (1961) 75-91.

[102] *Metaph.* IV 2.

[103] Cf. Porphyrius, *In Categ.* 65, 18ff.

[104] Speaking of Plato's First Principle, the Good, Aristotle himself had used τῷ ἀφ' ἑνὸς εἶναι (*E.N.* 1096 b 27).

[105] *S.Th.* I 13, 6: "Quod in omnibus nominibus quae de pluribus analogice dicuntur necesse est quod omnia dicuntur per respectum ad unum; et ideo illud unum oportet quod ponatur in definitione omnium"; *S.C.G.* I 34: "analogice, hoc est secundum ordinem vel respectum ad aliquid unum". See also *Comp. Theol.* I, c.27; *In IV Metaph.*, l.1, n.536.

[106] *The Logic of Analogy*, The Hague 1971, 78.

fifth article he uses the term 'healthy' in two different types of analogy. This is tantamount to saying that analogy changes according to the point of view we take. The same fact is also expressed in the well known text of the *Scriptum super libros Sententiarum* where Aquinas writes that a logician uses the term substance univocally of material and immaterial things, but that the metaphysician uses it analogously[107]. It is also intimated in a passus where St. Thomas describes how only at a later stage do we remove from God 'being' (which until then was the concept of being of created things), when we understand that God's being is altogether different[108]. The same conclusion follows from the subtle way in which St. Thomas corrects Aristotle in what he writes on the analogy of being: it is not so much the analogy of healthy which correctly describes the analogy of substantial and accidental being, but the fact that substance is the subject and the accidents exist in this subject[109]. Apparently we have to know precisely the relation of accidents to substance before we can meaningfully use the analogous term 'being' of both of them. How easily the use of words may shift from univocal to analogous signification and vice versa also appears from the fact that in the statement "all qualities are being (*ens*)" we use 'being' univocally[110]. On the other hand, that we make our concepts analogous is not the result of an inner dynamism of the intellect toward a reality which escapes from it[111], but the adaptation of the intellect to reality. Analogous uses of names is not random talk but the expression of a deep understanding of things.

We must now consider the division of analogy. In his treatise on the Analogy of Names Cajetanus presents a tripartite division of analogy: analogy of inequality, analogy of attribution and analogy of proportionality[112]. Although Cajetanus may claim some support for this division in an early work of St. Thomas[113], in most texts St. Thomas proposes a *twofold* division of analogy and writes explicitly that the mode of analogy is dual. This slight discrepancy in Aquinas' works can perhaps be explained[114], but we must here take for granted that St. Thomas' considered and definite view is that there is a *duplex modus analogiae*. In the *De veritate*, q.2, a.11 analogy is divided into analogy of proportion ("duobus quorum unum ad alterum habitudinem habet", as, for instance substance and accident) and of proportionality (vision of the eye and of the intellect). In this connection Aquinas points out that the proportion between God and created

---

[107] *In II Sent.*, d.3, q.1, a.1 ad 2.
[108] *In I Sent.*, d.8, q.1, a.1 ad 4.
[109] *In IV Metaph.*, lectio 1; *In Boetii De Trin.*, q.6, a.3; I 67, 1; 88, 2 ad 4.
[110] St. Thomas alludes to this in *In I De caelo et mundo*, 1.24, n.238.
[111] E. Schillebeeckx, *Offenbarung und Theologie*, Mainz 1965, 225ff.
[112] *De nominum analogia* 3 (8).
[113] *In I Sent.*, d.19, q.5, a.2 ad 1.
[114] See McInerny, *o.c.* (n.93), 80ff.

things is indeterminate and does not allow us to reach a determinate knowledge about God's being.

In three texts, which we are now going to discuss, St. Thomas proposes a twofold division of analogy: "(Analogy) can happen in two ways: either according as many things are proportioned to one (thus, for example 'healthy' is predicated of medicine and urine in relation and in proportion to health and body, of which the latter is the sign and the former the cause), or according as one thing is proportioned to another (thus 'healthy' is said of medicine and animals, since medicine is the cause of health in the animal body). And in this way some things are said of God and creatures analogically, and not in a purely equivocal nor in a purely univocal sense. For we can name God only from creatures. Hence, whatever is said of God and creatures is said according as there is some relation of the creature to God as to its principle and cause, wherein all the perfections of things pre-exist excellently"[115]. This division is also that of the *Quaestio disputata de potentia*[116] and of the *Summa contra Gentiles*[117].

For the understanding of this division which apparently replaces an earlier division into analogy of proportion and of proportionality[118], it is important to notice that there is a given correspondence in reality between things which we want to express by applying the same name to them. This correspondence or relationship can be manifold but we can divide it into two categories: (a) there are things which are totally different and have nothing in common except a relation to a same point of departure or final end, or a reference to the same subject. The notional contents of the analogous name belong only to that some one thing which is the point of reference but is entirely extrinsical to the other analogates, although the reference to it is always present in them (else we would have metaphorical language instead of analogy). There is a real relation or proportion (e.g. of origin, of final cause) to some one thing. Hence we speak of the same *res significata* and relate things to this. Thus we speak of 'military' vehicles, 'military' doctors etc. referring these things and persons to the military and signifying the same *res significata*. In a metaphorical use of names, however, there is no ontological connection between things except perhaps vague external similarity. In I 13, 2 and 5 St. Thomas excludes the use of this type of analogy to express the relationship between created things and God: the main *analogatum* would be something in the created order and the *res significata* would first be said of created things. (b) The second type of analogy concerns things which are different but which show a similarity

---

[115] I 13, 5.

[116] *De pot.*, q.7, a.7.

[117] *S.C.G.* I, c.34.

[118] Cajetanus thinks that this *duplex modus* is a subdivision of the analogy of attribution (*De nom. anal.* 17 (42)), but this position is not defendable.

which is intrinsical to them. Sometimes this similarity is a sort of proportionality: we call a dog smart when it shows a certain behaviour which agrees with the way in which a smart man behaves. Or the word 'seeing' is used to express the immediate grasping of its object by the eye and the intuition of its object by the intellect. But often such a proportionality is absent. For instance, it does not make much sense to say that an accident is to its being what a substance is to its being. Substance rather is the fundamental reality. An accident is real and is a being but in such a way that it exists in a subject which it determines. Yet there is an analogy.

This agreement or correspondence means that although the essential *ratio* of the two things compared is different[119], some characteristics or properties are nevertheless intrinsically present in each of them which allow us to use the same name. The unity of this analogous use of a name lies in the fact that the same *res significata* is intrinsically present in both things although in different ways.

We now come to the analogy between God and created things: the 'ontological situation' is clear: (a) God contains in himself the perfections found in the created world, (b) he does so in the simplicity and eminence of his divine being (*esse*). For this reason the essential contents of what we mean by 'wise' or 'good' are in God, even if in a totally different way. This analogy can hardly be signified by the term 'proportionality' and for this reason Aquinas resorts to a new terminology in the *S.C.G., the De Potentia* and the *Summa theologiae*. A confirmation is found in the *Commentary on the Nicomachean Ethics*[120]. This new terminology is preferable for the simple reason that we hardly have the means to verify a proportionality in God (as we do with 'seeing' or 'calm') for God is unknown to us and we cannot directly observe him. At the most one could say that the way in which God arranged the world is similar to that in which a wise man would organize his household, but even this comparison requires much reasoning and is not without some unknown factors. In the supernatural order one can more easily speak of such a proportionality because the faithful have a real experience of God's patience and goodness.

---

[119] This point was forcibly argued by Meister Eckhart: "Analogata nihil in se habent positive radicatum formae secundum quam analogantur" (quoted after J. Koch, "Zur Analogielehre Meister Eckharts", in K. Ruh, *Altdeutsche und altniederländische Mystik*, Darmstadt 1964, 275-307). Eckhart apparently reached the erroneous conclusion that in creatures there are no transcendental perfections, because he failed to notice that St. Thomas applies the second member of the division to the analogy between God and created things.

[120] *In I Ethic.*, lectio 7, St. Thomas distinguishes between four types of analogy. The first three correspond to the first member of the division in the *S.Th.* The fourth type is described as follows: "Quandoque vero secundum unam proportionem ad diversa subiecta; eandem enim proportionem habet visus ad corpus et intellectus ad animam". This analogy is said to apply to the predication of 'good' of God and of creatures.

The names of God: Whether Names Predicated of God are Predicated
Primarily of Creatures (I 13, 6)

In our study of analogy an important question must still be clarified. If the
relationship of God to created things is similar to that of medicine to health
in animals, are the analogous names not primarily predicated of creatures? St.
Thomas answers that metaphorical names applied to God are primarily said
of created things, for these names only signify that God acts somewhat like
created things. If, on the other hand, analogous names would only be
predicated of God as the cause of certain perfections (as was the opinion of
Alain of Lille) such terms would primarily be said of creatures and God would
be named after his causal relation to created things. But because these perfections of created things exist in God in a more excellent way, "these names are
applied primarily to God rather than to creatures, because these perfections
flow from God to creatures; but as regards the imposition of the names, they
are primarily applied by us to creatures, which we know first. Hence they have
a mode of signifying which belongs to creatures".

By this answer St. Thomas upholds at the same time the ontological
primacy of God and the psychological priority of our knowledge of created
things. Having arrived at the end of the discussion of analogy the question
which must be answered is that of the value of the use of such names to signify
God's being. Time and again St. Thomas reminds us that there is an infinite
distance between God and created things[121]. The effects of God do not lead
us to a quidditative knowledge of God because created perfections pre-exist
in God in an entirely different way.

Aquinas introduces a further distinction to define even better the limits of
our knowledge of God, viz. that between the mode of existence of a certain
perfection on the one hand and its notional contents on the other. With regard
to the first there is a greater distance between divine wisdom and human
wisdom than there is between "the laughter of a field made beautiful by
flowers" and "the laughter which makes the countenance of man beautiful",
because in God wisdom is infinite subsistent being (*esse*). But with regard to
the notion expressed there is greater correspondence between God and created
perfection for there is analogy with one *ratio communis*, whereas the laughter
of a meadow is only a metaphor[122].

St. Thomas' balanced solution of the problem of the analogous use of
names of God safeguards divine transcendence but also a certain similarity
between created things and their Cause[123]. The subtlety and perfect

---

[121] I-II 114, 1; *In I Sent.*, d.22, q.1, a.2 ad 3.

[122] *In I Sent.*, d.22, q.1, a.2 ad 3.

[123] See the excellent study by Th.A. Fay, "The Problem of God-language in Thomas Aquinas:
What can and cannot be said", in *Rivista di Filosofia neoscolastica* 69 (1977) 385-391.

equilibrium of this doctrine has not always been understood. In particular some analytical philosophers have been very critical of recourse to analogy to justify God language. They hold that philosophy is the criticism of language and has the task to replace misleading statements by other proportions which are less so. Instead of appreciating the care with which St. Thomas elaborated his grammar of God-language, they think that he tries to escape the refutation of sentences like "God is love" by adding ever new restrictions to their sense so that God dies the death of a thousand qualifications[124]. W. T. Blackstone argues that it is hardly enlightening to ascribe analogically goodness to God when we know nothing about his being. He feels that if we are to know something analogically about God, we must first know something literally[125]. When nothing literal is known about God, one analogy is invoked to explain another analogy. "When St. Thomas says that an effect resembles God solely according to analogy, not only goodness but also resemblence is viewed analogically"[126]. When God possesses the qualities of infinite goodness and infinite knowledge, the difference between these and human goodness and knowledge is not one of degree but of kind. "These 'infinite' qualities do not have the experiential grounding for meaningful comprehension"[127]. R. Swinburne argues that once we give analogical senses to words, proofs of coherence or incoherence become very difficult[128]. Furthermore, as the number of words used analogically increases, less information is conveyed[129]. Swinburne feels closer to Scotus and Ockham who claimed that predicates applied to both God and man are used univocally. Ian T. Ramsey proposes to resort to a rather loose use of analogy: we employ various words and models to get across a message about God, but we cannot apply these models too strictly[130].

It is not difficult to answer these criticisms: St. Thomas was facing the fact that in Christianity as well as in non-Christian religions God language does exist, so that the question of its value must be examined. Those who beforehand reject propositions about God as nonsensical (even if they are willing to assign to the latter an esthetical, ethical or emotional role) are obeying an ideology, which dictates the *a priori* exclusion of any rational knowledge of what lies beyond the realm of the senses. It must furthermore be kept in mind that St. Thomas does not begin his treatise by claiming that our language about God is analogical. He first establishes God's existence and

---

[124] Cf. A. Flew in A. Flew and A. MacIntyre (edit.), *New Essays in Philosophical Theology*, London 1955, 96-99.

[125] *The Problem of Religious Knowledge*, Englewood Cliffs 1963, 66.

[126] *O.c.*, 67.

[127] *Ibidem*.

[128] *The Coherence of Theism*, Oxford 1977, 61.

[129] *O.c.*, 70.

[130] *Religious Language*, London 1957, 81.

explains how God is or, rather, how he is not. Created beings, as the effects of God, must have some similarity to their Cause. Hence whatever perfection is found in them must pre-exist in the unity of divine Being. It follows that when we affirm wisdom or goodness of God, we do not use a metaphor but make an entirely literal assertion: wisdom and goodness are formally in God and much more so than they are in man. But the infinite simplicity and eminence of divine being remains hidden from our intellect, so that we know, without understanding how, that wisdom, goodness and the other perfections are taken up in the unity of divine being. Thus our concepts and the names we use become analogous when applied to God; they do not die "the death of a thousand qualifications" but touch the mystery of divine transcendence.

With regard to Swinburne's sympathy for Scotus' solution, we trust that our previous explanations have sufficiently shown that univocal predication between God and created things is to be excluded. We may add that there is no concept of a *res significata* without the connotation of a particular *modus significandi*. This mode of signifying is entirely different in the case of God and of created things, whereas in univocal predication the same *modus significandi* remains present throughout. The debate with Scotus is somewhat more than a technical subtlety, for it concerns the question whether our concepts of being and other perfections encompass both God and the created order. If one choses this position, one is moving into a direction which submits God to man's thought. Deism and modern subjectivism are no longer far away.

The Names of God: are Names which Imply Relation to Creatures Predicated of God Temporally (I 13, 7)

In God language and, in particular, in the Bible certain names are said of God which imply a relation to the world or man and connote a beginning in time. When we say that God is the Creator of heaven and earth or that he is the Lord of all men, we seem to signify something which has a beginning. This places us before a difficulty because God is eternal. To clarify this aspect of the philosophical grammar of God language St. Thomas first gives a description of what relations are, dividing them into three groups: logical relations which only exist in the apprehension of reason (for instance, relations between being and non-being); relations which are realities as regards both extremes (as is the case with all relations consequent upon quantity); relations between extremes in such a way that in one extreme they are real, while in the other they are only notional. An example of this last group is knowledge: the intellect and the senses have a real relation to the object which determines their knowledge, but the things which are known belong to the physical world and not to the order of knowledge and hence they have no real relation to the senses or the intellect which know them. This case applies whenever two extremes are not of one order.

St. Thomas then draws the conclusion: "Since ... God is outside the whole order of creation and all creatures are ordered to him and not conversely, it is manifest that creatures are really related to God himself whereas in God there is no real relation to creatures, but a relation only in thought inasmuch as creatures are related to him. Thus there is nothing to prevent such names which import relation to the creatures, from being predicated of God temporally, not by reason of any change in him, but by reason of the change in the creature''. In the replies to the five objections St. Thomas works this solution out in more detail. It must be kept in mind that when *real* relations to creatures are excluded from God, this is meant formally, viz. there are no accidental determinations added to God's being and relating him to the world, but God is "related" to created things inasmuch as he gives them being, allows them to act and is the final Good to which all their activities are directed.

On the Names of God: On the Precise Meaning of the Name 'God' (I 13, 8-10)

The eighth article treats the question whether the name 'God' signifies God's nature. As we have already indicated above, in this article St. Thomas explains the difference between that from which a name is imposed and that which a name signifies. Because God is not known to us in his nature, we impose a name from his operations, in particular from his universal providence over all things. But in doing so we nevertheless intend to signify God's nature as existing above all things.

For the etymology of the terms 'deus' and 'God' one may consult the first chapter. It could well be that the operation most commonly associated with God is that of imposing order on the world, governing the elements and giving fertility. Man tried to express this by the name 'God'.

The name 'God' cannot be communicated to other beings because it is intended to signify God's being which is most incommunicable[131]. In the tenth article St. Thomas draws attention to the fact that some people have wrong ideas about God's nature and conceive it as a specific essence which is attributed by them to different things. In Greece and Rome terms as 'god' and 'divine' were indeed applied to beings at different levels of reality, which show some likeness to God or share to some extent one or more of his attributes, at least according to the opinion of those who used the terms. This is an analogous use of the term. "Likewise, when we call an idol 'god', by this name 'god' we understand that something is signified which men think to be

---

[131] Cf. I 11, 3.

God"."If any name were given to signify God not as to his nature but as to his *suppositum* according as he is considered as *this something*, that name would be absolutely incommunicable as, for instance, perhaps the tetragrammaton among the Hebrews"[132]. To understand better what is meant by this remark of St. Thomas we should remember that the name J(a)hw(e)h occurs more than 6000 times in the Old Testament and became the proper name of God in Jewish tradition. Early mediaeval writers usually took their information about the name *Jhwh* from St. Hieronymus[133]. In the Middle Ages fantastic speculations about its meaning were sometimes proposed[134], but Aquinas remains very sober in his explanation but he does go so far as to suggest that the tetragrammaton might in a sense be more proper to God than the name 'He who is'. This concession of St. Thomas only occurs in the *S. Th.* and may have been inspired by a text of Maimonides[135].

The Names of God: Is the Name 'He Who Is' the Most Proper Name of God?
(I 13, 11)

In Exodus 3, 13-14 we read that when Moses asked the Lord what to answer when the people should say to him "What is his name?", the Lord answered him: "Thus shalt thou say to them: 'He who is' hath sent me to you". The meaning of this expression written in Hebrew has variously been understood: (a) I am the one who makes things be (and hence one may place one's trust in me). (b) I am being itself. (c) I am personal, active, free being. (d) A functional interpretation considers the answer evasive or as a refusal to answer now: "You will find out later".

Those who read these words in the Greek version of the *Septuagint* were inclined to understand the answer ontologically as a statement about God's deepest being. This understanding does not necessarily contradict the interpretations listed under (a), (c) and (d). Philo of Alexandria strongly supported this understanding: God alone is true being; all other things are perishable[136]. Outside the sphere of Biblical revelation Plutarch affirmed that "You are" is the only name which really belongs to God[137]. Returning to the interpreta-

---

[132] I 13, 9.

[133] *Epist. ad Marcellam; De decem nominibus Dei: PL* 22, 429.

[134] See A.M. Dubarle, "La signification du nom de YHWH", in *RScPhTh* 35 (1951) 5-21; G. Lambert, "Que signifie le nom divin de YHWH?", in *Nouvelle revue théologique* 74 (1952) 897-915.

[135] See *The Guide of the Perplexed* I 61 and F. Niewöhner, in *HWB* 6, 394-5; A. Maurer, "St. Thomas on the Sacred Name *Tetragrammaton*", in *Mediaeval Studies* 34 (1972) 275-286.

[136] Cf. *Mut.* 11; *Vita Moysi* 1, 75; *Det.* 160; *Conf. ling.* 137. See also A. de Libera et E. Zum Brunn (edit.), *Celui qui est. Interprétations juives et chrétiennes d'Exode 3, 14*, Paris 1986.

[137] *De E apud Delphos* 18 and 19. Plotinus, however, places God (the One) above being. Being is only given with *Noûs* and emanates from the One (*Enn.* 5, 9, 8). Porphyrius, on the other hand, identified being with God. See P. Hadot, *Porphyre et Victorinus*, Paris 1968, vol. II.

tion of the Exodus text we notice that the Fathers, both in the East and in the West, give a metaphysical meaning to these words and consider 'He who is' the most proper name of God. St. Gregory of Nazianze writes that being is proper to God in a most exclusive way; 'He who is' is the best name of God[138]; God is like an infinite ocean of being[139]. Similar affirmations are found in the works of St. Gregory of Nyssa[140]. It is true, however, that some of the Greek Fathers did not so much consider the name the real name of God as an expression of God's ineffability[141].

In the West St. Hilary insists on the importance of the name[142] as do St. Ambrose[143] and St. Augustine[144] who stress its implication of divine immutability In this they are followed by St. Anselm and St. Bonaventure, who likewise regard the name as an expression of divine immutability. St. Albert raises the question whether the name 'He who is' signifies God's essence; he refers to St. John Damascene who holds that none of the names said of God are as proper as 'He who is' but that nevertheless it does not signify the *quid* of God[145]. For St. Albert himself the name signifies the absence of determination[146].

Aquinas affirms that the best name we may give to God is that of being (*esse*) in this sense that God is self-subsistent being itself. He holds this doctrine from the early *Scriptum super libros Sententiarum*[147] to his last works and the *Quaestio disputata de potentia* 7, 7 as well as the *Summa theologicae* In the *Summa contra gentiles* St. Thomas, who is always so sober and formal in his language, calls this revelation of God's name to Moses a sublime truth[148]. St. Thomas understands the name in the meaning being (*esse*) has in his metaphysics, viz. the actuality of all acts and the perfection of all perfections[149]. Over the years Aquinas quotes different authorities in support of his understanding of this "sublime truth": Holy Scripture, St. John Damascene, St. Hilary, Boethius, etc.[150]. He even interprets Dionysius' doctrine of the primacy of the Good in such a way that goodness adds the aspect of desirability to being; being is the first effect caused by God and contains

---

[138] *Orat.* 30, 18.
[139] *Orat.* 45, 3: *PG* 36, 625C.
[140] *Contra Eunomium III 3: PG* 45, 768f.
[141] Cf. Origines, *De orat.* 24: *PG* 11, 491.
[142] *De Trin.* I 5: *PL* 10, 28.
[143] *In Ps.* 43, 19: *PL* 14, 1100: "Nihil tam proprium Deo quam esse semper'.
[144] *De Trin.* VII 5, 10; *In Ioan, Evang.* 38, 10; *Enn. in Ps.* 101. God is the 'ipsum esse': "vere esse est enim semper eodem modo esse".
[145] *De fide orthod* I 9: *PG* 94, 835. Cf. I 12.
[146] *In I Sent.*, d.2 D, a.13 ad q.2.
[147] *In I Sent.*, d.8, q.1, a.1.
[148] I, c.22.
[149] See volume I, chapter twelve.
[150] *De Trinitate*, c.2: (divina substantia) "esse ipsum est et ex qua esse est".

(*praehabet*) in itself the other perfections. In this way it expresses best divine being[151]. In the *S.Th.* Aquinas does not mention this argument, probably because it considers being more as a first participation than as self-subsistent reality itself. With three other arguments instead St. Thomas shows that 'He who is' is the most proper name of God. "First, because of its signification. For it does not signify some form, but being itself. Hence, since the being of God is his very essence (which can be said of no other being), it is clear that among other names this one most properly names God; for everything is named according to its essence.

Secondly, because of its universality. For all other names are either less universal, or, if convertible with it, add something above it at least in idea; hence in a certain way they inform and determine it. Now in this life our intellect cannot know the essence itself of God as it is in itself, but however it may determine what it understands about God it falls short of what God is in himself. Therefore the less determinate the names are, and the more universal and absolute they are, the more properly are they applied to God. Hence Damascene says that 'He who is' is the principal of all names applied to God; for comprehending all in itself, it contains being itself as an infinite and indeterminate sea of substance[152]. Now by any other name some mode of substance is expressed determinately, whereas this name 'He who is' determines no mode of being, but is related indeterminately to all; and that is why it names the infinite ocean of substance.

Thirdly, from its consignification, for it signifies being in the present; and this above all properly applies to God, whose being knows not past or future, as Augustine says"[153].

In his reply to the first objection St. Thomas adds that, in a sense, the name God is more proper as it is imposed to signify divine nature and still more proper is the tetragrammaton because it is imposed to signify the incommunicability of God.

The three arguments proposed by Aquinas are also a summary of the treatise on divine attributes: because there is no composition in God, God's essence is his being (*esse*) and this is proper to God alone. God's unity flows forth from it. God's omni-perfection is given with the fact that he is being itself. Likewise his immutability and eternity flow forth from the acutality and togetherness of his being. The arguments given by St. Thomas show that this

---

[151] *De div. nom.*, c.5. See *In I Sent.*, d.8, q.1, a.1.

[152] *De Fide orth.* I 9.

[153] Cf. Peter Lombard, *Sent.* I 8 (I 58); St. Isidore, *Etym.* VII 1: *PL* 82, 261; Rhabanus Maurus, *In Exod.*, I 6: *PL* 108, 21 (the references are those given in the Translation of the *S.Th.* by the English Dominicans. On the above see also R. Imbach, *"Deus est intelligere"*. *Das Verhältnis von Sein und Denken in seiner Bedeutung für das Gottesverständnis bei Thomas von Aquin und in den Pariser Quaestiones Meister Eckharts. Studia Friburgensia*, NF 53, Fribourg 1976.

"sublime truth" is accessible to man's natural reason, even if, as a matter of fact, it is only within the context of Revelation that this doctrine of God was worked out.

According to J. Owens the concept of being (*esse*) is unable to signify divine nature. The reason is that if we conceive God as an indeterminate sea of being, our concept is that of something existing in indefinite fashion. In other words we conceive being as a nature or a thing, but being is not known as a nature (in a concept). Therefore this name cannot express God's being in its transcendent greatness and otherness. Owens understands the name 'He who is' as an imperfect name and prefers to withdraw himself into negative theology[154].

While we must agree with Owens' insistence on the importance of the negative element of our knowledge of God, we cannot help pointing out that Gilson's theory that we have no concept of being (or that, if we have one, it no longer signifies real, individual being) is not correct[155]. It is, moreover, remarkable that St. Thomas himself has no difficulty here and considers 'He who is' the best name of God. It is true that when applying this name to God we must remain within the compass of negative theology. We do so in that we are aware of the fact that God's being is entirely different and that even if the *res significata* (actuality and perfection) is the same, the mode of signifying is entirely different in God and so much so that it transcends our understanding.

The 'Names of God: Whether Affirmative Propositions can be Formed of God (I 13, 12).

The question treated in this article closes the entire treatise. An ancient and sound theological tradition as well as St. Thomas himself so strongly insists on the negative character of our philosophical theology that one may wonder whether affirmative propositions about God are possible. Dionysius' maxim "negations about God are true, affirmations inconclusive"[156] raises serious doubts as to the value of positive statements about God. In order to show that affirmations are possible Aquinas first gives an analysis of what an affirmative proposition is: in a true affirmation we signify that something which in reality is one in some way or other, has a content which is formally distinguished by reason (*secundum rationem*). For instance, the proposition "this man is white" connects two different forms which are in one subject. The

---

[154] "Aquinas-"Darkness of Ignorance" in the most Refined Notion of God", in R.W. Shahan and Francis J. Kovack (edit.), *Bonaventure and Aquinas. Enquiring Philosophers*, University of Oklahoma Press 1976. 69-86.

[155] See volume I, chapter twelve.

[156] *De cael. hier.* II 3. For an explanation of the maxim see above, chapter IV, I on negative theology.

composition of our judgement expresses this real identity. In this way we know also when we speak about God that God is one and that the multiplicity of names we use and the duality of subject and predicate are only an aspect of our thinking about God and the composition of subject and predicate represent God's unity. The human "intellect cannot apprehend simple subsisting forms as they really are in themselves; but it apprehends them after the manner of composite things in which there is something taken as subject and something that is inherent. Therefore it apprehends the simple form as a subject and attributes something else to it". But it knows that these forms in themselves are not composite and thus far its affirmation of a predicate of God is true.

We may add that our affirmations concern reality. When we say that it is cold, we affirm something about reality. Our affirmations of God also regard God's being. In his reply to the first objection (which states Dionysius' maxim) St. Thomas observes that Dionysius intends to say that no name can be said of God according to the mode of signification it has in God, because God's being transcends our thinking. In the *De Potentia*[157] the answer is somewhat more explicit: Dionysius wanted to say that affirmations can be said of God with regard to the thing signified, but that they must be denied with regard to the way of signifying. For this reason they can absolutely be denied of God because they do not apply to him in the mode which is signified. Nonetheless, concludes Aquinas, they belong to him in a more sublime way.

---

[157] *De potentia* 7, 5 ad 2.

CHAPTER EIGHT

THE KNOWLEDGE AND LIFE OF GOD

In the introduction to his treatise of God's operation St. Thomas gives a survey of the contents of that part of the *Summa theologiae* which extends from question fourteen to twenty-six. "Having considered what belongs to divine substance, we have now to treat of what belongs to God's operation. And since one kind of operation is immanent, and another kind of operation proceeds to an exterior effect, we shall treat first of knowledge and will; and afterwards of the power of God, which is taken to be the principle of the divine operation as proceeding to an exterior effect. Now because to understand is a kind of life, after treating of the divine knowledge, we must consider the divine life".

The Knowledge of God (I 14)

Aquinas divides the treatise of divine knowledge into the study of God's knowledge proper, that of God's truth and of the divine ideas, viz. the essences of things are existing in God. The question of God's knowledge itself comprises sixteen articles. The first four concern God's understanding of himself, while the twelve following articles deal with God's knowledge of things other than himself. It must be noted that the Latin term for knowledge here is *scientia*, which signifies intellectual knowledge which is certain as it understands the causes of what it knows.

God's Knowledge of Himself (I 14, 1-14)

A first question is whether there is knowledge in God (I 14, 1). In Greek religion and philosophy knowledge was generally ascribed to the gods, even if in the later Platonic tradition the tendency prevailed to place the supreme principle above knowledge. Knowledge implies a certain duality of the knowing subject and the object known and for this reason Plotinus placed it outside the One. He holds that there is something higher than pure thinking. Although thought belongs to the divine, it is secondary[1]. Thinking is "in two"; it is otherness and sameness, and hence a sort of scission[2]. *Noûs* is

---

[1] *Enn.* VI 7, 41, 1-3.
[2] *Enn.* V 3, 11, 22; 3, 10, 23-25; 44-45.

multiple unity³. From this Plotinus infers that Aristotle in saying that the First Being knows itself, makes it a duality, so that it no longer is the First Being⁴.

St. Thomas rejects this Neoplatonic theory and solves the objection by pointing out that subsisting in oneself is self-knowledge⁵. Arguing that there is knowledge in God, he stresses the difference between beings with knowledge and those without it.

"The latter possess only their own form; whereas the knowing being is naturally adapted to have also the form of some other thing, for the species⁶ of the thing known is in the knower. Hence it is manifest that the nature of a non-knowing being is more contracted and limited; whereas the nature of knowing beings has a greater amplitude and extension. That is why the Philosopher says that the soul is in a sense all things⁷. Now the contraction of a form comes through the matter. Hence, as we said above, according as they are the more immaterial, forms approach more nearly to a kind of infinity⁸. Therefore it is clear that the immateriality of a thing is the reason why it is cognitive, and that according to the mode of immateriality is the mode of cognition. Hence it is said in *De anima* II that plants do not know because of their materiality⁹. But sense is cognitive because it can receive species free from matter; and the intellect is still further cognitive, because it is more "separated from matter and unmixed" as is said in *De anima* III¹⁰. Since therefore God is in the highest degree of immateriality, as was stated above¹¹, it follows that he occupies the highest place in knowledge".

Aquinas' argument is based on the doctrine of form and matter, act and potency as well as on the analysis of what knowledge is. The same demonstration was used by Avicenna¹² and Averroes¹³. St. Thomas himself points this out and with the great Arab philosophers he maintains that every immaterial being has knowledge¹⁴. Scotus, however, denies the validity of this argument from immateriality to knowledge, because immateriality is the essence of intellectual beings and essences are not demonstrated¹⁵. The answer is that in

---

³ *Enn.* V 4, 1.

⁴ *Enn.* V 1, 9, 7-9.

⁵ Cf. the *Expositio in librum de causis*, lectio 15; *S.Th.* I 14, 2 ad 1.

⁶ By 'species' is meant the cognoscible contents of the thing as communicated to the knower. It is sometimes called a similitude or form of the thing known and its function is to make the known present to the knower.

⁷ *De anima* III 2, 431 b 21.

⁸ This point was argued in question 7, a.2 where St. Thomas presents his own theory of infinity. The conclusion is of great importance for it sheds light on a fundamental characteristic of spiritual being, viz. its all embracing universality.

⁹ *De anima* II 12, 424 a 32.

¹⁰ *O.c.* III 4, 429 a 18; b 5.

¹¹ *S.Th.* I 7, 1. Cf. I 3, 4.

¹² *Metaphysica,* liber I, II, tr. 3, c.1.

¹³ *Destructio destructionum*, disp. VI.

¹⁴ *In II Sent.,* d.3, q.1, a.1. See St. Deandra, "L'identità dell'essere e del conoscere della Verità divina", in *Angelicum* 15 (1938) 465-514.

¹⁵ *Report. Paris.*, liber I, d.35, q.1, a.1: Vivès 22, 417b.

created intellectual beings a distinction obtains between their substance and
their intellectual operation, so that we may conclude that a substance of a certain degree of immateriality requires a like operation. In God, on the other
hand, substance and operation coincide. We may nevertheless make a distinction of reason between immateriality and thought, attributing to the first a
logical priority (not unlike the priority of God's immutability with regard to
his eternity). F. Van Steenberghen also finds fault with the argument: immateriality is a condition of knowledge but does not explain it. He prefers to
deduce the presence of knowledge in God from the fact that knowledge is a
perfection found among creatures. Since all perfections have their source in
God, God himself possesses knowledge[16]. The reply to this objection is not
difficult: knowledge is to have or to be forms in an immaterial way, i.e. objectively. God is an immaterial substance and possesses himself as such in full
actuality. Hence he is self-knowledge.

Some modern authors argue that the word knowledge has no literal common meaning when applied to God and man, so that we should avoid speaking of God's knowledge[17]. The previous chapter on the names of God and
analogy has sufficiently answered this difficulty[18].

The text of the first article sheds light on knowledge and its purpose: to
know is to acquire and to possess intentionally the contents of other beings
and so to go beyond the boundaries of one's own being. The text also suggests
that in the supreme instance of divine knowledge the order of being and that
of knowledge merge: knowledge is the highest form of self-possession of self-
subsistent being itself.

In his reply to the objections St. Thomas adds a number of observations
which proceed from the negative nature of our knowledge of God: whenever
we attribute the name of a perfection to God, we must remove from its
signification anything that belongs to the imperfect mode it has in creatures.
For this reason, knowledge in God is neither a quality nor a habitus, as it is
in man, but the divine substance itself and a pure act.

In man scientific knowledge is caused by principles. Thus we distinguish
between the understanding (*intellectus*) of the principles and the knowledge of
the conclusions. Knowledge of the highest cause is called wisdom. We furthermore speak of prudence, viz. knowledge applied to practical life. But what is
multiple and diversified in creatures, is one in God. We may use the above-
mentioned names to signify divine knowledge, but must leave out whatever
connotes limitation and imperfection. In this article St. Thomas also rejects

---

[16] *Le problème de Dieu* ..., 307.
[17] Charles Harthorne and William Reese, *Philosophers Speak of God*, Chicago 1953, 120.
[18] See in particular the commentary on I 13, 5.

implicitly St. Albert's view that God knows himself by means of a plurality of *rationes*, i.e. cognitive likenesses[19].

The first article concluded that there is knowledge in God and that God is his knowledge. The second article makes this conclusion more precise by nothing that God knows himself. The insight that God is "thinking of thinking" was reached by Aristotle[20]. The precise meaning of this expression is a matter for debate[21]. It has been criticised as a meaningless repetition. Others take its meaning to be "supreme thought". More recently R. Norman argued that the meaning of the expression is that the Unmoved Mover has only abstract thought and no self-knowledge[22], but this interpretation is wrong as is patent when we place the expression in its context: the First Unmoved Mover is for ever active in the happiest of lives; his activity is contemplation[23]. He is *noûs* thinking himself[24]. The text implies that the divine knower and the object of his knowledge are the same; moreover his very being is the act of knowing. Aristotle's doctrine of God as "thinking of thinking" had a profound influence on later philosophy, in particular on Middle Platonism[25] and on Plotinus[26].

St. Thomas seems to have some reservations with regard to this expression for neither in *S.C.G.* I 45-48 nor here does he mention it. In his *Commentary on the Metaphysics* the reason for this reserve is indicated: Aquinas understands the clause as having, in the context of chapter nine of Book XII, the role of an objection which restricts God's thinking to a reflection on his thinking to the exclusion of being himself the intelligible[27]. St. Thomas' interpretation has a certain probablity. Later Scholastics such as John of St. Thomas defined God as subsistent thinking of himself. Outside the tradition of Scholastic philosophy Hegel saw in Aristotle's words an anticipation of his own theory of the dialectical movement of the absolute Idea which is enacting itself as the Absolute Spirit, producing and enjoying itself[28].

Returning to St. Thomas' text we notice that the solution begins with the assertion that God knows himself through himself. To show this Aquinas recalls the difference between operations that remain in the operator (immanent actions) and those which pass into an external effect (transient actions).

---

[19] See St. Albert, *In I Sent.*, d.2, a.3.
[20] *Metaph.* XII 9, 1074 b 34.
[21] Cf. L. Elders, *Aristotle's Theology*, Assen 1972, 259.
[22] "Aristotle's Philosopher-God", in *Phronesis* 1969, 63-74.
[23] *Metaph.* 1072 b 18.
[24] *L.c.*, b 19.
[25] See Albinus, *Didaskalikos* X 3.
[26] Plotinus, *Enn.* V 3, 7, 18-19.
[27] *In XII Metaph.*, lectio 11, n.2617.
[28] *Enzykl.* III § 577.

In the former group of operations the object of the action (which is its term) is in the operator. When this object is in the operator, this activity is actually within him. Aristotle expressed this by saying that the sensible in act is the sense in act and the intelligible in act is the intellect in act[29]. We feel, see or know something when our senses are actually informed by its species (cognitive likeness). By these species the senses or the intellect, which were in potentiality to knowledge, have become actualised. However, God has nothing of potentiality in himself. He cannot be determined by an object but his intellect and the object must be altogether the same, so that the intelligible species is the divine intellect itself which is identical with God's being: God understands himself through himself.

St. Thomas' argument is based throughout on the doctrine of act and potency. God is pure actuality and therefore immaterial; he is himself in an immaterial way and thus he is self-knowledge. For his self-knowledge cannot be an addition to his being, but must be his substance. In his reply to the first objection Aquinas recalls that self-knowledge is a sort of returning to oneself. Now those cognitive powers which subsist in themselves (i.e., which do not need the organic whole of the body to exist, but which have existence by themselves) return to themselves and hence also have self-knowledge. "Now it supremely belongs to God to be self-subsisting. Hence ... he supremely returns to his own essence and knows himself"[30].

In his reply to the third objection St. Thomas explains why self-knowledge in man remains so imperfect: our intellect must be perfected by an intelligible species even with regard to itself, for it is in a state of potentiality. It knows its act of understanding and its intellectual power by understanding intelligible objects. God, on the other hand, is pure act in the order of being and of intelligible objects and so he understands himself through himself.—One might further add that man's intellect is directed to the knowledge of the physical world and only secondarily to self-knowledge. A corollary of this article is that the duality of subject and object is not essential to knowledge because it is absent in God.

There follows the question of whether God comprehends himself (I 14, 3). This article is introduced by two objections which are closely connected with one another. Their purpose is to provoke a reflection on what self-knowledge and self-comprehension of Infinite Being means. St. Augustine observes that whatever comprehends itself, is finite to itself[31]. Since God is infinite, this creates a difficulty, unless one is prepared to admit that he is both finite and

---

[29] *De anima* 426 a 16; 430 a 3.

[30] This argument may also be used in a different way, viz. starting from the presence of self-knowledge in man, we can conclude that man's soul is not material.

[31] *Lib. 83 quaest.*, q.15: *PL* 40, 15.

infinite. St. Thomas replies that it is obvious that God knows himself as perfectly as he is perfectly knowable:

"For everything is knowable according to the mode of its actuality, since a thing is not known according as it is in potentiality, but in so far as it is in actuality, as said in *Metaph.* IX (1051 a 31). Now the power of God in knowing is as great as his actuality in existing; because it is from the fact that he is in act and free from all matter and potentiality, that God is cognitive, as was shown above. Whence it is manifest, that he knows himself as much as he is knowable; and for that reason he perfectly comprehends himself".

The reply to the objections shows where the difficulty arises from: to comprehend suggests the idea that one thing *includes* and *possesses* another. But God's intellect is not a reality apart from God himself which would include and contain God. When we apply the verb 'to comprehend' to God, we must understand it along the lines of negative theology. God is in himself and comprehends himself insofar as nothing of himself remains hidden from him. God's essence does not exceed his intellect, for the latter is himself. But we should not say that he is finite to himself in the sense that he understands himself to be something finite.

The fourth article examines whether the act of God's intellect is his substance. It closes the first part of question fourteen which treats of God's knowledge of himself. Aquinas asserts the identity in God of intellect, the object known, the intelligible species and the act of understanding. In modern philosophy knowledge is sometimes described as the construction by the self of that which is not the self and a sharp opposition or even an unbridgeable gap is assumed to separate the knower and his object. Knowledge is regarded as a duality by Fichte[32]. The idea recurs in a somewhat modified form in existentialist phenomenology[33]. Realism, on the other hand, affirms that the greatest possible union (*unio omnium maxima*) obtains between the thinking subject and the thing known[34]. It sees a progressive realisation of this union, starting from sensitive knowledge and ending in the highest form of intellectual life in God in whom there is a total identity[35].

---

[32] According to Fichte the unity of the Absolute Self is ruptured by the duality of the Self and the Non-Self at the level of knowledge. See his *Wissenschaftslehre* (1794) I 270

[33] See M. Merleau-Ponty, *Phénoménologie de la perception*, 270: "Ce qui fait la "réalité" de la chose est donc justement ce qui la dérobe à notre possession. L'aséité de la chose, sa présence irrécusable et l'absence perpétuelle dans laquelle elle se retranche, sont deux aspects inséparables".

[34] This doctrine is derived from certain texts of Aristotle (*De anima* 424 a 25 and 431 b 21; *Metaph.* XII 7, 1072 b 20-22) and was formulated by Averroes, *In III De anima*, comm. V, disgr. in sol. q.2. Plotinus pointed out this identity in contemplative knowledge (*Enn.* V 8, 10; VI 9, 10). See also St. Gregory of Nyssa, *PG* 44, 1269 C and St. Augustine, *De Trin.* IX, 12, 18: "cognitum enim et cognitor ipsa est". St. Thomas observes that in man's intellectual knowledge the experience of one's self is concomitant on knowing something. See below I 14, 6 ad 1. Cf. *De verit.* 10, 8.

[35] See the sublime account in *De verit.* 2, 2.

In God there is no potency and no composition. Hence his intellect and his thinking are his substance[36]. Because God is without composition, there is in him no form and no intellectual species which is something other than his being. Hence his very essence is his intelligible species. The stupendous conclusion of the article is that "in God intellect, the thing understood, the intelligible species and the act of understanding are entirely one and the same". In other words, God's knowledge is wholly different from ours and surpasses our understanding.

God's knowledge of things other than himself (I 14, 5-16)

Articles five to sixteen treat the problem whether and how God knows the world, that is things other than himself. To religious man the answer to this question is obvious[37], but for the philosopher it is not without certain difficulties. Some argue that there is no divine knowledge of the world nor providence since god-fearing people sometimes suffer while murderers and tyrants wield power[38]. The Epicureans believed that the gods are impassible and entirely self-sufficient, so that there is no conceivable reason why they would concern themselves with human affairs[39]. Plato mentioned a view which admits the existence of the gods but denies divine providence[40].

While Plato vigorously affirms the prescience and loving care of the gods with regard to man, Aristotle stresses God's self-sufficiency and immutability. In his dialogue *De philosophia* he argues that the world cannot have a beginning because God cannot proceed from not-willing the world to a decision to make it[41]. In *Metaph.* XII 9 Aristotle attempts to show that God cannot have anything other than himself as the object of his thinking. For, if this were the case, his attention would shift from one object to another and God would be determined by something else which is less perfect. To deny that God knows the world is tantamount to a denial of providence. Hence it is not surprising that Christian authors criticised Aristotle's position. Tatianus writes that in his ignorance Aristotle sets limits to divine providence[42]. Athenagoras points out that Aristotle denies divine providence with regard to the sublunar world[43]. Similar criticisms are voiced by Clement of Alexandria[44] and Eusebius of Caesarea[45].

---

[36] St. Thomas refers to *Metaph.* XII 9, 1074 b 18.
[37] Cf. Homer, *Odyss.* 4, 468: θεοὶ δέ τε πάντα ἴσασιν.
[38] See Euripides, *Bellerophon*, fr. 286.
[39] Cf. Antiphon, fragm. 10.
[40] *Laws* 885 b; Xenophon, *Memor.* I 4, 10.
[41] Fr. 20: Cicero, *Lucullus* 38, 110.
[42] *Ad graecos* II 1, and 2.
[43] *Liber pro christianis* 26.
[44] *Strom.* V 14.
[45] *Praep. evang.* XV 2.

Some texts, however, of the *Corpus aristotelicum* intimate that God does have knowledge of the world[46]. Partly they are likely to be a concession to a popular way of speaking, but there are some passages which seem to go beyond such standard phrases: inasmuch as God contains in himself the plenitude of being and is the terminus of all process in the cosmos, in knowing himself he has a sort of grasp of the cosmos[47]. But the First Mover does not know himself as a model to be imitated. In the thirteenth century Aristotle's view was taken up again by some Parisian masters. One of the 219 theses condemned by Bishop Tempier asserts that God does not know things other than himself[48].

In his *Commentary on the Metaphysics* St. Thomas says that what Aristotle really intends to exclude from God is that anything else but divine being is the perfection of God's intellect[49]. Yet from this it does not follow that all other things than God are unknown to him. By knowing himself God knows all the effects contained in his power. Aquinas refers to some texts where Aristotle does indeed write that the universe depends on God[50]. St. Thomas understands this text as saying that the continued existence (and perpetuity of the substantial being of the heavens as well as the perpetuity of its movement depend on this principle. It would seem, however, that attributing the conservation of the being and movement of the celestial bodies to God goes beyond the text of Aristotle, although one might argue that it follows from certain of his principles[51].

Aquinas replies to Aristotle's objection that God could not concern himself with lower things by saying that the unworthiness (*vilitas*) of certain things does not derogate from the dignity of the intellect as long as the intellect does

---

[46] See *Metaph.* 983 a 8-10; 1000 b 3-6. Themistius declares that it would be absurd to exclude from God all knowledge of the world. See S. Pinas, in J. Wiesner (edit.), *Aristoteles Werk und Wirkung*, II, Berlin 1987, 184ff. Several modern commentators think that in these and similar texts Aristotle is taking over, for argument's sake, more popular ways of speaking. Aristotle's position is better understood if we consider that he could not assign a basis for God's knowledge of the world because he did not know God as the cause of the being of things.

[47] See *De caelo* 279 a 25-30; 284 a 4-11.

[48] Cf. R. Hissette, *Enquête sur les 219 articles condamnés à Paris le 7 mars 1277*, Louvain 1977, 37 (prop. 13). Siger of Brabant's doctrine seems to be meant.

[49] *In XII Metaph.*, lectio 11, n. 2614-2615.

[50] See 1072 b 13. Cf. *De caelo* 279 a 28-30 and our *Aristotle's Theology*, 179f.It is not clear which kind of dependence is meant by Aristotle. The text may not mean more than that the activity and the desire of the heavens turn to the First Principle, although a certain ontological dependence might be connoted (Cf. *Metaph.* 1003 b 17).

[51] In *De substantiis separatis*, c.14 St. Thomas proposes a somewhat different explanation: when Aristotle denies any knowledge of the world from God, he is arguing against the Platonists, according to whom the intelligible object is outside the knower. In *S.C.G.* I 49 Aquinas quotes the Aristotelian principle that we 'know' something when we know its cause, to show that God must know the world, but he does not refer to *Metaph.* XII 9. See M. Enrique Sacchi, "Utrum Deus cognoscat alia a se.—La teoría sobre el conocimiento divino del mundo y la exégesis de santo Tomás de Aquino", in *Divinitas* 26 (1982) 123-1611.

not rest in these things, so that it is kept from contemplating a worthier object.

Later authors insisted on the *causal* aspect of divine knowledge of the world. According to Plotinus, the *Noûs*, being the maker of the world, sees in itself what it produces[52]. A similar affirmation is found in Ammonius: because the gods are causes or "prior causes" of all beings, they cannot ignore what they have made[53]. In the Christian centuries it was considered obvious that God knows the world. St. Thomas presents the following argument: God perfectly understands himself (otherwise he would not be perfect since his being is his act of understanding). Hence God must perfectly know his power and that to which his power extends. Now God is the first effective cause, as was shown in the Second Way. He therefore knows things other than himself.

This argument avoids the formulation of the first proof of *S.C.G.* I 49: "God is by his essence the cause of the other things", an expression which might be understood along the lines of Neoplatonic pantheism; it fails to make explicit the distinction between God's essence as the object of divine understanding and created things.

Aquinas adds that God's being is his act of understanding. Now effects pre-exist in their cause, i.e., created things pre-exist in God and are necessarily in his act of understanding in an intelligible way, for everything which is in another is in it according to the mode of that in which it is. The importance of this passage cannot be strongly enough emphasised: God's knowledge of things other than himself can only be based on his causality. He knows things because he is their cause and he knows them in and through his causality. The causal nature of divine knowledge of the world was intimated by Plotinus. St. Augustine very strongly insisted on it: "Thus we see the things which you made, because they are, but because you see them, they are"[54].

The way in which God knows things other than himself must still be examined. St. Thomas proceeds as follows:

> "A thing is known in two ways: in itself, and in another. A thing is known in itself when it is known by the proper species adequate to the knowable object itself; as when the eye sees a man through the species of a man. A thing is seen in another through the species of that which contains it; as when a part is seen in the whole through the species of the whole, or when a man is seen in a mirror through the species of the mirror, or by any other way by which one thing is seen in another.
>
> So we say that God sees himself in himself, because he sees himself through his essence; and he sees other things not in themselves, but in himself, inasmuch as his essence contains the likeness of things other than himself"[55].

---

[52] *Enn.* V 9, 5.

[53] *In De interpret.* (*Comment. arist.* IV 5, 134, 4).

[54] *Conf.* XIII 38, 55; *De Trin.* XV 13: "Quod scivit creavit, non quod creavit scivit"; *De civ. Dei* XI 10. Cf. St. Gregory the Great, *Moral.* XX 23: "... ideo sunt quia videntur". See also Dionysius, *De div. nom.*, c.7, § 2.

[55] I 14, 5. On 'species' see note 6.

The reply to the second objection sheds further light on the argument: the thing understood is a perfection of the intellect not as a physical thing but by its species. Now the cognitive likeness or species in which created things are known by God is God's own essence. Hence it does not follow that these things are the perfection of the divine intellect.

A serious difficulty is presented in the third objection: if God knows created things, the latter specify God. This implies potentiality in God. The solution is that God's essence is the sole and sufficient species of all things, for it is God's essence which makes his intellect be in act[56]. It does so by the identity of its own being with the divine intellect. At the level of physical being God's essence cannot be the form of other things[57], but it can be so at the level of knowledge. For as an intelligible species the divine essence does not form a compound with the divine intellect[58].

If God knows things other than himself in his own essence, it would seem that he only knows them in a general way, viz. in his own being as the common and universal cause of creation. A good number of philosophers were keenly aware of this difficulty. Some even felt that it is below God's dignity to be concerned with particular and often trivial things[59]. Others believed that God would be changeable if he knows things in their incessant mutability. Avicenna in particular defended the view that God knows whatever he knows in a universal way, although his knowledge nevertheless extends to even the smallest of existing things[60]. Elsewhere Aquinas quotes Averroes as holding the view that God only knows things insofar as they are beings (for he is the cause of their being), but does not know the nature of their essences. One who knows heat in general knows the nature of the heat present in various things, but he does not know the nature of this particular form of heat[61]. Even some Christian authors were attracted by this theory as we shall see below.

"But this cannot be. For to know a thing in general, and not in particular, is to have an imperfect knowledge of it. Hence our intellect, when it is reduced from potentiality to act, acquires first a universal and confused knowledge of things,

---

[56] St. Thomas wrestled to find the perfect expression of this solution, as we may infer from the successive redactions of *S.C.G.* I 53. Cf. L.-B. Geiger, "Les rédactions successives de *Contra gentiles* I 53 d'après l'autographe", in *a.a.v.v., Saint Thomas d'Aquin aujourd'hui*, Paris 1963, 221-240. In the latter text Aquinas also considers the *verbum mentis* to conclude that God understands all things by one *verbum mentis*.

[57] See above chapter four on I 3, 8.

[58] Cf. *S.C.G.* III 51.

[59] See below chapter nine on God's providence.—For further details about the historical background of the question of God's omniscience, one may compare T. Rudavsky, *Divine Omniscience and Omnipotence in Medieval Philosophy. Islamic, Jewish and Christian Perspectives*, Dordrecht 1985.

[60] *Philosophia prima*, VIII, c.6 (*Avicenna Latinus. Liber de philosophia prima*, 2, Louvain-Leiden 1980, 418, 73-80 and 91-93).

[61] *In I Sent.*, d.35, q.1, a.3 Aquinas refers to Averroes' *Commentary on Metaph. II.*

before it knows them in particular, as proceeding from the imperfect to the perfect, as is clear from *Physics* I (184 a 22). If therefore the knowledge of God regarding things other than himself were only universal and not particular, it would follow that his understanding would not be absolutely perfect; therefore neither would be his being. And this is against what was said above (I 4, 1). We must therefore say that God knows things other than himself with a proper knowledge not only in so far as being is common to them, but in so far as one is distinguished from the other"[62].

By "proper knowledge" as distinguished from "knowledge in general" we understand a knowledge which fully grasps the quiddity of each thing with all its characteristics so that it is known as it is and as it differs from all other things. St. Thomas' argument is original inasmuch as he writes that to know things in general is to have an imperfect knowledge. In the dominant Platonic epistemology little importance was attached to the knowledge of individual things. Aquinas recalls that man's vocation is to know material reality. Material things, however, are individual substances. Hence our knowledge will be perfect if we know the individual things[63]. In Aquinas' realism knowledge reaches its perfection when things are known as they are.

A second novelty of this text is the inference from God's perfection: God's understanding is his being; his being is perfect; therefore his understanding is perfect. In this form the argument differs from that of *S.C.G.* I 65 which says that no kind of knowledge is lacking in God and that hence God knows the singular.

The affirmation that God knows all things with a proper knowledge must be understood in the light of the conclusion of the previous article, viz. that God knows all things in the intelligible species which is his own essence. Theologians such as Dionysius and Alexander of Hales used examples to illustrate how God knows things: the centre of a circle knows the lines proceeding from it; light knows the colours it contains[64]. But these comparisons are inadequate because neither the center nor the light is the only adequate cause of that which comes forth from it. For instance, the diversity of colours

---

[62] I, 14, 6.

[63] I, 84, 7: "... de ratione huius naturae est quod in aliquo individuo existat ... Unde natura lapis vel cuiuscumque materialis rei cognosci non potest complete et vere, nisi secundum quod cognoscitur ut in particulari existens".

[64] See *De div. nom.* II, § 5 and Alexander of Hales, *Summa theologica* I 166 (cf. I 249). The comparison of divine knowledge with the centre of a circle and the lines proceeding from it was probably inspired by Averroes, *In De anima* III 31: Crawford 471, who applies the image to the *sensus communis* in which the perceptions of the senses come together. The comparison occurs in Proclus, *In Parm*, IV 892, 20-28 (*Elem. theol.* 194-195): the sciences are contained in the soul as the radii of a circle are in the centre from which they issue. In the *De Veritate*, q.2, a.3, obi 11 Aquinas attributes the saying "Deus est sphaera intelligibilis cuius centrum est ubique, circumferentia vero nusquam" to Trismegistus. See Ps.-Trismegistus, *Liber 24 philosophorum* II (Bäumker, 208).

is not caused by the light only but by the diaphanous. St. Thomas rejects the rather popular comparison of God to the center of a circle[65]. Likewise we should not compare God's knowledge of things to the relation of the number one to the numbers following it, because the one does not perfectly contain what is consequent upon it. Rather God is like a perfect number which is equal to the sum of its own parts[66]. Whatever perfection exists in created things, pre-exists in God's essence and far more so[67]. God knows all the possible ways in which his own perfection can be shared by others.

The reply to the first objection offers an important clarification: one might understand the conclusion that God knows all other things in his own essence as saying that he knows them as they are in himself according to his own way of being as the primary and universal cause. In his answer St. Thomas recalls an insight of realism: the knower does not always know the thing known according to the being it has in the knower. An eye does not know a stone according to the being it has in the eye but (by the species of the stone) it knows it according to its being outside the eye. Because the human intellect does not create its knowledge of things but receives it, the intellect knows the things as they communicate themselves. The mode in which the thing is in the knower insomuch influences knowledge as the more perfectly a thing is in the knower, the more perfect the mode of knowledge becomes. The upshot of this passage is that if God knows things, he knows them with a proper knowledge because his own essence represents all and each of them in their most individual characteristics. This is the case because God's essence excels all creatures and pre-contains in itself whatever is found in the latter.

If God knows himself and the things other than himself, does his attention go from the one to the other, in other words, is his knowledge discursive? (I 14, 7). In man's intellectual knowledge there is a twofold discursiveness: (a) according to succession; (b) according to causality, when from principles we reach conclusions. Both kinds of discursive knowledge must be excluded from God: God sees all things in his own essence and hence he sees them simultaneously and not successively. The second mode of discursive knowledge cannot apply to God since it presupposes the first and because discursive knowledge in this sense means that one proceeds from principles to conclusions and that the latter are not known *in* but *from* the former. God, however, knows all things *in* his own essence.

---

[65] Such comparisons, sometimes accompanied by graphic representations, were current in the School of St. Victor.

[66] Euclides, Nicomachus and Theon of Smyrna describe these *perfect* numbers, of which there are only four, viz. 6, 28, 496, 8128. See Th. Heath, *A History of Greek Mathematics*, I, Oxford 1921, 74. The Pythagoreans, however, called the number 10 perfect, because it is the sum of 1, 2, 3 and 4 which form the tetractus.

[67] See I 4, 2.

The seventh article stresses that God's knowledge is very different from what we can conceive and so it takes us back to negative theology.

As we have established God's knowledge rests upon the fact that God is the cause of all things and that his being is his understanding. Aquinas now proceeds further and asks whether God's *knowledge* is the cause of things (I 14, 8). As Cajetanus writes in his commentary, this article is of great importance because St. Thomas here starts his consideration of how God produces things and so prepares for the treatise on creation. The production of things is the work of God's intellect. This article closes the series of four articles dealing with God's knowledge of things in general. From article nine onwards Aquinas discusses to which objects divine knowledge extends.

It is manifest that God causes things by his intellect, for God's being is his act of understanding. Now God's being is the cause of the world as is implied by the Second Way and will be elaborated in the treatise on creation. In this respect we may compare God's knowledge to that of an artisan who produces things by his art after their form conceived in his mind. The form in the intellect is the principle of action. It is understood that an intelligible form alone is not a principle of action unless there is an inclination to produce this effect. Hence God's intellect must be determined to precisely this effect by his will. Divine knowledge, therefore, is the measure of created things, which in their turn are the measure of the human intellect [68]. In conclusion we may say that God's knowledge of things is creative knowledge. It comprehends things and sees them as they are in their true exemplar. While our knowledge of things resembles vision in twilight, God's knowledge is full of clarity.

God's knowledge of vision comprehends all things which exist at any time, whether past, present or future, as objects present to him (I 14, 9). God's knowledge is measured by eternity, that is, it is in the unchangeable 'now' of eternity and so it knows whatever will come to be in the succession of time. On the other hand, God knows by his knowledge of simple intelligence (and not by his knowledge of vision) whatever is in the active or passive power of created things (and thus also what is in the power of thought and imagination) but which will never be realised. The basis for this knowledge is that he knows the faculties of created things, which as beings proceed from divine causality, and so he knows whatever they are capable of thinking or expressing. What is only possible and never becomes real, is not known in itself but in the active potency which is able to realise it (I 14, 9).

Whoever knows something perfectly, must also know all that can occur to it. By the very fact that God knows good things, he also knows the evil which deprives a thing of certain perfections. The knowledge of God is not the cause of evil; it is the cause of the good through which the evil is known (I 14, 10).

---

[68] Cf. *De ver.* q.1, a.2: "res naturaliter inter duos intellectus constituta est".

In his *Commentary on the De anima* 430 b 20-26 Averroes intimates that according to Aristotle God does not know privations. It follows that he does not know evil either and that divine providence is to be excluded. In his earlier works, when rejecting this error, Aquinas mentions Averroes by name[68a], but in this article he just proposes the correct interpretation of the passage: while the human intellect, which is in potentiality, knows simple and indivisible forms by means of a privation, God whose intellect is always in act, knows privations in the positive forms of which they are privations[68b]. Against this conclusion of St. Thomas, J. M. Garrigues argues that God does not know evil: he "is totally innocent". Evil does not exist and therefore it is radically opposed to God[69]. To this we say that evil does exist although not as a thing but as a privation; without the knowledge of evil, God would not understand the world.

In the eleventh article the question is raised whether God knows singular things. The article elaborates a topic already indicated in art. 6: God does not know individual things in general only, but by proper knowledge. In the latter article the question was studied from the standpoint of the perfection of God's knowledge: a general and confused knowledge is less perfect than a proper knowledge. There remains, however, a difficulty inasmuch as in human knowledge only the senses directly know the singular *qua* singular; the intellect only knows it due to its contact with the senses[70]. St. Thomas solves this difficulty by arguing that to know singular things is part of our perfection and that it is incongruous that anything known by us should be unknown to God. "Now the perfections which are found divided among inferior beings exist simply and unitedly in God", so that God knows universal and immaterial realities and singular and material things as well, for his knowledge extends as far as his causality[71].

As was pointed out above the great Arab philosophers hesitated to ascribe to God direct knowledge of singular things. In fact, in this article St. Thomas refers to the opinion of Avicenna who said that knowledge knows singular things through universal causes[72], and also to a view of Averroes according to whom God knows singular things by the application of universal causes to particular effects[73]. Aquinas shows that Avicenna's solution is inadequate:

[68a] See *In I Sent.*, d.36, q.1, a.2 ad1; *De ver.*, q.2, a.15; *S.C.G.* I 71.

[68b] Cf. R. Gauthier, *Sancti Thomae de Aquino Opera Omnia. Sentencia libri de anima* (Leonina XLV, 1) 232*.

[69] *Dieu sans idée du mal. La liberté de l'homme au coeur de Dieu*, Limoges 1982.

[70] Cf. I 86, 1: "Indirecte autem et quasi per quandam reflexionem potest cognoscere singulare". In this connection Aquinas speaks of a "continuationem quandam intellectus ad imaginationem et sensum" (*De ver.* 2, 6). See G. Klubertanz, "St. Thomas and the Knowledge of the Singular", in *The New Scholasticism* 26 (1952) 135-165.

[71] I 14, 11.

[72] *Metaph.* VIII, c.6 (100 rb).

[73] *Destructio destructionem* XI.

universal causes do not give knowledge of *this* thing as this particular thing, because the individual characteristics depend on matter and not on the universal cause.—Averroes suggested a slightly different solution which is also defective: no one applies a thing to another thing unless he first knows that other thing. The true solution of the problem, St. Thomas writes, is that God's knowledge extends as fas as his causality. Now the latter extends to whatever exists, even to matter[74]. God's knowledge is the likeness of whatever is real.

The following article deals with the question whether God can know infinite things. Raising this question does not mean that the existence of an infinite number of things is presupposed. Rather the infinite possibilities latent in created thing are envisaged. The difficulty lies in the fact that according to its definition the infinite is that which to those who measure it, leaves always something more to be measured, or, as another definition says, which it is impossible to traverse[75]. In his solution Aquinas recalls that there is no infinite number of actually existing things except in this sense that the thoughts and affections of men will be multiplied to infinity since rational beings will endure for ever in their immaterial substantial forms and intellectual activity. God knows this 'infinity in succession' by means of the science of vision. Moreover he knows the infinite possibilities in himself and in created things. He knows them all in his divine essence which is a sufficient likeness of all things that are or can be. Hence God does not know the infinite by counting its members (which would be impossible), but by comprehending his own power and the potentiality of created things. God himself is infinite; it is not contrary to the notion of the infinite to be comprehended by the infinite[76].

God's Knowledge of Future Contingent Things (I 14, 13)

In the thirteenth article St. Thomas pursues the study of the extent and mode of God's knowledge and deals with an extraordinarily difficult question, viz. if and how God knows future contigent things (FCT) such as man's free actions. If God's knowledge of them is certain, as God's perfection requires, does it not impose necessity on these contingent effects? The difficulty was already recognised in classical antiquity. In his commentary on Aristotle's *Peri hermeneias* Ammonius notes that the question of how to reconcile divine omniscience with the contingency of future events is a topic of frequent debate[77]. Boethius mentions the problem in his *De consolatione*

---

[74] See below Chapter Ten.

[75] Cf. *Phys.* 207 a 7; 204 a 3.

[76] I, 14, 12 ad i & 2.

[77] *In De interpretatione* 132, 8f. On the history of this problem see W. Lane Craig, *The problem of Divine Foreknowledge and Future Contingents from Aristotle to Suarez*, Leiden 1988.

philosophiae[78]. In St. Thomas' day some Parisian doctors denied that God has knowledge of FCT[79]. The question is not only if and how God knows the latter, but also why his knowledge does not take away their contingence. St. Thomas himself does not think that his explanation provides ultimate clarity[80]. The mystery of God's being and knowledge is far above our capacity of understanding.

By FCT Aquinas means things which have non-necessary secondary causes[81]. In his account he first recalls that God knows everything which is, because he is the first efficient cause: whatever is, participates in his being. Now FCT can be considered (a) in their causes; since these are not determined to one effect, they cannot give certitudinal knowledge; (b) in themselves; one knows FTC in themselves when one knows them as they actually are in themselves.

> "Although contingent things become actual successively, nevertheless God knows contingent things not successively, as they are in their own being, as we do, but simultaneously. The reason is because his knowledge is measured by eternity, as is also his being; and eternity, being simultaneously whole, comprises all time, as was said above. Hence all things that are in time are present to God from eternity, not only because he has the essence of things present within him, as some say[82], but because his glance is carried from eternity over all things as they are in their presentiality. Hence it is manifest that contingent things are infallibly known by God, inasmuch as they are subject to the divine sight in their presentiality; and yet they are future contingent things in their relation to their own causes"[83].

The argument used in this article is also found in other works of Aquinas[84]. It has given rise to divergent interpretations. The reason is that the text is couched in general terms, so that some sentences have been understood differently by different commentators.

As is obvious from the text and is confirmed by all the important commentators, the real, physical presence of the FCT in their own being in God's eternity is meant and not their presence in God's essence which virtually contains all things[85]. If future things would not be present in the now of God's eternity, they would be so at a future moment and so there would be a development

---

[78] *De consol.* V, prose 3.—Boethius' account of God's eternity, in which things are simultaneously present, is taken over by St. Anselm, *De concordia praescientiae et praedestinationis et gratiae Dei cum libero arbitrio*, q.1.

[79] See the 15th thesis of the 219 articles condemned in 1277 (Hissette, *o.c.*, 39ff.)

[80] In *S.C.G.* I 67 Aquinas writes that from these principles it can to a certain extent (*aliqualiter*) be made clear that God knows FCT with infallible certitude.

[81] See the reply to the first objection.

[82] Avicenna, *Metaphysica* VIII, c.6 (100rb).

[83] I 14, 13.

[84] *In I Sent.*, d.38, q.1, a.5; *S.C.G.* I 67; *De ver.* 2, 12. The solution was prepared by Boethius, *De consol. philos.* V, prose 6.

[85] See Bañez, *In I^{am}*, 14 (edit. Madrid-Valencia 1934, 353 b).

in God's knowledge. On the other hand, the fact that future things are present before God from eternity does not mean that these things exist themselves from eternity. This doctrine of the physical presence of FCT in God is proper to St. Thomas. St. Bonaventure, for instance, understands this presence in God's eternity as a knowledge by means of divine ideas, by which "God knows future things with as much certitude as when these would be present"[86].

This confronts us with the question of the meaning and scope of Aquinas' recourse to this presence of FCT in God's eternity in order to explain God's knowledge of them. The older commentators Capreolus and Cajetanus understand the presence of FCT in God's eternity as a requirement of their cognoscibility; without it FCT cannot be known with certitude. Bañez, John of St. Thomas and later commentators (e.g. Hugon, Garrigou-Lagrange) insist on the divine decrees as the medium in which God knows the FCT. The physical presence of the FCT serves the purpose of making an *intuitive* knowledge of them possible[87].

A first observation is that in this article it is understood that God's knowledge is a *causal* knowledge so that God knows things because he makes them[88]. God knows things by means of the cognitive species which is his own essence, inasmuch as this, by God's decision, is the cause of these beings[89]. With regard to this point, the same applies to God's knowledge of FCT as to that of other things. Although God knows things in himself, he knows these things as they exist in reality. There is no science without existing things as its object. God's knowledge is science, that is, certitudinal knowledge of reality. Because science is certain knowledge of reality, that which is known by science must be such that it cannot be otherwise[90]. If God is to have such a knowledge of the FCT, the latter must be real. As Cajetanus writes, a future contingent thing as such is not knowable by science[91]. It can only be the object

---

[86] *In I Sent.*, d.39, a.2, q.3 (Q.I 696): "... ita certitudinaliter sicut si essent praesentes". The term 'praesentialitas' is also used by Bonaventure.

[87] Cf. J. Groblicki, *De scientia Dei futurorum contingentium* (diss. Angelicum), Roma 1937; F. Schmitt, *Die Lehre des hl. Thomas von Aquin vom göttlichen Vorherwissen des Zukünftig Kontingenten bei seinen grossen Kommentatoren*, (diss. Nijmegen), 1950. See also L. Baudry, *La quérelle des futurs contingents (Louvain 1465-1475)*, Paris 1950; J. Mazzone, "De medio obiectivo in quo scientiae divinae circa futuribile", in *Divus Thomas* (Piac.) 1928, 231-248. That God's causality is the foundation of his knowledge of future events was already held by St. Augustine and St. Anselm.

[88] The Suarezian explanation (God knows the FCT in their objective truth: because the FCT are to exist, they possess truth which rests upon God's being) is insufficient: FCT are not from themselves but from God as their primary cause. Hence their truth must depend on God's causality.

[89] See I 14, 9 ad 3; I 16, 7 ad 3; *De ver.* 12, 11 ad 3.

[90] Cf. *In I Post. Anal.*, lectio 4, n32: "quia vero scientia est etiam certa cognitio *rei*..., oportet quod id quod scitur non possit aliter se habere".

[91] *In I^{am}* 14, 13, XXXVII.

of science, if it exists and is present. For if so, it is necessary in the sense of determined to one thing: if Socrates is sitting, then necessarily I see him sitting. As long as FCT only exist in their causes, they cannot be known with certitude.

What is novel in St. Thomas' treatment is that he requires that God's knowledge be perfect, i.e. certitudinal and unchangeable. Therefore the things he knows must be real to him; they must be present. Without their being present, God cannot know them with certitude, as the older commentators point out[92]. It is unfortunate that later the divine decrees came to be considered a sufficient basis for God's knowledge of FCT, for both the decrees and the presence of the FCT have a role to fulfil: the decrees are the medium by which God knows them, while the presence of the FCT means that the subject-matter of divine science exists and so it makes this science possible[93].

Aquinas explains this presence of FCT by means of God's eternity, in which there is no succession but which in its eternal 'now' comprizes all time. Hence God's being and knowledge actually bear upon all things which will ever be real. This does not mean that God sees future things before they are real: he sees them in the eternally present 'now' of his eternity. "God's glance", writes Aquinas, "is carried from eternity over all things as they are in their presentiality": this is not seeing of things *outside* him, because God's knowledge does not receive cognitive species from outside things. That God sees all things present means that his causal knowledge[94] is accompanied by its effects. Not in this way that from all eternity the effects exist in their own being, but that from his side God brings them to existence by his immutable causality from all eternity[95]. It is obvious that God's eternity transcends our thinking and cannot be known by us in this life. Here again our inquiry ends in a kind of negative theology.

A. Kenny calls this solution of St. Thomas misconceived and argues that on this view God does not know *future* events, for to know the future is to know more than a fact[96]. Kenny also rejects Aquinas' concept of eternity as

---

[92] M. Matthijs, "De ratione certitudinis divinae scientiae circa futura contingentia", in *Angelicum* 13 (1936) 493-497. Aquinas himself writes that we should not say: "If God knows something, it will be", but rather: "If God knows something, it is". The reason is that the antecedent proposition uses a statement about God's knowledge, so that the consequent proposition must be expressed from the point of view of God's knowledge. As has been shown, for God things are now, rather than in the future (*De ver.* 2, 12 ad 7).

[93] This position goes beyond that of John of St. Thomas who holds that the presence of things is required so that an *intuitive* knowledge is possible. The greater stress on God's decrees in later Thomism was probably due to the influence of Scotus' writings. Scotus rejects that God sees the FCT by inspection and makes God's decrees the sole cause of divine knowledge of future contingent events (*Ordin.*, q.39, q.1-3, n.44). On the aftermath of this debate see *The Cambridge History of Later Medieval Philosophy*, Cambridge 1982, 368-381.

[94] See article 8 of our question.

[95] Cf. John of St. Thomas, *In Iam*, disp. 9, art. 3, n.29 (edit. Solesmes II, 75).

incoherent, for it is ridiculous that "my typing of this paper is simultaneous with the whole of eternity". To this we reply that God sees a future fact as present, but he knows that it is a contingent fact taking place in a succession of events in time. Cajetanus pointed out that a contingent thing remains contingent even in the presence of God's infallible science[97]. Likewise God's knowledge does not take away from a thing that it is to be realised at a future moment of time. God's knowledge is not timeless in the sense that the things known by him are timeless. Kenny is mistaken in that he attributes to created things what belongs to God: it is not my typing which is simultaneous with the whole of eternity, but God's eternal now is simultaneous with this speck in the succession of time which is my typing. The deeper reason for Kenny's refusal of this doctrine is his empiricism which prevents him from understanding the stringent argumentation leading to the conclusion that God's being and knowledge cannot but be simultaneous with all things in a 'now' of reality which knows no succession.

The reply to the objections provides some further explanations: by virtue of God's free decision to the effect that FCT be, his knowledge of them is necessary, although the FCT are contingent because of their proximate causes. In his answer to the second objection Aquinas points out that although God's knowledge of the existence of the FCT is absolutely necessary, it does not follow that therefore these things themselves will be necessary. For the existence of FCT in God's knowledge is not their being as it is in itself. The reply to the third objection once more draws attention to the fact that God's knowledge is in eternity and transcends time, so that what is successively realised in time, is present to God. At this juncture Aquinas uses a comparison: a man overlooking a winding road from a height, sees different people walking on it, although these travellers, hidden as they are by the curves, do not see one another. In this connection St. Thomas raises a further objection: "Whatever is known by God must be (for God's knowledge is certain). But nothing which is future and contingent must be. Therefore nothing which is future and contingent is known by God". The solution of this difficulty runs as follows: if the *must* of the first statement is attributed to the *thing* (*res*), we do make indeed its existence necessary, but this attribution is wrong. The *must* must be applied to the proposition, so that the sense is: "This proposition, 'that which is known by God is', is necessary".

In addition to the FCT the Scholastics also speaks of *futuribilia*, i.e. things which will never actually exist but which would have come about if a specific condition had been fulfilled. This question received special attention because

---

[96] "Divine Foreknowledge and Human Freedom", in A. Kenny (edit.), *Aquinas. A Collection of Critical Essays*, London 1969, 255-270.
[97] *In I^{am}*, 14, 13, XXVII.

Holy Scripture mentions a number of such conditionally future things[98]. How can apparently certain statements be made about these *futuribilia* such as: "If this kind of miracle had happened in Sidon, the inhabitants would have converted themselves"? To explain God's knowledge of the *futuribilia* Molina resorted to the so-called *scientia media*, that is a knowledge of man's will which is not causal but a sort of comprehensive grasp of the will compared to the various situations in which it will be or could have been placed. By means of this knowledge God would infallibly know what the human will would do in particular circumstances[99]. But this explanation is wrong because it assumes that the will is determined by the circumstances and no longer free. God can only know these *futuribilia* if he is himself conditionally their cause. The foundation of his knowledge must be a conditional decree of his will.

Does God know whatever is enunciable by man! (I 14, 14). This question arises because enunciations are composed of a subject and predicate, whereas there is no composition in God's thought. The answer is that God knows whatever is in his own power or in that of creatures and so he knows all enunciations that can be made, but he does so in his own way and, not in our way. In one simple glance he understands whatever can be said of a certain subject. In our human knowledge, on the other hand, different predicates are successively attributed to it.

Is God's knowledge variable? (I 14, 15). The answer seems to be affirmative, because the things which are the object of God's knowledge are not permanent. Moreover God could have created more things than he actually did. If so, his knowledge would have been different. However, God's knowledge is his being which is totally immutable. His knowledge concerns created things inasmuch as they are in himself. Now they are in God in an invariable way, while they are variable in themselves.

One cannot say that God can know more than he actually knows: his knowledge of simple intelligence embraces whatever is possible, while he knows with the science of vision whatever from all eternity he decided to be.—The proposition 'whatever God knew, he knows' is not true if referred to what is enunciated, although God's knowledge itself does not change and is true.

A last question is whether God has a speculative or a practical knowledge of things (I 14, 16). Knowledge is called speculative when it is about such things as nature or God which cannot be made by man. Somewhat less properly it is called so if it has man-made things as its object, but in a theoretical

---

[98] Cf. I *Sam.* 23, 10-13; *Matthew* 11, 21.

[99] In his *Concordia* ... Molina coined the term *scientia media*: the latter would be between the science of vision and of simple understanding.—We cannot here discuss the debate between Thomists and Molinists. A careful study of St. Thomas' arguments shows the untenability of the Molinist position.

manner. For instance, one considers how a house is built but not in order to build one. In such cases the knowledge is also partly practical. Using this division Aquinas notes that God has a speculative knowledge of himself, but of other things he has both a speculative and a practical knowledge: his knowledge is non-practical with regard to its mode. Regarding things God never makes, his knowledge is non-practical in respect of the end.

The Ideas in God's Intellect (I 15)

In the Prologue to question fourteen St. Thomas introduces this subject as follows: "As everything known is in the knower, and the essences of things as existing in the knowledge of God are called *ideas*, to the consideration of knowledge there will have to be added a consideration of ideas".

By 'ideas' we understand the forms of things existing apart from these things themselves. They serve as exemplars of the forms (the formal contents) of things or as principles of knowledge. In Plato's thought the ideas are of fundamental importance: they are principles of knowledge and of reality. According to Plato the ideas are the supreme reality and subsist separately from the material world. Although manifold and distinct from one another they form a quasi-organic whole, but they are not the thoughts of God. Rather they are primordial objective principles of thought and of reality.

From the beginning of our Christian era, the view that the ideas are the thoughts of God begins to spread[100]. The theory probably originated from a contamination of Platonism with the Aristotelian concept of the First Unmoved Mover as well as by the growing conviction that there is one supreme God. In some texts Philo seems to express this view, although elsewhere he speaks of a creation of the intelligible world by God. Albinus proposes the theory in its fully developed form[101]. St. Augustine took over this theory of the ideas as the thoughts of God because it agrees so well with the teachings of Holy Scripture[102]. Dionysius wrestled with the problem of how

---

[100] Some historians place the start of this doctrinal development with Posidonius and Atticus. See W. Theiler, *Die Vorbereitung des Neuplatonismus*, Berlin 1934, 34ff. Cf. Seneca, *Epist.* 65, 7 and R. Miller Jones, "The Ideas as Thoughts of God", in *Class. Philol.* 21 (1926) 317-326; Audrey N.M. Rich, "The Platonic Ideas as the Thoughts of God", in *Mnemosyne* 4 (1954) 123-133. In Seneca's day the theory was widely accepted. See his *Epist.* 7, 28: "Haec exemplaria rerum omnium Deus intra se habet numerosque universorum quae agenda sunt et modos mente complexus est quas Plato ideas appellat, immortales, immutabiles, infatigabiles".—H. Tarrant believes that no additional metaphysical function is facilitated by confining the Ideas to the divine mind, for in this way they can no longer directly act upon the world. But T. overlooks the need for unification and a foundation for God's knowledge of the world. See his *Scepticism or Platonism. The Philosophy of the Fourth Academy*, Cambridge 1985, 117.

[101] *Didask.* (Hermann) 163, 30.

[102] See, for instance, his *De div. quaest. 83*, q.46, 1-2: "Singula igitur propriis sunt creata rationibus". Cf. M. Grabmann, "Des heiligen Augustinus Quaestio de Ideis (De div. quaest. 83, qu.46) in ihrer inhaltlichen Bedeutung und mittelalterlichen Weiterwirkung", in *Mittelalterliches Geistesleben* II, München 1936, 25-34.

God is strictly one while nevertheless containing the wealth of created things within himself. The doctrine of the ideas as the thoughts of God offered a solution[103]. In medieval theology the theory retained a central place[104]: the entire universe with all its laws must be present in God's intellect. In the commentaries on the *Sententiae* and in the *Summae* of the thirteenth century the doctrine of divine ideas was dealt with in the study of God's knowledge[105]. St. Bonaventure and Henry of Ghent defend it against those Aristotelians who rejected the ideas in God's intellect[106]. The question whether these ideas in God are distinguished from one another *ab intra* or *ab extra* was much discussed in the last decennia of the century. The simplicity of God's being seems to exclude a plurality of objects in God's mind. Furthermore, God's own essence must be the primary object of his intellect, so that the ideas of created things must constitute the secondary object. But is such a distinction possible[107]?

Returning now to St. Thomas' text we must recall that Gilson considers question fifteen a concession to a theological language which is not that of Aquinas himself; St. Thomas could have wanted to insert this discussion into his text only because of the authority of St. Augustine[108]. One may call the exemplariness of God's essence 'divine ideas' Gilson adds, but this does not help us very much: God's essence remains God's own being, as St. Thomas himself writes in I 15, 1 ad 3[109]. Sertillanges had been equally severe in his criticism of question fifteen: except for their exemplarity the ideas serve no purpose whatever; they give rise to misunderstandings and are a liability rather than an asset to the treatise on God[110]. The position of Gilson and Sertillanges was criticised by L. B. Geiger who argues that if Aquinas kept the theory of the divine ideas from his earliest to his last works, he did so to avoid the contradiction between the thesis of God's simplicity and the affirmation of God's distinct knowledge of a multiplicity of objects[111]. St. Thomas himself clearly states his intention: because the distinction between created

---

[103] Cf. O. Semmelroth, "Gottes geeinte Vielheit. Zur Gotteslehre des Ps.-Dionysius Areopagita", *Gregorianum* 25 (1950) 389-403.

[104] Se J.M. Parent, *La doctrine de la création dans l'Ecole de Chartres*, Paris-Ottawa 1938, 44-48 (l'exemplarisme divin du monde). See also W. Norris Clarke, "The problem of the Reality and Multiplicity of Divine Ideas in Christian Neoplatonism", in D.J. O'Meara (edit.), *Neoplatonism and Christian Thought*, Albany 1982, 109-127.

[105] Cf. Alexander of Hales, *Summa theol.* I 258ff.; St. Bonaventure, *In I Sent.*, d.36, a.2, q.1 (Q.I 623).

[106] St. Bonaventure, *In Hexaem.*, coll. 6, a.2 (Q.5, 360); Henry of Ghent, *Quodl.* IX, 15.

[107] See E. Hocedez, "La théologie de Pierre d'Auvergne", in *Gregorianum* 11 (1930) 531ff. Cf. also Scotus, *Oxon.* I, d.35 (Vivès 10, 536f.).

[108] *Introduction à la philosophie chrétienne*, Paris 1960, 174.

[109] *O.c.*, 183.

[110] *Le christianisme et les philosophes*, Paris 1939, I 276.

[111] L.-B. Geiger, "Les idées divines dans l'oeuvre de S. Thomas", in *St. Thomas Aquinas 1274-1974: Commemorative Studies*, Toronto 1974, I 175-209, 179.

things is God's work, we must place the proper *rationes* of the different things in God and therefore also a plurality of ideas[112].

In the first article of this question the presence of ideas in God's intellect is affirmed. Ideas are forms of things existing apart from the things themselves. They can be exemplars or principles of knowledge. In both senses we must posit ideas in God: the agent acts for the sake of the form insofar as he intends to realise a likeness to what he himself has in mind. Now in making the world God acts by his intellect[113]. Hence "there must exist in the divine mind a form to the likeness of which the world was made. And in this the notion of an idea consists". In his reply to the objections Aquinas adds that God knows everything else by his own essence which is the likeness of all things. His essence is also the operative principle. The ideas in God are nothing other than God's essence. Ideas are said to be principles of knowledge not in the sense of a cognitive species by means of which things are known, but as the objective form of a thing which is known. St. Thomas makes this plain by the apposition "according as the forms of knowable things are said to be in him who knows them". The same is stated clearly in the second article[114].

In the first article the emphasis is on God's essence being the likeness of all things. The question of the multiplicity of divine ideas is discussed in the following article. St. Thomas affirms the multiplicity of ideas in God's intellect: God brings about the good of the universe which consists in the order of a great number of different things[115]. It follows, Aquinas concludes, that God must have proper ideas of all things. Why does St. Thomas resort to the concept of the *order* of things to prove that there is a plurality of ideas in God instead of affirming that different things require different ideas as their exemplars? The reason is that one might think that one comprehensive idea could be the model of the variety of things, for instance, the idea of being. But to bring about an order consisting of different things which by their particular characteristics and actions cooperate with one another a proper and precise knowledge of each of them is required.

With the help of a subtle distinction Aquinas proceeds to show that a multiplicity of ideas is not repugnant to the simplicity of God: an idea is not that by means of which God knows things (as would be an intentional species), but that which is known, i.e. ideas are objects of knowledge. God's own essence is the sole cognitive species by means of which he knows all things, but understanding his essence perfectly he also knows all the modes

---

[112] *De ver.* 3, 2.
[113] See below, the commentary on question 47, a.1.
[114] Cf. Cajetanus, *In I^{am}* 15, 1, V.
[115] This affirmation is based upon the insight that the being of all things is caused by God himself. Creation through intermediate causes is not possible as will be shown in chapter ten.

in which it can be participated in by things outside himself. If God decides to make some of these things, he has ideas of them as exemplars. Of possible things there are ideas in the sense of objects known. This formulation of the doctrine of the plurality of ideas in God's intellect is more pronounced here than in the *S.C.G.* I 54 where Aquinas writes that the *rationes* (cognitive contents) of the various things in God are not several or distinct unless insofar as God knows that things can be made similar to him in various ways.

In the third article St. Thomas determines in more detail the extent of this multiplicity of ideas in God's intellect: there is no idea of evil, but evil is known through the likeness of the good in which it exists; primary matter is known through the idea of the composite thing in which it is. On this point Aquinas corrects his position of *De veritate* q. 3, a. 5 where he admitted a divine idea of primary matter itself, inasmuch as idea means *ratio*, that is the cognitive content, and not its realisation.

The distinction between ideas as exemplars and as likenesses makes it possible to solve the difficult problem whether there are ideas in God of genera, species and individuals. Nebridius, a correspondent of St. Augustine, raised the question whether God has an idea of each man or of the species 'man' only[116]. Henry of Ghent answers that as such a species has one idea in God, but with regard to the plurality of supposita in which the species is realised, there are more ideas[117]. St. Thomas solves the problem by means of the distinction between ideas as cognitive contents and ideas as exemplars[118]. Inasmuch as an idea is that which is known (and does not bear on something existing) it signifies a mode of being. Now God's essence is known by God as representing many possible ways in which his being can be imitated and shared in,—generic and specific modes as well as individually realised modes.

Insofar as God's essence is the exemplar of existing things, there are ideas in God of all things which exist, even of accidents which are, but need not be, added to substances (but not of those accidents which are always together with their respective substances, such as the cognitive faculties). On this point Aquinas' view differs from that of Plato, since he does not admit ideas of such accidents as the intellect while, on the other hand, he asserts that there are ideas (as exemplars) of individual things. That St. Thomas admits ideas of individual things follows from his answer to the fourth objection, especially if we read it against the background of question fourteen, article eleven and the *De veritate*, q. 3, a. 8 where he most expliticly says that we must hold that God has ideas of individual things.

---

[116] See *Epist.* 14, n.4: *PL* 33, 80.
[117] Cf. R. Wielockx (edit.), *Henrici de Gandavo Quodlibetum II*, Leuven 1983, 4-8.
[118] This distinction is used by St. Albert the Great in his *De div. nom.*, VII (edit. Simon, 350, 38ff): 'exempla' are directed to the things to be made, while 'rationes' remain speculative.

God is Truth (I 16, 5 and 6)

The first articles of question sixteen treat of truth in general and serve as an introduction to the theme of God as truth. Truth resides primarily in the intellect, insofar as the intellect is conformed to the thing known: truth is the agreement of the intellect with reality[119]. In a secondary sense things are said to be true if they have the likeness of the form in the mind of their maker and bring it about in other intellects. Because everything is knowable insofar as it has being, all things are true. Hence 'true' and 'being' are convertible terms, but 'true' adds to being a relation to the intellect. In the fifth article these insights are applied to God.

> "As was said above, truth is found in the intellect according as it apprehends a thing as it is; and in things according as they have being conformable to an intellect. This is to the greatest degree found in God. For his being is not only conformed to his intellect, but it is the very act of his intellect; and his act of understanding is the measure and cause of every other being and of every other intellect; and he himself is his own being and act of understanding. Whence it follows not only that truth is in him, but that he is the highest and first truth himself".

One of the earliest theologians to affirm that God is truth itself, was St. Augustine[120]. St. Thomas accepts this theological tradition issued from *John* 14, 6 where Jesus calls himself the Truth. The conclusion that God is truth is far from trivial. Truth is the summit of reality, for it is being come to awareness and conscious possession of itself. "Truth must be the ultimate end of the universe"[121]. All other things outside God share in God's truth and God is the source of the different ways of being; all things receive their intelligibility and truth from him. Now the vision and "possession" of God is man's fulfilment. This doctrine confirms again that knowledge is man's noblest activity[122].

This takes us to the theme of the sixth article: In St. Augustine's theology, marked by Plato's exemplarism and his theory of participation, things are true because of their conformity with their source, that is with God's ideas; the human intellect acquires its truth from God, who is the spiritual sun of our mind and God's light makes us share in the truth he placed in created things. St. Thomas affirms that all things are true by the primary truth of God, to which each thing is assimilated according to its degree of being. However, with regard to the truth of the intellect Aquinas points out that we cannot simply reduce this to one truth common to all men, for each intellect must acquire its own conformity to reality which is *its* logical truth.

---

[119] See volume one, chapter five for more details.

[120] Cf. Ch. Boyer, *L'idée de vérité dans la philosophie de saint Augustin*, Paris 1920, c.2: "La vérité subsistante".

[121] *S.C.G.* I, 1.

[122] See P. Rousselot, *L'intellectualisme de saint Thomas*[2], Paris 1937.

God is Life (XVIII (I 18, 3)

In the third article of the eighteenth question St. Thomas argues that life is properly said of God. Plato admitted a special idea of life but later he identified it with soul and placed it immediately below the ideas in the hierarchy of being[123]. In his *Sophistes* 248c Plato ascribes life to that which is altogether or in every respect being. This text is understood by some as a declaration to the effect that life is to be found in the world of ideas[124]. Aristotle develops a scientific treatise of what it means to be a living being[125]. Intellectual activity is the highest form of life[126] and thus he ascribes life to God[127], the First Unmoved Mover whose knowledge is self-contemplation[128]. Aristotle's insight that the activity of *noûs* is life, was taken up by Plotinus[129] who, however, combined 'life' with the process of emanation from the One and the returning of diversity to unity[130]. In the Middle Ages God was said to be life itself[131]. From the lengthy discussions of the theme by Alexander of Hales and St. Albert we may conclude that much importance was attached to it[132]. While in the Aristotelean tradition life is conceived of as the first and highest act of living beings and as a concentration of reality, modern philosophers frequently consider it as a never ceasing process in opposition to speculative thought.

In keeping with Aristotle and the Bible, which calls God a living God, St. Thomas asserts that life most properly belongs to God. His argument is based on an analysis of what 'to be alive' means. Its prime characteristic is to move and to be active by oneself and not because someone else moves us. This self-motion can be realised on three levels which go from less perfect to more per-

---

[123] *Phaedo* 106 d. Cf. H. Morin, *Der Begriff des Lebens im 'Timaios' Platons unter Berücksichtigung seiner früheren Philosophie*, Uppsala 1965, 28-32.

[124] See C.J. de Vogel, "A la recherche des étapes précises entre Platon et le néoplatonisme", in *Mnemosyne* 1954, 111-122, 118. In *Soph.* 248c Plato rejects the view of the total unchangeableness of being. In ascribing life to the world of ideas he connects the latter with living things. Plato's reference to being, life, intellect, was developed into a triad in Neoplatonism. See P. Hadot, "Etre, vie, pensée chez Plotin et avant Plotin", in *Les Sources de Plotin. Entretiens sur l'Antiquité classique*, Vandoeuvres-Genève 1957, 107-141.

[125] *De anima* 413 b 22.

[126] *E.N.* 1170 a 18.

[127] *Metaph.* 1072 b 26.

[128] L. Elders, *Aristotle's Theology*, 198f.

[129] *Enn.* VI 9, 9, 17.

[130] Cf. *Enn.* VI, 7, 16 and 17. According to Proclus life is the synthesis of a triad of principles. See W. Beierwaltes, *Proklos. Grundzüge seiner Metaphysik*, Frankfurt a.M. 1965, 93ff.

[131] Cf. St. Anselm, *Proslogium*, c.13; Hugh of St. Victor, *De sacramentis* II, 2, c.4.

[132] See A.E. Wingel, "Vivere viventibus est esse in Aristotle and St. Thomas", in *The Modern Schoolman* 38 (1961) 85-120; L.-B. Geiger, "La vie, acte essentielle de l'âme, l'*esse*, acte de l'essence d'après Albert le Grand", in *Etudes d'histoire doctrinale et littéraire*, Montréal-Paris 1962, 49-116; J. Kohlmeier, "Vita est actus primus. Ein Beitrag zur Erhellung der Geschichte der Philosophie der ersten Hälfte des 13. Jahrhunderts anhand der Lebens-Metaphysik des Petrus Hispanus", *FrZPhTh* 16 (1969) 40-91; 287-320.

fect forms of life, viz. vegetative, sensitive and intellectual life. Intellectual life has a possibility of self-determination in the sense that man can assign certain ends to his actions. Nevertheless his intellect is predetermined by nature with regard to the first principles and the final end, which it cannot help aiming at. However, God's being is his thinking and what he has by nature is not determined by someone else. Hence God possesses life in the highest degree.—St. Thòmas' argument is based on the fact that God possesses and knows himself entirely in a never interrupted act of contemplation and love.

In the following article Aquinas develops this doctrine somewhat more. God's life is his understanding. Now God's intellect, what he knows and his actual understanding are the same thing. It follows that the things which are present in God's knowledge are his life[133]. In this way we can say that created things have being more truly in God than in themselves, because in God they have an uncreated existence. St. Thomas adds, however, that as this or that particular thing (e.g. as a man) created things are more truly what they are in their own nature than in God, for their nature is to be material beings. As such they are not in God. An example may explain this: a house which has been built is more truly a house than that which is in the mind of the architect.

The remark hints at the splendour of God's intellectual life in which all created things are present and shine in the clarity of their essence as this is a mode of participating in God's being. Elsewhere Aquinas writes that each form is a certain participation in the brilliance of God's being[134]. A form is a likeness to God's being and shares in God's actuality[135].

---

[133] With the help of philosophical arguments this article develops the thought stated in *John* I, 4, in its mediaeval reading ("What has been made, was life in him").

[134] *In De div. nom.*, c.4, lectio 5, n.349.

[135] *In I Phys.*, lectio 15, n.135.

CHAPTER NINE

DIVINE WILL AND LOVE, PROVIDENCE AND POWER OF GOD

I. *God's Will and Love (I 19 & 20)*

In Question 19 Aquinas presents a considerable number of insights about God which are also relevant for philosophical psychology. Because of the difficulty of its subject matter as well as the depth and subtlety of its text, the interpretation of this question is beset with difficulties.

We cannot here develop St. Thomas' doctrine of will, but only recall that the fact that the will is said to be consequent upon the intellect does not mean that Aquinas subscribes to a brand of rationalism in which the will and its striving have only a secondary role. Question 19 gives a profound view of the significance of will and its relationship with the intellect which treads a middle path between rationalism and voluntarism. Compared to earlier texts Question 19 shows a certain development of doctrine.

We know by experience that we ourselves strive to attain certain things, that we love or detest and so on, so that it hardly needs proof that there is such a faculty as will. But we have no experience of the inner life of God. Aristotle does not speak of will in God and in Plato's theory the highest idea, the Good or the One, can hardly be said to love, desire or take decisions. The Christian concept of God is altogether different. Aquinas shows that it is possible to establish by reason that God's being is full of love.

Demonstrating in the *De veritate* 23, 1 that it is proper to God to possess will St. Thomas starts from the principle that the spiritual mind has two different relationships with things: one relationship consists in a certain presence of things in the mind (although not a presence in their physical reality). This takes place in knowledge. But because all things, whether they are material or immaterial, are related to other things, there results in the knowing subject an inclination to the things it knows. On the level of sensitive cognition this inclination is spontaneous but not free. In intellectual beings it is perfectly free. Such a free inclination is the act of the faculty we call will. The central part of this argument is that each individual thing has a relation to other things. As Aquinas explains in *SCG* I 72, it is because of their form that things have a relation of likeness or dissimilarity to other things. At first sight it is not obvious how the argument passes from this relation of likeness or difference to acts of the will. Furthermore, in God the things known by him, toward which a relation is said to arise, are not an *alia res* but God himself. Nevertheless the principle enuntiated is one of the first, self-evident principles:

things cannot be conceived without this relationship. The principle points to the fact that the knowing subject has a rapport with the form it knows.

In Question 19, 1 this insight is further developed by St. Thomas:

> I answer that there is will in God, just as there is intellect, since will follows upon the intellect. For as natural things have actual being by their form, so the intellect is actually knowing by its intelligible form. Now everything has this disposition towards its natural form, that when it does not have it, it tends towards it; and when it has it, it is at rest therein. It is the same with every natural perfection, which is a natural good. This disposition to good in things without knowledge is called *natural appetite*. Whence also intellectual natures have a like disposition to good as apprehended through an intelligible form, so as to rest therein when possessed, and when not possessed to seek to possess it; both of which pertain to the will. Hence in every intellectual being there is will, just as in every sensible being there is *animal appetite*. And so there must be will in God, since there is intellect in him. And as his knowing is his own being, so is his willing. [1]

In this demonstration the basic insight is that everything has such a disposition (habitudo) towards its natural form that when it does not have it, it tends towards it and when it has it, it is at rest therein. Aquinas points out that each substance strives to keep its own being (esse) according to its nature[2]. The principle is particularly evident in living beings, whose "substantiality" is much more pronounced that that of minerals. Certain elements of the periodic system, for instance, are eager to enter into a combination with other elements rather than to remain what they are. St. Thomas probably means substantial natures as called for by the conditions of their cosmic environment. Certain elements should perhaps be considered pre-substances rather than substances, at least in their present state, for they are meant to form compounds.

As so often in the *Summa theologiae* St. Thomas argues from what is proper to (created) being in general to what belongs to God's nature. The difficulty in the argument is that it passes from an inclination which is the nature of the thing itself to an inclination which is an accidental act (actus elicitus). It also seems to jump from an inclination to the object perceived in cognition to an inclination to the latter's goodness[3]. These difficulties disappear when one keeps in mind that the contents of cognition are a form of being. Thus what is proper to the substance inasmuch as it is being, also applies to accidents (at least in an analogous way). Hence a substance endowed with knowledge will 'accept' and 'affirm' the form which is the object of its thought (and a reality accidental to it) by means of an inclination which is also at the level of accidental being. Furthermore, just as the inclination of a

---

[1] I 19, 1. The argument was anticipated in the third proof of *S.C.G.* I 72: all things strive to attain their perfection.

[2] I-II 94, 2: "Quaelibet substantia appetit conservationem sui esse secundum suam naturam".

[3] See Cajetanus, *In I*^{am} 19, 1 IV.

substance to its own being is an inclination to its perfection, so the striving of the faculty of the will is directed towards the perceived good inasmuch as it is good.

St. Thomas ends this first article by recalling God's simplicity: God's understanding is his being, hence also his will is. It is obvious that his will does not desire what it does not have, but loves God's infinite perfection. God's will is not moved by anything outside God, but by itself alone in this sense that it is the joyful affirmation and love of God's perfection in identity of being. It is obvious that we do not here reach a real understanding of God's will and hardly go beyond the affirmation that there is will in God.

Scotus rejects the dependence of God's will on the divine intellect. For in his view this would diminish the freedom of God. However, if with Scotus we conceive will as a dynamic force which stands by itself and is not consequent upon the intellect, God's will is no longer bound by the nature of the things he created. The only 'limitation' of this boundless freedom of God, proposed by Scotus, is that God cannot will anything which is contradictory[4]. Pursuing Scotus' line of thought Ockham drew the conclusion that once God created man, he is not bound by man's nature in his providential dealings with the world. Ockham's view of total liberty of the will contributed to the rise of modern subjectivism. On the other hand, his view paradoxically also promoted a theory with considers the intellect as separate from natural inclinations and thus it led to an exaggerated rationalism. An unexpected witness to these tendencies is Newton who in line with the voluntaristic trend in English philosophy subordinated God's intellect to God's will in this sense that he emphasized God's power much more than divine wisdom in the creation of the world.

If God's will is love and joy in the infinite perfection of his being, can it also direct itself to imperfect beings which are not God himself? In Aristotle's theology an affirmative answer would attribute an imperfection to God. Plotinus likewise denies that One wills directly that which proceeds from it. When Plotinus occasionally applies terms expressing 'will' to the One, he means that the One wills its procession, but not that which proceeds from it[5]. As J. M. Rist observes, "the One does not concern itself directly with the second hypostasis; it concerns itself with itself. But the *result* of willing itself is its production of the second hypostasis"[6].

In the second article of Question 19 St. Thomas demonstrates that God also wills things other than himself by means of the principle that every agent in so far as it is perfect and in act, produces its like. "It pertains, therefore, to

---

[4] Scotus, *Op. Oxon.* I, d.1, 1.4.

[5] See *Enn.* VI 8, 20, 18. As J. Trouillard points out, we should not reduce the Plotinian procession of hypostases to a mechanical operation. See his *La procession plotinienne*, Paris 1955, 76f.

[6] *Plotinus: the Road to Reality*, Cambridge 1967, 83.

the nature of the will to communicate to others as far as possible the good possessed". This holds true even more for God's will, for God is the source of being. Hence God "wills both himself to be and other things to be; but himself as the end and other things as ordained to that end inasmuch as it befits divine goodness that other things should partake therein".

The argument proceeds in three stages: its formulates a principle of being (all things tend to produce their like), applies this to the will in general, and concludes that it is also proper to divine will to communicate God's being. As he did in the first article Aquinas avails himself of the analogy between created things and God. The basis for such a use of analogy was laid in the Fourth Question (the perfections encountered in created beings must also exist in God who is their cause). However, in applying this insight to God, one must not overlook the fact that the divine being is totally different from created things and, secondly, that God wills things voluntarily and not by natural necessity. This last point will become clear in the remaining articles of this question. The general law of being, formulated by St. Thomas, is based on experience: things communicate what they are and what they have with other things. Telling examples are procreation, the exchange of energy (entropy) and the communication of their likeness by things to the knowing subject. Things exist with one another and for one another.

When we transfer the deepest tendencies of created things to God, we must leave out whatever is imperfect: God's love is not split into a multitude of acts nor can it be intermittent. Moreover God must love things outside himself because of his own goodness which is the adequate object of his love. This does not imply that God's love of things other than himself is not authentic. On the contrary, it is infinite in depth as well as in motivation and it is directed towards that which is deepest in creatures and which constitutes their real goodness, viz. their participation in God's goodness.

Aquinas emphasises that God wills other things as ordained to the end he is himself. Thus his will is not moved by anything else except his own goodness. This means that just "as the divine knowledge is one, because it sees the many in the one, in the same way the divine willing is one and simple, as willing the many only through its own goodness"[7].

The argument of the Second Article might seem to some as forcing us to hold that God's love of created things is necessary, since it is God's nature to communicate himself. Hence he must necessarily create things other than himself and create whatever he can. Several philosophers did, in fact, deny that there is freedom in God with regard to the creation of the world. Not only the Neoplatonists but also such Christian thinkers as Abaelard considered creation necessary. If God's love were not necessary, a good would be

---

[7] I 19, 2 ad 4.

lacking[8]. This difficulty is solved in the Third Article: Does God will necessarily whatever he wills? St. Thomas first distinguishes between two ways in which a thing can be said to be necessary, namely absolutely and by supposition. Absolutely necessary is what cannot not be (for instance, the proposition "man is an animal"). Necessary by supposition is what under a given supposition cannot not be (granted that Socrates is sitting, he cannot not be sitting).

God's will has a necessary relation to divine goodness, its proper object. Hence God wills it necessarily.

> "But God wills things other than himself in so far as they are ordered to his own goodness as their end. Now in willing an end we do not necessarily will things that conduce to it, unless they are such that the end cannot be attained without them... Hence, since the goodness of God is perfect and can exist without other things, inasmuch as no perfection can accrue to him from them, it follows that for him to will things other than himself is not absolutely necessary. Yet it can be necessary by supposition, for supposing that he wills a thing then he is unable not to will it, as his will cannot change".

God wills his own goodness necessarily, but, as St. Thomas explains, this does not exclude that God wills himself freely. Freedom is opposed to violence or compulsion. When God loves his goodness in keeping with his nature, he freely, that is willingly loves himself, although he does so necessarily[9]. In this connection St. Thomas uses 'free will' in a sense which goes beyond the freedom of choice which characterises man's freedom. The latter is based on the grandeur of the spiritual will, by reason of which it is not necessarily inclined to choose a particular, limited good, but freely decides to will or not to will it. Because the will is a spiritual faculty it possesses itself in spontaneity. St. Thomas calls this intimate, willed concurrence with itself freedom. Indeed, it is a form of freedom superior to free choice such as man has.

In his reply to the fourth objection Aquinas observes that God's willing created things is contingent: God's will as the act of his being, is necessary, but it has a non-necessary relation to created things, because the latter are not so perfect as to be willed necessarily. God's will is not determined by that which is outside God, but determines itself to will things to which it has no necessary relation.

Aquinas finally draws attention to the fact that God knows the things as they exist in himself and that things have necessary being inasmuch as they exist in God[10]. But since the will is related to things as they exist in themselves

---

[8] *Introductio ad theol.* II 17; *Theol. christ.* V (PL 178, 1329f.).

[9] Cf. *Q.d. de potentia* 10, 2 ad 5; *De ver. 23, 1* & 4; *In II Sent.*, d.25, q.1, a.4.

[10] Cajetanus comments that every knowable thing necessarily has being in God, although the knowability of some of these things is not necessary (*In I^am* 19, 3 VI).

and things are not absolutely necessary, God does not will necessarily whatever he wills.

Is God's will the cause of things or should we say that God's essence or knowledge makes them? The question is discussed in the fourth article. The text deals with the important issue whether God creates things by a natural causality (not unlike the way in which the sun spreads its light and warmth) or because he wills. The Neoplatonic tradition speaks of creation in terms of a natural process[11]. The maxim "bonum est diffusivum sui" was understood as referring to efficient causality. St. Thomas vigorously opposes this view tainted by a pantheistic monism. He brings three arguments against it:

(a) causality by means of a natural process such as emanation or radiation, cannot be the original and primary form of efficient causality in the universe, because nature acts in view of an end. In order to do so it must be directed to this end by an intellect[12]. Hence the agent acting with intellect and will precedes the agent that acts by nature.

(b) an agent of a particular nature produces effects according to its nature. But God has no determinate nature[13]. Hence he could not act by natural causality unless he were to produce something undetermined and indefinite in being.

(c) the agent produces its like so far as possible. Its effects proceed from it in so far as they pre-exist in it, that is, after the manner of the agent's being. Since God's being is his own intellect, the effects pre-exist in him after the mode of the intellect and proceed from him by a decision of the will, for "his inclination to put in act what his intellect has conceived pertains to the will".

In his reply to the first objection St. Thomas explains that the causality of the Good as formulated by Dionysius ("the good is self-diffusive")[14] must not be understood as a mechanical causality. God acts by choice and decision and thus the good is a final cause[15].

In Articles Five to Eight the nature and properties of God's will are further determined. In particular differences with man's will are pointed out. A first question is whether any cause can be assigned to God's will. When *we* choose to do something, we always have a reason why we do it. In the last analysis all our willing is in view of happiness. It would seem that God would act unreasonably if his willing was not determined by an end. On the other hand,

---

[11] *Enn.* II 9, 8. According to Plotinus things have a natural inclination to produce the being which is ontologically consequent upon them (*Enn.* IV 8, 6).

[12] See Chapter Three, the commentary on the Fifth Way.

[13] As has been shown in Chapter Four, God has no determinate nature. His nature is to be self-subsisting being itself.

[14] *De div. nom.*, 4.

[15] See I 5, 4 ad 2: "Goodness is described as self-diffusive in the sense that an end is said to move".

such a determination of God's will would seem to introduce a dependence and potentiality in God.

In his solution of the problem St. Thomas vigorously denies that God's will has a cause. In order to explain this he insists on the parallelism between the operation of the intellect and of the will: the will, indeed, follows the intellect.

"The case with the intellect is that if the principle and its conclusion are understood separately from each other, the understanding of the principle is the cause that the conclusion is known. But if the intellect perceives the conclusion in the principle itself, apprehending both the one and the other at the same glance, in this case the knowledge of the conclusion would not be caused by understanding the principles, since a thing cannot be its own cause; and yet it would be true that the intellect would understand the principles to be the cause of the conclusion"[16].

Aquinas applies this insight to the will:

"If anyone in one act wills an end, and in another the means to that end, his willing the end will be cause of his willing the means. This cannot be the case if in one act he wills both end and means, for a thing cannot be its own cause. Yet it will be true to say that he wills to order to the end the things that are means to it. Now as God by one act understands all things in his essence, so by one act he wills all things in his goodness"[17].

It follows that willing the end (his own goodness) is not the *cause* of his willing the means; yet God wills the ordering of the means to the end.

God wills created things because of his own goodness, but in one single act he wills himself necessarily, the created things freely and this act has no cause. Aquinas maintains the secret of God's will, which is its own explanation[18]. St. Thomas' doctrine differs sharply from that of the so-called *Loquentes in Lege Maurorum*[19]. The latter simply said that God makes things because he wants to make them. Aquinas rejects their view observing that we can indicate a threefold reason (ratio) why God makes things: his own goodness (he creates the world out of love of his own goodness); the good of the universe is the reason why God wants each particular thing; when, thirdly, a thing needs other things in order to be and to work, that is the reason why God wills these other things. This reason is not absolute but conditional: if God wills things

---

[16] I 19, 5.

[17] Ibidem.

[18] St. Thomas statement "vult ergo hoc esse propter hoc, sed non propter hoc vult hoc" means that God's goodness is the reason (*ratio*) why he wills the world, but that willing the world is not a new act of will caused by the love of his own goodness. Cf. the comment by Cajetanus (*In I^am* 19, 5, III): "Actus voluntatis divinae attingens hoc volitum, puta universum vel hominem, ex parte actus caret causa, non solum ut tale ens est sed etiam ut attingens tale volitum ..." See also John of St. Thomas, *Cursus theologicus, In I^am* 19, disp. 4, a.4, n.10.

[19] See Maimonides, *The Guide of the Perplexed*, I, c.73 and G. Anawati, "Saint Thomas d'Aquin et les penseurs arabes: Les "Loquentes in lege Maurorum" et leur philosophie", in L. Elders (edit.), *La philosophie de la nature de saint Thomas d'Aquin*, Città del Vaticano 1982, 155-171.

outside himself, then he wills them because of his own goodness[20]. There is a reason why God wills things other than himself, but there is no cause that makes him will[21]. This implies that one cannot say that God's will is arbitrary: we call arbitrary what depends on the will alone. However, God's will is his being and his intellect.

The Sixth Article examines the question whether God's will is so efficacious that it is always fulfilled: Our human will encounters obstacles and often we cannot attain or do what we want to attain or to do. Does God's will meet with impediments? This question is not without importance in sacred theology: God wills that all men be saved, but are they really? The answer of Aquinas presupposes that God is the first efficient cause of all things. It would seem that intermediate causes hinder the working of the First Cause, for in our world not all good, which is possible, actually exists. However, St. Thomas argues that God's will must always be fulfilled: existing things are always something, that is, they have some essential contents even if they are not what other things are (e.g., they may not be living beings). Things are the effects of efficient causes and their forms are conformed to them. Hence

> "something may escape the order of any particular agent, but not the order of the universal cause under which all particular causes are included; if any particular cause fails its effect, this is because of the hindrance of some other particular cause which is included within the order of the universal cause. Therefore an effect cannot possibly escape the order of the universal cause"[22].

Since the will of God is the universal cause of all things, it is impossible that the divine will should not produce its effect. Hence that which seems to depart from it in one order, returns to it in another[23]. What St. Thomas says is illustrated by the evil in the world: in one way this evil is not according to God's will, but it is being used by him for some good, so that it re-enters into God's plan in another respect. No being, indeed, exists without God's sustaining force. God includes under his activity all causes and hence nothing escapes his causality[24].

The Seventh Article considers the question whether God's will is changeable. In his reply Aquinas lays down that the will of God is entirely unchangeable.

---

[20] *S.C.G.* I 87. See also III 97 where St. Thomas rejects the view that God does everything according to his simple willing without reason. The *Loquentes in lege Saracenorum* felt that one can only say "God wills things".

[21] *S.C.G.* I 87.

[22] I 19, 6.

[23] *Ibidem.*

[24] In his answer to the first objection Aquinas distinguishes between the antecedent will of God and his consequent will. The first concerns things absolutely considered, the second things considered together with some additional circumstances. This distinction is not a division of God's will itself, but concerns the things willed.

The reason is that a change of will does not happen, unless because of some change (a) in the disposition of the substance of the person who wills (by reason of which something which was a good to him no longer is, or vice versa), or (b) in his knowledge, for instance, when he learns that something is good for him. Such changes cannot take place in God[25]. God's plan with regard to the world remains the same, but this plan includes that certain things change into other things.

The foregoing articles allow us to conclude that God's will is always infallibly fulfilled. This takes us to the question whether God's will imposes necessity on things so that, whatever happens is necessary. According to a view which was rather widely held in antiquity, all things and all process in the world depend on an absolute and unchangeable necessity. Democritus was the first philosopher to give expression to total determinism: "All things that were, are and are to come are foreordained by necessity"[26]. By his rejection of any causes of process in the world other than mechanical Democritus prepared the way for scientific mechanism. In Stoic philosophy the ancient religious belief in *Heimarmene* was transformed into a coherent philosophical theory: man cannot change external events; his own inner life is also predetermined[27]. Even the gods are subject to this necessity[28].

Fatalism, particularly in its astrological form, was fought by Plotinus, Alexander of Aphrodisias and Christian authors. The sermons of St. Augustine witness to the diffusion of fatalism in the ancient world: "You will be an adulterer because that is the way you have (the planet) Venus; you will be a homicide, because it is in this way that you have (the planet) Mars"[29]. Some centuries later a number of Islamic theologians developed a particular form of determinism. One of the reasons of its rise was the decision by political power to impose jabarism (the theory of divine constraint of man's will) so that the authority of the reigning khalif would be unassailable: whatever happens results from a divine decree[30]. Religious fatalism is at the centre of the occasionalism of the Mutakallims who held that the only true cause acting in the universe is God. In keeping with this the philosopher Al-

---

[25] See Chapter Six on divine immutability.

[26] Plutarchus, *Strom.* 7. See C. Bailey, *The Greek Atomists and Epicurus*, Oxford 1928, 120ff.

[27] See M. Pohlenz, *Die Stoa*, Göttingen 1948, 103-106. The Stoic theory of fate provoked an abundant literature. One may quote Cicero's *De fato*, Pseudo-Plutarchus' *De Fato*, Alexander of Aphrodisias' *De Fato*, etc.

[28] See Seneca, *De prov.* 5, 8: "quid est boni viri? praebere se fato. Grande solacium est cum universo rapi: quicquid est quod nos sic vivere, sic mori iussit, eadem necessitate et deos alligat ... Ille ipse omnium conditor et rector scripsit quidem fata, sed sequitur: semper paret, semel iussit".

[29] *Enn. in ps.*140: *PL* 37, 1821.

[30] L. Gardet and M. G. Anawati, *Introduction à la théologie musulmane*, Paris 1948, 37f.

Ghazali teaches that God is the sole agent in the world[31]. For Avicenna who was steeped in Neoplatonism, only that which is necessary is intelligible: the entire chain of being is necessary by the power of the First Being. There is no divine free will. Nevertheless each essence has an accidental and contingent connection with its existence.

In St. Thomas' day some philosophers held that everything which is preordained by the First Cause will happen by necessity and that secondary causes are needed in order to bring about contingency[32]. Their view goes back to Avicenna and thus to Neoplatonism: the emanation of beings from God is a necessary process. Avicenna conceived the production of the world as the actualisation of a series of possible essences, but this actualizing force emanates from God eternally and necessarily. Contingence is excluded[33]. Scotus adapted this theory to Christian doctrine by making this emanation dependent on a free decision of God. In fact he places contingency in God's causality: because God is self-sufficient he produces the world by a free decision. Contingence is a condition which intrinsically affects God's will[34].

St. Thomas states his position in this article: necessity and contingence in the world must be dependent on God, but contingence depends on God's will not as a condition affecting it, but as an effect, Aquinas' argument runs as follows: (a) nothing escapes God's knowledge and will; (b) nothing can frustrate his causality. "Hence it is not because the proximate causes are contingent that the effects willed by God happen contingently, but God has prepared contingent causes for them, because he has willed that they should happen contingently"[35]. But how can the same comprehensive act of divine will produce both necessary and contingent things? Aquinas solves this difficulty by recalling that the more efficacious an agent is, the more he determines the effect. This principle is deduced from what we observe in nature: in procreation the more vigorous parents produce offspring that has a greater likeness with them and is more fully developed. Although St. Thomas' example is hardly convincing in view of the hereditary factors not dependent on the parents, the principle imposes itself as evident: the more efficacious the agent, the more it will influence the effect and model it. In this way God lets things happen contingently or necessarily. Scotus, on the other hand, stresses God's liberty so much that it becomes difficult to explain how the universe proceeds from God as an agent who acts with decision and knowledge.

---

[31] Cf. M. Fakhry, *Islamic Occasionalism*, London 1958, 77.

[32] See Articles 93 and 94 of the propositions condemned in Paris in 1277 (Hissette, *o.c.*, 160ff.).

[33] See L. Gardet, *La pensée religieuse d'Avicenne*, Paris 1951, 48-68.

[34] Scotus, *Opus oxon.* I, d.2, q.1. Cf. E. Gilson, *Jean Duns Scott. Introduction à ses positions fondamentales*, Paris 1952, 270ff.

[35] I 19, 8.

In the Ninth Article St. Thomas shows that God wills accidentally some forms
of evil in nature, such as the passing away of living beings, in so far as he wills
a good to which these forms of evil are attached. In fact, no natural agent
intends a privation or corruption, but he intends to produce the form to which
this privation is annexed. An example illustrates this: when a lion kills a stag,
his object is food, not the killing of the stag[36]. However, God in no way wills
the evil of sin, because he wills his own goodness above anything else, whereas
sin is precisely a privation of the right order toward the divine good. Moral
evil deprives man of his ordination to God.

In the reply to the objections Aquinas adds a clarification about the way
in which we may speak of how God's will is related to evil: one should not
say that God wills evil to be done[37], because evil is not of itself ordained to
a good, but only accidentally. The correct way of expressing God's attitude
with regard to evil is to say that he wills to permit that evil is done.
In the Tenth Article of this Question St. Thomas points out that since God
wills things other than himself not necessarily, he freely chooses to will
whatever he wills.

After he has established that there is will in God St. Thomas examines what
belongs to God's will as such. Thus he deals successively with God's love
(Question 20) and God's justice and pity (Question 21). The way in which
Aquinas treats these themes here differs considerably from that in the S.C.G.
I 89-96. In the S.Th. he does not mention the passions nor the moral virtues
(except justice and pity), apparently because he felt that the previous discussions have made it clear that whatever belongs to material being or the senses
must be excluded from God.

Love is the first movement of the will and of the other appetitive faculties,
directed to the good in whatever form it is found. Thus the object of love
simply is the good without any restriction, i.e., regardless even of whether the
good is present or absent. Love is the first act of the will and the appetite and
is presupposed by all other acts such as joy, desire, sadness, hatred. A distinction must be made between acts of the will and those of the sensitive appetite.
The acts of the latter (the passions) involve a modification in the body. They
are marred by imperfection and cannot be said of God[38]. But love is present
in God, for love is the first act of the will. Moreover, God's love of his own
goodness is his being.

One might raise the objection that spiritual love is love of a person; now
God is just himself in the simplicity of his being; thus it would seem that we
can hardly speak of divine love. Aquinas solves this difficulty by means of a

---

[36] For a more detailed treatment of evil see Volume One, ch. 7.

[37] Hugh of St. Victor expressed himself in this way. See his De sacr. I 4, 13 (PL 176, 239).

[38] Some of the passions are imperfect precisely because of their formal nature. For instance,
fear of a threatening evil, desire of an absent good.

distinction between the good one wills and the person for whom one wants this good. For to love someone is to want what is food for him. Now God wants what is good to himself and that good is no other than himself, because he is good by his essence[39]. Elsewhere Aquinas adds that God's goodness is intimately united with him so that his love is the very heart of his being[40].

God's love extends to all existing things[41], for God is the cause of all things: their being and goodness are willed by God, that is, God loves all things. However, his love differs from ours: our love is ignited by the good present in others, but God's love precedes this good, making and creating it. God's love is from all eternity as is his knowledge. On the assumption of the ontological dependence of all things of God[42], it is evident that the universe and man owe their existence to an act of love. From this results that all created things are directed to and attracted by the Infinite Good. God impresses his own love of his goodness on his creatures and he moves them so that they love him in whatever finite good they pursue. As Etienne Gilson has shown, this doctrine is the source of the dialectics of love elaborated by such medieval theologians as St. Bernard[43].

God governs the world with equal wisdom and love, although he loves those things more, on which he confers greater goods[44]. Because God cannot but will what is according to his wisdom, he acts justly: his wisdom is his end and our law[45]. Since God acts to remove the misery of man, he also acts out of pity. His goodness and pity are the source of whatever God does for his creatures, for he owes nothing to them[46].

II. *The Providence of God (I 22)*

After he has dealt with what relates to God's will absolutely, Aquinas proceeds to examine God's action in so far as it is related to both the intellect and the will, in other words he treats God's providence. The term "providence" means to know beforehand, to foresee, to look after, to govern. In Greek religion and poetry we encounter the concept of Fate, to which man's life is subject. Homer sometimes depicts this Moira as placed above Zeus and the gods, but on other occasions he suggests that it depends on Zeus. A similar lack of clarity is found in the description of Fate's relation to man: in certain cases it leaves man the liberty to act against reason, but elsewhere it opposes

---

[39] I 20, 1 ad 3.
[40] *S.C.G.* I 91.
[41] I 20, 2.
[42] See below Chapter Ten.
[43] See E. Gilson, *The Spirit of Mediaeval Philosophy*, New York 1940, ch. 14.
[44] I 20, 3 ad 2.
[45] I 21, 1 ad 2.
[46] I 21, 3.

itself to the will of man. A proper concept of a supreme provident God was
unknown in classical Greece, although in popular religion people addressed
supplications to the gods; local deities were felt to protect the cities, where
their shrines were located. In his *Hecabe* Euripides writes that for the pious
man belief in providence is a powerful comfort, but when one considers the
vicissitudes of life, everyone seems to be a victim of fate. It is true, however,
that Socrates and Plato rejected the view of some Sophists[47] and the Atomists,
who argued that the gods are not interested in man[48]. Plato writes that the
gods extend a loving care to man[49]. But Aristotle's theory of the First
Unmoved Mover, who does not concern himself with the world, takes away
the foundation of the theory of divine providence. Nevertheless the dox-
ographic tradition ascribes to him the view that God's providence extends to
the supralunar bodies, but does not reach the sublunar elements[50]. This position provoked the sharp criticism of the Church Fathers.

Epicurus denies that the gods concern themselves with man[51]. On the other
hand, the Stoa admitted divine providence in the sense of an unchangeable
plan which governs all events, even the smallest, and from which there is no
escape. This providence is a necessity immanent in the universe[52]. Certain
Stoic philosophers distinguish between Fate (*Heimarmene*) and Providence
(*Pronoia*). Although the world order has been established definitely, man may
nevertheless pray to the gods[53].

Carneades criticised the Stoic position: if everything is determined by fate,
law and punishment as well as prayer are superfluous[54]. Authors such as Alexander of Aphrodisias tried to reconcile both positions by suggesting that the
causality of fate can be obstructed[55]. Alexander also defends Aristotle against
the criticism we mentioned above: through an intermediary the providence of
God can extend to the sublunar region, although not to individuals. The basis
for this assertion is that God is the cause of the circular movement of the sun
on which the preservation of the species depends. Alexander seems to assume
that the Prime Mover knows the forms of material things in general. The
(view) according to which providence concerns itself only with species and not
with individuals "removes difficulties over how the divine can attend simulta-

---

[47] Antiphon. See Xenophon, *Memor.* I 4, 5.

[48] Plato, *Apol*, 41 d; Xenophon, *Memor.* I 4, 5.

[49] See *Tim.* 36 b and *Laws* X.

[50] See Diogenes Laertius 5, 32; *Doxogr. graeci* (Berlin 1929) 592, 11. It is somewhat surprising
that the relation of the First Mover to the heavenly spheres is described by means of the term
πρόνοια.

[51] See *Kyr. Dox.* I and Lucretius, *De natura deorum* II 646ff.

[52] Seneca, *De providentia* 5, 8.

[53] Seneca rejects prayer as meaningless. Cf. his *Nat. quaest.* II 36.

[54] Apud Ciceronem, *De fato* XI 23.

[55] *De fato*, in *Scripta minora* (Bruns), vol. 2, 2, 164ff. Cf. G. Verbeke, *The Presence* of
Stoicism in Medieval Thought, Washington 1983, 73ff.

neously to a multiplicity of details and over the injustice suffered by some particular individuals"[56].

Plotinus rejects the rigorous concept of fate of the Atomists and the adepts of astrology. He admits providence at the level of soul: the universal soul exercises providence and individual souls govern the material world by touching the bodies[57]. In a different sense *noûs* is providence inasmuch as it produces the general order of the world. The law of providence cannot be changed, so that prayer is useless, except in so far as it expresses cosmic sympathy[58]. Neoplatonism was attentive to man's religious nature and attempted to recuperate as much as possible of the spontaneous belief or religious people in the loving care of the gods. "Proclus regards the reconciliation of providence with transcendence as the especial glory of Platonism[59], Aristotle having maintained the second without the first, the Stoics the first without the second"[60]. To Epicurus' objection (concern with human affairs would hamper the happiness of the gods) the Platonists answer that the divine bestows its gifts without losing its transcendence, for it does not acquire a relation to those who partake in its good[61].

In his treatise *On providence* the Jewish philosopher Philo presents the biblical teaching on Providence, which is based on the doctrine of creation. God is the maker of all things and so he cares for plants, animals and man. The Christian apologist Athenagoras expresses his conviction as follows: the belief in creation implies belief in Providence[62]. Nevertheless the influence of non-Christian thinking remained quite strong. According to Boethius God's government of the world shows itself as providence with regard to higher things, but as *fatum* (destiny) with regard to lower things. The further a being is removed from mind, the more it is ensnared in necessity and fate[63].

---

[56] R.W. Sharples, "Alexander of Aprhodisias on Divine Providence: Two Problems", in *Class. Quart.* 32 (1982) 198-211, 198. The author quotes the *De providentia*, known to us by two Arab translations. Cf. H.-J. Ruland, *Die arabischen Fassungen von zwei Schriften des Alexander von Aphrodisias*, diss. Saarbrücken 1976. It is not clear to which extent Alexander attributes to the First Mover knowledge of the beneficial effects of its providence on sublunar things.

[57] *Enn.* III 1; IV 8, 2.

[58] Cf. Ch. Parma, *Pronoia und Providentia. Der Vorsehungsbegriff Plotins und Augustins*, Leiden 1971; H.P. Esser, *Untersuchungen zu Gebet und Gottesverehrung der Neuplatoniker*, diss. Köln 1967.

[59] *Theol. Plat.* 42.

[60] E.R. Dodds, *Proclus. The Elements of Theology*[2], Oxford 1963, 264f.

[61] *O.c.*, prop. 122.

[62] *De resurr. mort.* XVI.

[63] *De consol. philos.* IV, prosa 6, 37. This division by Boethius probably goes back to Proclus and possibly to the Stoa. With regard to the precise meaning of *fatum* we may recall Cicero's definition "ordo seriesque causarum" (*De div.* I 125). St. Isidorus derives the term from the verb *fateor*; its original meaning would be "utterance", "that which has been decided". According to St. Thomas the question of fate must be examined in the treatise on creation. He insists on the meaning of *series causarum*: the concatenation of secondary causes acting in the universe may be called *fatum* (I 116, 1 & 2; *In I Perih.*, 1.14).

In later ages when the divorce between philosophy and the Christian faith became widespread, philosophers admitted at best a general world order, dependent on God, but rejected God's providence for individuals[64].

In the First Article of Question 22 Aquinas argues that providence must be attributed to God: whatever is good in things has been created by God and therefore also the good which is their order to their end. Since God is the cause of things by his intellect, the exemplar of every effect preexists in him. The exemplar of things ordered to their last end is God's providence. Using Boethius' definition we may say that "providence is the divine reason itself which, seated in the Supreme Ruler, disposes all things". When we attribute providence to God, we must exclude whatever is imperfect in our human notion of it, as are uncertainty and deliberation. We must furthermore distinguish between the exemplar of order in God's mind and the execution of this plan. The latter takes place in time, whereas the former is eternal. Providence resides in the intellect, but it presupposes the decision to will the end.

An important question is whether all things are subject to God's providence (Article 2). The Stoa stressed the universality of providence but tended to overlook its care of individual things. In the second century A.D. some philosophers felt that just like law divine providence does not concern itself with all individual events. The view probably depends on Aristotle's cosmology: God's influence extends so far as there are spheres moved by the First Unmoved Mover. Opposing the determinism of the Stoa the Peripatetics held that God does not concern himself with details in the sublunar world[65]. This view is upheld by Alexander of Aphrodisias[66]. Averroes also subscribes to it[67].

In his solution of the question Aquinas evokes the views of Avicenna and Averroes and then sets forth his own doctrine: *all* things are subject to divine providence, not only in general, but also in their own individual being. This follows from the fact that God is the First Cause, whose causality extends to all beings in their individual characteristics. Hence all things are directed by God to their ends. The fact that everything is subject to God's providence, does not do away with *chance* at the level of created causality. Certain things may happen which to man are fortuitous, because they are outside his intention, while they are foreseen and intended by God's encompassing causality.

This conclusion seems to be contradicted by the existence of evil in the

---

[64] One may compare Voltaire's text on Providence in his *Questions sur l'Encyclopédie* (1771).

[65] See P. Moraux, *Der Aristotelismus bei den Griechen von Andronikos bis Alexander von Aphrodisias*, II, Berlin 1984, 498. See also Critolaus, fr. 3 Wehrli.

[66] *De anima mant.* 113, 12-15 (Bruns).

[67] Averroes, *In Metaph.* XII, comm. 52 (VIII, 158). See St. Thomas, *In I Sent.*, d.39, q.2, a.2 and Maimonides, *Dux perplexorum* III, c.17 (Five Theories concerning Providence).

world: a wise provider excludes defects and evil from those over whom he exercises his care. Thus it would seem that God's providence does not extend to all individual things. This objection was raised time and again in the course of the ages. Voltaire sees in the presence of evil an argument against providence rather than against the existence of God[68]. John Stuart Mill believes that the permission of evil is incompatible with God's goodness[69]. St. Thomas solves the difficulty by means of a distinction: one who is in charge of a particular thing tries to exclude all defects from it. However, when one is in charge of the whole of being, one can allow small defects to remain, inasmuch as the defects of one thing lead to the good of another or even to the universal good. This is illustrated by an example: a lion would cease to live if there were no slaying of animals. The patience of the martyrs would not be exercised, if there were no tyrannical persecution[70]. St. Thomas closes his reply with a quotation from St. Augustine: almighty God would in no way permit evil to exist in his world, unless he were so almighty and good as to produce good from evil.

Against this solution Anthony Flew raises the objection that "a God who is prepared to allow such a volume of evil as there actually is in the world, because this is the necessary price of securing certain special goods which have been and will be achieved, cannot after all possibly be called good"[71]. The objection repeats what such authors as J. S. Mill, W. James and others already said. Our answer is that experience shows that in many cases evil leads to some good. This allows us to make the assumption that in general evil is the road to some good. Does that "justify" evil, especially in the case of human suffering, tragic death, etc.? The difficulty is enhanced when one considers everything from the point of view of bodily existence. If, on the other hand, this life is seen as the first part of a continuing existence, our evaluation of evil becomes different and evil loses much of its importance. There nevertheless remains a mystery: we are baffled by some horrible forms of moral evil. We know that God does not will this evil at all, but only wills to permit it to take place. If we cannot see how it fits in God's plan, we may nevertheless assume that it has a meaning and a good will follow for those who suffer. Else God who is good and almighty would not allow this evil to happen.

In the Third Article of this Question St. Thomas sets forth that God has immediate care of everything, but that with regard to the execution of his plan he may use certain intermediary causes. He does so not because his own power is defective, but because he wants other things to share in his causality.

---

[68] See his *Poème sur le désastre de Lisbonne*, Oeuvres (Pléiade) 308.

[69] *Three Essays on Religion*, London 1874, 52.

[70] I 22, 2 ad 2.

[71] "Divine Omnipotence and Human Freedom", in Anthony Flew and Alasdair MacIntyre (edit.), *New Essays in Philosophical Theology*, London 1955, 144-169, 147.

The next Article considers from a slightly different angle a theme already discussed in I 19, 8 (whether God's will imposes necessity on the things willed). In Article Four the emphasis is on the execution of God's will in the government of the world: does this execution impose necessity on what God foresees? Several Greek philosophers held that causes linked to form a chain, are connected necessarily to one another. The effect flows from the first cause and passes through the intermediate causes with ineluctable necessity. This theory, which was predominant in Stoic philosophy[72], was also defended by some Neoplatonists. According to Avicenna only what is necessary is intelligible. Hence the entire chain of beings must be necessary by the power of the First Cause, even though the existence of things is only contingently connected with their essence.

St. Thomas argues that the perfection of the universe requires that all degrees of being are found in things, so that certain things have necessary, other things contingent causes. Nevertheless Aquinas adds in his reply to the first objection that what God has decided shall happen, either necessarily or contingently, happens infallibly. It would contradict the efficacy of God's power and the universality and certitude of his knowledge if the effects he decides to bring into existence, would not come about infallibly. In his commentary on this text Cajetanus observes that these lines contain a mystery which is perhaps insoluble to the human intellect[73]: how is that which inevitably comes about, compatible with such contingent causes as free will? The answer lies in the fact that created intermediate causes, such as man's free will, while producing a certain effect, possess the power not to produce it but something else instead. Although the event takes place unerringly, its created cause nevertheless does not have a necessary causal connection with its effect. The infallibility of the event is only given in God's transcendent causality which comprehends all causes and all modalities of causal action.

Connected with the theme of God's providence are the questions of the meaning of prayer and the possibility of miracles. By prayer we understand the elevation of the mind to God to pay him respect and express gratitude as well as to invoke his help. Prayer is the most elementary form of religion. The practice of prayer lies outside philosophical theology, because it is no longer an act of the speculative intellect alone. Yet the analysis of the meaning and possibility of prayer has its place in the treatise on God's providence.

It has been argued by some that prayer is something of an embarrassment to classical theism: if God orders and controls all things in accordance with his eternal purpose, what difference can human prayers make? How can we

---

[72] Cf. Seneca, *Natur. quaest.* II 36, 1: "Necessitas rerum omnium actionumque quam nulla vis rumpat". See also Nemesius, *De natura hominis* 37 and D. Amand, *Fatalisme et liberté dans l'antiquité grecque*, Louvain 1945.

[73] *In I*^{am} 22, 1, III.

presume to beg God to alter that what in his infinite wisdom he has decided to do?[74]. Some authors think that classical theism is unable to handle the prayer of intercession and adoration. God does not change his decisions and in his perfect bliss he has no need of our adoration.

The solution of this difficulty is simple. Divine providence does not exclude created causes, rather it orders and uses them in such a way that they collaborate with God and carry out his plan. Granted that man is a being who needs protection and help, it is to be expected that God wills certain things to be given to man in answer to prayer. "So it is the same thing to say that we should not pray in order to obtain something from God, as to say that we should not walk in order to get to a certain place" (God having decided from all eternity that we shall be in that place)[75]. In St. Thomas' view, prayer is a secondary cause. If we place prayer in the context of God's love for man, the convenience of prayer becomes even more telling[76]. Prayer of thanksgiving and adoration is an expression of man's metaphysical awareness of his situation. It is man's loving answer to God's goodness and an ascent of the mind to the Fountain of all being[77].

In process theology prayer is considered an expression of the creative advance, that is of the common development and growth of God and man. But, as was shown in Chapter Six, the concept of an evolving God is untenable.

A second question is what to think of miracles. The word 'miracle' signifies something which makes us wonder because it lies outside the ordinary course of events. In the strict sense of the term a miracle is an observable event (effect) which surpasses the forces of nature. St. Thomas distinguishes between three types of miracles[78].

Some argue against the definition of a miracle as given above that we simply do not know what nature is capable of doing. If at this moment we do not yet have a scientific explanation of a certain event, this does not mean that it has a supernatural cause. Much that was considered miraculous in the past

---

[74] L. Ford, "Our Prayers as God's Passions", edited by H.J. Cargas and B. Lee, *Religious Experience and Process Theology*, New York 1976, 429. The objection was already raised by such rationalists as Voltaire. See n.64. Aquinas himself formulates it in II-II 83, 2; I 23, 8.

[75] *S.C.G.* III 96 (transl. V. Bourke).

[76] This point is stressed by J.F.X. Knasas in his excellent study "Aquinas: Prayer to an Immutable God", in *The New Scholasticism* 57 (1983) 196-221.

[77] *Ibid.*: "It pertains to the essential meaning of friendship for the lover to will the fulfilment of the desire of the beloved, because he wishes the good and the perfect for the beloved ..."

[78] The three classes of miracles are: those with regard to the *manner* in which something happens (a sudden cure); events happening in a subject which is not naturally capable of receiving this effect (to give back life to a dead body); miracles which natural causes can never bring about, because the effect simply is above nature (the glorification of Christ's body). See I 105, 8; I-II 113, 10; *S.C.G.* III 101 ff.

has now found a natural explanation. Moreover, resorting to the supernatural
is tantamount to the introduction of something which cannot be verified. A
further factor which made the admission of miracles more difficult was the
rise of mechanism in physics. Scientists felt that God would contradict
himself, if he would violate the laws he had established[79]. David Hume, for
his part, voiced doubt with regard to the value of the testimony of people who
claim to have witnessed miracles. To counter the objections voiced by the
mechanists some Christians suggested that material nature is both immutable
and changeable: mathematical and physical lawa are without exception, but
changes in quantity and quality may occur. Miracles do not affect the
immutable part of nature[80]. This view is neatly expressed in the following text
of P. Tourlemont: "In performing a miracle providence does not disturb this
order or suspend the operation of physical laws; rather it uses the laws,
neutralizing their effect in a particular case as a hand neutralizing the effect
of weight in stopping a falling stone"[81]. The philosopher E. Le Roy argued
that science gives only a distant view of reality; it shows us determinable
rather than determined natures. Physical laws are marked by a restricted
application[82].

Obviously it is not the task of the metaphysician to enter into a discussion
of the validity and scope of the laws which physical science discerns in the
material universe. Philosophy, moreover, does not pronounce itself on the
question whether miracles have occurred. It does not use miraculous events
to demonstrate God's existence. It does, however, reflect on certain events
which *appear* not to be subject to an explanation by natural causes. It raises
the question whether in some cases a special intervention of God in the world,
besides and sometimes in contrast with the forces and laws of nature, is possible. Would God contradict himself when he would cause a miracle?

If we identify God with nature, miracles are unthinkable, but if God is a
transcendent, free Person and the material world only one mode of being, it
no longer seems impossible that exceptional things such as miracles happen.
Rather than being against the laws of nature, miracles transcend them[83].
Material things have a certain capacity to be subservient to higher beings.
Because of the sublime unity of things and their cooperation, physical and
biological facts will also be ordered toward or, have at least a non-repugnancy

---

[79] Cf. R.S. Westfall, *Science and Religion*.

[80] This was Lacordaire's position. See the *Revue du Clergé français* 87 (1916) 507f.

[81] Quoted after Harry W. Paul, *The Edge of Contingency. French Catholic Reaction to Scientific Change from Darwin to Duhem*, Gainesville 1979, 17.

[82] "Essai sur la notion du miracle", in *Annales de philosophie chrétienne* IV 3 (1906-1907).

[83] As a matter of fact certain Scholastics did describe miracles as being *contra naturam*, but
understood this in such a way that God produces effects in a manner different from the ordinary
course of things. Cf. St. Bonaventure, *In II Sent.*, d.18, a.1, q.2, concl. 5 (Q.II 438).

to being ordered toward man as he proceeds on his spiritual itinerary[84]. It follows that if a miracle is sometimes opposed to a specific tendency or disposition of a body, it is not opposed to the latter's deep-seated capacity to serve what is higher.

III. *The Power of God (I 25)*

The treatise of God's power logically follows that of divine knowledge and will. Thus far God's intellect and love were considered in so far as they are God's intradivine activity. In this Question God's being is studied inasmuch as it is the foundation of the creation and conservation of the world. In the *S.Th.* Aquinas considers God's power immediately after the treatment of divine science and will, but in the *S.C.G.* he places the study of this subject in the Second Book which deals with the production of things by God. The first argument concludes from the fact that God is a principle of the being of things outside himself that he must have power. In the *S.Th.* St. Thomas takes a somewhat different starting point: when we consider God's being in the light of the analyses thus far carried out, does God have the capacity to act on other things and to produce them in being?

The idea of the power of the gods was not very prominent in Greek philosophy. Aristotle contributed to the elaboration of the treatise of divine power by his theory of the First Unmoved Mover, who moves in infinite time and must possess an infinite power[85]. However, Posidonius was the first philosopher to assign a central place to the study of the theme. Power is the vital cause which keeps the cosmos together and is active in all its parts[86]. Another text witnessing to the growing importance attached to divine power is the pseudo-Aristotelian treatise *De mundo*: God is compared to a king who although invisible in the various parts of his realm, makes his influence felt everywhere[87]. According to Philo God rules over all things and everything is subject to his power[88]. In Neoplatonism power is an important concept in the metaphysics of emanation: through the intermediary lower beings the One

---

[84] See *In II Sent.*, d.18, q.1, a.3 and *De pot.* 6, 2 ad 3, where St. Thomas limits miracles *contra naturam* to those miracles where in the bodies undergoing the miraculous action, a tendency to do the opposite remains latent, so that they return to their natural condition when God's intervention ceases (Christ walking upon the waters). This implies that God's action stands in a limited opposition to their nature and to the laws which govern them. But there is no opposition to the deep-seated disposition of things to be subservient to what is higher.

[85] *Metaph.* 1073 a 7-11.

[86] K. Reinhardt, *Poseidonios*, München 1921, 11. See fr. 18 and 106 in Edelstein and Kidd, *Posidonius I: The Fragments*, Cambridge 1972.

[87] *De mundo* 397 b 19. In the *De mundo* as well as in Hellenistic circles intermediate things were often assumed to have a role in passing on this divine power. See M.P. Nilsson, *Geschichte der griechischen Religion. II* (1950) 446.

[88] *De opif. mundi, passim.* See H.A. Wolfson, in *Harvard Theol. Review*, 1960, 109.

and *Noûs* are active. The power of the latter is not limited by matter[89]. In keeping with the numerous texts of Holy Scripture on God's power the Christian authors express their belief in divine omnipotence[90].

In the First Article of this Question St. Thomas demonstrates that there is active power in God in the highest degree[91]:

> "For it is manifest that everything, according as it is in act and is perfect, is the active principle of something; whereas everything is passive according as it is deficient and imperfect. Now it was shown above that God is pure act, absolutely and universally perfect, and completely without any imperfection[92]. Whence it most fittingly belongs to him to be an active principle, and in no way whatsoever to be passive. On the other hand, the nature of active principle belongs to active power. For active power is the principle of acting upon something else; whereas passive power is the principle of being acted upon by something else, as the Philosopher says[93]. It remains, therefore, that in God there is active power in the highest degree"[94].

Aquinas' demonstration is based upon an insight which we acquire by experience: everything according as it is in act, is perfect and is the active principle of something. We observe, indeed, that the things which act do so because of a force and a capacity proper to them or communicated by some other being. The greater its capacity, the more a thing can act in the various fields in which it is apt to do so. This holds true of agents in the physical world, of the crafts, administrative capacities and acquired knowledge. God is pure act and universal aptitude to act. At the end of his demonstration St. Thomas observes that "active power" means precisely that what it is to be an active principle. For by "active power" we mean the principle by which the possesser acts. God is pure act and thus he possesses power in the highest degree.

In his reply to three objections Aquinas removes imperfections from the concept of God's power: it does not include any potentiality; God's action is not distinct from his power (as is the case in created agents) for both are God's essence[95]. For this reason God's power is the principle, not of an action, but of effects outside God. In his answer to the fourth objection St. Thomas points out that God's power is logically and not really distinct from his

---

[89] *Enn.* 2, 2; V 5, 12; VI 9, 16. Cf. R.T. Wallis, *Neoplatonism*, London 1972, 156.

[90] Cf. Irenaeus, *Adv. Haer.* I 10, 1; Tertullianus, *De virg. vel.* 1. See also Boethius, *De consol. philos.* III prosa 12.

[91] Passive power to undergo something must be excluded from God, as was shown in the conclusion of the First Way. Active power is the principle which acts upon something else (*S.C.G.* II 7: principium agendi in aliud).

[92] Q. 3, a.1 & 2; q.4, q.1 and 2.

[93] *Metaph.* 1019 a 19.

[94] I 25, 1.

[95] In the *De mundo* a sharp distinction is drawn between God's being and his power. Their precise relationship does not become very clear.

knowledge and will "inasmuch as power implies the notion of a principle putting into execution what the will commands and what the intellect directs".

Is God's power infinite? (I 25, 2). Active power exists in God according to the measure in which he is actual. Since God's being is infinite, his power is as well. St. Thomas illustrates this argument by means of an induction: the hotter a thing is, the greater will be its power to heat; the more learned a person is, the more knowledge he has to share. From these examples we conclude that the more perfectly an agent possesses the form by which it acts, the greater is its power to act. Since God acts through his essence, which is infinite, his power cannot but be infinite.

This does not mean that God produces infinite effects. God is a non-univocal agent; nothing can agree with God who is above all categories. His effects bear only a remote likeness to him.

If God's power is not limited, God will be omnipotent (I 25, 3). The term 'almighty' (παντοκράτωρ, omnipotens) is occasionally used in Greek and Latin literature to describe the great power of Hermes, Jupiter or Fortune, but there is no specific theory of divine omnipotence. The Christian creed, on the other hand, confesses that God, the Creator of heaven and earth, is almighty. Thus St. Thomas can write that "all confess that God is omnipotent, but it seems difficult to explain in what his omnipotence precisely consists". Power is said in relation to that which is possible. God is not said to be omnipotent in reference to his own being, for this would be a vicious circle. God can do all things that are possible to his power. This includes whatever is possible absolutely speaking. In this sense God is omnipotent.

Aquinas adds some further observations: "to each active power there corresponds a thing possible as its power object according to the nature of that act on which its active power is founded". Since God's being is not limited to any class of being, his power extends to anything whatsoever which has or can have the nature of being. What is contradictory, does not have the nature of being and "does not come under the divine omnipotence, not because of any defect in the power of God, but because it has not the nature of a feasible or possible thing.... Hence it is more appropriate to say that such things cannot be done than that God cannot do them"[96].

---

[96] This answer solves the paradox of the stone mentioned by R. Swinburne (*The Coherence of Theism*, Oxford 1977, 152f.): Can God make a stone too heavy for himself to lift? The question itself and the concept of such a stone imply a contradiction. In his *Providence and Evil*, Peter Geach argues that there are logically possible things which, according to Aquinas, God cannot do. However, a closer look at what God is solves this objection: self-contradictory things are not doable; certain doable things involve a contradiction if God does them. See R. McInerny, "Aquinas on Divine Omnipotence", in Ch. Wenin (edit.), *L'homme et son univers au Moyen Age. Actes du 7me congrès international de philosophie médiévale* (1982), Louvain-la-Neuve 1986, I 440-440.

The doctrine of God's omnipotence was strongly affirmed by Descartes although he introduced a revolutionary change in formulating it: God's power, he said, cannot in any way be limited; this also means that there is no truth which is not subject to God's will. What is contradictory for us, must not be considered impossible for God[97]. Gilson considered this position the most important innovation by Descartes in philosophical thinking. Descartes' view had been prepared by the theory of the *potentia Dei absoluta* of the Nominalists[98]. Descartes' position tends to deprive the world of logical consistency.

Can God undo the past? (I 25, 4). The question may seem purely academic to us. However, it has been debated by philosophers from the fifth century B.C. until the dawn of the modern age. Plain common sense, based upon experience, tends to hold that the past cannot return. Plato formulated this conviction in the *Republic*: human life is irreversible[99]. However, Empedocles' theory of the cosmic cycle implies the periodic return of the past. This view is related to the Pythagorean doctrine of reincarnation. Plato and Aristotle assume that there is a periodic rise and fall of civilisations. Quoting the belief of people at large Aristotle writes that time is cyclical[100]. Meteorological events occur in cycles[101] and the same truth appears at frequent intervals in human history[102]. An extreme form of this belief in cyclical return is found in the works of Eudemus of Rhodos who asserted that after a set cosmic period he would be teaching again the same students[103]. The Early Stoa, on the other hand, taught that it is a law of the cosmos that that which is past, is past[104]. Although St. Augustine rejected the theory of the return of the past[105], some Mediaeval authors such as Peter Damianus[106], Gilbert of la Porrée[107] and William of Auvergne[108] taught that in his omnipotence God could allow the past to return. After St. Thomas' time the debate on God's *potentia absoluta* and *potentis ordinata* (see below) made this question gain in importance[109].

---

[97] See his *Letter to Mersenne*, April 15, 1630 (Adam et Tannery I 145f.).

[98] Arab occasionalists hold a similar view: all natural events depend on the arbitrary decrees of God's will. See M. Fakhry, *o.c.*, 87.

[99] *Rep.* 620e.—However, Plato knows the theory of the Great Year, a cosmic period in which the celestial bodies return to the same positions (*Polit.* 273a. Cf. *Tim.* 22bff.; *Laws* 677a; *Critias* 109d).

[100] *Phys.* 223 b 28.

[101] *Meteor.* 352 a 30.

[102] *Meteor.* 339 b 27; *De coelo* 270 b 19; *Metaph.* 1074 b 10, etc.

[103] Fragm. 88 Wehrli.—Simplicius, *In Phys.* 732, 23ff.

[104] Chrysippus, *S.V.F.* II 913.

[105] *Contra Faustum* 26, 5: PL 42, 481.

[106] *De divina omnipotentia*, c.15: PL 145, 620B.

[107] *In Boethii De Trinitate*: PL 64, 1287A.

[108] *Summa aurea* I, c.11, q.5 and q.6.

[109] See W.J. Courtency, "John of Mirecourt and Gregory of Rimini on whether God can undo the Past", in *Rech. théol. anc. et médiév.* 40 (1973) 147ff.

In his solution St. Thomas considers the question in a strictly formal way: can God bring it about that a past event is no longer past or that it did not happen? He answers that this implies a contradiction and even an absolute contradiction. Hence to undo the past is not possible and not subject to God's power. This does not mean that God cannot change or take away the effects of past events or return to life dead people. What must be excluded is that he could bring about that what once happened did not happen.

The next question is whether God can make other things than those he actually has made (I 25, 5). Peter Abelard thought that the answer is negative: God can only make what he has actually made and act in the manner he has actually acted and at the very moment he did so[110]. The reason is that God does whatever he does in the most perfect way so that he cannot do any better and even does so necessarily. This theory was condemned by Innocent II[111].

Aquinas rejects Abelard's view because it tends to reduce God's operation to a natural process: God is only able to produce a certain effect, just as a particular seed cannot but produce this particular plant. But, as has been shown above, God's will does not act by necessity in the production of the world. One cannot say that since God acts with supreme wisdom, he cannot act in a different way, for God's wisdom surpasses so much the order of created things that it is not bound by it. In his reply to the first objection St. Thomas adds that God's power, will and being are the same, but that nevertheless something can be in God's power which he does not will to come into existence. At this juncture Aquinas introduces the distinction between God's absolute and his ordinary power: by his absolute power God can make other things than he actually made. One must not say that God can do something because he wills it, but because God is omnipotent in his nature he can make whatever he conceives. The purpose of St. Thomas' observation is to exclude any arbitrariness from God.

The distinction between the *potentia absoluta* and the *potentia ordinaria Dei* was current in St. Thomas' day[112], but after the condemnation of certain theories in 1277 it was given a more prominent place by Scotus and the Nominalists[113]. In the fourteenth century the question of God's absolute power even occupied the centre of philosophical and theological speculation: attention was drawn away from the actual order of things to speculations on

---

[110] *Theologia christiana* V: *PL* 178, 1321; *Theologia scholarum* III 4-5: *PL* 178, 1091C. Cf. also St. Bernard, *Tract. vel epist.* 190: *PL* 182, 106.

[111] See D.E. Luscombe, *The School of Peter Abelard*, Cambridge 1970, 109.

[112] It was used by Hugh of St. Victor in his De *Sacramentis* I 22: *PL* 176, 214. On the origin of the distinction see A. Lang, *Die Wege der Glaubensbegründung bei den Scholastikern des 14. Jahrhunderts, in BGPTMA* 20, Münster 1930.

[113] Cf. Mary A. Pernoud, "The Theory of the *Potentia Dei* according to Aquinas, Scotus and Ockham", in *Antonianum* 47 (1972) 69-95. See also E. Grant, "The Effects of the Condemnation of 1277", in *The Cambridge History of Later Medieval Philosophy*, 1982, 537-539.

what could have been done by God. While this provided some theologians with the opportunity to praise God's love and pity which are at the origin of the established order, it led others to turn their attention away from the latter and to seek immediate contact with God himself. The established order is something contingent which could have been different. Human reason could never have predicted it. In this way a sceptical attitude began to prevail; man felt himself at a greater distance from the world and quite autonomous. This brought about a greater freedom with regard to Aristotle's physics and helped prepare the rise of modern science. The supernatural world was now experienced as an extra addition to the physical world rather than as an encompassing society in which man lives[114]. Nature no longer seemed to offer access to God. The distinction between God's absolute and his ordinary power had a considerable impact on the theology of G. Biehl and through Biehl on Luther.

Connected with this theme is the question whether God could have made a better world (I 25, 6). Is our universe the best possible one? Peter Abelard thought that Plato was right when he said that God made things as well as they could be made[115]. However, mediaeval authors hesitated to follow Abelard because his position tends to restrict God's omnipotence[116]. But later philosophers had no such hesitations. Malebranche asserts that this world is best because we cannot understand why God would have made a less perfect one[117]. Leibniz presents a similar argument: God is morally obliged to make the best world; else there would be something that could be corrected in God's work[118].

In *In I Sent.*, d.44 St. Thomas makes an elaborate study of the issue. He distinguishes between several questions (whether God could have made a creature better than it is; whether he could have made the universe better; whether he could have made the human nature of Christ better, etc.). In the *S.Th.* these questions are grouped together and receive an answer in a lucid synthesis. Aquinas begins his solution with a distinction: the goodness of things is that of their essence and the accidental goodness which lies outside their essence (such as, in man, knowledge and virtue). With regard to the

---

[114] See P. Vignaux, *Nominalisme au XIVᵉ siècle*, Montréal-Paris 1948, 12ff.; H. Obermann, "Some Notes on the Theology of Nominalism", in *Harvard Theol. Review* 53 (1960) 47-76; *idem, The Harvest of Medieval Theology*, Cambridge 1963, 38-50; F. Oakley, "Pierre D'Ailly and the Absolute Power of God", in *HThR* 56 (1963) 59-73.

[115] *Theol. schol.* III: *PL* 178, 1094B.

[116] J.M. Parent, *La création dans l'Ecole de Chartres*, Paris-Ottawa 1938, 65. Proposition 66 of the 219 articles condemned in 1277 (Hissette, *o.c.*, 118f.) was apparently censured because it limited divine omnipotence to the creation of this universe only.

[117] *Entretiens sur la métaphysique* IX, 8.

[118] *Theodicea II* 201: "Il y aurait quelque chose à corriger dans les actions de Dieu, s'il y avait moyen de mieux faire" (*o.c.*, I 8).

former things cannot be improved upon. God cannot maker a better man in
the sense of a being which is essentially more man, although he could always
make things of a different specific nature, better than those he actually has
made. This is an obvious conclusion from the fact that God is infinitely perfect and powerful.

The goodness of created things which lies outside their essence can be
increased. To stress God's all-surpassing greatness and power Aquinas closes
this article with the observation that God could always make better things
than any of those created. In his reply to the first objection St. Thomas adds
that with regard to his mode of operation God could not have worked with
greater wisdom and goodness than he did. The second objection is concerned
with a difficulty raised by Epicurus[119] and taken up again by Hume:
"Epicurus' old questions are yet unanswered. Is he (God) willing to prevent
evil, but not able? then he is impotent. Is he able but not willing? then he is
malevolent. Is he both able and willing? whence then is evil?"[120]. As has been
shown above, the answer to this difficulty is that God wills certain goods to
which evil may be attached, in order to attain a greater good in our universe
which comprises decay, corruption and suffering. As a matter of fact, more
power is required to construct such a universe.

The answer to the third objection is no less important. In a sense our
universe can be said to be the best one possible inasmuch as the things which
make it up together constitute the best world order. In St. Thomas' view this
comprises the accidental goodness of things, so that limited perfections,
defects and evil, when taken together, yield the best order. The reason is that
God is the wisest efficient cause[121]. In his answer Aquinas expresses his Christian optimism and admiration for God's creation. He safeguards God's
freedom and omnipotence which are not bound to the creation of the things
which make up our world. But St. Thomas also brings in God's wisdom and
goodness which obtain the best possible order with the things he decided to
make[122].

IV. *God's Beatitude (I 26)*

In a well-known passus of the *Metaphysics* Aristotle writes that God's activity
is joy[123]. This conclusion follows from a comparison of God's activity with

[119] On Epicurus' view see Lactantius, *De ira Dei*, 13.
[120] *Dialogues Concerning Natural Religion* (edit. Longmans, London 1909, X 440).
[121] See I 47, 2 ad 1: "optimi agentis est producere totum effectum suum optimum".
[122] As A. Rozwadowski, "De optimismo universali secundum S. Thomam", *Gregorianum* 17
(1936) 254-264 pointed out, the doctrine of Aquinas implies that the existing universe has the best
possible order given its constituents, and cannot be improved accidentally; however, an individual
created thing can be accidentally improved. This position goes beyond that expressed in *In I Sent.*,
d.44, q.1, a.2.
[123] *Metaph.* 1072 b 16.

the best which man temporarily enjoys. But Aristotle also argued that all beings strive for pleasure. In doing so they imitate the supreme pleasure of the First Mover whose very activity is pleasure[124]. This activity is contemplation[125]. In his theology Aristotle transposes the popular concept of the blessed life of the gods: God's life consists in self-knowledge accompanied by joy[126].

Some critics find fault with the idea of a Being shut up in unceasing and changeless contemplation of itself and cannot "imagine that such a contemplation is worthy of the names of perfect activity, of life, of blessedness"[127]. But this criticism betrays a lack of metaphysical insight and of the capacity to think along the lines of the *via negativa* and the *via eminentiae*.

St. Thomas takes over Aristotle's definition of pleasure as the unhampered act of a habitus in conformity with the nature to which this habitus belongs[128]. In view of this definition the conclusion imposes itself that God's self-knowledge and love are joy. Thus Aquinas closes his treatise of God with the theme of God's bliss. This question is not explicitly announced in the introduction to the previous questions, so that it has been suggested that St. Thomas added it as an afterthought[129]. But this can hardly be correct. In the *S.C.G.* the chapters on divine beatitude are preceded by cc.97-99 on God's life, but in the *S.Th.* the question whether life belongs to God follows that about divine knowledge. The reason for this change is that "to know" is a certain way of being alive. But this creates a difficulty: beatitude is also a form of intellectual life, as St. Thomas intimates[130]. Why did he not examine divine beatitude before treating God's will, providence and power? To answer this question we must recall the opposition between the Christian doctrine of happiness and other views. St. Augustine describes happiness as a state in which one has whatever one wants[131]. The Stoa, on the other hand, said that virtue constitutes the essence of happiness. In Abelard's *Dialogue Between a Philosopher, a Jew and a Christian* the debate on the various theories of happiness

---

[124] See *Met*. XII, cc.7 & 9 and *E.N.* 1178 b 3-10; 1134 b 27.

[125] *Met*. 1072 b 24-30.

[126] The precise relationship between activity and pleasure is expressed differently by Aristotle in his works. In *E.N.* VII, cc.12-15 the view is defended that pleasure is an activity. See A.-J—Festugière, *Aristote. Le plaisir*, Paris 1946, xxi and R.A. Gauthier & J.Y. Jolif, *L'Ethique à Nicomaque*, Louvain 1959, 779. However, in *E.N.* X, c.4 Aristotle only says that pleasure accompanies, completes and intensifies activity. In his *Commentary on the N.E.* St. Thomas does not show himself aware of an opposition between these two views. The text of 1072 b 17 need not be understood as affirming the full identity of activity and pleasure (Gauthier and Jolif, *l.c.*). To the contrary, however, J. Léonard, *Le bonheur chez Aristote*, Bruxelles 1948, 80.

[127] F. Cornford, *From Religion to Philosophy*, Harper Torch edit., New York 1957, 261.

[128] *In VII Ethicorum*, lectio 12.

[129] R. Guindon, *Béatitude et théologie morale chez saint Thomas d'Aquin*, Ottawa 1956, 257.

[130] I 26, 2.

[131] Cf. St. Augustine, *De Trin*. XII 5.

is vividly depicted. St. Thomas brings clarity. He points out that Aristotle's description of happiness in the *Nicomachean Ethics* concerns the imperfect happiness possible in this life. He stresses more than Aristotle that the *possession of the good* belongs to happiness [132], but maintains the dominant role of the intellect: by our knowledge we possess things and are aware of our possessing them.

In our question Aquinas sets out from a definition of the happiness proper to man [133]: beatitude is the perfect good of an intellectual nature which knows its own self-sufficiency in the good it has,—to which something good or bad may happen and which has the mastery over its own operations [134]. This definition minus the human limitation has two main elements: to be perfect and to possess knowledge. Both are proper to God in a most excellent way. Hence bliss is proper to God in a superlative manner. The elements of this definition are taken from the *Nicomachean Ethics*, where Aristotle defines happiness as a good which is self-sufficient [135] and as an activity of the soul implying a rational principle [136]. The perception of one's own goodness is pleasant [137]; misfortune reduces or destroys happiness [138]. In taking over this definition Aquinas lays greater stress than Aristotle had done on the good in which and through which happiness is found. He also adds the domination over one's operation and in this way introduces the will. This explains the place of our question at the end of the treatise on God's operation.

As all things strive to attain their perfection, a being endowed with intellect seeks happiness, which consists in its intellectual operation by which it graps, in a sense, all things. This also applies to God. It must be noted that his thinking and being are the same reality and both can only be distinguised by reason (I 26, 2). The implication of the Second Article is that one is only happy through knowledge and through awareness of perfection and goodness.

In the last two articles of this Question St. Thomas argues that God is the beatitude of the blessed in heaven and that divine bliss comprises any happiness. For whatever good is desirable, it is present in God in a more excellent way. Aquinas furthermore makes a distinction between the object of the act by which we are happy and the act of understanding itself. With regard to the object, only God is the beatitude of man, but inasfar as our beatitude is knowledge, it consists in an act of the intellect.

---

[132] See L. Elders, "St. Thomas Aquinas' Commentary on the Nicomachean Ethics", in L. J. Elders and K. Hedwig, *The Ethics of St. Thomas Aquinas*, Città del Vaticano 1984, 9-49, 15ff.

[133] See G. Wieland, "The Perfection of Man", in *The Cambridge History of Later Medieval Philosophy*, 1982, 673-686.

[134] I 26, 2.

[135] *E.N.* I, c.5ff. Cf. *In X Ethicorum*, l.9, n.2069: "de ratione felicitatis est quod sit per se sufficiens et non indigeat aliquo alio".

[136] *E.N.* 1098 a 13ff.

[137] *E.N.* 1170 b 8ff.

[138] *E.N.* 1100 b 22ff.

CHAPTER TEN

CREATION (I 44-47)

Man has always shown a great curiosity with regard to the origin of the world. A great number of myths tell us about the genesis of the universe and of man himself. This raises the question whether philosophical reflection must deal with the issue of creation. There are theologians who hold that the concept of creation has not been acquired from experience but was communicated to man by revelation[1]. The fact that creation in the sense of the production of the universe from nothing by a free decision of God, is unknown to philosophers, favours this view[2]. As a matter of fact, in this particular sense the term is only used by Christian authors, who seem to borrow if from the Bible. However, it is an altogether different question whether, absolutely speaking, natural reason by its own force, can reach the concept of creation. St. Thomas gives an affirmative answer in four sections: the procession of creatures from God, the mode of emanation, the beginning of the duration of things and the distinction of things.

I. The Procession of Things from God and the First Cause of All Things (I 44)

One may distinguish between four different views on the origin of the world. A first theory is monistic and considers the material universe as the only reality and as derived from a single principle such as water, air, fire or homogeneous atoms or elementary particles. This view sometimes develops into a dynamic and evolutionary monism. For instance, Neoplatonism holds that all things proceed through emanation from the One in serial order: each nature produces necessarily that which follows upon it and the world is not the product of a divine Spirit who creates by a free decision[3]. The Neoplatonic theory is attractive: Spinoza, Hegel, Henri Bergson[4] and others subscribe to it in one way or another.

---

[1] Cf. J. Auer and J. Ratzinger, *Kleine Katholische Dogmatik*, III, 65.

[2] This point is stressed by E. Gibson all through his *The Spirit of Mediaeval Philosophy*, New York 1940. Cf. also C. Tresmontant, *La métaphysique du christianisme et la naissance de la philosophie chrétienne*, Paris 1961.

[3] Cf. Plotinus, *Enn.* V 8, 7.

[4] *Evolution créatrice*, 270: "... je parle d'un centre d'où les mondes jailliraient comme les fusées d'un immense bouquet, pourvu toutefois que je ne donne pas ce centre pour une *chose*, mais pour une continuité de jaillissement. Dieu ainsi défini n'a rien de tout fait; il est vie incessante, action, liberté. La création ainsi conçue n'est pas un mystère, nous l'expérimentons en nous dès que nous agissons librement".

A second theory juxtaposes the universe to a Supreme Being. The world is subordinated to and to a certain extent dependent on this Being, although it is eternal and not created. The question of an absolute beginning of matter is not raised. This position is held by Plato and Aristotle[5]. The former admitted two opposite principles: the Ideas and the Receptacle (or Matter). While for Plato the formal being of things depends on the Ideas, in Aristotle's view the dependence of the world on the First Mover is less pronounced: God is the final cause and as such the cause of all process in the world. The elements and the celestial bodies are eternal[6]. This doctrine was so wide-spread that even Philo[7] and some early Christian authors admitted eternal matter[8]. However, very soon the Fathers began to point out that, unlike human craftsmen, God does not need preexistent matter[9].

Some thinkers denied the reality of the world either by reducing it to sense perceptions which are connected with one another by the knowing subject[10] or by asserting that being is an act of thinking[11]. Somewhat related to this phenomenalism is the doctrine of Mahayana Buddhism according to which the phenomena are without any substance. There exists an underlying reality which cannot be conceived and which has no cause[12].

A fourth group of theories admit two equipollent principles which are antagonistic. The Early Pythagoreans held the view of two ultimate contrary principles, the limit and the unlimited[13]. As we have seen, Plato's philosophy shows dualistic features[14], but dualism reached its most pronounced expression in gnosticism and in some Eastern religions.

Against this background the Biblical concept of creation, as understood by the Christian Church, asserts something wholly novel: the celestial bodies as

---

[5] See *Tim.* 30 a: "Desiring, then, that all things should be good, and, so far as might be, nothing imperfect, the god took over all that is visible—not at rest, but in discordant and unordered motion—and brought it from disorder into order, since he judged that order was in every way the better" (transl. by Cornford). For the interpretation of the text see the historical survey.

[6] Cf. *De caelo* I 9; II 1, 283 b 26: "That the heaven as a whole neither came into being nor admits of destruction as some assert, but is one and eternal, with no end or beginning of its total duration, containing and embracing in itself the infinity of time ..." (Oxford translation). E. Zeller qualifies Aristotle's doctrine as a dualistic theism (*Die Philosophie der Griechen* II, 2, 384).

[7] Cf. E. Bréhier, *Les idées philosophiques et religieuses de Philon d'Alexandrie*, Paris 1925, 78-82

[8] Cf. Justinus, *1 Apol.*, 10: *PG* 6, 340. On Clement of Alexandria's view see S. Lilla, *Clement of Alexandria*, Oxford 1971, 193.

[9] St. Irenaeus, *Adv. Haer*, II 10, 4: *PG* 7, 736. Tertullian wrote his *Adversus Hermogenem* to refute the theory of pre-existent matter.

[10] This is J. Stuart Mill's position in his *An Examination of Sir W. Hamilton's Philosophy*, London 1865, ch. 11.

[11] This thesis is defended by so-called absolute idealism.

[12] Cf. H. Zimmer, *Philosophies of India*, New York 1956, 520ff.

[13] W.K.C. Guthrie, *HGrPh* I 246.

[14] See S. Pétrement, *Le dualisme chez Platon, les gnostiques et les manichéens*, Paris 1947.

well as the sublunar elements are neither gods nor divine; they have been made by God who produced them from nothing by a free decision of his will. Creation is not a necessary process such as spontaneous emanation[15]. God's freedom in making the world is frequently stressed by the Fathers[16]. Time and again they also point out that God made the world from nothing[17], without resorting to the help of intermediary beings[18]. However, we are not now concerned with the faith but with the philosophical aspects of creation.

The term creation (χτίσις) is used to denote the production of something in whatever way it is made. More specifically it signifies artistic production. In the strict sense of the term creation denotes the production of beings from nothing. As we proceed with the study of questions 44, 45, 46 and 47 the various aspects of this latter notion of creation will be brought to light. Before we begin to study of the text of St. Thomas, however a concise historical survey of philosophical theories of the origin of the world will be helpful.

It has often been ponted out that the outstanding Greek philosophers Plato, Aristotle and Plotinus did not reach the insight that the universe receives its being from God, so that it has a beginning in time. It is true that in his description of the becoming of the world in the *Timaeus* Plato seems to refer to creation by the demiurge, but the majority of scholars take this story to be a myth. Plato wants to present an analysis of the structure of things by means of a genetic description. However, in his renowned *A History of Greek Philosophy* W. K. C. Guthrie is reluctant to pronounce himself on the precise meaning of this passage in the *Timaeus*[19]. Indeed, it is not so clear what Plato really intends to say. A. E. Taylor moved from his initial interpretation (creation of the world is meant) to an admission of the eternity of the universe in Plato[20]. R. Hackforth, on the other hand, followed the opposite road: from his initial denial that the soul for Plato was created in time he went all the way to admitting such creation[21].

We cannot enter here into a full discussion of the issue and must limit ourselves to a number of observations. In the first place we must distinguish between the question of the eternity of soul and of the physical world on the one hand and the eternal existence of a second principle on the other. The

---

[15] Cf. Eusebius, *Praep. evang.* VII 3.

[16] St. Athanasius, *Or. adv. Arianos* I 29; *De fide orth.* I 8 (ἠθέλησεν). In his *Hexaemeron* St. Basil rejects the Platonic view according to which God is a non-free cause of the world. St. Irenaeus expresses the Christian concept pregnantly in his *Adv. Haer.* II 1, 1: "sua sententia et libere fecit omnia".

[17] See the second part of this chapter.

[18] Cf. St. Augustine, *De gen. ad litt.* IX 26.

[19] *O.c.* V 302ff.

[20] See his *Plato*, London 1908 and *A Commentary on Plato's Timaeus*, Oxford 1928, 79 where Taylor emphatically warns his reader that according to Plato the world has existed for ever.

[21] See his "Plato's Theism" (1936) in R.E. Allen, *Studies in Plato's Metaphysics*, London 1956, 439-447 and his "Plato's Cosmogony", in *Class. Quart.* 1959, 17-22.

Receptacle or Space in which things are formed, is eternal. The divine craftsman of the *Timaeus* is confronted with matter and chaos and seeks to bring
them to order. As F. Cornford writes, throughout the *Timaeus* it is implied
that the activity of the Demiurge is restricted by an extrinsical factor called
Necessity[22]. The Demiurge does not create the Receptacle of becoming in
which the forms are reflected. This also holds true for the second principle of
Plato's later theory, viz. the Great and the Small or the Indeterminate Dyad.
This second principle is at work also in the ideas and, therefore, it must be
eternal. Plato does not have the biblical notion of creation. It would seem that
the story of the creation of soul and the world is an allegorical expression of
their dependence on the Ideas. The image of the divine craftsman must be
explained by Plato's intention to oppose the cosmogony of Hesiod[23].

Aristotle most explicitly teaches the eternity of the world and restricts its
dependence on God: all movements in the universe ultimately depend on God.
But he also writes on two occasions that the world is dependent on the First
Principle[24]. The First Principle is the final and exemplary cause, but it is not
clear to what extent it also exercises efficient causality.

Is the Neoplatonic doctrine of emanation from the One comparable to the
Christian Idea of creation, as has been suggested by some?[25] The emanation
of *Noûs* and Soul from the One is a necessary process, consequent on the very
nature of the One. It does not entail any degradation of the One, but is pure
redundancy or generosity. As Plato taught, the divine is not jealous. If in a
certain sense the One "wills" this emanation, it does so necessarily and does
not will its effects. Emanation is a necessary process: what proceeds is out of
the substance of the One itself, even if it falls far short of its perfection.
Plotinus' theory remains within the compass of monism, although it is a
somewhat differentiated and evolutionary monism. Even matter appears to be
a sort of by-product and negative limit which accompanies the descent of
soul[26]. St. Augustine expressed in terse terms the difference between this
monism and the Christian doctrine of creation: "All other good things are

---

[22] *Plato's Cosmology*, London 1937, 36.

[23] Cf. A.-J. Festugière, *La révélation d'Hermès Trismégiste, II: Le dieu cosmique*, Paris 1949,
147f.

[24] *Metaph.* 1072 b 13. Cf. *De caelo* 279 a 28-30. In a recent essay Ch. H. Kahn suggests to
attribute a broader causality to God than is commonly done ("The Place of the Prime Mover in
Aristotle's Teleology", in A. Gotthelf (ed.), *Aristotle on Nature and Living Things*, Pittsburgh
PA-Bristol 1985, 183-205).

[25] See K. Kremer, *Die neuplatonische Seinsphilosophie und ihre Wirkung auf Thomas von
Aquin*, Leiden 1966, The author attempts to show that emanation is basically the same as the
Christian concept of creation. For a refutation see W. Beierwaltes, *Proklos. Grundzüge seiner
Metaphysik*, Frankfurt a.M. 1965, 137; 143; L. Elders, in *Revue thomiste* 67 (1967) 610-617.

[26] See J.M. Rist, *Plotinus. The Road to Reality*, Cambridge 1967, 118ff. Neoplatonism shows
the tendency to leave behind the (mitigated) dualism of Plato and to move to an integral monism.
With Proclus this monism becomes a fact. In the West Boethius is tempted by this monism.

only by him (*ab illo*), but they are not of his being (*de illo*)''²⁷. In Neoplatonism emanation is an impersonal process taking place within the One and somewhat similar to the generation of numbers²⁸. The Christian doctrine of creation by a free decision of God is entirely different. Neoplatonist philosophers saw in Judaeo-Christian creationism an anthropomorphic model and they attributed a greater interiority to their own theory of emanation²⁹. In reality, however, Christian creationism considers God a loving person who makes the world and man out of love.

Plotinus' thought exercised a powerful influence on the Christian West. For example, John Scot Eriugena is in many ways close to Neoplatonism: creation is a necessary process and God does not exist before creation³⁰. In thinking the intelligibles God places them before him³¹. Thus creation is the unfolding of divine unity. The apparition of the sensible world is due to sin: without sin there would not be material things³².

According to classical Mohammedanism God created the world by an act of free will at the beginning of time. Against this backdrop of orthodoxy several divergent interpretations were developed³³. The Mu'tazalites admitted God's transcendence but insisted at the same time on man's free will and responsibility. Opposing them the Ash'arites denied man's free choice in order to secure God's sovereignty. They subscribed to a rather primitive atomism: God creates the atoms from instant to instant; adding new atoms he annihilates others. A third current of thought, the Falāsifa, combined Greek, that is mainly Neoplatonic, philosophy and the coran: God is transcendent; soul and the world are eternal; the sublunar region is marked by corruptibility. From the Supreme Principle, the One, proceeds only what is one, so that intermediaries are required to produce the variety of beings. The explanation of creation lies in the principle that the good is self-diffusive.

Avicenna's theory of creation is complex, subtle and impressive: whatever comes into existence after absolute non-existence, has been created. Even matter has been created. God continues to create, for without his causal influence

---

²⁷ *De natura boni* I.

²⁸ A.-J. Festugière, *La révélation d'Hermès trismégiste, IV: Le dieu inconnu et la gnose*, Paris 1951, 18-53 argues that the Neoplatonic concept of emanation was derived from mathematical speculations.

²⁹ As Proclus writes, emanation is production in unity and precedes being; the One radiates unity (*In Parmenidem* I 641). On the view of Philoponus and Christian Neoplatonists one may compare G. Verbeke, "Some Later Neoplatonic Views on Divine Creation and the Eternity of the World", in D.J. O'Meara (edit.), *Neoplatonism and Christian Thought*, Albany 1982, 45-53.

³⁰ *De div. nat.* III 8: *PL* 122, 639; I 72.

³¹ *O.c.*, II 20. Cf. Proclus, *Elem. theol.*, prop. 174.

³² Cf. T. Gregory, "Dall'Uno al Molteplice", in *Giornale Critico della filosofia italiana* 37 (1958) 319-332.

³³ Cf. Georges C. Anawati, "La notion de création dans l'Islam", in *Studia Missionalia* 18 (1969) 271-295.

all beings would return to non-existence. One must, however, distinguish between the essence and the existence of things. Essences as such are not produced by God but "exist" as possibles[34]. God's causal influence passes through intermediaries. The Necessary First Being causes by emanation a first intellect. In its contemplation of God this intellect produces a second and in this way the stream of being spreads out up to the sphere of the moon[35]. Here resides the last intellect in this chain, the *Dator formarum*. This process of emanation is necessary and eternal.

It would seem that Averroes at first admitted Avicenna's theory of emanation and identified the first intellect with the mover of the outermost sphere of the universe. He also held that creation is from all eternity, but contrary to Avicenna, he asserted that it requires a substrate which is not created, viz. primary matter. Influenced by Al-Ghazālī's criticism Averroes seems later to have abandoned this scheme and identified God with the first intellect, ascribing to God only final and exemplary causality. He did maintain, however, a chain of causal connections between the separate intelligences and the celestial spheres[36].

Averroes's theory of creation plainly contradicts Christian dogma but it nevertheless influenced several Parisian masters as appears from the condemnation in 1277[37]. The School of Chartres uses a Platonic terminology to express the Christian doctrine of creation: the Demiurge made the world and matter; God's goodness is the final cause of creation. However creation is not a necessary emanation but depends on God's free decision[38]. Such medieval doctors as St. Albert could stay clear only with difficulty from certain aspects of the Neoplatonic theory of emanation. In particular the principle that from the One only what is one proceeds caused some problems[39].

In the great mediaeval *Summae*, in particular in St. Thomas' works, the treatise of creation is the crowning piece of metaphysics. Instead of monism or dualism an entirely new doctrine of God and creation is developed. A loving decision by a spiritual being to make the world replaces the natural process

---

[34] L. Gardet, *La pensée religieuse d'Avicenne*, Paris 1951, 38-68.
[35] Differentiation is caused according as the intellect considers its cause, its own essence or its existence.
[36] See B. Sherman Kogan, "Averroes and the Theory of Emanation", in *Mediaeval Studies* 43 (1981) 384-404.
[37] See in particular the articles 27-32 (Hissette, *o.c.*, 64ff.). Cf. M.-M. Gorce, "La lutte *Contre Gentiles* à Paris", in *Mélanges Mandonnet* II, Paris 1930, 234-243.
[38] J.M. Parent, *La doctrine de la création dans l'Ecole de Chartres*, Ottawa 1938, 44-64. See also N.M. Häring, "The Creation and Creator of the World according to Thierry of Chartres", *AHLDMA* 30 (1955) 137-216.
[39] See M. Grabmann, "Die Lehre des hl.Albertus vom Grunde der Vielheit der Dinge und der lateinische Averroismus", in *Mittelalterliches Geistesleben II*, München 1936, 287-312.

of emanation[40]. The study of creation also leads us to a new understanding of created beings[41].

In Descartes' works creation is considered in a novel way. Descartes admits the creation of his own self by God, but God's task ends when man has reached intellectual certitude. Once process in the universe has started, it continues according to immanent laws. God is almost foreign to the world[42].

Spinoza transposes God as a Free Person into nature and rejects the Christian idea of creation. In order to explain the transition from God's infinity to finite creatures Spinoza uses the concept of *modi*, through which God's nature is expressed. These *modi* affect God as finite modifications of his being[43]. The world and man are immanent in God and result from him with the same necessity by which the three angles of a triangle are equal to two right angles[44]. Things do not depend on God's will but come forth from God with the necesity of a logical deduction.

According to Kant the beginning of the world is a truth to be believed in. At the end of the 18th century, however, several authors rejected creation. Matter was held to be eternal and if God is really the supreme Being, perfect in every possible way then, it was argued, there is no conceivable reason why he should ever have created anything at all[45]. Neglect or rejection of creation was facilitated by the rise of deism which severed the metaphysical ties between God and the world. Fichte constructed his philosophy on the Self which at the beginning posits its own being. Man can escape from solipsism because consciousness has as its correlative the Non-Self. In Fichte's later philosophy this Non-Self is declared to be God, so that the atheistic character of his thought became less conspicuous. Fichte's philosophy is an expression of Western voluntarism, in which man is hardly aware of his limits and autonomy is prefered to communion with others. According to Fichte God is reality understood in a spiritual way. Hence nothing comes from God; in him there is nothing else but an eternal "is"; what is to come into being must be originally in him and must be himself[46]. Creation, if one conceives it as different from an immanent process, is "the absolute and fundamental error of all wrong metaphysics and doctrine of religion"[47].

Hegel enlarges Fichte's Self into the Absolute Spirit. Creation is an immanent process in this Spirit. It is not a unique act resulting from a decision, but

---

[40] Cf. J. Chevalier, *Histoire de la pensée, II: La pensée chrétienne*, Paris 1976, 8f.

[41] F. De Viana, "Noción y causa de la creación filosóficamente", in *Angelicum* 37 (1960) 411-430.

[42] Cf. A. Ganoczy, *Der schöpferische Mensch und die Schöpfung Gottes*, Mainz 1976.

[43] *Ethica* I, prop. 28

[44] *O.c.*, II 62.

[45] A. O. Lovejoy, *The Great Chain of Being*, New York 1960, 73-85.

[46] *J.G. Fichte, Werke. Auswahl in sechs Bänden*, hrsg. von F. Medicus, Leipzig *s.a.*, V 192.

[47] *O.c.*, 191.

it belongs to the Spirit's very essence. Creation is the alienation of the Absolute Spirit, that is, a dialectical process[48]: in order to be itself the Spirit must render itself finite and make its appearance in time. Creation is part of the process of divine self-realisation. Hegel distinguishes between a first stage (the Spirit itself), a second stage, at which the Spirit makes itself objective in history and society. Finally, the Spirit becomes again the Absolute in art, religion and philosophy. God is process and without the world and man God is not God.

Karl Marx belonged to the Hegelian Left. He declares that man is not autonomous when he lives by the grace of another to whom he would owe his existence. He admitted that it is very difficult to extirpate the idea of creation from the mind of man, for man does not yet have the experience of full self-sufficiency. When this is attained, the idea of creation will fade. In fact, man strives to attain aseity[49]. Marx even conceives the formation of the earth (*Erd-bildung*) as an auto-production. It is somewhat astonishing to see how flippantly he identifies cosmic evolution with ontological self-sufficiency[50].

About the middle of the century positivism was on the rise and several scientists felt that divine intervention in nature is incompatible with the requirements of science. Natural science cannot but seek homogeneous explanations and must avoid recourse to immaterial causes. The existence of God is wholly unnecessary to explain the phenomena observed in the universe. Religious belief in creation hampers the development of science. Thus God was removed from nature and the scientists neutralised his existence almost as effectively as did the atheists[51].

In process philosophy God is conceived in an entirely novel way. He is the unlimited realisation of the absolute wealth of potentiality and does not exist before but together with creation. God is the principle by which a definite outcome is initiated. God's so-called derivative nature is even consequent upon the creative advance of the world. Apparently Whitehead professes a sort of evolutionistic monism[52].

One of the rare twentieth century philosophers to discuss creation is J.-P. Sartre. He rejects the very possibility of conceiving a Creator of the world.

---

[48] *Vorlesungen über die Philosophie der Religion,* II, c.I (Suhrkamp 54ff,); III. Die absolute Religion, B (Suhrkamp 205ff.); C II 1 (Suhrkamp 243ff.).
[49] Cf. *Marx-Engels, Kleine ökonomische Schriften (Bücherei des Marxismus-Leninismus,* B.42), Berlin 1955, 138f.; G. Cottier, *L'athéisme du jeune Marx. Ses origines hégéliennes,* Paris 1959, 145ff.; 342f.
[50] Cf. Cl. Tresmontant, *Les idées maîtresses de la métaphysique chrétienne,* Paris 1962, 131.
[51] Cf. Neal C. Gillespie, *Charles Darwin and the Problem of Creation,* Chicago, 1979, Epilogue; Charles C. Gillispie, *Genesis and Geology,* Cambridge MA 1969.
[52] *Process and Reality,* New York 1929, 520-523; H.J. Nelson, "The Resting Place of Process Theology", in *Harvard Theol. Review* 72 (1979) 1-21 argues that certain philosophical preconceptions are at the origin of this theory.

For if God existed, his being would be intrasubjective and exclude the will to create objective being. If there is no God, the world just emerges and is itself active[53].—A view to be mentioned in this connection is that of P. Teilhard de Chardin. This author is of the opinion that the concept of creation as an absolute beginning is not admissible[54]. Creation must be the evolution of what is already present. Rather, it is the perfection and fulfilment of God himself. Classical metaphysics with its distinction between the *ens a se* and *ens ab alio* makes the world contingent so that it loses its inner force and drive. Teilhard is apparently groping his way to a Hegelian synthesis of God and the world which takes place not in the Absolute Spirit but in matter[55].

After this excursion into the history of the concept of creation we must now examine St. Thomas' position with regard to the procession of things from God. The *First Article* deals with the question whether it is necessary that every being is created by God, in other words whether all things are dependent on God as their cause. Three objections are raised against the affirmative answer: (a) dependence on God does not seem to belong to the essence of things; hence things can exist without such dependence; (b) necessary beings cannot not be and thus they do not require an efficient cause; (c) mathematical entities do not have an efficient cause. Hence not all beings have God as their cause.

St. Thomas' argument in defence of creation is surprising at first sight: God is self-subsistent being itself[56] and this can only be one. The reader is referred to questions 3 and 11: God must be his own *esse*, because else it would have been caused by an agent outside God and there would be a composition in God. Since he is the First Efficient Cause and the Principle from which all process and activity begins, God can in no way depend on another cause. Hence he is his own being and this is exclusively proper to him. Now self-subsistent being, that is being which is itself and exists by itself, is only one. For multiplication requires a cause. Being (*esse*) as such signifies plenitude of

[53] *L'être et le néant*, 31f.

[54] Several physicists are of the opinion that an absolute beginning is meaningless. Although certain facts of the physical universe (such as entropy) suggest that the universe in its present state cannot have existed for ever, yet the limited approach of modern physical science does not require one to consider the question of the origin of the world. Ironically some historians suggest that the reason why natural science developed so much in the West, is that the doctrine of creation provided favourable conditions for its rise: the world is no longer considered divine, but has a history; it is man's task to acquire understanding and to introduce more order into the world. See S. Jaki, *The Road of Science and the Ways to God*, Chicago 1978, 153. See also F. Kraft, "Wissensschaft und 'Weltbild II", in N. Luyten (hrsg.), *Naturwissenschaft und Theologie*, Düsseldorf 1981, 79-117, 86f.

[55] Cf. N. Luyten, "Schöpfung und Evolution", in *Freib. Zeitschr. f. Philos. u. Theol.* 27 (1980) 437-456.—Some physicists resorted to the hypothesis of continuous creation to ensure that the structure of the universe remains the same under expansion (Bondi, Gold and Hoyle). However, the theory of a "steady state universe" has found very little support.

[56] See Chapter Four, *S.Th.* I 3, 4.

actuality, concentration of reality and perfection in unity. Plurality and multiplication can only come about by means of a subject which participates in being, in other words, by a potency[57]. This is precisely what St. Thomas means by the example of whiteness: "if whiteness were self-subsisting, it would be one, since whiteness is multiplied by its recipients"[58].

At the end of his demonstration Aquinas invokes the support of Plato and Aristotle. "Plato said that unity must come before multitude".—These words are a reference to the theory of ideas which holds that if there are several things possessing a perfection, they participate in the exemplar which is this perfection principally[59]. The quotation given from Aristotle's *Metaphysics* II 1 has been discussed in the Third Chapter, under the Fourth Way.

The argument can be completed by a reference to God's infinity and unity: self-subsistent being is infinite and thus it comprehends in itself the whole perfection of being. If God is infinite, he possesses in himself whatever perfection a second infinite being has, so that there would be absolutely nothing by which they differ[60]. "Therefore all beings other than God are not their own being (*esse*), but are beings by participation". With this inference St. Thomas has shown that all beings other than God receive their being from the First Cause[61]. The conclusion implies that things which receive their being, never become it, that is, they never have it of themselves. In other words, being is continuously given to them by God.

Participating in being is a lasting communion with the First Cause. In this way the philosophical argument brought forward by St. Thomas arrives at the truth of the faith, expressed in the *Sed contra*: "Of him, by him and in him are all things" (*Rom.* 11, 36). Although the being (*esse*) of things is continuously communicated to them by God, St. Thomas considers this created *esse* as something stable and perfect: it is the very act, that is the reality of created things[62].

In the reply to the first objection Aquinas sets forth that the relation to its cause is not part of the definition of a thing caused, but follows "as a result of what belongs to its nature. For from the fact that a thing is being by participation, it follows that it is caused. But, since to be caused does not enter

---

[57] See volume I, chapter XI, the third argument.

[58] The example of whiteness is quoted also in I 7, 1 ad 3.

[59] St. Thomas probably refers to *Metaph.* A 9, where Aristotle discusses the argument of "the one over the many". See Alexander, *In Metaph.* 83, 34-84, 2.

[60] I 11, 3.

[61] Cf. *De pot.*, 7, 4: "In qualibet autem creatura invenitur differentia habentis et habiti ... in Deo autem nulla"; *Quodl.* II, art. 3: "nulla creatura est suum esse, sed est habens esse".

[62] St. Thomas' doctrine is quite different from Eckhart's position. The latter did not attribute to the *esse* any inherence in created things, but stresses only how it flows from outside towards creatures (*In Gen.* II, n.3: *Latein. Werke* I, Stuttgart 1936, 493. See also J. Koch, *Altdeutsche und altniederländische Mystik, Wege der Forschung*, Bd. XXIII, Darmstadt 1964, 275-308).

into the nature of being (*ens*) taken absolutely, that is why there exists a being that is uncaused".—Heidegger's assertion that in the mediaeval doctrine of being to be created is a structural element[63] is clearly not quite correct.

Turning now to the second objection St. Thomas first recalls that according to Democritus that which is eternal and necessary does not need a cause[64]. However against this we maintain that some necessary things do have a cause of their necessity. Hence the effect would not be, if the cause were not.—That the efficient cause has no place in mathematics is because this discipline considers its objects in abstraction. Metaphysics, on the other hand, deals with real beings and considers their efficient cause: all things, except God, *have* their being and thus they have an efficient cause.

After having established in the First Article that all existing things receive their being from God who is their efficient cause, St. Thomas now investigates the extent and modality of God's causality with regard to the world. To this effect he follows the scheme of the four causes. This provides him with the opportunity to refute successively a number of positions, contrary to the faith, upheld by renowned philosophers. Aquinas is perhaps following a suggestion made by St. Albert the Great who observed that God's causality with regard to the world is threefold[65]. St. Albert attributes the theory of uncreated matter to Plato: the First Principle would create the forms according to the disposition of matter (*dator formarum* theory). St. Albert himself prefers "to follow Aristotle whose view is more Catholic" because he admits an efficient production of forms according to the exemplary model, although we must also hold, he adds, that the First Cause produces the whole being, that is both form and matter[66].

In the Second Article St. Thomas discusses the issue of the creation of primary matter. The three objections suggest that primary matter is not created by God because (a) it has no subject or substrate, (b) being passive, matter must be divided against God, and (c) matter is only potentiality and therefore unlike God, who like every other agent, only works that which is his like.

In his solution St. Thomas first recalls the main theories of matter which were upheld by the earliest philosophers, who thought that only material things exist and that all changes are at the level of accidental being, so that corporeal substance itself is uncreated. "An advance was made when they understood that there was a distinction between the substantial form and matter, which latter they held to be uncreated, and when they perceived

---

[63] *Sein und Zeit*, 24.
[64] Aristotle, *Phys.* 252 a 35ff.
[65] *In Dionysii De div. nom.*, c.2 (edit. Simon 73, 42). St. Albert aligns Aristotle (*Metaph.* XII 4, 1070 b 30-35?) and Averroes (*in hoc loco*, Venetiis 1562, r.309) as in favour of his explanation.
[66] *L.c.*, 73, 28-74, 10.

transmutation to take place in bodies in regard to essential forms. These transmutations they attributed to certain more universal causes, such as the oblique circle, according to Aristotle, or the ideas according to Plato''[67]. The ''advance'' consists in the better understanding of change which is now seen to take place also at the level of substances, viz. as concerning the substantial form; Plato attributed it to the causality of the ideas which are participated in[68]. Aristotle explains coming-into-being in the physical universe by means of changes in the accidental dispositions (such as hot-cold, humid-dry) brought about by the movement of the sun in the inclined circle (the ecliptic) which prepares the condition for substantial mutation: ''it generates by approaching and being near; this same thing destroys by retreating and coming to be further away''[69].

St. Thomas criticizes both explanations, for they account only for a particular aspect of being, viz. as *this* being or as *such* a being. He clearly means that they left the presence of matter and therefore of the whole being as being unexplained. Aquinas grants Plato's view the benefit of explaining (by participation) the presence of certain qualities and that of Aristotles that of accounting for the occurrence of generation in the world and thus of the presence of substances (*this* being) belonging to the various species of material things.

For all its concision this is a masterly qualification of Plato's and Aristotle's respective positions[70]. The wording of the text, however, causes a problem. In the following lines (''others, advancing further, raised themselves to the consideration of being as being and assigned a cause to things, not only according as they are *these* or *such* but according as they are *beings*'') St.

---

[67] I 44, 2 (transl. of the English Dominicans).

[68] In his *Phaedo* 96 a ff. Plato rejects the explanations the physicists gave of coming-into-being and proposes his own theory of formal causality and participation. For his description of Plato's view St. Thomas probably relies on the numerous passages in the *Metaphysics* where Aristotle shows the inadequacy of Plato's explanation of generation (*Metaph.* 1045 a 14-22; *Metaph.* A 7 and A 9). Aristotle points out that the hypothesis of the forms does not explain changes in things nor their unity and even less why generation is intermittent.

[69] The locus classicus of this doctrine is Aristotle's *De gen. et corr.*, ch. 10, 336 a 14ff. The translation is that of Williams. See his *Aristotle's De generatione et corruptione*, translation with notes by C.J.F. Williams, Oxford 1982, 186-195.

[70] A presentation of the history of philosophy in stages is not unsusual. Aristotle does this in *Metaph.* A. Philoponus presents one in his *Vestigium* I 19ff. (Heiland). St. Bonaventure also offers such a survey in *In II Sent.*, d.1, p.1, a.1, q.1. His judgement on Aristotle's theory of the origin of the world is mild (''... veritati magis appropinquantes''), although, he says, A. did not quite reach the insight that matter and form have been created. St. Thomas makes such a survey also in other texts, e.g., in *De substantiis separatis.*—It is now generally admitted that Aristotle did not know of the creation of the world. See J. Chevalier, *Trois conférences, I: Aristote, saint Thomas et l'idée de création*, Paris 1928, 20; R. Jolivet, *Essai sur les rapports entre la pensée grecque et la pensée chrétienne. Aristote et saint Thomas ou l'idée de création. Plotin et saint Augustin ou l'idée du mal*, Paris 1931, 72-82.

Thomas intimates that Plato and Aristotle did *not* understand the dependence of the being of things on God, that is, they did not know about creation. As we have seen, this agrees with a sober evaluation of the evidence. But before we examine this question, the conclusion reached by St. Thomas must be dealt with.

The consideration of the being of things shows that it cannot but be a participation in God's being and thus be caused. Now being (*esse*) is the first act; if it is created, then so is matter for it is a component of the existing whole. This conclusion is an application of the insight gained in the First Article of Question 44.—The objections are easily answered: matter is the first passive principle and as such it must be the effect of the first active principle. However, matter never exists by itself, but it is always together with form.

The description of Plato's and Aristotle's views of the cause of being differs, it would seem, from the evaluation Aquinas gives in other texts. In the *Commentary on the Physics*[71] he writes that Plato and Aristotle arrived at the knowledge of the principle of all being (*principium totius esse*). In the *De potentia*[72] the following summary is given: the first philosophers only knew accidental changes; others added some external agents such as Love and Hatred. Later philosophers, namely Plato, Aristotle and their followers, arrived at the consideration of universal being (*esse*) itself and thus they alone posited the existence of some universal cause of things from which all other things came forth into being as appears from what Augustine says in the *De civitate Dei* II 4[73].

The differences between this text and that of *S.Th.* I 44, 2 are obvious. However, we need not see any contradiction between them. For I 44, 2 does not say that Plato and Aristotle did not acknowledge the existence of God, but that they did not see that all beings as beings depend on God. The *De potentia* seems to say the opposite, but upon closer inspection the text can be understood in such a way that *only the followers* (*sequaces*) actually reached the insight of the dependence of all things. Apparently these followers are the same as "the others"[74] of the subsequent lines of I 44, 2 who "advanced further and raised themselves to the consideration of being as being and who assigned a cause to things not only according as they are *these* or *such*, but

[71] *In VIII Phys.*, 1.2, n.975.

[72] *De potentia* 3, 5.

[73] In this remarkable chapter St. Augustine praises Plato who brought the philosophy of the Pythagoreans and Socrates to perfection, dividing it into three branches (moral, natural and rational philosophy). St. Augustine notes that it is difficult to interpret Plato, but those who are praised for having followed Plato, who penetrated deeper into the truth than other philosophers, reached a view about God which considers him the cause of being, the ground of understanding and the order of living (correctly). St. Augustine does not ascribe the doctrine of creation to Plato himself.

[74] The "others" are apparently Christian authors and some Arab philosophers.

according as they are beings''. In St. Thomas' eyes these followers reached
this insight using the principles of Plato and Aristotle. For this reason one can
also say that the doctrine of creation is prepared for or intimated in the
writings of the two great philosophers. When St. Thomas understands them
according to the principles they themselves enounced, he almost attributes the
doctrine of creation to Aristotle. One of these texts referred to is *De caelo* 279
a 28ff. where Aristotle says that the being and life in the lower regions of the
universe depend on eternal principles. The precise meaning of the text is not
certain: formal, final and some efficient causality seem to be meant. St.
Thomas' interpretation stays close to the text[75]. The reason why the *De potentia* is more positive than I 44, 2 has no easy answer. It would not do to say
that at this stage of St. Thomas' development he was not certain whether
Aristotle or Plato taught the doctrine of creation of the world from nothing[76]:
chronologically both works are very close and not much reading of Aristotle
is needed to see that he attributes only a limited causality to the First Mover.
A possible explanation is that in question 3 of the *De potentia* St. Thomas is
dealing with the divergent philosophical views of such philosophers as
Avicebron and Maimonides and that he did not want to jeopardize the use of
Plato and Aristotle by his students. The reference to the *De civitate Dei* could
well have a tactical purpose, viz. to protect Aristotle against the criticism or
outright rejection by associating him with the praise St. Augustine is lavishing
on Platonism.

In the Third Article St. Thomas shows that God is also the *exemplary* cause
of created things, God's causality communicating being (*esse*) must be determined in order that the effect may receive a determinate form. A comparison
is made with an artificer who produces a determinate form in matter by reason
of the exemplar before him, whether it be the exemplar beheld externally or
the one interiorly conceived in the mind. Now God's effects do have determinate forms which must therefore result from God's wisdom. Indeed, as was
shown above[77], in God are the ideas of all things which "are not really distinct
from the divine essence, inasmuch as the likeness of that essence can be shared
diversely by different things. In this manner, therefore, God himself is the
first exemplar of all things"[78]. It is understood that God's efficient action is
his own essence and his exemplarity.

Is God also the *final* cause of all things, as Plato and Aristotle affirm? A
difficulty lies in the fact that the agent who acts for an end strives to reach
this end in order to attain a certain fulfilment. However, God cannot desire

---

[75] *In I De caelo*, l.21, n.216: "Unde cum ista entia habeant vitam optimam et per se sufficien-
tissimam et esse sempiternum, consequens est quod inde communicetur aliis esse et vivere".
[76] James A. Weisheipl, *Friar Thomas D'Aquino*[2], Washington D.C., 1983, 203.
[77] I 15, 1.
[78] I 44, 3.

to acquire anything at all and therefore cannot work for an end. In this connection one may mention that Kant, Hegel and others do not admit that God
creates for himself. In his solution Aquinas recalls the principle that every
agent acts for an end, otherwise one thing would not follow more than
another from the action of the agent. Hence God cannot but work for an end.
Now certain agents are at the same time patients: in their actions they intend
to aquire something. But this is not the case with God, whose end can only
be to communicate his own goodness. If God acts as a final cause, it follows
that all created things strive for God and that the divine goodness is the end
of all things. All beings desire God [79].

Aquinas explains this further in his reply to the third objection: "All things
desire God as their end in desiring any particular good, whether this desire be
intellectual or sensible or natural (i.e., without knowledge); for nothing is
good and desirable except inasmuch as it participates in the likeness to
God" [80].—The fourth objection argues that God cannot be at the same time
the efficient and the final cause of things, because as a final cause he must
be prior to himself as the efficient cause. St. Thomas replies that God is the
efficient, the exemplary and final cause of all things in the transcendent unity
of his being. "From the standpoint of our reason there are many things in
God, of which we come to know some before others".—Against this conclusion H. E. Hengstenberg argued that creation is the opposite of causation and
therefore cannot be denoted by that term [81].—However, although it is obvious
that God is a cause in a different and unique way, the definition of "cause"
applies to him in the strict sense of the term, for God is a positive principle
from which something comes forth in such a way that its being depends on
him.

II. *The Mode of Emanation of Things from the First Principle (I 45)*

This question clarifies the nature and manner of divine causality with regard
to created things. It comprises eight articles, of which the main points will be
discussed in this section. In this question St. Thomas defines the word "creation" as the emanation of the whole being [82] from the universal cause which
is God. This definition of the term is approximative and is rendered more
precise in the subsequent explanation. Besides denoting God's action produc-
tive of the world "creation" is also used in a passive sense to signify the effect
of creation, viz. the world as made by God.

---

[79] I 44, 4.

[80] The fundamentral inclination of all things to attain God, is treated in *S.C.G.* III 17-21.

[81] *Das Band zwischen Gott und Schöpfung*, Regensburg 1948, 129; *id., Sein und Ursprünglichkeit*, München 1959, 106.

[82] The expression "totius entis" means both "the whole being" and "the whole reality". In the following lines Aquinas stresses the second sense.

The first article argues that creation is "to produce from nothing". This doctrine is that of the Christian faith and it is found in some texts of Holy Scripture either implicitly (cf. *Prov.* 8, 22-32; *Ecclesiasticus* 42, 15) or explicitly (2 *Macch.* 7, 28: "God made them out of what did not exist". Cf. also *Acts* 14, 14; 17, 18 etc.). In their debate with pagan authors and the gnostics Christian theologians strongly affirmed that God created the world from nothing[83]. Faith in God's omnipotence and awareness of the total dependence of everything on God imposed this conclusion[84]. But St. Thomas is convinced that creation from nothing can be demonstrated by reason[85].

If we consider that the totality of being (*totum ens universale*) proceeds from God, there cannot be any preexistent substrate or material God used in creating things. Before the world came into being there simply was nothing (*nullum ens*). In his reply to the third objection Aquinas explains that ex (from) in *ex nihilo* does not signify the material from which God makes the world, but order: before God creates there is nothing; there is no subject or substrate on which he works[86]. This conclusion confronts us with an entirely novel idea which is at variance with our experience of the becoming or making of things.

In the Second Article some difficulties are raised against the very possibility of the concept of creation. Creation seems to contradict the principle "nothing comes into being from nothing". Furthermore, creation is a kind of becoming, but all becoming takes place in a subject. In creation, however, the presence of such a subject is denied. Furthermore, becoming precedes "having been made" and takes place in a subject.—Finally, it is not clear how created things can traverse the infinite distance from not-being to being.—These difficulties show that creation is utterly different from the coming-into-being in the physical world. The concept of creation apparently belongs to negative theology.

Aquinas argues that not only is creation possible, but that one must say that everything which exists has been created by God. The reason is that things cannot exist but by participating in God's being (*esse*). This means that they have been created. A substrate which is independent of God, is not possible. In his reply to the objections Aquinas first points out that the principle that

---

[83] Origines, *De princ.* II 1, 5.

[84] It would seem that G. May, *Schöpfung aus dem Nichts. Die Entstehung der Lehre von der creatio ex nihilo*, Berlin 1978, does not consider the implicit presence of the doctrine of creation in the early teaching of the church. He refers to the philosophical debate with started with Basilides.

[85] This is not only the gist of questions 44 and 45. Aquinas says so explicitly in *In II Sent.*, d.1, q.1, a.2: "creationem esse, non tantum fides tenet, sed etiam ratio demonstrat".

[86] The expression *ex nihilo* can be understood as indicating an order of succession ("before" there was nothing) or as the negation of a subject out of which being is made. In *De pot.* 3, 1 ad 7 this distinction is attributed to St. Anselm, *Monologion*, chapters 5 and 8.

all becoming requires a subject applies to particular causes but not to the emanation of beings from the universal cause. This means that the principle is not a so-called *first* principle which holds true for all beings.—That "creation" is a novel and transcendent form of causality is further explained in the reply to the second objection: because creation is the production of the entire reality of a thing it does not involve any change, although in our way of expressing it we use the terminology of change ("from nothing")[86a].— Likewise, contrary to what the third objection suggested, in the becoming without any change which creation is, becoming and having become are the same.—Finally there is no infinite intermediary distance between nothing and being[87]. Imagination easily betrays us when we try to speak about the creation of beings by God[88]. A.-D. Sertillanges summarised the Second Article as follows: creation is not a change; it is not a transition nor a becoming or an arrival at being. There is no anteriority to it and no transient action passing from God to his effects[89]. In short, the very concept of creation is a challenge to our way of conceiving causality and becoming.

The concept of creation is further determined in the Third Article. In as much as creation is God's action, it does not signify an emanation from God's substance, but God's free decision to make creatures be. For this reason it is not surprising that several of St. Thomas' contemporaries considered creation in its passive sense a mutation from not-being, that is a *mutatio ad esse*[90]. However, St. Thomas holds that we must not call creation a mutation. He adds that formally speaking 'being created' is not the very being of created

---

[86a] Although creation itself not does not imply any change in God's being or in created things, one must nevertheless say with Cajetanus that "before creation God was one and there was nowhere not God. But after the other beings had been created the division between God and not-God is present in the world" (*In I^am*, 11, 2).

[87] Aquinas does say that there is an infinite distance between God and man (I-II 114, 1). He means the total otherness and diversity of finite creatures from God's infinite perfection. But between "being" and "nothing" there is no comparison and no distance to be traversed, because "nothing" is not an opposite pole. See I 45, 5 ad 3: "there is no proportion between being and not-being". In order to produce something from no presupposed substrate an infinite power is required.— This way of stating the issue seems more formal than that of the *De potentia* 3, 4: "non esse autem simpliciter in infinitum ab esse distat".

[88] On imagination as a source of error see *S.C.G.* I 4.—In *In VIII Phys.*, 1,2, n.973ff. St. Thomas argues against Averroes. The later concluded from the maxim that all changes require a subject that creation from nothing is impossible. Aquinas observes that Averroes failed to notice the difference between the operation of the First, Universal Agent and that of particular agents. The latter presuppose matter, God does not.

[89] "La création", in *Revue thomiste* 33 (1928) 97-115.

[90] Alexander of Hales, *Summa* II q.9, m.1. St. Bonaventure, *In II Sent.*, d.1, p.1, a.3, q.1. On the distinction between the active and passive sense of creation in modern literature see L. Dümpelmann, *Kreation als ontisch-ontologisches Verhältnis. Symposion. Philosophische Schriftenreihe*, Freiburg-München 1969. The author identifies God's act of creation with the act of the created *esse* (105).

things, but a relation of dependence. Scotus and others identify this relation with its foundation, that is with created being itself.

It is obvious that created being is participated being and essentially dependent on God. But the question is not whether God's creative action produces an effect,—this is obvious—, but whether this coming-into-being of things takes place by means of a special receiving (*passio*) which is the correlative of all created transient causality. This must be excluded, because there is nothing which receives: the created being is created in its entirety. It does however, have a relation of dependence resulting from its being caused, as every effect has a real relation to its cause. This relation, like other accidents, is inherent in the created substance[91].

If one understands this subtle doctrine of Aquinas correctly, the reproach by L. Scheffczyk that the theology of the Middle Ages deprived the term creation of its rich contents is without object. Moreover, the doctrine that the being of created things ontologically precedes its predicamental relation of dependence[92] finds an interesting application in the field of ethics: while the Franciscan School holds that our actions are virtuous because they are prescribed[93], St. Thomas teaches that they fall under law because they are virtuous.

That God does not have a relation of causality to the world does not mean that he is unconcerned with his creation, as Aristotle's First Mover is, or devoid of knowledge and love for his creatures as Plotinus holds. On the contrary, it means that what in creatures is a predicamental relation of causality, in God is actually God's being itself[94].

Creation is the production of beings from nothing. In the Fourth Article Aquinas explains that properly speaking those things are created to which being primarily belongs, that is substances. Forms and accidents do not exist by themselves and thus they are concreated rather than created.

A major problem is dealt with in the Fifth Article: does it belong to God alone to create? In Gnosticism creation of the material world is attributed to

---

[91] Inasmuch as this relation refers the entire being of creatures to God as their cause, it differs from other relations of causal dependence. Nevertheless I do not see why we should make it something so very mysterious as James F. Anderson does, "Creation as a Relation", in *The New Scholasticism* 24 (1950) 263-283. See also J. Thyrion, "La notion de création passive dans le thomisme", in *Revue thomiste* 34 (1929) 303-319 who correctly points out that in some of his earlier works Sertillanges is not quite clear with regard to this point. He quotes *S.C.G.* II 18; *De pot.* 7, 9 and Ferrariensis, *In S.C.G.* II 18 ("creatio est accidens realiter distinctum a creatura quae refertur"). Sertillanges later revised his interpretation ("La notion de création", in *Revue thom*, 35 (1930) 48-57).

[92] In another respect the relation may be called prior, inasmuch as it recalls God's causality which is the origin of creatures (I 45, 3 ad 3).

[93] See Alexander of Hales, *Summa* III, 2, inq.3, tr.2, sect.1, q.1, tit.1, c.4, a.1: Quar. IV 418ff.

[94] G. Siewerth, *Der Thomismus als Identitätssystem*, 1939, 131-133, apparently did not understand this point.

intermediary beings. In Middle and Neoplatonism the First Principle is not in immediate contact with the material universe, but several intermediaries are placed between the One and matter. For instance, Albinus posits a cosmic intellect below the Supreme Intellect which governs nature[95]. Over and against the materialism of the Stoics Neoplatonism stressed the transcendence and remoteness of God from the world. To bridge the gulf between the One and the material universe intermediaries were needed. Jamblichus in particular tended to multiply ontological levels. Proclus' theory of serial intermediates is wellknown. Dionysius also strongly insisted on a metaphysical hierarchy of beings between God and matter. In this "he echoed the ambivalent tendencies of pagan Neoplatonism... He seems equally equivocal on the fundamental point separating Neoplatonic and Christian world views, whether creation is a result of the divine nature or a gratuitous act of grace"[96].

Avicenna conceived the emanation from God as a series of processions from eternal substances above time down to perennial bodies in time and the corruptible things of the sublunar world. The first intellect shares in the clarity of the Supreme Principle, but there is composition in it because it has received its being. According to the manner in which it thinks itself, three different beings flow forth from it: the soul of the ninth celestial sphere, the body of the latter and the second separate intellect. This intellect in its turn produces the soul and body of the eighth sphere as well as the third separate intellect. This process is repeated until the sphere of the moon is reached. Its intellect is the agent intellect from which the human souls, the four elements and all forms proceed[97].

Averroes discarded the complex theory of Avicenna, himself allowing four intermediate causes between God and matter, viz. the first intellect, the agent intellect, soul and form[98]. The Christian theologians rejected these views[99]. However, Peter Lombard held that God can communicate the power to create to a creature so that it becomes an instrument of God[100]. Out of respect for the Master of the *Sentences* St. Thomas initially tried to give an acceptable

---

[95] *Didaskalikos* X 164, 16-165, 4. The Word-Soul of the *Timaeus* was understood as such an intermediary. Philo places the Logos and divine power between God and the cosmos. In popular religion the daemons filled the gap. On the intermediaries in Philo's philosophy see E. Bréhier, *Les idées philosophiques et religieuses de Philon d'Alexandrie*[2], Paris 1925, 112ff.; H.A. Wolfson, *Philo. I*, Cambridge Ma. 1948, 282ff.

[96] R.T. Wallies, *Neoplatonism*, London 1972, 161.

[97] L. Gardet, *La pensée religieuse d'Avicenne*, Paris 1951, 51f. With regard to the influence of this theory in the West see Giles of Rome, *De erroribus philosophorum* (edit. Koch VI 8-9) of approximately 1270 and propositions 56-58 of the Articles condemned in 1277 (Hissette, *o.c.*, 110ff). The text of the condemnation was taken from Siger's commentary on the *De causis*.

[98] *Destructio destr.* III (Zedler, 173ff.).

[99] R. De Vaux, *Notes et textes sur l'avicennisme latin aux confins des XIIe et XIIIe siècles*, Paris 1934, 37ff.

[100] *Sent.* IV 5, 3.

meaning to this opinion but in his later writings he consistently rejects it[101].
The Fifth Article of Question 45 treats the issue with clarity and conciseness.

The text first recalls that to create is the proper action of God alone. Only
God is subsistent being itself, whereas all things other than God are not their
being, but have received it. To exclude the theory which places an
intermediary between God and creatures through which being is communicated to the latter Aquinas adds the following argument: the more
universal effect must be reduced to the more universal and prior cause. Now
among all effects being is most universal; and hence it must be reduced to God
himself. This argument is subtle and is an application of the principle that
every agent produces its like. To understand St. Thomas' reasoning better one
must keep in mind that in being (*esse*) different aspects are to be distinguished,
such as being real, being a substance, being man, being this human individual.
Although the being of a man is not that of a horse, and each man has his own
being, every being (*esse*) nevertheless has in common with all other *esse* that
it is the actuality and perfection of a thing. This common aspect requires a
cause which extends to all the instances of being (*esse*), that is a universal
cause, which encompasses all being.

The argument may be illustrated by human procreation: parents are the
cause that a new human individual comes into being, but they do not produce
human nature as such, for they cannot produce themselves. Hence human
nature must be reduced to a more universal cause.

An opponent might argue that the argument does not yet prove that no
intermediary can be used, even if it has become clear that God must be the
per se efficient cause of the *esse* of created things. St. Thomas excludes that
creatures can be used as instruments in creation: an instrumental cause con-
tributes to the causal action of the main cause by disposing the subject on
which the main cause works. St. Thomas gives the example of the instrumental action of a tool. But in creation there is no subject to be disposed, for this
results from God's causality. Hence there simply is no room for instrumental
causality.

The answer to the first objection shows that this conclusion applies also to
spiritual beings. Created things produce what is like to themselves, but they
cannot do so in an absolute way. If so, they would be making themselves.
They can only bring about that their like exists in a given subject. Spiritual
beings have no matter, so that there is no substrate in which their form can
be produced. "Hence they cannot produce another similar immaterial

---

[101] See A.R. Motte, "Théodicée et théologie chez s. Thomas d'Aquin", in *RScPhTh* 26 (1937)
5-26, 13. In *In IV Sent.*, d.5, q.1, a.3, ql.3 St. Thomas clearly maintains that creative power is
in no way communicable. In *De pot.* 3, 4 five reasons are brought forward to show this, in this
article only one. Cf. *S.C.G.* II 21.

substance as regards its being".—In his reply to the second and third objections St. Thomas argues that in order to create something, that is to make it without a pre-existing potency or subject, infinite power is required.

III. *The Beginning of Creation (I 46)*

According to Kant the question whether the world is eternal or has a beginning in time is the first and basic problem of human reason. Awareness of this problem was enhanced by the confrontation of the dogma of the beginning of the world in time with the impressive Aristotelian demonstration of the eternity of the world. The historical background of Aristotle's theory is Greek religious thought in general. The Greek philosophers assumed that matter is eternal. Aristotle gave a definite, scientific form to the theory of the eternity of the world and its structure: changes in size, movement and number of the stars have never been observed[102]. Moreover, what has a beginning cannot continue to exist for ever; an absolute beginning is unthinkable. Furthermore, there are no contraries in the celestial spheres and hence no corruption and generation. The movement of the spheres is cyclical, but a circle has neither beginning nor end. This cyclical revolution is the expression of their being[103].

At the closing of the 4th century B.C. Aristotle's theory was challenged by the Stoics and the Epicureans: we observe change in our region of the universe; if part of the whole is perishable, the whole must be so too. In the atomism of the Epicureans the structure of the world is not permanent: chance which led to the present organisation of the world. will also destroy it. A century later the conviction that the world is eternal began to gain ground again[104].

For Plotinus the eternity of the world is an essential thesis of philosophy. He felt that the Judaeo-Christian doctrine of creation in the beginning of time imputes a change of mind to God, which Aristotle already rejected and which it is blasphemous to accept[105]. Proclus adduced no less than 18 arguments against the Christian doctrine of the beginning of the world, but did not exclude a certain dependence of the world on God[106].

---

[102] *De caelo* 270 a 2-20.

[103] *O.c.*, i cc.11 and 12. See also *Phys.* VIII, 1, 250 b 13: movement has always existed and cannot have been preceded by rest.

[104] See J. Baudry, *Le problème de l'origine et de l'éternité du monde de Platon à l'ère chrétienne*, Paris 1931.

[105] Plotinus, *Enn.* II 1, 4; 9, 4 etc.; Aristotle, *De phil.*, fr. 19c Ross.

[106] In the lost treatise *De aeternitate mundi* against which Philoponus wrote his *De aeternitate mundi contra Proclum* (edit. Rabe, Leipzig 1899). See also G.C. Anawati, "Un fragment perdu du *De aeternitate Mundi* de Proclus", in *Mélanges Auguste Diès*, Paris 1956, 21ff.; W. O'Neill, "Time and Eternity in Proclus", in *Phronesis* 7 (1962) 161-165. See also Proclus, *In Tim.* I 294, 9-28.

Maimonides summarised the arguments of Aristotle and his followers[107]: all philosophers hold that it is impossible that God produce anything from nothing. Arab philosophers attempted to reconcile Aristotle's theory of the eternity of the world with religious belief by resorting to Neoplatonic emanation. According to Avicenna the world is produced from all eternity. In itself it is not necessary, but its emanation is necessary. Analogous views of the eternity of the world are proposed by Al-Farabi and Avicebron. Other authors, in particular Al-Gazali, attempted to demonstrate the impossibility of an eternal world[108]. The confrontation between orthodox Aristotelianism and the dogma of the creation of the world in the beginning of time comes to the fore in Averroes' works[109]. Averroes rejected Avicenna's theory of emanation from God and of the real distinction between essence and existence in created things. He holds the eternity of movement and of the world. In his *Destructio destructionum* he refutes Al-Gazali's arguments against the theory of eternity of the world. Some think that in his philosophical writings Averroes does not positively affirm the eternity of the world, but only says that its is possible that the world has existed from all eternity[110].

In the Christian West a benign interpretation of Aristotle understood the latter's arguments against the theory of a beginning of the world as excluding only a natural beginning of things, but not a supernatural origin. However, the growing influence of the Arab philosophers brought a number of masters in the Faculty of Arts in Paris to the view that although the world was created by God, it has always existed. They found a vigorous opponent in St. Bonaventure[111].

St. Thomas devotes much attention to the question of the eternity of the world. In the *De potentia*, q.3, a.17 and the *S.Th.* I 46, 1 he adduces a host of arguments in favour of the eternity of the world (respectively 30 and 10). In the *S.C.G.* II eight chapters are devoted to the issue. Aquinas proceeds very carefully keeping faith and reason separate[112]. The main points he makes are

---

[107] *Dux perplexorum* II 14.
[108] See E. Behler, *Die Ewigkeit der Welt. Problemgeschichtliche Untersuchungen zu den Kontroversen um Weltanfang und Weltunendlichkeit in der arabischen und jüdischen Philosophie des Mittelalters*, München-Paderborn-Wien 1965, 146ff.
[109] E. Gilson, *L'être et l'essence*, Paris 1948, 66ff.
[110] Behler, *o.c.*, (n.108) 206ff. Cf. *Destructio destr.* (edit. Zedler) 136f.
[111] Cf. the Fifth Proposition condemned in 1270: M.-M. Gorce, "La lutte *Contra Gentiles* à Paris", in *Mélanges Mandonnet*. II, Paris 1930, 235-234 and the Articles 83-85 condemned in 1277 (Hissette, *o.c.*, 147ff). See also F. Van Steenberghen, *La controverse sur l'éternité du monde au XIIIe siècle. Académie Royale de Belgique. Bulletin de la Classe des Lettres* 1972, 5e série, tome 58. Cf. *id.*, *Introduction à l'étude de la philosophie médiévale*, Louvain 1974, 512ff. *id.*, "Saint Bonaventure contre l'éternité du monde" and A. Coccia, "De aeternitate mundi apud S. Bonaventuram et recentiores", in *S. Bonaventura IV*, Grottaferrata 1973, 259-278; 279-306.
[112] In 46, 2 he writes "by faith alone".

the following: (a) nothing other than God has existed from all eternity[113]. This proposition we hold by faith alone, although reason can show that it is not impossible, for the existence of the world depends on God's will. But it is not necessary for God to will anything other than himself. (b) If so, the eternity of the world cannot be demonstrated. Consequently the arguments advanced by Aristotle are not absolute. They only have a relative value as directed against some of the ancients who tried to show by means of faulty proofs that the world has a beginning. (c) Aristotle's arguments in favour of the eternity of the world are dialectical or probable. (d) St. Thomas finally rejects, in his reply to the objections, the more important of the arguments in favour of the eternity of the world. As the editors of the English edition of the *Summa* point out, these arguments are found in the works of Aristotle, Averroes, Avicenna and Maimonides.

The Second Article asserts that it is only by faith that we hold that the world did not always exist. The arguments used by some theologians to show the incompatibility of creation and eternal existence are at best only probable. St. Thomas notes that we should not use arguments which are not cogent, to defend the faith, for this gives unbelievers occasion to ridicule it.

Aquinas proves his point in the following way: (a) the fact of the origin of the world cannot be demonstrated from the world itself, for the principle of a demonstration is the essence of a thing[114]. But the essence abstracts from here and now and is a universal. Thus it simply is not contained in the essence of things that they cannot have been from all eternity, just as it is not in the essence of created things to show that God is a Trinity of Persons[115]. St. Thomas does not mean here that single, material things can exist for ever (this is excluded because they have matter in their essence): the totality of things, in which generation and passing-away is in continuous succession, could be from all eternity, when one considers them from the point of view of material reality.

(b) Likewise the originating of the world cannot be demonstrated from the efficient cause which acts by will, for we do not know God's will, unless with regard to what God necessarily wills. Thus one must say that it is in God's power to effect that that which he causes never does not exist[116].—St. Thomas

---

[113] St. Thomas does not resort here to the distinction made by Boethius between eternity as proper to God and perpetuity as the possible property of the world (*De consol.* V, prose 6). William of Conches, however, did use it to reconcile Chalcidius' view of a world coeternal with God and the Christian doctrine (Parent, *o.c.*, 105). In his reply to the fifth objection St. Thomas observes that in the assumption of a perennial world its duration is characterised by succession and is entirely different from God's eternity.

[114] Cf. *In I Anal. post.*, l.23.

[115] In producing the world God's action belongs to his essence which is common to the divine Persons and thus his effects do not reflect divine Trinity.

[116] *De aeternitate mundi*, n.302; *De potentia* 3, 14: "in Deo non deest potentia ab aeterno essentiam aliam a se producendi".

insists that it is important to realize that one cannot demonstrate that the world has a beginning. However, his position was rejected by many theologians. Abelard discarded Boethius' solution[117]: things which have been created, are not eternal[118]. Alexander of Hales concurs. St. Bonaventure also agrees with Abelard's position. In 1273 he writes that the learned admit that whatever becomes of nothing, begins to exist[119]: *esse creatum* and *esse aeternum* are contradictory. St. Albert the Great is wavering, but Siger of Brabant, on the other hand, felt that there is no contradiction between being eternal and having been caused[120].

St. Thomas reviews the arguments of his opponents in his reply to the objections, which he formulates in this Article and in the *De potentia* q.3, a.14:

(a) a thing which has been made need not be posterior in time to its cause, provided the latter's action is instantaneous and not successive.

(b) that the world was created from nothing does not mean that it was made *after* nothing.

(c) the opponent argues that everything which works by intellect, works from some principle. Aquinas replies that this does not hold true for God's intellect.

(d) a more formidable objection is the evidence of a certain evolution of knowledge and the handicrafts. In an eternal world such an evolution would not make sense. St. Thomas knows, of course, that this argument has a certain probability. However it is not convincing for one may conceive a cyclical development in which progress is followed by decay. Incidentally this reply also takes care of the view that the "big bang theory" shows that the world has a beginning: The present expansion may just be one of a series.

(e) even if the world exists from all eternity it would not be equal to God in eternity for the divine being is entirely simultaneous without any succession, but this is not the case with the world.

(f) it is objected that if the world is eternal, an infinite number of days will have passed. But it is impossible to traverse the infinite. The argument is based on the idea that given two extremes there is an infinite number of mean terms. The objection is raised by St. Bonaventure[121] and taken up again by F. Van Steenberghen[122]. According to the latter, in his reply St. Thomas

---

[117] See n.113.

[118] *Theologia* I 20: *PL* 178, 1026A.

[119] In *In II Sent.* d.1, B, a.10 St. Albert writes: "absque dubio nihil probabilius etiam secundum rationem est quam quod mundus inceperit, sicut dixit Moyses et hoc fide tenendum". St. Bonaventure, *Hexaëm.*, coll. 4, 13 (V 351): Alexander of Hales, *Summa theol.* I 64; I 95.

[120] *Quaestiones de anima intellectiva*, in P. Mandonnet, *Siger de Brabant et l'averroïsme latin au XIIIe siècle*, tome II, Louvain 1908, 159. Cf. the works quoted in n. 111.

[121] *In II Sent.*, d.1, p.1, a.1, q.2 (II 20).

[122] Quoted in n.111.

would contradict his own denial, in I 7, 4, of the possibility of an infinite multitude in act.—But this does not seem to be correct. In Aquinas' cosmology the expression "an infinite number of days" refers to the circular movement of the sun and the sphere of fixed stars. Characteristic of such a circular movement is that there is no point of departure, no arrival term and that its trajectory is finite. When we say that the infinite cannot be traversed, we mean a passage from term to term and not a circular movement. Aristotle was aware of this for he asserted both the axiom in question and the eternity of the revolutions of the celestial spheres. The opponent assigns points on the trajectory, between which a star or planet would have executed endless revolutions and covered an infinite distance. St. Thomas replies that "whatever bygone day we choose, from it to the present day there is a finite number of days which can be traversed". St. Thomas' answer also solves the question whether an infinite succession, such as an infinite number of revolutions is possible. Such as infinite is not an infinite in act, as F. Van Steenberghen seems to think[123]: the infinite revolutions are nowhere real, except perhaps in the divine intellect which oversees all time.

(g) this takes us to the next objection: if the world is eternal, there is an infinite series of generations, in which what comes later depends on what comes before as on its efficient cause. Now an infinite series of efficient causes is impossible. The solution of this difficulty lies in the distinction between causes *per se* and causes *per accidens*, as was explained in Chapter Three, The First Way.

(h) the final objection points to the fact that in the hypothesis of an eternal world, an infinite number of human individuals will have lived, whose immortal souls survive and constitute an actually infinite number of souls. But the possibility of an actually infinite number was disproved in Question Seven, Article Four: "No species of number is infinite, for every number is multitude numbered by one".The concept of an infinite number of *things* is contradictory for an infinite multitude of things (of a certain species) do not make up a mutually related, determinate group, which can be counted. A real number is not an abstraction but a group of things which have something in common, inasmuch as they can be counted.

Aquinas observes that the argument considers a particular case and hence does not disprove the possibility that the world is eternal. He intimates that he himself considers it impossible that there is an infinite number of souls[124]. It is true that in the *De aeternitate* he writes that it has not yet been shown that God cannot make such an infinite number of souls to exist. This observation stands in a dialectical context: Aquinas has never seen any of his adver-

---

[123] "Le mythe d'un monde éternel", in *RPL* 76 (1978) 157-179, 167.
[124] This is also stated in I 7,4: "Species multitudinis sunt secundum species numerorum".

saries bring forward a proof of such impossibility. Moreover, his own argument in I 7, 4 is only probable, for it concludes from the impossibility of an infinite number in the order of material things to that of an infinite multitude of spiritual beings[125].

At first sight it seems astonishing that Aquinas insists on demonstrating the possibility of creation *ab aeterno* over and against a vociferous group of theologians. In addition to the reason indicated above (not to expose the faith to ridicule through using faulty argument to prove that the world has a beginning) one may also assume that St. Thomas felt that he was defending solid principles of Aristotelian philosophy against the risk of their total rejection and a return to the Platonic cosmology of the *Timaeus*. The reproach levelled against Aristotle by Maimonides and the *De erroribus philosophorum* was that the Stagirite explained all becoming by means of his theory of primary matter. Hence it was important for St. Thomas to introduce the necessary distinctions and to show what the faith implies and what reason has to tell us.

The Third Article of this Question discusses the meaning of creation in the beginning of time: the universe was created together with time. For time only exists according to some "now", that is the instant of a movement. Time begins as from the first "now".

IV. *On the Distinction of Things in General (I 47)*

After treating the question of the production of beings Aquinas turns to the consideration of the distinction between them. Is the multitude and the distinction of things from God? Above in discussing 45, 5 the theory was mentioned according to which only the first intellect proceeds from God. The principle "ab uno non procedit nisi unum", which is frequently used in Arab philosophy, occurs in Proclus: The Demiurge is a monad and the Paradigm is one also. Consequently, since the universe emanates from a monad, it is one[126]. On its significance in Arab philosophy, see above (I 45, 5). In his *De*

---

[125] In his excellent essay "Mundus est aeternus. Zur Auslegung dieser These bei Bonaventura und Thomas von Aquin" in *Die Auseinandersetzungen an der Pariser Universität im XIIIᵉ Jahrhundert (Miscellanea Mediaevalia*, 10), Berlin 1976, 317-330 A. Zimmermann suggests that such an infinite multitude is possible if the beings which compose it are independent of one another (*l.c.,* 325). However, this does not seem possible: whenever there are two or more substances they must be determined by relations of similitude and difference. Cf. I 47, 3: "Whatever things come from God have relation of order to each other".—On this problem see also A. Zimmermann's "Alberts Kritik an einem Argument für den Anfang der Welt", in A. Zimmermann (hrsg.) *Albert der Grosse. Seine Zeit, seine Wirkung (Miscellanea Mediaevalia*, 14), Berlin 1981, 78-88.

[126] See his commentary on the *Timaeus* I 447, 17-32 Diehl. Proclus repeatedly points out that the intelligible exemplar of the world is one and hence also the world itself. He reads this view in Plato's *Timaeus* 31 a.

necessitate Siger explains that according to the philosophers God is the immediate cause of the first intellect only[127].

In the First Article St. Thomas gives a historical survey of the explanations which have been proposed of the distinction of things: some philosophers made matter the sole cause, others matter together with an agent (Anaxagoras) or secondary agents (Avicenna). St. Thomas lays it down that the distinction of things cannot come from matter, but is from form, for matter is formless and is for the sake of form. In Avicenna's view the distinction between things depends on secondary agents, viz the first and successive intellects[128]. But this opinion cannot stand "because creation belongs to God alone and hence whatever can be caused only by creation is produced by God alone". It follows that all spiritual substances as well as the first appearance of material substances depend on God and not on intermediate causes[129]. Furthermore in Avicenna's view "the universe would proceed from many concurring causes and such an effect is an effect produced by chance", but it is in conflict with the fact that the world is well organised and that things work together. This can only be explained if there is one supreme cause. One should note that the argument of St. Thomas does not exclude the use of intermediary causes in the government of the world, but only concludes that the distinction between things must be intended by God.

Because his goodness cannot adequately be represented by one creature alone, God produced many and diverse creatures[130]. The multitude and variety of things reflect God's goodness more perfectly.—In his reply to the objections Aquinas rejects the argument that what is one produces only one thing. The axiom applies to natural things which act by their own (limited) form. But God acts by his intellect and will: it was shown that God can understand many things, but if so, he can also make many things.—It is true that the exemplar of the world in God is only one, but no single creature can adequately represent this exemplar because of its transcendent perfection.

If God wills the distinction between things, he also wills their inequality (Article Two). A difficulty lies in the fact that the notion of inequality evokes that of injustice and discrimination. Although mediaeval society was hierarchically organised, the ideal of the equality of men was always present, in particular in respect to the common eschatological hope. Inequality among men

---

[127] Edited by J.J. Duin, Louvain 1954 in *La doctrine de la providence dans les écrits de Siger de Brabant (Phil. Médiév.* III). See also Hissette. *o.c.*, 66 and 70f.

[128] See above the commentary on I 45, 5.

[129] The conclusion follows from the solution in I 44, 1 & 2 and 45, 5.

[130] Cf. *In De div. nom.*, c.1, l.1, n.29; *S.C.G.* IV 7: "nulla creatura recipit totam plenitudinem divinae bonitatis, quia perfectiones a Deo in creaturas per modum cuiusdam descensus procedunt".

is the result of sin. The inequality of the material universe is willed by God[131].

Aquinas first rejects the eccentric opinion of Origenes on the cause of inequality to show that formal distinction always requires inequality, because the forms of things are like numbers, in which species vary by the addition or subtraction of unities. In fact, natural things are arranged in a hierarchy, proceeding from less perfect to more perfect forms. "Just as the divine wisdom is the cause of the distinction of things, so it is the cause of inequality. For the universe would not be perfect, if only one grade of goodness were found in things". The different parts of the universe are not best absolutely, but they are in respect of the whole: the different parts of a body or those of a house may differ in value and perfection, yet each of them is useful and good for the whole.

If a variety of creatures is required to express God's perfection, must one not also assume that there are innumerable worlds? God's power is not limited and many worlds are better than one.—Hence in the Third Article the question is discussed whether God created only one world. By "world" the totality of existing things as mutually related is meant. In Greek antiquity the atomists assumed that there are innumerable worlds of different sizes, at irregular distances, some of which are flourishing, others declining[132]. Aristotle discusses this question in the *De caelo* I 8. In his view, which is taken over by Averroes, only one world is possible. In an anonymous commentary on the *Physics*, dating from approximately 1273, the argument is advanced that more worlds would require more Prime Movers. Now the latter cannot be multiplied because they lack matter. Moreover the heavy elements of the other worlds would move toward the centre, that is our earth[133]. Article 27 of the articles condemned in 1277 seems to refer to this or similar texts. Its censors saw in it a limitation of God's power.

St. Thomas adduces an important argument: whatever things come from God have a relation of order to each other and to God, and therefore they must belong to one world. Aquinas means that God has a comprehensive plan and therefore connects things with another and himself. But one can also argue from experience: all material things are related by gravity and other fundamental forces. Moreover the concept of two or more worlds separated the one from the other by nothingness is inconceivable: everything is communicative. A mere multiplication of worlds would not glorify God, for

---

[131] Cf. St. Augustine, *De civ. Dei* XIX 15. On the ideology of equality see S.A. Lakoff, *Equality in Political Philosophy*, Cambridge Ma. 1964.

[132] Cf. Hippolytus, *Refutatio* I 13, 2 (Diels, *FVS*, Democritus A 40). Diogenes of Apollonia seems to have taken over their view. On classical theories of innumerable worlds and Aristotle's treatment of the subject see L. Elders, *Aristotle's Cosmology*, Assen 1966, 127-136.

[133] Cf. A. Zimmermann, *Ein Kommentar zur Physik des Aristoteles aus der Pariser Artistenfakultät um 1273. Quellen und Studien zur Geschichte der Philosophie*, 11, Berlin 1968, 78.

"material multitude has no certain limit but of itself tends to infinity and the infinite is opposed to the notion of end"[134].

The third objection insisted that whatever has form in matter can be multiplied. Hence the world also can.—St. Thomas replies that the world is composed of the whole matter and that there is only one centre in world space, which is already occupied by the earth[135].—Aquinas' answer is defective because of its cosmological assumptions. However, one might perhaps say that the entire universe with all its matter forms a system and that parts of it cannot be multiplied without disturbing its organisation.

St. Thomas does not deny God's power to create other worlds[136], but says that God's effects must show a unity of order. In later centuries the view that God can make more worlds was accepted by John Buridan and Nicholas Oresme[137]. In the seventeenth century the question of the plurality of worlds was widely discussed in popular literature[138].

---

[134] I 47, 3 ad 2.

[135] The text follows Aristotle's *De caelo* I 8, 277 b 12-24. Aristotle puts forward a subtle argument based on his theory of natural places.

[136] I 25, 6.

[137] See F. Kraft, "Wissenschaft und Weltbild, I: Die Wende von der Einheit zur Vielfalt", in N. Luyten (hrsg), *Naturwissenschaft und Theologie*, Düsseldorf 1981, 53-78, 66ff.

[138] See G. McColley, "The Seventeenth Century Doctrine of a Plurality of Worlds" in *The Annals of Science* 1 (1936) 385-430; M.J. Crowe, *The Extraterrestrial Life Debate 1750-1900. The Idea of a Plurality of Worlds from Kant to Lowell*, Cambridge 1986.

CHAPTER ELEVEN

GOD AND HIS CREATURES

In the previous chapter the conclusion was reached that a multitude of finite and different beings have been created by Self-subsistent Being Itself. The question whether creatures continuously depend on God in their being and actions must now be examined. Furthermore, the co-existence of the infinite Absolute Principle and the world is not without its problems. Some have called it totally meaningless. These are the questions to be considered in this chapter.

I. *On the Preservation of Things in Being (I 104)*

The Greek natural philosophers use the term σωτηρία to denote the preserving influence of the whole animal organism on the individual organs[1]. In the *De Caelo* Aristotle writes that according to some authors the sky needs the sustaining force of Atlas lest it collapses. He himself, however, rejects the theory that a soul is needed to keep the universe in being[2]. Stoic philosophers admit a permanent causal influence to keep the world in existence. In particular Posidonius attached much importance to such a preserving force[3]. Cicero echoes the same doctrine[4] and Philo knows the concept of preservation[5]. Numenius holds that an immaterial power must maintain the celestial bodies in motion along their orbits[6].

In the ps.-Aristotelian treatise *De mundo* a divine power is said to keep the world together[7]. Plotinus knows this doctrine[8]. In fact, the theory of the necessity of preservation is Platonic rather than Aristotelian[9]. Early Christian

---

[1] Cf. Plato, *Protagoras* 320 e; 321 b and W. Theiler, *Geschichte der teleologischen Naturbetrachtung bis auf Aristoteles*[2], Berlin 1965, 75.

[2] *De caelo* 284 a 20-27.

[3] See K. Reinhardt, *Kosmos und Sympathie*, München 1926, 129 and *SVF* II 439 (the pneuma is the preserving power).

[4] *De natura deorum* II 51: "caelestium ergo admirabilem ordinem incredibilemque constantiam, ex qua conservatio et salus omnium omnis oritur".—The Second Book of the *De natura deorum* repeatedly mentions this divine power which keeps thing in being.

[5] *De spec. leg.* I 16; *De prov.* II 49.

[6] Eusebius, *P.E.* XV 17.

[7] *De mundo* VII 401 a 25. See also 398 a 4ff.

[8] *Enn.* IV 7, 8-9.

[9] P. Moraux, *Der Aristotelismus bei den Griechen*, II 47.

authors assert that divine Providence keeps all things in existence[10]. St. John Damascene explicitly affirms the preservation of the world by God[11]. In the Christian ages all admitted this doctrine, but the formulation of the principle of conservation of energy in seventeenth century physics and the rise of positivism led certain physicists to the belief that natural bodies keep themselves in being. While Descartes still considered the tendency of physical bodies to persevere in their status to be dependent on the immutability of God[12], Newton no longer mentions such a dependence[13]. Spinoza even identified continued existence with the very essence of things[14].

St. Thomas devotes ample space to this question. In fact, the issue is of paramount importance for religious life: the dialogue with God in prayer is based on the acknowledgement of an ontological dependence. If this doctrine of preservation is abandoned, man stands on his own and is no longer an *ens ab alio* in the full sense of the term. Religious life is bound to wither away as happened when deism held its sway.

The First Article of this question first distinguishes between indirect and accidental preservation on the one hand and direct and *per se* preservation on the other. The former obtains when one removes the cause of corruption (e.g. by sterilizing food), the latter when a thing depends on another being for its very existence. In his government of the world God also keeps things in being protecting them from what might destroy them, inasmuch as he organizes the world in such a way as to shield certain beings from destructive influences. (One may recall the defensive systems of organisms, the ozon layer in the stratosphere, etc.). But St. Thomas here considers direct preservation.

In the second manner all creatures need to be kept in being by God. To make this clear, St. Thomas does not just insist on the fact that no creature has its being of itself, but that all things participate in God's being[15]. Rather he avails himself of the opportunity to compare God's causality with the various ways in which in the physical universe things may keep other things in existence. A distinction is made between causes of the *becoming* of an effect and causes of its *being*. Examples are taken both from natural processes and from artificial production.

---

[10] Athenagoras, *De resurrectione* 16; Irenaeus, *Adv. Haer.* IV, 34, 1; Origines, *Contra Celsum* IV 87.

[11] *De fide orthodoxa* I 3.

[12] *Les principes de la philosophie* II 36 (AT VIII 1, 61ff.). However, for Descartes the preservation of things no longer has the same sense, because time is conceived by him as discontinuous; its "now"s are no longer connected the one with the other. See F. Alquié, *La découverte métaphysique de l'homme chez Descartes*, Paris 1950, 128f.

[13] *Principia naturae*, def. 3 & 4.

[14] See H. Blumenberg, *Selbsterhaltung und Beharrung. Zur Konstitution der neuzeitlichen Rationalität. Abh. Mainz. Akad. d. Wiss.*, Geistes u. soz.-wiss. Kl. 1969, n.11, Mainz 1970, 333-383.

[15] Neo-scholastic authors show a tendency to follow this short-cut. See Gredt. *Elementa* II 850.

(a) in artificial production, such as making a machine or building a house, the builders are the cause of the becoming, but not the cause of the being of their product, for a house or a machine exists, once it exists, because of its parts having been put together in a certain order.

(b) in natural homogeneous generation a thing can be the cause that this matter receives this form, but it cannot be the cause of the form as such, because then it would be its own cause, for it also has itself this form it is assumed to produce.

When we now consider heterogenous generation, i.e. the production of a thing of a particular species by a universal encompassing cause, it appears that in this case the production of the specific form obtains. St. Thomas, who was misled by insufficient observation, thinks that lower organisms, such as those found in rotting organic material, may be caused by a universal cosmic agent such as the sun. Whatever be the value of this theory, it helps, by analogy, to make clear that God is a universal cause which produces the form as well as the whole being of created things. This is demonstrated as follows: God alone is being by virtue of his own essence, since his essence is his existence, while other things *have* being by participating in it. Their being (*esse*) never turns into an *esse* they have of themselves[16], but it remains always participated, receiving being. Hence they need to receive it continuously from its source.

St. Thomas explains this further by means of a comparison with the sun which enlightens the air: as soon as the sun sets, the air becomes dark because it does not possess light of itself. A text of St. Augustine is quoted to confirm this: if God would withdraw his power, all natural things would collapse[17]. This conclusion is a warning not to yield to the temptation of extrapolating into the field of metaphysics our observations of what is at the surface of things: the being of created things is never to be cut loose from its source.

In his reply to the first and the second objection Aquinas explicitly states that without divine causality things cannot continue to exist: "God cannot grant to a creature to be preserved in being after the cessation of divine influence". The fact that by their very nature spiritual creatures are not subject to corruption and cannot not exist, does not do away with the dependence of their being on God. Likewise God's causal influence is not opposed to a creature's inclination to self-preservation, for this inclination concerns the removal of what causes decay and only indirectly the act of existing[18].

Finally St. Thomas observes that the preservation of things by God is not a new activity of the First Cause, as some theologians believe it is[19], but the

[16] See volume I, chapter XI.
[17] *De gen. ad litt.* 4, 12.
[18] For more objections see the *Q.d. de potentia*, 15, 1.
[19] Cf. Descartes' *Third Meditation*.

continuation of the act of creation, which is without either motion or time. Because God's continued causal influence which keeps things in existence does not make a new being, it is not called creation.

The argument of the First Article leads to the conclusion that God *immediately* preserves every creature. But in the Second Article St. Thomas explains that in keeping things in being God may also avail himself of secondary causes, both with regard to indirect and with regard to direct preservation. For instance, certain preservatives hinder the action of corrupting agents and things may depend on other creatures for their being, as organic substances need outside energy and food. In point of fact in the physical universe this dependence on others is the rule. The action of the First Cause is always present and contains and sustains that of secondary causes. The latter give being only inasmuch as they are instruments of God's action[20].

God freely creates the world and keeps it in being and, therefore, he could also let it return into nothingness. Aquinas deals with this question in the Third Article. The chapter on creation made it abundantly clear that the production of things by God is not a necessary process of emanation from divine substance, but rests on God's free decision. "Therefore, just as before things existed, God was free not to give them existence, and so not to make them; so after they have been made, he is free not to continue their existence, and thus they would cease to exist; and this would be to annihilate them ". On the other hand, one must not go so far as to assume that in created things there is a tendency to non-being: non-existence has no direct cause.

Although God is free not to keep things in being, in reality he does not annihilate anything. The reason is that God treats things according to their nature. Now it is not according to their nature to be annihilated: incorruptible things demand to exist for ever and material things are composed of primary matter, which is the imperishable and indeterminate subject of generation and corruption. Moreover God's power and goodness are manifested more by the preservation of things than by their annihilation.

Some critics object that substantial forms and accidents of material things return to nothingness, so that there is some form of annihilation. To this Aquinas replies that these forms and accidents are not beings themselves but something *of being*, viz. forms and accidents of substances. Furthermore, these forms and accidents are not entirely reduced to nothingness, but remain in the potentiality of primary matter or of the substance.

The preservation of all things by God is the basis of religious life. Man receives his being from God and acknowledges his dependence in rites and prayer.

---

[20] See *De pot.* 3, 7 and *S.Th.* I 105, 5.

II. *The Change of Creatures by God (I 105)*

In the previous question Aquinas demonstrates the preservation of all things by God. Related to this issue is the problem of God's further influence on created things besides this preservation. The question is raised against a theological background: *Genesis* 2, 7 and other Biblical texts attribute to God a causal influence on things in general as well as on man's intellect and will in particular. The arguments brought forward by Aquinas affirm that there is such a causality and show that it pervades all motion and activity.

A first problem raised by St. Thomas is whether God can immediately move matter to form (Article 1). The Bible gives an affirmative answer, which is exemplified by a number of instances of divine intervention. The doctrine of divine omnipotence lays the foundation of this view. As against this Biblical metaphysics positivism considers it to be the purpose of science to discover laws which reflect the operation of purely natural or "secondary" causes only. The positivist frame of mind tends to exclude any divine intervention, the possibility and reality of which are defended by Aquinas in q.105. The issue was much debated in the 19th century. Many scientists felt "that everything can be explained in a natural way" and that "There can no longer be anymore doubt that the existence of God is wholly unnecessary to explain any of the phenomena of the universe, than there is doubt that if I leave go of my pen it will fall upon the table ... the knowledge that a Deity is superfluous as an explanation of anything, being grounded on the doctrine of the persistence of force, is grounded on an *a priori* of reason,—i.e., if the fact were not so, our science, our thought, our very existence itself, would be scientifically impossible"[21].

Although it is true that the debate between creationists and positivists was partly due to a misunderstanding of the approach used by the sciences on the one hand and that of philosophy (theology) on the other, it cannot be denied that in their attempt to exclude God's causality from the world scientists were driven by materialism. They extrapolated the conclusions reached in the field of science to consider these the sole adequate explanation of all aspects of reality. The spirit of the Enlightenment shows in the belief that nature and reason are sufficient. An unlimited confidence in the power and autonomy of reason made these scientists feel satisfied with the valuable, but nonetheless superficial knowledge reached in the positive sciences, so that they overlooked the true nature of being and its source[22].

Question 105 provides a refutation of the positivist creed. Aquinas arranges artfully the issues to be examined in the successive articles. We pass from

---

[21] Quoted after N.C. Gillespie, *Charles Darwin and the Problem of Creation*, Chicago 1979, 151.

[22] See G. Cottier, *Questions de la modernité*, Paris 1985, 32ff.

God's causality giving shape to matter and making bodies move, to his influence on man's thinking and willing. The Fifth Article establishes the principle that God works in every worker. After considering God's ordinary influence Aquinas next argues that God can also intervene outside the natural order of things.

The First Article answers a question about the so-called adornment of the world after its initial creation, viz. the introduction of the various classes of beings. For this reason it directly bears upon the debate between evolutionists and creationists. "God can move matter immediately to a form; because whatever is in passive potentiality can be reduced to act by the active power which extends over that potentiality. Therefore, since the divine power extends over matter as produced by God, it can be reduced to act by the divine power". St. Thomas by no means intends to exclude that ordinarily particular effects are produced by secondary causes (objection 3). He rejects the extrinsicism of Ibn Gebirol and Avicenna, "who place the cause of material forms and movements in the ideas or in a separate intellect"[23]. But the secondary causes are ordered by God to determinate effects and their causality is carried and encompassed by that of God who, therefore, can also himself produce certain effects without the collaboration of any other cause.

It follows from the conclusion reached in the First Article that God can move immediately any body whatever, for he "can himself produce all the determinate effects which are produced by any created cause" (Second Article). "For every movement either results from a form ... or else tends to a form". Since God can imprint immediately a form in matter, he can also supply the movements resulting from such a form or disposing to it.—This argument sees movement as connected with the form, that is with the deeper nature of things, a view which is in keeping with the insights reached in contemporary physical theory.

The conclusion established in this article does not conflict with God's spiritual nature: in order to move a body, God does not need to be in *bodily* contact with it: his causal contact is of a higher order.

In the next two articles the operation of God on the created intellect and will is considered. In Neoplatonic philosophy a cascade of light is said to descend from a First Intellect to lower intellects, but there is no direct influence of the Supreme Mind on man The Bible, on the other hand, speaks of a divine revelation given to the prophets and asserts that there is a direct causality of God on the human mind. It also teaches that man's beatitude consists in the vision of God without any intermediary.

However, such a causality seems to contradict the nature of the mind's operation, which is wholly immanent and self-contained. In fact, thinking is

---

[23] Cf. E. Gilson, *Le thomisme*[6], Paris 1972, 238.

a supreme form of life, that is of self-movement (Objection 1). The second objection proceeds from the assumption that the intellect's own light is sufficient for its operation, while the third objection points to the fact that God exceeds by far the object of the intellect.

In his solution Aquinas takes up the distinction implied in the previous objections, between the intellectual power or light on the one hand and the likeness of the thing understood on the other[24]. God moves the intellect in respect of both factors: (a) God is the first intelligent being[25] and "in each order the first is the cause of all that follows"[26]; hence "we must conclude that from him proceeds all intellectual power". Hence God works in the intellect in that he gives it its intellectual power, which he can also augment (e.g. in prophetic illumination and in the beatific vision). (b) All things intelligibly pre-exist in God, their First Cause. Hence all intelligible likenesses which render the intellect to be in act, are ultimately derived from God who consequently can also impress these species on the intellect without mediation.

In his reply to the objections Aquinas points out that God is the First Cause whereas the natural intellectual light and the intelligible species are secondary principles.

The argument set forth in the Third Article belongs to the metaphysics of participation: "It must be said that everything that in any way is, is from God. For whatever is found in anything by participation, must be caused in it by that to which it belongs essentially"[27]. Participated being can neither exist nor work without God's sustaining influence. This entails that man cannot think and reason without God's prevenient and accompanying help.

This takes us to the difficult and much debated question whether God moves the will (Article 4). At this juncture St. Thomas deals with the problem in the general context of God's causality, of which his influence on the will is an instance. The objections show the perplexity of the philosopher who is wrestling with this question: 1. The will cannot be forced; hence it cannot be moved from without. 2. To be voluntarily moved means to be moved from within and not by another. 3. If God moves the will, God is responsible for man's voluntary actions.

As in the previous article Aquinas distinguishes between the object of the will and its power to act:

(a) the object of the will is the good by which the will is moved in that it is desired by the will. Since God alone is the universal good, he alone can fill the will's capacity and elicit the love with which it loves necessarily. But this only occurs when God is seen by the intellect as he is in himself. It is the nature

---

[24] This distinction is repeatedly used by Aquinas. See his treatise on prophetic knowledge.
[25] See above chapter VIII.
[26] On this principle see chapter III, the Fourth Way.
[27] I 44, 1. Cf. *In I Sent.*, d.37, q.1, a.1.

ot the will to tend toward the good and to will it: all the objects presented to
it in this life are limited goods (or, at least, represented to it as limited), so
that its infinite amplitude[28] cannot be filled and irresistibly attracted by them.
God alone can move the will in this way, when he is known as he is in himself.

(b) God also causes the power of willing (*virtus volendi*). "For to will is
nothing but to be inclined towards the object of the will, which is the universal
good. But to incline towards the universal good belongs to the First Mover,
to whom the ultimate end is proportionate". The act of willing is a movement
of the will and, as has been shown in Chapter Three (the First Way), every
movement depends on the causality of the First Mover. In the case of a free
decision of the will, this is even more obvious, since external (created) causes
cannot directly influence it: it must freely decide itself and to this effect *pass
from potency to actuality*[29]. The principle "whatever is moved, is moved by
another" is indeed a universal law of being.

The dynamism with which the will seeks to attain the good as well as the
will's innermost self-determination have thus their source in God. God's
causal influence, however, does not force the will, for it agrees with the very
exigencies of the will's own nature. God's motion makes the will determine
itself and thus retain the command over and responsibility for its actions.
Clearly God's causality is entirely different from a mechanical energy which
gives material things an impulse. The manner of God's motion must be
examined further although this will lead us once more to negative theology.

In the Fifth Article St. Thomas inquires into the *fact* of God's causal influence on created agents. The previous articles, on the other hand, studied the
question whether God *can* move bodies immediately and whether he *can* act
directly upon the intellect and will. The title of the Fifth Article is "Whether
God works in every agent?". The argument rejects two opposite theories,
occasionalism and the theory of the auto-sufficiency of creatures in their
operations.

(a) Some Arab theologians, the Mutakallimun and in particular the School
of the Ash'arites, taught the radical discontinuity of the beings which make
up the universe[30] and attributed all causality to God's operation alone. To
them an activity is but an isolated accident and must be created, each instant

---

[28] Cf. *S.Th.* I 7, 2 ad 2: "virtus intellectus extendit se quodammodo ad infinita".

[29] The senses cannot directly move the will, because they are not at the level of the immaterial
mind. The intellect does not efficiently act upon the will, because it is a cognitive faculty.

[30] See Majid Fakhry, *Islamic Occasionalism and its Critique by Averroës and Aquinas*, London 1958, 22ff. For a survery of the theories of the Mutakallimun see Maimonides, *The Guide
of the Perplexed*, I, 73. In I 115, 1 Aquinas ascribes occasionalism to Avicebron. Occasionalism
also spread in the West. Malebranche regarded the Scholastics as pagans because they attributed
activity to creatures (*De le recherche de la vérité* VII 2, 3); *Dialogues sur la métaphysique et la
religion* VII 12.).

again, by God[31]. St. Thomas gives a lenghty refutation of this view in *S.C.G.*
III 69 and 70 and places the origin of the theory in Plato's minimalistic view
of sensible things. In the *S.Th.* two arguments are brought forward against
occasionalism: it takes causality away from created things and this implies
that there is a lack of power in God, who is credited with creating crippled
beings[32]. In the second place, the active powers things possess would have
been given to them for no purpose, for they would never act. We must, therefore, maintain that things have their own operations.

(b) Nevertheless religiously minded people are aware of a total dependence
on God. The text of Isaiah, quoted in the *Sed contra* argument, expresses this
conviction: "Lord, Thou hast wrought all our works for us". This insight is
also found in non-Christian literature. The poet Pindar writes that whatever
man is and does, comes from the gods[33]. In order to prove that God does
work in all things St. Thomas passes in review the four genera of causality.

Material causality does not act itself, so that here the question whether God
co-operates with created agents does not apply.

God works for an end, for "every operation is for the sake of some good,
real or apparent; and nothing is good either really or apparently, except in as
far as it participates in a likeness to the Supreme Good which is God".

In order to act the agent must pass from potentiality to actuality, so that
in the last analysis, the First Mover is the source of all activity. Aquinas uses
on purpose the example of a carpenter and his tools to describe how God co-
operates with secondary causes. It helps to indicate that with regard to the
production of being, every created cause is an instrument of God[34].

Thirdly, God gives created things their forms and preserves them in being.
Thus he works intimately in all things.

In his reply to the objections Aquinas lays down that when God works in
created things, the latters' own operation does not become superfluous. For
God's causality is at an entirely different level from theirs.

The motion imparted by God at the level of efficient causality is that causal

---

[31] See G.C. Anawati, "Saint Thomas d'Aquin et les penseurs arabes: les "loquentes in lege
maurorum" et leur philosophie de la nature", in L. Elders (edit.), *La philosophie de la nature
de saint Thomas d'Aquin*, Città del Vaticano 1982, 155-177; 160.

[32] If things exist, they also have activity: "Agere autem, quod nihil aliud est quam facere aliquid actu, est per se proprium actus in quantum est actus" (*S.Th.* I 115, 1).

[33] *Ne.* 1, 9: *Isth.* 5, 23; *Ol.* 9, 28; D. Roloff, *Gottähnlichkeit, Vergöttlichung und Ergöhung
zum seligen Leben*, Berlin 1970, 141.—One may compare such texts of Holy Scripture as *1 Cor.*
12, 6: God "is working everything in all" and *Phil.* 2, 13: (God) "puts both the will and the action
into you". Cf. also St. Augustine, *De gratia et libero arbitrio* 16, 32-17, 33; *De gen. ad litt.* 9,
15, 26; *De Trinitate* 3, 8, 14.

[34] Cf. De potentia 3, 7: "... prout quodlibet agens est instrumentum divinae virtutis
operantis".

influence which *applies* an agent to his action[35]. This "impression", caused by the First Mover[36], reduces the created agent from potentiality to actuality. Wherever a created agent begins to work, such a causal impulse is necessary. It comes to it from God either immediately or through intermediary agents. Ontologically this "motion" is an entity, a power which is given fleetingly (*transeunter*) to the created cause.

Although this doctrine of St. Thomas results from the principle of causality and does justice to a good number of otherwise unexplainable texts of Holy Scripture, it has come under sharp criticism, in particular in its application to the human will. In the 16th century L. Molina proposed a different explanation: he admits that God produces the effect together with the created agent, but he denies a direct causal influence on this agent, that is, on the human will. For such an influence on the human will itself would determine it, but in this way there no longer is real freedom of will[37].

Molina developed his theory to do justice to a growing awareness of man's autonomy and power, so typical of his age, and to fight the determinism of the will taught by some Protestant leaders. But Molina's theory does not explain at all how a created cause *begins* to work, and so it rests on a contradiction. The Spanish philosopher, however, rightly draws attention to a difficulty: how is God's causal influence on the will, which brings it from potentiality to its free decision, compatible with the will's most typical characteristic, viz. its capacity to determine itself?

In the last analysis this cooperation of God and man in man's free decisions remains hidden from us[38]. Nevertheless the analysis can be pushed a little further:

(a) Molina does not explain how the will is brought from potency to actuality. His later recourse to a neutral causal impulse by God (the so-called *concursus oblatus*) which has to be determined by the will so that it turns into an actual causal assistance (*concursus collatus*) does not explain how this determination by the will comes about. Furthermore, Molina's theory jeopardizes or even denies God's actual knowledge of man's heart[39] as well as his government of the world.

Needless to add that the *object* proposed to the will by the intellect, cannot move the will as an *efficient* cause such as is needed to make it act. Moreover,

---

[35] Cf. *De pot.* 3, 7: "... applicat actioni"; I 36, 3 ad 4: "virtus causae primae coniungit causam secundam suo effectui".

[36] I 103, 8: "impressio a primo movente".

[37] See his *Concordia liberi arbitrii cum gratiae donis, divina praescientia, providentia, praedestinatione et reprobatione*, Lisboa 1588.

[38] God's causality by far exceeds our understanding. See Th.-G. Chifflot, "L'avoir, condition de la créature", in *RScPhTh* 28 (1939) 40-57.

[39] God's knowledge can only be a causal knowledge.

such an object is always a finite good whereas the will has an infinite amplitude.

(b) It must be God who moves the human will. He does so by removing its potentiality and by placing it in an act which is at the same time the autonomously willed decision of the will itself. God can give such a self-determination to the will, because he is a universal cause which produces the entire scale of beings and their differences[40]. His causal power is so great that he produces his effects according to particular modalities and adapts them to the nature of the creatures in which he works, and also to man's free will[41].

Because man remains free under God's motion, he can will something else other than that which he does choose (*in sensu divisio*), but given this motion, he cannot carry out such a choice (*in sensu composito*). God's motion is so much adapted to the nature of the things to which it is imparted, that it is not God who acts, but the created cause. Consequently, if the will sins, this act is not to be connected with God. In this case, God moves to the entity of the sinful act, but not to the privation which makes up its sinful character. The reason is that God causes the effect under the aspect of being, and not under that of a limitation or privation. An evil act does not have an efficient cause *per se*, but only a deficient cause.

If one would insist and make God responsible of man's sinful acts because he does not give that efficacious motion, which would infallibly lead to a good act[42], the reply would be that the initiative for the evil act comes from man himself. God only allows evil to happen and, in the order of material causality, this permission is subsequent upon the will's failure to insert the good it wants to attain into the context of man's moral duties[43]. According to the axiom "causae sunt sibi invicem causae" the deficiency of the human will precedes God's motion in the order of dispositive (material) causality[44].

Jacques Maritain calls attention to the dissymetry between the causation of the morally good acts and that of sinful acts[45]. The former are expressed in terms of being, the latter in terms of non-being. In an attempt to penetrate deeper into the question of the origin of man's sinful acts, he introduces the

---

[40] *In I Periherm*, 1.14, n.197: "(causa universalis) "profundens totum ens et omnes eius differentias".

[41] I 19, 8. Cf. I 83, 1 ad 3: "God, therefore, is the first cause, who moves causes both natural and voluntary. And just as by moving natural causes he does not prevent their actions from being natural, so by moving voluntary causes he does not deprive their actions of being voluntary, but rather is he the cause of this very thing in them, for he operates in each thing according to its nature.

[42] This is the way Bañez states the issue.

[43] *De malo* 3, 2 ad 2. St. Thomas speaks of an absence of consideration of the moral law. For this absence the will's liberty is sufficient.

[44] See R. Garrigou-Lagrange, *Dieu, son existence et sa nature*[6], 699. G. refers to the main commentators, in particular to John of St. Thomas, *Cursus theol.*, In I[am], q.19, disp. V, art.6.

[45] *Court traité de l'existence et de l'existant*, Paris 1947, 153ff.

notion of a divine motion, offered to all, which can be frustrated by the
human will (*une motion brisable*), that is by the deficiency we spoke about.
If the human will does not frustrate it, this fragile motion is turned into an
efficacious help. But this theory creates more problems than it solves: how
does God know that a created will is going to refuse his offer? The theory
seems to imply that, in a sense, man must determine God's motion. It is better
to admit that the cooperation of God's motion and the human free will
remains shrouded in a seemingly impenetrable mystery.

III. *The Antinomies of the Coexistence of the Infinite Being and Finite Creatures*

It is a basic assumption of atheistic existentialism that man's autonomy is
incompatible with the existence of God. Jean-Paul Sartre often mentions God
but only to deny his existence: God does not exist, for man is free. God means
the death of my subjectivity. The very idea of God is intolerable[46].

Maurice Merleau-Ponty also sees an irreconcilable opposition between God
and man. The world and man exist by themselves: if they would depend on
God, they would lose their subsistence[47]. The hypothesis of creation deprives
things of their perfection and original sufficiency[48]. Merleau-Ponty thinks
that the assumption of a First Necessary Being is a vain attempt at an escape
which does not solve anything. Rather it destroys temporality and contingence. The French philosopher adds that if God exists in his infinite perfection or being, nothing is left to man to accomplish.

These objections are not new. The problem of the coexistence of the Infinite
Being with finite things has been a challenge to philosophers over the centuries. A first observation is that the deduction of the existence of God as a
necessary and infinite Being is compelling for our reason. There is no rational
justification for denying God's existence because of the alleged irrecon-
cilability of an Infinite Absolute and finite things. In the second place, it
would seem that in the theory which assumes an incompatibility between God
and his creatures imagination interferes with the work of reason, presenting
divine being as an infinite expanse which leaves no room for other things and
which makes superfluous whatever is finite.

A first remark is that God and created things are not at the same level at
all. They cannot be compared. Created things are an expression of God which
lies outside God's being. The Scholastics say that after creation there are more

---

[46] Cf. J.-P. Sartre, *L'être et le néant*, 321; Hegel, *Vorlesungen über die Philosophie der Religion*, III, C II 2 (die Welt).

[47] M. Merleau-Ponty, *Sens et non-sens* 193.

[48] *Eloge de la philosophie*, 61-62. See R. Jolivet, "Le problème de l'Absolu dans la philosophie de M. Merleau-Ponty", in *Tijdschrift voor Philos.* 19 (1957) 53-100, 90.

beings, but not more being (*non plus entis*)[49]. Indeed, creation does not produce a novel degree of being, wisdom or love, because whatever comes into being, pre-exists in God in a higher and more perfect way. But creation does produce more wisdom, more love and joy, since it multiplies finite participations in God.

This helps us to understand something of the coexistence of God and his creatures. God creates out of love of his goodness; his creatures share in his goodness and in his life. As Christian theology teaches, this sharing in God reaches it highest point in man's supernatural vocation: man is invited to take part in God's innermost life, his knowledge, his love and his joy.

According to Plato the world is not true being but only a shadowy existence. Some Christian authors followed him and denied real being and subsistence to created things[50], which are no more than a reflection of God. But St. Thomas has a more positive view: things really exist and themselves act. They are substances and accidents, although they receive their being from God.

Aquinas' metaphysics is a metaphysics of interiority in this sense that in their most intimate depth things are touched by God and flow forth from his causal action. They strive to attain God in whatever they do and pursue. Thus St. Thomas' philosophical theology discloses a dimension forgotten by deism and positivism, viz. that things exist and act sustained by God. This divine causality and cooperation is not the assistance of a juxtaposed cause, but works from the inside and depth of things and their actions. One may recall Proclus' proposition that the effect is within its cause according to the power of the cause[51].

Aquinas rejoins St. Augustine's metaphysics of interiority as it is developed in the *Confessions*, where God is said to be "intimior intimo meo" and the "vita vitae meae"[52]. God is the truth in which and by which we know whatever we know and the Love which moves every desire. Those who fail to discover this metaphysical dimension of reality and their own being, remain at the surface of things. To them St. Augustine's words seem to apply: "Et ecce intus eras et ego foris ... Mecum eras et tecum non eram"[53].

---

[49] Cf. M. Blondel, *L'être et les êtres*, Paris 1935, 466-467.—Cf. *De ver.* 2, 3 ad 11: "non enim aliquid Deo deperit, si eius creatura ponatur non esse".

[50] Cf. John Scot Eriugena, *De div. nat.* II 2: *PL* 122, 528AB. To these Platonizing theologians the universe is not the true reality (Parent, *o.c.*, 90ff.).

[51] *Liber de causis*, prop. 24. Cf. St. Thomas, *In librum de causis*, 1. 24, n.391.

[52] See C. Giacone, *Interiotità e metafisica*, Bologna 1964; P. Blanchard, "L'espace intérieur chez saint Augustin d'après le Livre X des *Confessions*", in *Augustinus Magister* I 535-542; R.L. Petz, *Ontologie der Innerlichkeit, Reditio completa und Processio interior bei Thomas von Aquin*, Fribourg 1979.

[53] *Conf.* X 27, 38.

That all things strive to attain God is a Neoplatonic dogma, which is taken up by Dionysius[54]. This seeking of God is not juxtaposed to other pursuits but its constitutes the very core of every desire. The reason is that in striving for a good, things strive for the Source of good, God. St. Thomas recalls that the more perfect a good is, the more it is loved. Therefore, in seeking their particular ends, things seek and love God above anything else[55].

---

[54] *De div. nom*, c.4: *PG* 3, 700 AB.

[55] Cf. *S.Th.* I 44, 4 ad 3: "omnia appetunt Deum appetendo quodcumque bonum"; *Quodl.* I 8: "Qualibet creatura plus amat Deum quam seipsam". See L.-B. Gillon, "Primacía del apetito universal de Dios según Santo Tomás", in *Ciencìa tomista* 63 (1942) 328-341, who points out the novelty of St. Thomas' doctrine that even irrational things have such a universal desire of God.

EPILOGUE

Aquinas's philosophical theology is a coherent whole, solidly based on daily experience and unassailable general principles of being which are self-evident and are admitted by common sense. Its conclusions, however, take us to summits shrouded in the clouds of negative theology. The mystery and transcendence of Self-subsistent Being Itself are left intact. Nevertheless, despite his infinite perfection, God is not far from his creatures, but always present to them as their Cause, their Ideal and their End.

Critics say that St. Thomas's philosophy of God contains the seeds of God's objectification[1], but this is a mistake. God is not brought down to the level of the abstract, the universal or the impersonal, unless by those who fail to understand the depth of Aquinas's doctrine.

In his quest of the Absolute and the Cause of everything the metaphysician reaches a borderline he cannot cross: God's essence is inaccessible. St. Thomas's philosophical theology preserves him from the temptation of monism and invites him to contemplate and adore a Personal Being to whose greatness there are no limits. It also prepares the mind for grateful acceptance of the gift of faith and of the promise of an eschatological fulfilment of its thirst for knowledge and love. In this way Aquinas's metaphysics is a *praeambulum fidei* in a most eminent way.

At the same time this study has presented an overview of the intellectual history of Western man who, by his strenuous efforts and enlightened by divine revelation, reached correct philosophical knowledge about the world and its transcendent Cause. More than 1600 years of philosophical speculation came together in the natural theology of St. Thomas and were transposed and integrated into his metaphysics of being. However, this study has also given an afflicting picture of decline and abandonment of acquired insights. Deism, agnosticism and atheism developed. As a result modern philosophical thought has lost its centre, Western man has forfeited the truth about his origin and destination and human life has been deprived of its deepest meaning. What is left is little more than the illusion of being autonomous.

---

[1] Cl. Geffré, "Sens et non-sens d'une théologie non-métaphysique", in *Concilium* 1972, n.76, 89-98. 93.

INDEX NOMINUM

INDEX RERUM

DATE DUE

JAN 1 '92			
JAN 1 '92			
MAR 1 '92			
APR 1 1 2001			